INTENTION IN LAW AND PHILOSOPHY

Intention in Law and Philosophy

Edited by

NGAIRE NAFFINE
Professor of Law, Adelaide University

ROSEMARY OWENS
Senior Lecturer in Law, Adelaide University

JOHN WILLIAMS
Senior Lecturer in Law, Adelaide University

DARTMOUTH
Aldershot • Burlington USA • Singapore • Sydney

© Ngaire Naffine, Rosemary Owens, John Williams 2001

Published by
Dartmouth Publishing Company
Ashgate Publishing Limited
Gower House
Croft Road
Aldershot
Hampshire GU11 3HR
England

Ashgate Publishing Company
131 Main Street
Burlington, VT 05401-5600 USA

Ashgate website: http://www.ashgate.com

British Library Cataloguing in Publication Data
Intention in law and philosophy. - (Applied legal
    philosophy)
    1.Intention 2.Criminal intent
    I.Naffine, Ngaire II.Owens, Rosemary III.Williams, John
    345'.001

Library of Congress Cataloging-in-Publication Data
Intention in law and philosophy / edited by Ngaire Naffine, Rosemary Owens, John Williams.
        p. cm. -- (Applied legal philosophy)
    Includes bibliographical references.
    ISBN 0-7546-2171-5
        1. Intention. 2. Law--Philosophy. I. Naffine, Ngaire. II. Owens, Rosemary III.
    Williams, John (John Matthew), 1967- IV. Series

K272 .I58 2001
340'.1--dc21

                                                                                2001032799

ISBN 0 7546 2171 5

Printed and bound by Athenaeum Press, Ltd.,
Gateshead, Tyne & Wear.

Contents

Torts

Contracts

PART III: INTENTION AND THE COLLECTIVE

Intention in Groups

Intention in Legal Texts

PART IV: BEYOND INTENTION?

List of Contributors

Sandra Berns is Professor of Law at Griffith University and a former Dean of the Faculty (1996–99). She was formerly an Associate Professor at the University of Tasmania. Her publications include three books, most recently *To Speak as a Judge: Difference, Voice and Power* (1999) and numerous journal articles and book chapters, most recently 'Folktales of Legality: Family Law in the Procedural Republic' (2000) 11 *Law and Critique* 1. Her current research interests include family law (particularly strategies and tactics in parenting disputes), gender equity and equality issues, and legal history.

John Braithwaite is a Professor and Chair of the Regulatory Institutions Network (RegNet) in the Law Program, Research School of Social Sciences, Australian National University. He is interested in restorative justice, responsive regulation and the globalisation of regulation. His new books are *Global Business Regulation* (with P Drahos), *Restorative Justice and Responsive Regulation, Shame Management Through Reintegration* (with E Ahmed, N Harris and V Braithwaite) and *Regulation, Crime, Freedom.*

Tom Campbell is Professor of Law at the Australian National University. He is author of *The Legal Theory of Ethical Positivism* (Dartmouth, 1996), and *Justice* (2nd ed, Macmillan, 2001). He was Professor of Jurisprudence at the University of Glasgow (1980–90) and Professor of Philosophy at the University of Stirling (1973–79). He is currently working on the protection of human rights in Australia.

Peter Cane has been Professor of Law in the Research School of Social Sciences at the Australian National University since 1997. For twenty years before that he taught at Corpus Christi College, Oxford. His main research interests lie in the law of obligations (especially tort law) and in public law (especially administrative law). He is author of *An Introduction to Administrative Law* (3rd ed, 1996), *Tort Law and Economic Interests* (2nd ed, 1996), *The Anatomy of Tort Law* (1997), *Atiyah's Accidents,*

Compensation and the Law (5ᵗʰ ed, 1999) and (with Francis Trindade) *The Law of Torts in Australia* (3ʳᵈ ed, 1999). His contribution to this volume is part of a larger project entitled 'Responsibility in Law: A Functional and Relational Analysis'.

Suzanne Corcoran is Professor of Law at Flinders University. She has written primarily in the area of company law, university corporations and legal history. She is the author of 'Dividends on Shares' and 'Company Accounts and Audit' as well as other titles in *Halsburys The Laws of Australia*.

Michael Detmold is Professor of Law at Adelaide University. His research interest is in the philosophy of law. He is the author of *The Unity of Law and Morality: A Refutation of Legal Positivism* (1984), *The Australian Commonwealth: A Fundamental Analysis of its Constitution* (1985) and *Courts and Administrators: A Study of Jurisprudence* (1989). He is currently working on a theory of law as the structure of love.

Grant Gillett is Professor of Bioethics, Otago Bioethics Centre, University of Otago, Dunedin, New Zealand as well as a practising neurosurgeon. His research interests are in bioethics and philosophy. His books include *The Mind and its Discontents* (1999); *The Discursive Mind* (1994) with HR Harre; and *Representation, Meaning and Thought* (1992).

Frank Jackson is Director of The Institute of Advanced Studies and Professor of Philosophy, The Australian National University. His most recent book is *From Metaphysics to Ethics* (1998). His interests include metaphysics and epistemology, and ethics.

Ian Leader-Elliott is Senior Lecturer in Law at Adelaide University. He has published extensively in the areas of criminal law and criminal responsibility. He is also a consultant to the Commonwealth Attorney General, Criminal Law Reform Unit, advising on the preparation of a Model Criminal Code for Australia. He has had primary responsibility in the preparation of Chapter 4 'Damage and Computer Offences' (2001, forthcoming) and 'Serious Drug Offences' (1998).

The Honourable **Sir Anthony Mason** AC KBE was Chief Justice of the High Court of Australia from 1987 to 1995. Until recently, he was

Chancellor of UNSW, National Fellow at the Research School of Social Sciences at the ANU, a Judge of the Supreme Court of Fiji and President of the Solomon Islands Court of Appeal. In 1996–97 he was Arthur Goodhart Professor in Legal Science at Cambridge University. Sir Anthony holds Honorary Doctorates from Deakin, ANU, Sydney, Melbourne, Monash, Griffith, UNSW and Oxford Universities. Sir Anthony's former positions in Australia include Commonwealth Solicitor-General and Justice of the NSW Court of Appeal. Sir Anthony has been a non-permanent Judge of the Hong Kong Court of Final Appeal since 1997. His major research interests include constitutional and public law, equity and contract. His most recent publications include: 'The relationship between freedom of expression and freedom of information' in Jack Beatson and Yvonne Cripps (eds), *Essays in Honour of Sir David Williams QC* (2000); 'The Evolving Role and Function of the High Court' in Brian Opeskin and Fiona Wheeler (eds), *The Australian Federal Judicial System* (2000); 'Contract, Good Faith and Equitable Standards in Fair Dealing' (2000) 116 *Law Quarterly Review* 66; 'The Impact of Equitable Doctrine on the Law of Contract' (1998) 27 *Anglo-American Law Review* 1.

Ngaire Naffine is Professor of Law at Adelaide University. Her research interests are criminal law, legal theory, feminism and medical law. Her books include *Female Crime: The Construction of Women in Criminology* (1987); *Law and the Sexes: Explorations in Feminist Jurisprudence* (1990) and *Feminism and Criminology* (1996). Her forthcoming books include *Are Persons Property? Legal Debates about Property and Personality* (with Margaret Davies).

Rosemary Owens is a Senior Lecturer in Law at Adelaide University. She has published numerous articles in the field of industrial relations law, most recently 'Equality and Flexibility for Workers with Family Responsibilities: A Troubled Union?' (2000) 13 *Australian Journal of Labour Law* 278 (with Therese MacDermott) and she is co-editor of *Sexing the Subject of Law* (1997). She is currently working on a project concerning fundamental concepts in the law of work relations.

Philip Pettit is Professor of Social and Political Theory at the Research School of Social Sciences, Australian National University, and a regular Visiting Professor of Philosophy at Columbia University. He is author of a number of books, including *Republicanism: A Theory of Freedom and Government* (1997), *Three Methods of Ethics* (with M Baron and M Slote,

1997) and *The Common Mind: An Essay on Psychology, Society and Politics* (1993). He also has a new book in press *A Theory of Freedom: From Psychology to Politics* (2001).

Michael Smith is Professor of Philosophy at the Research School of Social Sciences, Australian National University. He is the author of *The Moral Problem* (1994) which won the First American Philosophical Association Book Prize in 2000. His major research interests include ethics, moral psychology, philosophy of mind, political philosophy and philosophy of law.

Natalie Stoljar is a Senior Lecturer specialising in legal philosophy in the Faculty of Law at the University of Melbourne. She has published articles in legal philosophy, moral philosophy and feminist theory and is co-editor (with Catriona Mackenzie) of *Relational Autonomy. Feminist Perspectives on Autonomy, Agency and the Social Self* (2000). She is working on a book on legal interpretation.

Margaret Thornton is a Professor of Law and Legal Studies at La Trobe University, Melbourne. Her publications include *The Liberal Promise: Anti-Discrimination Legislation in Australia* (1990), *Dissonance and Distrust: Women in the Legal Profession* (1996), and an edited collection *Public and Private: Feminist Legal Debates* (1995), all published with Oxford University Press. She is a Fellow of the Academy of the Social Sciences in Australia.

John Williams is a Senior Lecturer in Law at Adelaide University. He is co-editor of *Makers of Miracles: The Cast of the Federal Story* (with David Headon, 2000) and *Manning Clark's Ideal of De Tocqueville* (with Dyphmna Clark and David Headon, 2000). His major research interests include constitutional law and Australian legal history.

Series Preface

The objective of the Dartmouth Series in Applied Legal Philosophy is to publish work which adopts a theoretical approach to the study of particular areas or aspects of law or deals with general theories of law in a way which focuses on issues of practical moral and political concern in specific legal contexts.

In recent years there has been an encouraging tendency for legal philosophers to utilize detailed knowledge of the substance and practicalities of law and a noteworthy development in the theoretical sophistication of much legal research. The series seeks to encourage these trends and to make available studies in law which are both genuinely philosophical in approach and at the same time based on appropriate legal knowledge and directed towards issues in the criticism and reform of actual laws and legal systems.

The series will include studies of all the main areas of law, presented in a manner which relates to the concerns of specialist legal academics and practitioners. Each book makes an original contribution to an area of legal study while being comprehensible to those engaged in a wide variety of disciplines. Their legal content is principally Anglo-American, but a wide-ranging comparative approach is encouraged and authors are drawn from a variety of jurisdictions.

TOM D. CAMPBELL
Series Editor
The Faculty of Law
The Australian National University

Thanks and Acknowledgements

This book is the outcome of a seminar series on intention in law and philosophy conducted at the Law School, Adelaide University in 1999. We are grateful to the Law School for funding the seminar series and we would like particularly to thank our colleagues at Adelaide University, especially those in the Philosophy Department and the Law School, for their lively contributions to discussions at each of the seminars. The Adelaide Law School also provided a small research grant to assist in the preparation of this volume of essays. We are also grateful to the Research School of Social Sciences at the Australian National University for its financial support for its scholars who contributed to the project.

In preparing the essays for publication, we have been assisted by Kate Leeson who has extensive editorial experience. We are grateful to her for the intelligence and meticulous care and general professionalism she brought to the task of helping us in the preparation of the essays to camera-ready copy. We also thank Andreas Schloenhardt.

The material in Chapter 7 has previously been published in the *Oxford Journal of Legal Studies* (Volume 20, Number 4, Winter 2000, 533–556). We thank the editors of the journal for their permission to reproduce the material in this collection.

1 The Intention Project

NGAIRE NAFFINE, ROSEMARY OWENS AND JOHN WILLIAMS

Why Consider Intention?

In Western thought, the concept of intention is fundamental to our understanding of human behaviour. And yet explication of the concept remains elusive. Intention is at the core of human achievement, the essence of purposive action, of agency, the means by which humankind constructs and makes sense of itself within the social world. The concept of intention helps us to explain and describe what it is we do. Indeed, all meaningful human action presupposes an intentional actor, someone who is in control of their actions. Intention thus also underpins moral responsibility for human action.

The assumption that people are rational intentional agents, who can freely choose either to obey or to break the law, or to honour or dishonour their legal agreements, may also be said to underpin the entire legal system. This is precisely why people are held legally responsible and accountable for their actions and why of, course, duress and other forms of coercion may relieve persons of their legal responsibilities. As we intend to demonstrate in this volume, the concept of intention, in one way or another, and variously interpreted, is relevant to all parts of law.

The Intention Project

Intention is vital to many bodies of knowledge, not just to law. Artists and literary theorists, theologians and psychologists all draw on their version of the concept in different ways and to different ends. However lawyers, as well as philosophers of mind, have perhaps thought more than others about the concept of intention, refining its meaning and its application.

Intention has always been a central interest of lawyers. Constitutional lawyers in Australia and the United States, for example, are still concerned

1

with the legal significance of the founders' intentions. Criminal lawyers remain preoccupied with the intention of the defendant as the paradigm mental state that forms the basis of criminal responsibility. Contract lawyers still look to the intention of the parties as the basis of a legal agreement. Even where intention plays a less decisive role in the determination of legal responsibility, as in the law of torts, intention remains the benchmark fault element. That is to say, much of modern tort law rests on a deliberate and defended determination to exclude intention as a basis of liability. Philosophers too have demonstrated a considerable and sustained interest in intention: indeed an entire branch of their discipline is dedicated to the study of the mind and its states.

In some ways, the disciplines of philosophy and law are strikingly different in their approach to intention. Philosophers have the luxury of theorising a concept in abstraction. Some of the more bizarre thought experiments conducted by philosophers of mind (such as tele-transportation and brain bisection) are perhaps symptomatic of this lack of practical discipline. By contrast, lawyers are always obliged to consider the practical implications of their organising concepts. For lawyers, concepts always ultimately have a real application and outcome (though, as we will see, this does not prevent them from engaging in their own peculiar, though perhaps less far-fetched, thought experiments). In their defence, philosophers would no doubt argue that it is impossible to have a developed theory of intention, in law or in any other discipline, without a developed philosophy of mind.

It may also be said that philosophers and lawyers share many concerns in their study and deployment of the concept of intention. Perhaps their most fundamental common concern about intention is its relation to responsibility. Both philosophers and lawyers want to know whether responsibility for an action should always depend on intention, conventionally defined, or whether negligence or culpable ignorance should suffice. Philosophers, like lawyers, also debate whether the concept of intention should depend on technical or ordinary language usage. Philosophers and lawyers have considered the problems raised by group action and the allocation of responsibility for it. And, as we observe throughout this volume, philosophers share with lawyers a fundamental interest in whether intention is a private individual mental event or whether it is a function of public behaviour, or social character, or public discourse. Both types of scholar also want to know whether the concept is subjectively or objectively determined. Over the course of this book, we will touch on all of these matters and discover that the lawyers as well as the philosophers of intention have arrived at some surprisingly similar conclusions about the concept, but that there also remain important differences of interpretation both between and indeed among them.

In view of their common (as well as divergent) concerns, it is perhaps surprising that there has been so little systematic work done on the relationship between the legal and the philosophical meanings of intention. Nor has there been the expected open dialogue between philosophers and lawyers about the meaning of the concept. A consequence has been that legal debates have sometimes lacked the theoretical sophistication of the more abstract philosophical debates about intention; while the philosophical debates have on occasion lacked the lawyers' discipline that comes from the obligation always to arrive at an actual determination of responsibility in a particular case.

This book seeks to bridge this intellectual gap between the two disciplines, to get the philosophers to think in practical terms and to get the lawyers to give a theoretical justification for their practical legal decision. The purpose of the volume is to foster a focussed dialogue between theorists of intention from law and philosophy and to consider connections between legal and non-legal understandings of the concept.

This collection is the outcome of a project conducted at the Law School, Adelaide University, in which eminent international philosophers and lawyers were commissioned to write an essay that specifically connected the interests of philosophers and lawyers. They were asked to think and write about intention from the point of view of their discipline, but also to consider any possible connections with the understandings of the concept deriving from the other discipline. In juxtaposing the work of philosophers and lawyers, this collection seeks to bring the two disciplines closer together.

Part I: The Philosophy of Intention

The book begins with the philosophy of intention. While the three philosophers who commence our discussion offer rather different accounts of intention, they are all concerned with the moral and legal problem of assigning responsibility to human agents. All want to know when and why a person can be said to be acting as an agent to whom blame can be assigned.

Frank Jackson and Michael Smith both employ a Humean account of human action. While suggesting certain refinements to Hume's theory, both philosophers accept that intentional acts arise from what an actor believes and desires. As Jackson illustrates, 'my intentional action of opening my mail is caused by my desire to learn what is inside my letters and my belief that a good way to learn what is inside my letters is by opening them'.

In the opening essay, Jackson considers 'how decision theory illuminates assignments of moral responsibility'. For Jackson there is an inevitable mental component to moral responsibility, but it is not limited to intention or foresight, conventionally understood. An actor may also be morally responsible for ignorance that may have no obvious intentional element. With Hume, Jackson asserts that intentional actions arise from beliefs and desires. Jackson also insists, however, that beliefs and desires come in degrees and that this is important for the calibration of moral responsibility. Jackson's application of decision theory shows how and why this is so. According to decision theory, intentional acts depend on a combination of an agent's subjective probability function (the agent's degree of belief that a state of affairs will occur) and their preference function (the desirability that the agent places on an outcome). From the range of acts available to an agent, the agent will do that which has maximum expected desirability. For Jackson, 'agents are morally responsible when they fail to maximise expected desirability according to the *right* desirability or preference function' (our emphasis). As he shows in his brief analysis of the famous rape case of *Morgan*,[1] the practical effect of his deployment of decision theory is to extend the compass of agency and hence of responsibility.

Smith investigates another important dimension of the problem of human agency: the 'irresistible' impulse. It is generally supposed that if we cannot control our behaviour, we cannot be said to intend it and so we cannot be held morally responsible. Smith takes the view, however, that irresistible impulse has been given too great a scope to excuse. Developing the standard Humean account of action, Smith argues that an irresistible impulse that excuses is one that undermines the agent's capacity to act in

---

1   [1976] AC 182.

response to his beliefs about what he would want if he had a 'maximally informed and coherent set of desires'. The mere existence of irresistible impulses, therefore, does not necessarily excuse bad behaviour. Critical to Smith's analysis is a distinction between what he terms 'synchronic' self-control (self-control at a particular moment of vulnerability, say gross intoxication by drugs) and 'diachronic' exercise of self-control (that is, self-control at a period before vulnerability or before the drugs were consumed). It is within the period prior to the loss of control that a person may be said to have the opportunity to deliberate, to bring into play their desires, knowledge, beliefs and preferences, and so to select an appropriate course of action in a right way. If there is at this stage a capacity within the agent to select a moral course of action, then they can be said to be accountable if they take the path which leads to ultimate loss of control. Again, this analysis enlarges the scope of responsibility.

Grant Gillett adopts a rather different approach to the determination of intention. He quite explicitly rejects the idea that intention is a causal and 'datable' mental event, antecedent to a public action. He suggests, instead, that good or bad intentions are always an expression of an individual's social and moral character and that the individual plays a vital role in the construction and development of that character. In this view, we are 'the situated narrators' of our own lives. Our situation is our particular (linguistic) community, which provides the rules and conventions that govern our lives but which we are also able to deploy, adapt and manipulate, according to our own life projects. To discern intention, therefore, we must look to the person's own understandings of themselves, their sense of their own character, within their particular situation. To Gillett, 'Every action I do is in its own way both formative of, and expressive of, my character as an agent.' This conception of the individual agent bears an interesting resemblance to the criminal legal subject theorised by Ian Leader-Elliott later in the volume.

Part II: Intention and Individual Responsibility

The second part of the book is the work of lawyers who consider the application of intention to a particular branch of law. Here we are able to observe the various ways in which criminal, contract and tort law allocate responsibility to individual legal actors and the role assigned to the concept of intention. A number of important themes emerge from this discussion.

We discover a strong critical concern with the orthodox legal understanding of intention as a mental state, or event, an activity residing in the recesses of the human mind, which is neither physical nor tangible, and which therefore cannot be observed. What is problematic about this view, we learn, is that only the individual can know their own intentions and therefore an individual subject may disavow an intention ascribed to them by another. An individual can also be misinterpreted by another. Thus understood, intention poses an epistemological question: how can intention be known?

Many of the essays in this book are highly sceptical of the orthodoxy that intention is private and subjective. This scepticism leads to further critical scrutiny of a number of dualisms which are so much a part of the complex structure of our intellectual and legal traditions: subjective and objective, mind and body, individual and collective, and private and public.

Crimes

While, as a matter of practice, crimes are now increasingly based on strict liability,[2] the mental state of intention remains the paradigmatic case of *mens rea* (loosely translated as mental state) and it is still absolutely central to legal understandings of criminal responsibility. As William Blackstone phrased it late in the eighteenth century, 'as a vicious will without a vicious act is no civil crime, so on the other hand, an unwarrantable act without a vicious will is no crime at all'.[3] Accordingly the common law has long recognised defences such as infancy, duress and insanity because the evil will is thought to be missing. It was for this reason that the famous animal trials of the Middle Ages were brought to an end.

Though there is broad agreement among criminal lawyers about the central role of intention in the determination of responsibility, there remains considerable controversy about what precisely it means to intend a criminal act. Does it refer to a private mental event to which only the defendant is privy and which must be divined from her statements (that is,

---

2   The prosecution does not have to prove intention, recklessness or even negligence.
3   William Blackstone, *Commentaries on the Laws of England Vol 4* (first published 1765–69, 1979 ed) 21.

from what she says she meant to do, notwithstanding appearances) as well as her actions and the broader context of her actions?

Certainly the classical division in criminal law between the mental state of the offender and the physical act suggests that the mental state of intention is something private and invisible: something quite other than the observable and therefore public physical manifestation of behaviour. Indeed, the establishment of two conceptually distinct elements to a crime, the *actus reus* and the *mens rea*, necessarily suggests the separation of an abstract mind from a material body. 'Almost all expositions of criminal law theory accept, without discussion, the Cartesian theory of mind and body', as Waller and Williams discern. 'That is to say, they treat mental operations as being related to physical activity as cause is related to effect.'[4]

This divided view of the person is one that many philosophers and the more critical criminal lawyers have long rejected as implausibly mechanistic. And yet the continuing use made by criminal lawyers of thought experiments which beggar belief, experiments in which hypothetical criminal actors conduct themselves in almost robotic and amoral ways (documented both by Leader-Elliott and Sir Anthony Mason), reveals the lawyers' ongoing commitment to a fairly unreflective mind–body dualism.

Although criminal law still purports to have recourse to the interior mental state, paradoxically it offers a simultaneous challenge to the idea of intention as a mental event, which only the individual knows for sure (and who can therefore always say 'I didn't mean to do that'). It does this by assigning meanings to intention which are quite distinct from ordinary language usage. As Mason explains in his essay on the law of murder, this is most evident when the accused's knowledge of certain consequences, which may not be desired, are nevertheless equated with criminal intention.

Leader-Elliott also considers the manner in which criminal law may make it impossible for an individual accused of a crime to disavow intention. Instead the criminal law may impose a 'conclusive characterisation of intention' which means that the individual is obliged to adopt law's meaning, not his own. By way of illustration, Leader-Elliott observes: 'Frequently ... defendants' descriptions of their intentions do not

---

4   Waller and Williams, *Brett, Waller and Williams Criminal Law: Text and Cases* (7th ed, 1993) 9.

prevail. Offenders who are convicted of theft as a consequence of "borrowing" another's property must be surprised, on occasion, to discover that what they intended was a permanent deprivation of the victim's property.'

Torts

Criminal law, as public law, demands self-control because of our moral responsibility to the community at large. By contrast, the law of torts is usually concerned with private legal actions—with citizen litigating against citizen. And yet, paradoxically, tort appears to be even less concerned than criminal law with a search for the private or subjective intentions of the individual tortfeasor and more concerned with public or 'objective' standards of behaviour. In the law of torts, individuals who cause harm by ignorance or inadvertence are often as culpable as those who intend their actions. A reason for this distinction between crimes and torts is provided by Peter Cane. He argues that, while criminal law focuses on the individual as a moral agent, the law of torts is more concerned with the external consequences of actions. It is concerned with the harm done to individual victims, and with the wrong done to society at large. As Cane explains, intention in tort law has therefore received comparatively little attention. Indeed when determining liability negligence has been far more influential than intention. Cane assesses the meaning of intention within this area of law and its relationship to other mental concepts such as voluntariness, recklessness, motive and belief.

Although the action for negligence has become pre-eminent among the modern torts, intention has not been entirely forsaken. Sandra Berns considers two of the so-called 'intentional torts': trespass to the person and action on the case for intentionally causing nervous shock. Intention in the law of torts is decidedly not concerned with the subjective mental state of the defendant, as Berns explains. Rather, intention is a formal device, a legal construct, whose symbolic purpose is to recognise human dignity and to assign responsibility for its infringement. A central concern for Berns is that the tortious construction of intention does not operate in a gender-neutral or objective manner. Instead it interprets the harms done to the bodies of men and women in quite different ways, working as it does within various sex-stereotypical narrative forms.

Contracts

Intention still plays a critical role within the law of contract, even though it is well accepted that the classical age of contract has come and gone. The underlying assumption within this branch of law is that the contracting parties, through their chosen contracts, declare and impose their intentions and thereby govern themselves and assert their autonomy as legal subjects. In the classical theory, prominent in the nineteenth century,[5] contract was an agreement based on the intentions of two or more parties. According to this theory, the law ensured that the parties honoured their stated intentions and provided damages when they departed from their agreement. The problem of how one is ever to know the 'private' subjective intent of the other person is therefore integral to the law of contract. For, in this classical view, it is the duty of the court to discover the individual wills of the parties—what they wanted from the agreement and what they said they would do as a consequence—and then impose their willed legal agreement.

By the end of the nineteenth century, the 'will theory' of contract had given way to the idea that the will objectified was the true measure of contract, as Margaret Thornton notes in her essay. The introduction of implied terms to contracts further removed the legal agreement from the actual intentions of the parties. And yet even today there remains a continuing legal commitment to the idea that a contract represents the wills of the respective parties; it is just that now the law is more likely to dictate those intentions, and impute them to the parties. However the process of interpretation employed by courts is still regarded as a neutral or transparent method of divining the will of the individual subject.

It is this classical view, that contract is concerned with the subjective will of the parties, that Michael Detmold also disputes in his account of intention. For Detmold, all lawful relations are contractual. He maintains that there is never a true contract if the parties remain fixed in their private understanding of what it is they wanted. Though he concedes that a contract is a meeting of minds, he insists that the making of a contract is a public, and therefore highly social, activity. It is only by making one's own intentions manifest to the other and simultaneously coming to know and respect the intention of the other person, and responding accordingly, that

---

5 P S Atiyah, *The Rise and Fall of Freedom of Contract* (1979) 405–8 traces this development of contract theory.

there is a true contract, that is a mutuality of understanding, which the court should enforce. To Detmold, the word 'intention' does no more than identify a discourse in which the sole issue is the construction, maintenance or breach of the relations of minds. Thus the terms 'intentional', 'reckless' and 'negligent' all identify degrees of exclusion of the other from one's mental life (in other words, the degree of one's reversion to the private). (Detmold no doubt would add that the private is not a place to be; it is actually madness, of which no account is available.)

Detmold's account of contract nonetheless adheres to a view that law is always neutral between the individual parties. By contrast, Thornton, like Berns, seeks to uncover the ideological dimensions of law's construction of intention in contract. Using the private world of the marriage contract as a counterpoint to the contracts of the commercial world of the public marketplace, she argues that there is nothing necessary, or natural, in law's attribution of intention to its actors. The marriage contract, as she observes, is an admixture of (chosen or intentional) contract and (state-assigned) status. And, through this selective use of intention, law helps to preserve and enforce the separation of family and market, and the private and the public spheres of life, in ways which do harm to women. The resurgence of neo-liberal ideology, with its emphasis on individual agency, lends added complexity to Thornton's argument, as the law seeks to accommodate new forms of contract in the private sphere, such as cohabitation agreements, and even possibly same-sex marriages.

Part III: Intention and the Collective

The individualistic nature of intention—its starting premise that an individual mind is doing the intending—generates further legal problems for the attribution of collective responsibility. These are tackled in the third part of this book. When it is a group, not an individual, which is responsible for anti-social behaviour, how does one allocate fault? Whose is the relevant mind and is there such a thing as a collective mind? Even with the refinements of the concept of intention identified and implemented in the preceding chapters, the concept seems to remain ineluctably individual in nature. Only the person has a mind, and intention is a mental characteristic. Intention is always tied to an individual person who exhibits a capacity for rational thought which is employed in the guidance of actions (or sometimes not, as the case may be) for which the individual then bears responsibility. Intention, we could say, is naturalised to the individual. Even when it is artificially assigned to non-human beings, it is the intentional individual person who supplies the ideal type.

Intention in Groups

The emphasis on the individual mind generates a problem in the case of group behaviour, particularly with the attribution of a purposive character to a group action and then the assignment of collective responsibility for it. Yet one of the most striking characteristics of human beings is their ability to work and act together in groups, and therefore the attribution of intention to groups is a common phenomenon. We are all familiar with the anthropomorphisation of the group; we recognise the way in which intention draws its meaning from the human person.

In his essay on collective intention, Philip Pettit accepts that reason is integral to intention. Thus he maintains a link between intention and the individual deliberating person in control of their actions. However, from this first premise, Pettit goes on to argue that when the agent is a collective, not an individual, it must 'collectivise' reason if it is to be said to have a collective intention. Collective intention is therefore essentially a procedural matter: the process of collectivising reason is a necessary precursor to the attribution of intention to any group. For lawyers, it is therefore instructive to reflect on the problems of assigning intention to a parliament, in the enactment of legislation, or of stating the *ratio decidendi* of a case that contains several (individual) judgments from the members of the court. Pettit's delineation of the conditions for collective intention enables him to state precisely the necessary relation between the individuals who comprise the group and the group as an entity, their respective roles and hence their respective responsibilities. While there can be collective responsibility for the actions of the group, Pettit shows that there can be no simple elision of individual and group responsibility.

The complex nature of many organisations makes the ascription of responsibility to them particularly difficult, as Suzanne Corcoran reveals in her essay. Although the law treats the corporation as a single entity, indeed explicitly anthropomorphises it as a legal 'person', the modern corporation often takes the form of a complex matrix of groups (especially, say, in its multinational form). Corcoran's essay is full of practical illustrations of the various ways corporate law has sought to overcome the individualistic nature of intention and to attribute responsibility, both collectively and individually (for the corporation can only act through individual human persons), for corporate misbehaviour. Corcoran reveals that legal intention as it pertains to the corporation has been obliged to develop a number of characteristics not usually associated with intention in individuals.

Discerning Collective Intention in Legal Texts

The legal attribution of intention, and thus the assignment of responsibility for 'group' action, is an important part of law's governance in the modern world in which corporations play such a significant role. But the legal problems of divining collective intention are not confined to the corporation. Positivism is the dominant organising theory of modern law and for positivists (and also for many others to a lesser or varying degree) the law is contained in texts that have been produced by collectives. Texts that take the form of statutes (including constitutions) are produced by groups of people. The judgments of courts are often produced by a group of judges. The intention of the legal text has thus come to be thought of as part of the very structure of law, though it has remained largely inscrutable. Lawyers are therefore always trying to make sense of what a group meant, be it the legislature or the judiciary.

The analysis of the intention of written law, of statute or constitution, necessarily raises a number of issues already considered in this collection. In particular, the debate about whether intention is a 'private' mental event, or whether it is a function of public meaning and interpretation, is especially acute where intentions are expressed within a text (including posited law) to which a community of language users must give meaning.

Because the very idea of the intention of a text seems so counter intuitive (we spoke earlier of the naturalising of intention to the human actor), the search for legislative intent might be thought to entail a search for the intention of the human author *behind* the text. Perhaps this is why the early approach to statutory interpretation, which precluded examination of extrinsic material such as statements made in parliamentary debates leading up to enactment, has been abandoned in recent years in some jurisdictions.[6] However modern legislation is generally the product of a

---

6   See, for example, *Acts Interpretation Act 1901* (Cth) s 15AB.

democratic assembly comprised of many, indeed often hundreds of, individuals. It is therefore now generally accepted that a search for the intention of individual legislators may do little to aid in the explication of their collective intention.

A rather different approach to the construction of statutes has been adopted by postmodern interpreters of law. They have tended to focus on the *reader* of the text of the law, not the writer, and in proclaiming 'the death of the author'[7] some have eschewed the role of intention altogether. Much of the recent scholarly legal literature on intention has been heavily influenced by literary theorists who have questioned the very idea of authorial intention. In this broad school of thought, debates have tended to focus solely on the reading of texts, and have paid little attention to the concept of intention.

And yet lawyers have not abandoned the search for parliamentary intent or 'the mind of parliament'. In her essay, Natalie Stoljar explores three influential theories of intention that are used to explain the meaning of a legal text, each of which relies on the idea of a 'hypothetical intention of a postulated author'. Implicitly, each concedes the impossibility of divining the intention of the actual author, hence the recourse to a fictional author. In the course of her essay, Stoljar reflects critically on the work of a number of prominent legal theorists: Ronald Dworkin, Stanley Fish, Michael Moore, John Rawls, Frederick Schauer and Jeremy Waldron.

Both Tom Campbell and John Williams deal with the problem of intention in text-dependent law: they consider ordinary and constitutional legislation respectively. While both recognise the importance of intention in the interpretation of the text of the law, each provides a distinctive account of its meaning.

Campbell offers a theory of statutory interpretation that is in some senses 'originalist': that is, it goes back to the origins of the text, to the intentions of the authors. However he eschews the idea that the intention of the statute is the same as the subjective intent of individual legislators. Rather, legislative intent is to be found in the ordinary meaning of the words as understood within the community at the time of enactment. Campbell explains that in the legislative process the only agreement is in relation to the words; the disagreements between individual legislators

---

7   Roland Barthes, 'The Death of the Author' in Roland Barthes, *Image, Music, Text* (Stephen Heath (trans)) (1977) 142.

about objectives and motives are never necessarily resolved. In this account, intention is incorporated into a theory of legitimacy that includes the democratic foundation of statutes, the rule of law and the distinctive roles of legislators and judges.

Williams is concerned with constitutions, rather than with ordinary statutes. In this the centenary year of the Australian Constitution, there is a heightened awareness of the historical foundations of the constitutional text, including the intentions of the 'founding fathers'. However, Williams questions the relevance for law of the recovery of the framers' intentions as an exclusively historical exercise. Because constitutions are designed to endure, it is inappropriate, in his view, to rely primarily on the founders' specific intentions. He argues instead that we should consider the broad legal purposes of the framers. His is a 'soft originalism', in that he accepts that the framers intended to create a framework for the political and legal institutions of the community, but they did not, and could not, anticipate the particular meanings of constitutional terms that must necessarily evolve and change over time.

Part IV: Beyond Intention?

Many of the papers in this volume have documented the problems with the concept of intention. So can we do without it completely? Can we assign responsibility in the absence of an intentional actor?

In the final essay of the volume, Braithwaite takes us beyond intention. This is not simply another challenge to the idea of intention as a 'private' mental state. Rather Braithwaite suggests that for the majority of wrongs intention need not concern us. Specifically, Braithwaite considers whether it is possible to have a legal system that focuses on the public consequences of harmful actions, rather than on an individual's wrongful intentions, ultimately with a view to 'the cultivation of restorative virtues' or a good society. Thus he is concerned more with the wrong done (say the *actus reus*) than with the mind behind it (say the *mens rea*). Braithwaite finds our legal system to be too backward looking, too preoccupied with the imposition of fault. As he explains, '[a]ttempts to impose intentionality-based fault lead to vicious circles of mutual recrimination, condemnation of the condemners in what shame scholars call shame-rage spirals'. The law should therefore attend less to the assignment of individual blame than to putting right the wrong.

The significance of this movement beyond intention is powerfully demonstrated by the Truth and Reconciliation Commission hearings, which have played such an important and symbolic role in facilitating the emergence of the new South Africa. It is arguably also a part of the efforts to effect a reconciliation between white and indigenous Australians. And so it is fitting to conclude the collection with Braithwaite's contribution.

PART I:
THE PHILOSOPHY OF
INTENTION

2 How Decision Theory Illuminates Assignments of Moral Responsibility

FRANK JACKSON

There is a mental element in moral responsibility. If Jones dies when I turn on the light because, unknown to me, the light circuit is connected to a bomb in Jones's house on the other side of the street, I am causally responsible for his death. But I am not morally responsible for his death. (Unless my lack of knowledge is culpable; we will return to this issue later.) And the reason is, as we might say it, that I am not 'mentally the right way' to be morally responsible. We all agree, also, that what it takes to be mentally 'right' to be morally responsible is closely tied up with the intentional nature of the action in question. Roughly—very roughly—I am not morally responsible for Jones's death because I did not in any way intend it.

The controversies start when we seek to make things less rough. Is the crucial point about the example that I did not and could not foresee that turning on the light would lead to Jones's death? Or do we need to distinguish between what is intended and what is merely foreseen when we address issues of moral responsibility, and is it the former that is really important? Or is the key distinction that between what is directly, and what is only obliquely, intended? Or is the really important distinction that between doing and allowing, or equivalently between acts and omissions?

We are all familiar with this cluster of issues. I will simply record my view that the whole area is a disaster. It is hard enough to make good sense of the various distinctions in the philosophy of action and mind, but when we examine attempts to explain *why* they matter for the moral issues to do with holding people responsible, things go from bad to worse, or so it seems to me.

What I will do is describe one simple way of making good general sense of *why* there is an intentional action requirement for moral responsibility. We will see, though, that the way to understand the requirement allows that we can be responsible for something we do not intend. The act must be an intentional one, but the outcome need not be an intended (or foreseen) one. I will also show how this approach explains why acting under a constraint or under coercion can affect one's moral liability, and explains why you can be morally responsible for reckless behaviour and for culpable ignorance. I conclude with a brief discussion of *Morgan*.[1]

I would particularly advertise the ability of the approach to *explain* how culpable ignorance is possible in a way that makes clear sense in the light of the mental element, the *mens rea*, in being morally responsible. When we seek an account of moral responsibility, an account of when A is morally responsible for B, we need, as noted above, to add to A's being causally responsible for B, clauses of one kind or another concerning the agent's mental state when acting. In many cases, it seems plausible to add clauses concerning A's knowledge or belief about what would result, or A's intending in some way or other what resulted.[2] However, in cases of culpable ignorance, B need not be an intended or expected result for there to be moral responsibility. A doctor who kills someone because he or she cannot be bothered to check the right dosage of a drug is held morally (and legally) responsible even though he or she may well neither have intended nor expected nor foreseen the result. But often culpable ignorance is handled by simply tacking on, as a kind of afterthought, a further clause at the end of the account to the effect that B must be intended or foreseen *except* when the case is one involving culpable ignorance; for, in such a case, A can be properly held morally responsible when B is neither intended nor foreseen. Unfortunately, the connection of this clause with the clauses about the mental element in being morally responsible is, at best, obscure. Indeed, typically there is a definite tension. The discussion of the mental element seems to point to the need for an intention to do something bad, or maybe some kind of foreseeing that something bad will happen. But then it is noted that there is such a thing as culpable ignorance, and that in such cases there need not be the relevant intention, expectation or foresight. One is left wondering where this leaves the earlier argument about the need for something like intention, expectation or foresight. Indeed, some have been so concerned with this tension that

---

1   *R v Morgan* [1976] AC 182.
2   For one example among many, see John Mackie, *Ethics: Inventing Right and Wrong* (1977) 208 ff.

they have been tempted with the idea that the only way to make sense of culpable ignorance is to treat it as a form of strict liability. Or they at least have thought that culpable ignorance and negligence involve some kind of departure from the *mens rea* requirement. Sometimes they have even been tempted to propose that we should delete culpable ignorance and negligence from the category of acts for which agents may be held morally (and legally) responsible.[3] Be all this as it may, on the approach I will propose the why and wherefore of culpable ignorance follows naturally from an understanding of the mental element in moral responsibility.

Hume on Action

The approach takes off from a picture of intentional action that David Hume most especially made explicit.[4]

Intentional acts arise from what we believe and desire. Indeed, on most views including Hume's, they arise in the straightforward sense of being caused by what we believe and desire. For example, my intentional action of opening my mail is caused by my desire to learn what is inside my letters and my belief that a good way to learn what is inside my letters is by opening them.[5] But, for our purposes here, it does not matter whether or not the relation is causation. What matters is that when people act intentionally, they always have a belief and a desire that give rise to, or which explain in some sense or other, the act. Of course, we often do not cite both the belief and the desire. We cite one or the other, and let context supply the missing term. Why did Fred take an umbrella? We might say, 'Because he thought it was going to rain'. There is no need to mention explicitly his desire not to get wet. We take the desire for granted once the belief is given. Or instead we might answer the question by saying, 'Because he did not want to get wet'. There is no need to mention his belief that umbrellas keep one dry. We take the belief for granted once the desire is given. All the same, there must have been both a belief and a desire.

---

3   See the discussion of the views of J W C Turner and G Williams in H L A Hart, *Punishment and Responsibility* (1968) ch VI. Hart himself insists that holding agents responsible for negligent acts does not involve a departure from *mens rea*. His reasons are distinct from those I will be offering.

4   David Hume, *A Treatise of Human Nature* (1888). See, eg, Book II, pt III, sec III.

5   Donald Davidson, 'Actions, Reasons and Causes', reprinted in his *Essays on Actions and Events* (1980) 3–19, is a classic contemporary source of this view.

It is also part of the Humean picture that the belief and desire are distinct: any belief can go with any desire. This is more controversial. Some insist, for example, that if you believe that some action is right, you *must* have at least some tendency to desire to do it. But it is relatively non-controversial that there must always be both belief and desire. True, some philosophers insist that sometimes belief alone can explain action; but it turns out that the sense in which they hold that desire may sometimes be absent is the sense of desire tied to bodily desires, not desire in the wide sense that Hume and modern day Humeans like Davidson have in mind. In this wide sense, desire is a generic pro-attitude which may or may not go along with anything like a yearning. A desire for water arising from medical advice that we should drink more water is just as much a desire for water in this wide sense as is thirst. Or sometimes, when they say that belief alone can explain action, it turns out that they allow that there must be desire in the wide sense; their point is rather that desire may not be a separate ingredient in the picture. The fact of desire follows from the nature of the belief, or sometimes from the way the belief leads to action. It is not, in their view, something extra to be added to the story. This is certainly an anti-Humean view but not one we need to quarrel with here. All we need is that there is both belief and desire when we act intentionally.

Indeed, the only objection to the view that intentional action requires both belief and desire that has any significant currency is the claim that more or less mindless actions like drumming one's fingers on the table can be intentional but are not typically backed by a belief-desire pair. But in fact there is a belief-desire pair backing drumming one's fingers on the table (when it is intentional). The belief will be, say, that time will pass that little bit faster if I drum my fingers, or maybe that I will feel that little bit more at ease if I drum my fingers, or something along these general lines. And the desire will be to have time pass that little bit faster, or to be a bit more at ease, or something along these lines. The same goes for familiar actions like shifting in one's chair during a meeting. In these cases, there may not be conscious reflection on the relevant beliefs and desires, but they will be present all the same provided that the action is intentional.

We need, however, to make a major addition or refinement to the core of the Humean picture. Belief and desire come in degrees, and that must be included in more refined accounts of intentional action. When we act, we balance our degrees of belief with the strength of our desires or preferences, and this has to be taken into account in order to explain actions. In many cases, it is not the case that agents' actions may be explained by their desiring some outcome that they believe their actions will realise. For example, often it is wrong to explain why someone applies for a job in terms of their belief that applying will lead to getting the job, and their desire to get the job. Many job applicants do not believe that they will get the job. What is true, rather, is that they give enough credence or subjective probability to getting the job to explain why they apply when we take into account how much they prefer being employed to being unemployed, or having that particular job to the one they currently have. The point is even more obvious if we consider how we explain gambling behaviour. Most horses we bet on are ones we do *not* expect to win; what explains our behaviour is how much we desire the possible winnings (and the thrill of betting) along with our judgement that, although the horse most likely will not win, its chances nevertheless justify betting at the odds on offer. The same goes even more obviously for betting at roulette.

The way to refine and extend Hume to take account of the fact that belief and desire come in degrees and that this matters for understanding what explains intentional action is given by decision theory. In what follows, I draw on one version of decision theory, known as Jeffrey-style or evidential decision theory. There are controversies over, *inter alia*, whether this style of decision theory should be replaced by a more causal style, but they do not matter for present purposes and it is easiest to work with a well-known, highly developed version of decision theory.[6]

Decision Theory

Agents have credences or degrees of belief or subjective probability functions defined on a space of possible worlds or possible states of affairs, or an event space in the language of statistics. Every possible world or state of affairs has a subjective probability between 0 and 1, which measures an agent's degree of belief that it is the actual world or the way things actually are. The probabilities across the space sum to 1. An agent's probability that it will rain tomorrow, or degree of belief in that state of affairs obtaining, is then given by summing the probabilities of all the worlds where it rains tomorrow. More generally, in symbols

---

6   Richard Jeffrey, *The Logic of Decision* (1965). For the debate between evidential and causal decision theory, see, eg, Ellery Eells, *Rational Decision and Causality* (1982).

$$Pr(X) = E_WPr(w \text{ at which } X)$$

for any proposition X, where '$Pr(X)$' is the probability of X, and '$E_WPr(w$ at which $X)$' is: $Pr(w_1) + Pr(w_2) + Pr(w_3) + Pr(w_4) + ...$ for all the w_i such that X obtains at w_i.

Agents also have preference functions which assign a desirability to every possible world according to how much they would like that world to be the actual world. The desirability may be positive or negative, or zero in the special case where the subject is indifferent to whether or not the world obtains. The desirability of a proposition or state of affairs or outcome of an action is then the probabilistically weighted sum of the desirability of the worlds where it obtains. In symbols

$$Des(X) = E_WDes(w).Pr(w/X)$$

where '$Des(X)$' is the desirability of proposition X obtaining, '$Pr(w/X)$' is the probability of world w given X, and '$E_WDes(w).Pr(w/X)$' is: $Des(w_1).Pr(w_1/X) + Des(w_2).Pr(w_2/X) + ...$, where the w_1, w_2, ... are all the worlds.

Intuitively, the point is that how desirable something, X, is depends on how desirable the various ways it might be realised are, weighted by how likely each way is to be the way X is realised. Thus, the contribution of some possible wonderful results of an operation to its desirability get dragged down to the extent that they are unlikely; similarly, the negative contribution of some possible very bad results get moderated to the extent that they are unlikely. We could express $Des(X)$ as the probabilistically weighted sum for all w where X obtains, but as the w where X does not obtain are ones where $Pr(w/X) = 0$, this is otiose.

The refinement of Hume is that, instead of simply saying that intentional acts arise from belief-desire pairs, we say that intentional acts arise from subjective probability function-preference function pairs, from, that is, degrees of belief and desirability. Where the simple picture says that what agents do is determined by what they believe and desire, the refinement says that what they do is determined by their preference and credence functions. But how is it so determined?

For each available action, X, at some given time, there is an expected desirability for the agent determined by multiplying the desirability of the action's various possible outcomes for the agent by their probability for the agent given the action is performed, and summing. In symbols

$$EDes(X) = E_iDes(O_i).Pr(O_i/X)^7$$

where '$EDes(X)$' is the expected desirability of action X, and '$E_iDes(O_i).Pr(O_i/X)$' is: the desirability of O_1 times the probability of O_1 given X plus the desirability of O_2 times the probability of O_2 given X plus ..., where the O_i are all the possible outcomes.

Decision theory says that, out of the acts available to an agent at a time, the agent will do that which has maximum expected desirability. This is the needed refinement on the too simple formula that agents do that which they believe will realise that which they desire. The refinement is required in order to take account of the way belief and desire come in degrees.

We can use this picture of how intentional actions arise from agents' probability and preference functions to give a straightforward account of when agents are morally responsible for what they do.[8] There is a right way and a wrong way to rank worlds or states of affairs in terms of desirability; there are right and wrong preference functions. Worlds which involve equitable distributions are, by and large, better than those which involve inequitable distributions—though exactly why is a matter of controversy. Worlds which involve great pain and suffering are worse than those which involve much happiness. And so on. So, in addition to how people actually rank various possible worlds, there is how they ought to rank them; there is how desirable they find them, and how desirable they ought to find them. Let us say that the 'right' preference function is the one that ranks w_1 ahead of w_2 exactly when w_1 is in fact better than w_2. Now we can give the core idea of this paper:

> Agents are morally responsible when they fail to maximise expected desirability according to the right desirability or preference function.

---

7   In causal versions, we get something along the lines of: $EDes(X) = E_i Des(O_i).Pr(X$ $—>O_i)$, where the '—>' is given a causal reading. Sometimes, '$Des(O_i)$' is replaced by '$Des(X.O_i)$' to allow for the possibility that the desirability of an outcome may be affected by the nature of the action that gives rise to it. For our purposes here, we can read outcomes as including the actions that they arise from when appropriate.

8   In the negative sense; we are thinking of blameworthiness rather than praiseworthiness throughout.

We might call expected desirability according to the right preference function *expected moral value* (EMV), and we can then state the view that agents are morally responsible when they fail to maximise expected moral value.

The core idea is that moral responsibility is a matter of something bad about agents' preference functions—that is, what they desire, taking account of the way it comes in degrees—leading to their doing the wrong thing; that is how to understand the *mens rea* of moral responsibility. Of course, none of us has the right preference function—unless there is a saint among us. But the suggestion is that only when the failings of our preference function lead to our doing the wrong thing in some given situation are we morally responsible for the bad that results. It is when we do bad *because* we have bad preferences that we are morally liable.

All this may sound rather abstract. But when we consider some examples, it is very straightforward. I will start with how this approach explains why coercion makes a difference to moral responsibility.

How to be Blameworthy Despite Intending the Good

There are a number of cases which show that we can be morally responsible even when we intend that something good occurs. These are cases where we seek after the good but take unacceptable risks in doing so, and we do not get away with it and something bad happens. In these cases, we are rightly held morally responsible for the bad that happens but, obviously, the explanation cannot be that we intended the bad that happens.

Here is a case. I want to cure someone of a rather unpleasant but in no way life-threatening skin condition. I give them a drug which I know is very likely to cure them without any harmful side effects but I know it has a 5 per cent chance of killing them. It kills them. I intended to cure them—which is to intend something good—but I am rightly held responsible for their death. It might be objected that I did not intend to cure them because I knew there was 5 per cent chance of failure. But consider what happens when we play golf. We may intend to hole a putt longer that one metre despite there being a 5 per cent chance of failure.

The approach via decision theory explains why I am morally responsible in terms of the great disvalue of death according to the right value function. This means that the action of my giving the drug did not have the greatest expected moral value. To see this, note that the relevant possible actions are: administering the drug versus not doing so, and the relevant possible outcomes are: dying versus being cured. So we need to look at the relationship between

EMV(drug administered) = Pr(death/drug administered).V(death) + Pr(cure/drug administered).V(cure)

and

EMV(drug not administered) = Pr(death/drug not administered).V(death) + Pr(cure/drug not administered).V(cure).

In the case as stated, EMV(drug not administered) will be greater than EMV(drug administered), so I failed to maximise moral value when I administered the drug. This is why I am morally responsible for the death.

How Coercion Exculpates

An action which is wrong in the absence of coercion can be right in the presence of coercion. It is wrong for a bank teller to give Clyde some of the bank's money because he asks nicely. But the teller is not held morally responsible for giving Clyde money at the point of a gun. Why does the gun make the difference? One popular answer is that the action is not free in that case. But the teller is not in a straightjacket or anything like that. The sense in which the gun alters matters is that it alters what is likely to happen if no money is forthcoming; we can say if we like that the teller's hand is forced, but the teller still has the option of not handing the money over. The sense in which the action is forced is simply that the outcome involves something very unpleasant.

However, if we approach the question via the question of which act maximises expected moral value, there is a simple answer as to why the gun makes a difference. When there is no gun, handing over the money fails to maximise expected moral value; when there is a gun, handing over the money maximises expected moral value. The reason is that the gun, or more precisely the teller's knowledge of it, changes the likely outcomes of the courses of action available to the teller. To make the point transparent, let's look at a simplified, schematic picture of how one might do an expected moral value calculation in the case where there is a gun and where there is not.

In the case where there is no gun, we need to look at the relationship between

> EMV(handing over money) = Pr(bank loses money and Clyde happy/hand over).V(bank loses money and Clyde happy) + Pr(bank does not lose money and Clyde unhappy/hand over).V(bank does not lose money and Clyde unhappy).

and

> EMV(not handing over money) = Pr(bank loses money and Clyde happy/do not hand over).V(bank loses money and Clyde happy) + Pr(bank does not lose money and Clyde unhappy/do not hand over).V(bank does not lose money and Clyde unhappy).

It is obvious that the EMV of not handing over exceeds that of handing over. Clyde's unhappiness counts for little against the bank's loss. This is why the teller who handed over the money in this case would be morally responsible.

In the case where there is a gun, we need to look at the relationship between

> EMV(handing over money) = Pr(bank loses money and Clyde happy and teller lives/hand over).V(bank loses money and Clyde happy and teller lives) + Pr(bank does not lose money and Clyde unhappy and teller does not live/do not hand over).V(bank does not lose money and Clyde unhappy and teller does not live).

and

> EMV(not handing over money) = Pr(bank loses money and Clyde happy and teller lives/do not hand over).V(bank loses money and Clyde happy and teller lives) + Pr(bank does not lose money and Clyde unhappy and teller lives/do not hand over).V(bank does not lose money and Clyde unhappy and teller does not live).

In this case, because of the high value that attaches to the teller's remaining alive, the action with the highest expected moral value is handing over the money. Adding the gun into the equation changes the act with the greatest EMV from being that of not handing over to being that of handing over. This is why what the teller ought to do changes and why the conditions under which he or she is morally responsible changes.

Reckless Behaviour and Culpable Ignorance

We hold people morally—and legally—responsible for the bad that results from reckless behaviour despite the fact that the bad need not be intended. When someone dies because I am driving too fast or because I fail to write the words 'highly poisonous' on a bottle, I may very well be morally responsible for their death—which is not, of course, to say that I should be treated as a murderer—but I need not have intended their death. The same goes when someone dies because I failed to check something out that I should have checked. There are certain things doctors ought to find out about before they carry out certain operations or prescribe certain drugs, and if bad happens when they do not, they are held morally responsible. As we noted above, it need not be the case, and typically is not the case, that the bad was in any way intended. This is why there is a puzzle about how to find the requisite *mens rea* in such cases. The approach in terms of decision theory explains how we can be held morally responsible in such cases.

In many cases which we naturally describe in terms of recklessness, the agent is aware of the possibility of a bad result but disregards or suppresses it in his thinking. The agent knows that a bad result may happen but goes ahead anyway, not because he or she wants the bad result but because its possibility does not loom large enough in their thinking and action. It is easy to handle these cases via decision theory. Clearly, the agent does give a small chance to bad happening, and, if the bad is bad enough, this can mean that the reckless act has a lower expected moral value than its alternative. Here is an example to make the point transparent.

Suppose that I like driving fast down narrow, winding streets. I know that this increases the chance that I will hit someone but, although I do not want to hit someone, this knowledge does not dissuade me from driving fast down narrow, winding streets. In this case, the expected value calculation, in highly schematic form, would look as follows:

EMV(driving fast) = Pr(fun for me and death for another/I drive fast).V(fun for me and death for another) + Pr(fun for me and no death for another/I drive fast).V(fun for me and no death for another).

EMV(not driving fast) = Pr(less fun for me and death for another/I do not drive fast).V(less fun for me and death for another) + Pr(less fun for me and no death for another/I do not drive fast).V(less fun for me and no death for another).

It is obvious that the EMV of my driving fast will be lower that that of my not driving fast—a small chance of another dying more than cancels out the high probability of more fun for me—and so, if I drive too fast in the kind of case under discussion, I will be someone with a value function that does not give enough weight to the lives of others over my own pleasure—which is the *mens rea* we were looking for. This is why if bad results from my driving fast down narrow, winding streets I am rightly held responsible.

However, some cases that we naturally describe in terms of negligence or culpable ignorance are not ones in which the possibility of something bad happening is noted but fails to exercise the pull it should. They seem more to be ones where the relevant possible bad result is not in any sense before the mind at all. Because the agent is ignorant—culpably but nevertheless genuinely ignorant—the possible bad result is not plausibly thought of as before their mind. Here is an example. I am a doctor prescribing a certain drug to a patient. I have no idea that in a small number of cases this drug causes blindness in a certain kind of patient. I prescribe the drug. I am unlucky and the drug makes the patient blind. Although this possibility was in no way before my mind—I literally had no idea that the drug could make anyone blind—I may still be properly held morally responsible by virtue of being culpably ignorant or negligent. It may be, as we say, that I ought to have known of the possibility of a disastrous result. Perhaps I should have checked the standard drug manual before writing the prescription or I should have consulted the experts in the relevant field and, if I had, I would have known of the problem. Of course, I need not be morally responsible—we cannot double or triple check everything. But I may be. We need, therefore, to understand how it is possible to be morally responsible despite the lack of anything like evil intent or even a sense that something might go wrong of the kind that is arguably always present in reckless behaviour. However, our account must also allow that, though I may be responsible, it does not have to be the case that I am. There is such a thing as bad luck that carries with it no element of culpability. Cases like these can—and should—also be handled via decision theory but it takes a little more work.

The key insight is that very often agents have, among their options, getting more information before making the decision that really interests them. Before people buy shares or a house they very often do some research. They first get more information, and then choose between buying or not buying in the light of the information obtained. There is a stage at which they decide not to get more information, of course. Otherwise, they would never get to buy anything! There has to be a point at which we stop getting information and simply act on what we have.

This raises the question of the conditions under which we should make our decision between *A* and *B* on the basis of what we know, and when we should get more information and decide between *A* and *B* on the basis of what we then know. And decision theory gives us the answer by noting that we can compare the expected value of acting on the information we have to hand versus getting more information and acting on the basis of the information we then have. Sometimes getting more information and proceeding to act on what then has, as a result, the highest expected value is the act with the highest expected value. Sometimes acting on the act which has the highest expected value before getting additional information is the act with the highest expected value. And, following the rule of maximising expected value, this means that when getting the additional information and acting in the light of it has the highest expected value we should get additional information, and when doing the act which has the highest expected value to start with has the highest expected value we should not get additional information before acting.

We can now say when agents count as morally responsible for a bad outcome through being culpably ignorant: it is when what they do (a) gives rise to something bad, and (b) the expected moral value of getting more information and acting on it is higher than the expected moral value of what they did.

Let me give an outline of the key calculation in a very simple case.[9] Suppose that *A* and *B* are the substantive options that concern me. Suppose that getting more information will either determine that *E* for sure, or not-*E* for sure. This means that we know what will happen to the expected moral

---

9   What follows is an elementary presentation of a familiar result. For a more detailed discussion and references to the sources, see Paul Horwich, *Probability and Evidence* (1982) 122 ff.

values of *A* and of *B*, after getting the additional information. Either they will be the original values except that the probabilities are conditionalised on *E* or else they will be the original values except that the probabilities are conditionalised on not-*E*. Finally, suppose that, before getting more information, it is *A* that has the highest expected moral value. We are concerned with the relationship between

(Immed): the expected value of acting right away

versus

(Wait): the expected value of acting after determining that *E*, or that not-*E*.

The expected value of the first is, of course, simply EMV(*A*).

To calculate the second, we start by distinguishing two cases: one where the further information cannot alter the relative ranking between *A* and *B*, and the other where it can. In the first case, we have both EMV(*A*/*E*) > EMV(*B*/*E*), and EMV(*A*/not-*E*) > EMV(*B*/not-*E*), where the EMV(—/—)'s are the expected moral values except the original probabilities are conditionalised on —. It follows that

(Wait) = Pr(*E*).EMV(*A*/*E*) + Pr(not-*E*).EMV(*A*/not-*E*).

It is easy to show that this equals EMV(*A*). Thus, when getting the additional information cannot change the relativities between *A* and *B*, that is, cannot change which is the right thing to do, (Immed) and (Wait) are the same. The expected moral value of acting straight off on what has the highest expected value versus acting on what would have the highest expected value after the new information has been obtained are one and the same. This is intuitively right. If the additional information cannot change the ranking between *A* and *B*, there could be no requirement to obtain it.

Now for case two, where the additional information may change the ranking between *A* and *B*. That is, either EMV (*B*/*E*) > EMV(*A*/*E*), or EMV(*B*/not-*E*) > EMV(*A*/not-*E*). It is easy to prove that both cannot obtain together. Again, this is intuitively the right result. If *B* would have the higher expected value both if *E* turned out to be the case, and if not-*E* turned out to be the case, we could say without actually carrying out the investigation that *B* was the right thing to do, contradicting the hypothesis that *A* is the right thing to do in the absence of the additional information.

So, if the investigation turning out one way reverses the ranking as between *A* and *B*, its turning out the other way does not. Suppose it is *E* turning out to be the case that reverses the ranking; that is, that EMV(*B*/*E*) > EMV(*A*/*E*), while EMV(*A*/not-*E*) > EMV(*B*/not-*E*). We can now calculate

(Wait) = Pr(*E*).EMV(*B*/*E*) + Pr(not-*E*).EMV(*A*/not-*E*).

It is easy to prove that (Wait) must, in case two, be larger than (Immed). And, in general, if getting more evidence can change the ranking between available options, the expected value of getting more information and acting on what then has the highest expected value is always higher than the expected value of acting on the evidence to hand. However, this does not mean that you should always get the additional information in such cases—it means you should do so provided the cost of getting the information is not too high.

In fact, we can be more precise. The difference between (Immed) and (Wait), that is, the amount by which (Wait) exceeds (Immed), is given by, as it is easy to prove,

(Z) = Pr(*E*).[EMV(*B*/*E*) - EMV(*A*/*E*)].

This means that the approach to moral responsibility via decision theory implies that the question of culpable ignorance turns on four factors. (i) Whether or not gathering new evidence can change which option has the highest ranking. (ii) How likely it is that any new evidence will change which option has the highest ranking—this is the 'Pr(*E*)' factor in (Z). (iii) How big a change would be involved—this is the 'EMV(*B*/*E*) - EMV(*A*/*E*)' factor in (Z). (iv) How costly it would be to obtain the new evidence—more particularly, whether (Z) is greater than the cost of determining whether *E* or not-*E* obtains.

It is interesting that none of this is really news to anyone. These four factors are those we all would have given after a little reflection as being key ones. What is striking—and confirming of our basic approach—is that we have deduced them from our basic approach.

Postscript: *Morgan*

What does our approach say about *Morgan*?

In *Morgan*, the Law Lords ruled three to two in favour[10] of the principle that if someone accused of rape in fact believed that the woman—or man, but it was a woman in the case—was consenting, be that belief a reasonable one or not, then they could not be found guilty of rape. This ruling created a furore, in part because of fears about its import in practice. It was feared that the ruling would make it too easy for rapists to escape conviction by arguing that they believed their victims were consenting. An interesting feature of the ensuing debate was that, although many commentators felt that, quite apart from the problem that the ruling might make rape convictions too hard to secure in practice, there was something deeply mistaken in principle about the ruling, they had considerable trouble saying precisely where the mistake was.[11]

To give one example, Kenny argued that the key mistake was that it was clear from the transcript that, independently of whether the defendants believed their victim was consenting, their intention was 'to have intercourse willy-nilly, ie *whether or not she consents*'.[12] This is no doubt true, but its relevance to the key issue is obscure. Suppose I keep one hundred dollars I find lying in my driveway, thinking it to have fallen out of my pocket. You may think that I would still have kept the money if I had thought it fell out of someone else's pocket, but that does not obviously make me a thief. It makes me, rather, someone of poor character who would be a thief in a case where I believed that the money was not mine.

On our approach to moral responsibility, it is easy to see where the Law Lords went wrong. The key issue is not whether or not the defendants believed their victim was consenting; it is whether or not they gave any significant degree of belief to her not consenting. Many people who agree to be operated on believe they will survive the operation—they would not agree otherwise—while giving the possibility that they will not a significant degree of belief. In *Morgan*, it is impossible to believe that the defendants did not give a significant degree of belief to their victim not consenting. But this means that they failed to maximise expected moral value. The defendants faced a choice between going ahead and stopping,

---

10   Lord Cross of Chelsea, Lord Hailsham of St Marylebone and Lord Fraser of Tullynelton; Lord Simon of Glaisdale and Lord Edmund-Davies dissenting.

11   E Curley, 'Excusing Rape' (1976) 5 *Philosophy and Public Affairs* 325 makes this case in detail. I am indebted to his discussion. I believe that the account I give here is the decision-theoretic version of his account of why the Law Lords were wrong in *Morgan*.

12   A J P Kenny, *Freewill and Responsibility* (1978) 65.

and we can give in very crude form the relevant expected value calculation as follows

EMV(go ahead) = Pr(rape/go ahead).V(rape) + Pr(intercourse between consenting adults/go ahead).V(intercourse between consenting adults).

EMV(stop) = Pr(dual disappointment/stop).V(dual disappointment) + Pr(rape avoided/stop).V(rape avoided).

Even this grossly over-simplified schema makes it clear that the defendants could not possibly have maximised expected moral value by going ahead. The circumstances of the case make it very clear that the probability of rape given they went ahead was not sufficiently low when multiplied by the very high disvalue of rape to allow the expected moral value of going ahead to be higher than that of stopping. This is so whether they believed in consent or not. The Law Lords majority principle focused on the wrong question. What was crucial was not the fact of belief but the degree of belief.

In the discussions that followed the Law Lords' ruling, much was made of the fact that the Law Lords did not think it crucial whether or not the defendants' belief was a reasonable one or one based on reasonable grounds. Many allowed that if the defendants had in fact believed that there was consent *and* if their belief had been a reasonable one, they were not guilty of rape. But even if their belief had been a reasonable one, it would still have been the case that they must have given a significant degree of belief—a significant degree of reasonable belief in this case—to their victim not consenting. And that is enough to make them guilty, as the decision-theoretic approach makes clear.

On this approach, reasonableness comes into the picture only when we address the question of when a belief is a reasonable one to act upon. A belief can be a reasonable one to hold but not a reasonable one to act upon having regard to the possible outcomes. It may be reasonable to hold that a certain branch will hold my weight but, if the branch is thirty metres above the ground, it may not be reasonable to put the matter to the test. The question of the reasonableness of a belief is distinct from the question of the reasonableness of acting on a belief. What is crucial in *Morgan* is that the defendants' action was unreasonable; and unreasonable independently of whether they believed in consent, and whether if they did (which they almost certainly did not, as the courts noted, which is why the Law Lords' principle did not lead to their acquittal) their belief was reasonable.[13]

---

13 I discussed some of these issues in 'A Probabilistic Approach to Moral Responsibility' in Ruth Barcan Marcus *et al* (eds), *Proceedings of the Seventh International Congress of Logic, Methodology, and Philosophy of Science* (1986) 351–66. I am indebted to the many discussions the earlier paper prompted, and must mention discussions with Philip Pettit and Stephanie Lewis.

3 Irresistible Impulse

MICHAEL SMITH

According to the McNaghten Rules of 1843, those charged with a criminal offence may be found not guilty by reason of insanity if they are so affected by a mental disease or defect that, at the time of the offence, they are either unable to understand the criminality of their act or are unable to conform their behaviour to the law. The precise interpretation of the rules is, however, a matter of some legitimate dispute.

In Australian criminal law the McNaghten Rules have been given a fairly wide interpretation. In *R v Porter* Justice Dixon said:

> If through the disordered condition of his mind [the accused] could not reason about the matter with a moderate degree of sense and composure it may be said that he could not know that what he was doing was wrong.[1]

Thus, in Dixon's view, people suffering from delusions, from brainwashing, and even those suffering from emotions and anxiety, should be excused to the extent that their delusory or brainwashed or discombobulated beliefs played a causal role in their conduct.

However some have argued that even Dixon's wide interpretation of the McNaghten Rules is unnecessarily narrow.[2] Dixon's gloss focuses exclusively on *cognitive* impairments, but there would seem to be *non-cognitive* impairments that impact on conduct as well. For example, those who suffer from an irresistible impulse, lacking all self-control, may know perfectly well that what they do is wrong. But if they are literally unable to translate their beliefs into action then, the suggestion goes, their conduct should be excused too. It should be excused because they are just as incapable of conforming their behaviour to the law as those whose reasoning capacities are impaired. Moreover, if there are people who, while not lacking the capacity for self-control entirely, have a capacity that

---

1   *R v Porter* (1933) 55 CLR 182, 189–190. Dixon J's judgment is quoted in Herbert Fingarette, *The Meaning of Criminal Insanity* (1972) 204 fn 17.
2   C L Ten, *Crime, Guilt and Punishment* (1987) 125.

is none the less diminished or limited in some way, then their liability too should be correspondingly limited.

There is no denying that this even wider interpretation of the McNaghten Rules accords with commonsense. But the mere fact that it accords with commonsense is no guarantee that the idea of an irresistible impulse, and the correlative idea of an agent's lacking all capacity for self-control, or having a diminished capacity for self-control, can be spelled out in a coherent and plausible way. My aim in the present essay is to focus attention on whether or not this can be done. To anticipate, I will argue that though these ideas make good sense, once we understand why they make good sense we also see some reason to suppose that they have only a limited application as excuses.

The Standard Humean Account of Action

In general terms our topic is to be the sense in which we have control over our actions. A natural starting point is therefore our ordinary conception of human action.

By nearly all accounts, an agent's actions are those of her bodily movements that spring in an appropriate way from her will. Non-bodily movements, and bodily movements that are caused in some other way—the movement of a leaf on a tree that is blown by the wind, say, or the bodily movement of someone who gets tossed about in the surf—are not actions at all. The crucial question that thus arises is what precisely it means to say that a bodily movement 'springs in an appropriate way' from an agent's 'will'. The distinctive feature of philosophical accounts of human action lies in the answer they give to this question.[3]

According to the standard Humean account of human action, for example, an agent's will is to be identified with her *system of desires and means-end beliefs*. The relation in which certain of her desires and means-end beliefs must stand to her bodily movements, for those bodily movements to count as actions of hers, is the *causal* relation. Thus, very roughly speaking, an agent's actions are those of her bodily movements that are caused by her desire for some outcome and her belief that that outcome can be produced by her moving her body in the way she does.

---

3   David Hume, *A Treatise of Human Nature* (1888). See, eg, Book II, pt III, sec III.

These are the bodily movements over which the agent is supposed to have control.[4]

Unfortunately, however, this rough characterisation is still a little too rough. For suppose that a budding actor desires to sound embarrassed and believes that she can sound embarrassed by saying 'Ugh!', but that this desire and belief cause her to say 'Ugh!' by causing her actually to become embarrassed. She makes an 'Ugh!' sound not as a pretence of embarrassment, but rather as an expression of embarrassment, embarrassment she feels at the prospect of acting on this particular desire and means-end belief. Then it seems that she doesn't have control over what she does despite the fact that her saying 'Ugh!' is caused by a relevant desire and means-end belief.

More precisely, then, the standard Humean account of action tells us that an agent's actions are those of her bodily movements that are caused *in the right kind of way* by her desires and means-end beliefs, where causation in the right kind of way is a matter of the agent's behaviours being not just caused by certain of her desires and beliefs, but also being differentially explainable by them, where differential explanation is a matter of the counterfactual sensitivity of her bodily movements to a whole host of the ever so slightly different desires and ever so slightly different means-end beliefs that she might have had instead. The agent's bodily movement is *counterfactually* sensitive to these slight differences because what *would have happened*, contrary to fact, *would have been different* if, contrary to fact, the agent had had ever so slightly different desires and means-end beliefs.[5]

In the case under discussion, for example, the agent's saying 'Ugh!' counts as an action only if it is not just caused by her desire to sound embarrassed and her belief that she can sound embarrassed by saying 'Ugh!', but it is also the case that, if she had believed that in order to sound embarrassed she would have to say 'Ooooh!', then she would have said 'Ooooh!'; and if she had believed that in order to sound embarrassed she would have to say 'Eeeeh!', then she would have said 'Eeeeh!'; and if she had desired to sound tired as well as embarrassed, and believed that the way to do that was to say 'Ugh!' through a yawn, then she would have said 'Ugh!' through a yawn; and so on and so forth. The reason the budding actor's saying 'Ugh!' as an expression of actual embarrassment doesn't count as an action, and hence isn't something over which she has control,

---

4   Donald Davidson, 'Actions, Reasons and Causes', reprinted in his *Essays on Actions and Events* (1980) 3–19, is the classic contemporary source of the standard account.

5   Christopher Peacocke, *Holistic Explanation* (1979).

is thus that her saying 'Ugh!' is not differentially explainable by her system of desires and beliefs. Even if she had believed that in order to sound embarrassed she would have to say 'Ooooh!', she would still just have said 'Ugh!'; and even if she had desired to sound tired as well as embarrassed, and believed that the way to do that was to say 'Ugh!' through a yawn, she would still just have said 'Ugh!'; and so on.

More generally, this more precise version of the standard account suggests that the following is a sufficient condition for an agent's having control over what she does: the agent's body moves in a certain way; that bodily movement is caused by a relevant desire and means-end belief the agent possesses; and the agent's bodily movement is also differentially explainable by her desires and means-end beliefs. With this conception of human action and control in the background, let's now ask what it might mean to say that an agent acts on an irresistible impulse, or that she acts but lacks all self-control.

What is an Irresistible Impulse?

A first conjecture would be that an irresistible impulse is an impulse that functions much like embarrassment functions in the situation just described. The reasoning might go like this.

Embarrassment in that case both caused the agent to say 'Ugh!' and would have caused the agent to say 'Ugh!' no matter what small differences we imagine in the desires and beliefs she possesses. In this sense, the impulse does seem both to be irresistible and to cause her to behave in a way that she cannot control. So, by analogy, an impulse that is irresistible must be one which both causes an agent to move her body in a certain way and which would have caused her to move her body in that way no matter what small differences we imagine in the desires she has and the means-end beliefs she has.

The problem with this first conjecture is, however, perhaps already clear. But in order to make the problem with it vivid, let's consider an agent who, depending on how we embellish his story, does plausibly act on an irresistible impulse. Suppose that Bob is a habitual drug user. He desires very strongly to take some heroin in the next short while and believes that, in order to do so, he will have to get some money. He considers the various ways in which he could get the money he needs in the time he has available and concludes that the most efficient method is to break into a certain house and steal it. As a result, let's suppose he breaks into the house and gets the needed money.

Now consider the conjecture. Is it at all plausible to suppose that Bob's desire to take heroin both causes him to move his body in a certain way—that is, in the break-into-the-house-and-steal-a-particular-amount-of-money way—and would have caused him to move his body in that way no matter what small differences we imagine in his wants and means-end beliefs? It most certainly is not plausible to suppose this. For Bob's bodily movement is, after all, an action, from which it follows straight away that it is a bodily movement which is not just caused by his desire for heroin and his belief that the way to get the money he needs is to break into a house and steal it, but is also differentially explainable by his desires and means-end beliefs. In other words, if Bob had thought that the most efficient way to get the money required for heroin was to break into the house a few minutes later than he had originally planned, then he would have broken into the house a few minutes later than he had originally planned; if he had desired to take a slightly higher dose of heroin, then he would have stolen the slightly larger amount of money required for the larger dose; and so on and so forth.

The upshot is thus that the mere fact that Bob acts at all on his desire to take heroin in the next short while and his belief about how that is to be accomplished suffices to falsify the first conjecture. The mere fact that an agent acts at all would seem to guarantee that he exerts a good deal of control over his bodily movement, precisely by ensuring the counterfactual sensitivity of what he does to small changes in his desires and means-end beliefs. Whatever an irresistible impulse is, then, it is nothing much like uncontrollable embarrassment.

A second conjecture therefore suggests itself, and this is that an irresistible impulse is a desire which both causes and differentially explains an agent's action, but which, in addition, is so strong that it is impossible for the agent who possesses it to have had an even stronger desire which would have outweighed it. In the case of Bob, the idea is thus that his desire for heroin is irresistible if it is so strong that it would be impossible for him to have an even stronger desire to do something else instead.

But this conjecture is hard to take seriously. For no matter how strong we imagine Bob's desire for heroin to be, it seems that we can always imagine a desire that is a little stronger. Indeed, it seems that we can often imagine circumstances in which an agent who plausibly has an irresistible impulse has actual desires which, in the right circumstances, would outweigh his impulse. Suppose, for example, that at the moment that he was about to break into the house Bob had seen a swarm of bees flying around inside. Is it supposed to follow from the fact that Bob's desire for heroin is irresistible that he would have gone ahead and broken into the house anyway? That seems manifestly implausible. But if this is right then not only is it possible for Bob to have a stronger desire than his desire to take heroin, he in fact has such a desire, whether or not his desire is irresistible: the desire not to be repeatedly stung by a swarm of bees.

This brings me to a third and final conjecture, which is that in order to make sense of the idea of an irresistible impulse we will have to go beyond the standard Humean account of action within which we have so far been trying to make sense of the idea. In particular, we will need to recognise the fact that the desires that agents have are themselves often arrived at on the basis of deliberation, that is, on the basis of reflection about what it would be good to do, or what they should do, or what it would be rationally justifiable for them to do. Here, accordingly, we find a further sense in which an agent can exercise control over what she does. To be in control, in this further sense, it suffices that an agent's desires are suitably explainable by her deliberations, that is, by her beliefs about what it would be good to do, or what she should do, or what it would be rationally justifiable for her to do. An irresistible impulse would then be a desire that, in a yet to be specified way, eludes control by these beliefs in the circumstances in which she acts. The further detail that we need to add to Bob's story, in order to establish whether his desire for heroin is or is not irresistible, is thus whether his desire is suitably controlled by his deliberative beliefs.

Going Beyond the Standard Humean Account of Action

At this point, however, we run into a familiar difficulty. For a defining feature of the standard Humean account of action is that beliefs are incapable of playing the kind of explanatory role we have just envisaged for them.

This is not to say that beliefs are inert, on the Humean account. Rather it is to say that, on that account, much as with desires, beliefs are incapable of explaining actions all by themselves. An agent who merely had beliefs is, according to the Humean account, incapable of acting because the mere fact that she believes that the world is a certain way doesn't tell us whether or not she is disposed to make it that way, or some other way. Equally, an agent who merely had desires would be incapable of acting because the mere fact that she is disposed to make the world a certain way doesn't tell us how she thinks the world needs to be changed, or even if it needs to be changed at all, in order to make it that way. To be capable of acting at all, then, the standard Humean account of action insists that an agent must have both desires and beliefs. But in that case an agent's beliefs about what it would be good to do, or what she should do, or what it would be rationally justifiable for her to do, must be incapable of playing the explanatory role suggested. For, the suggestion goes, such beliefs would have to be capable of both causing and rationalising an agent's having certain desires rather than others all by themselves, and this is something no belief can do.

To respond to this familiar difficulty it seems to me that we must do two things. First, we must say what exactly it is that an agent believes when she believes that she should or shouldn't behave in a certain way, and then, second, we must explain how beliefs with that sort of content are able to play the role we have imagined for them in explaining an agent's desires. What is it about the content of such beliefs that enables them to play that explanatory role? Once we have answered both these questions then it seems to me that we will be in a position to explain the further sense in which an agent can have control over what she does, and this, in turn, will enable us to define the idea of an irresistible impulse.

Let me therefore begin with the first question. What is it that an agent believes when she reflects on her options and comes to the conclusion that it would be good to act in a certain way, or that she should act in that way, or that it would be rationally justifiable for her to act in that way?

I want to approach this question somewhat obliquely by first describing Bob's case in a little more detail. Assume that Bob has two intrinsic desires: a stronger desire that his children fare well and a weaker desire to experience pleasure. Given that he also has various means-end beliefs it follows that, if he were fully instrumentally rational—that is to say, if he were a creature with the ability to perfectly satisfy his intrinsic desires in the light of his means-end beliefs—then he would have extra extrinsic desires as well. That is to say he would have extra desires for things that he doesn't desire intrinsically, but merely as a means to the things that he does desire intrinsically. So let's assume further that, because he intrinsically desires pleasure and believes that taking heroin is pleasurable, Bob would, if he were fully instrumentally rational, extrinsically desire to take heroin, and let's also assume that, because he intrinsically desires that his children fare well and believes that taking heroin will prevent them from doing so (perhaps because he believes that doing so will cause him to neglect them), he would also, if he were fully instrumentally rational, extrinsically desire not to take heroin.

With this background in mind, let's now ask what conclusion Bob might come to if he were to reflect on his options and ask himself what it would be good to do, or what he should do, or what it would be rationally justifiable for him to do. A natural interpretation of this question now suggests itself, an interpretation according to which we imagine Bob asking himself what he would most want himself to do, in his present circumstances, *if he were fully instrumentally rational*. Moreover, when we interpret the question in this way the answer also becomes clear. For what Bob plainly should do, in this sense—that is, what he would want himself to do, in his present circumstances, if he were fully instrumentally rational—is to refrain from taking heroin. He should refrain from taking heroin because his intrinsic desire that his children fare well is stronger than his intrinsic desire to experience pleasure, and so, if he were fully instrumentally rational, the strengths of his extrinsic desires to take heroin and not to take heroin would simply follow suit.

However even though this is what Bob *should* do, in the sense just explained, it doesn't follow that it is what he *will* do. For what an agent will do is a function of the extrinsic desires she in fact has, not those she would have if she were fully instrumentally rational. Bob's stronger desire that his children fare well will have no impact whatsoever upon his behaviour if it doesn't first combine with a means-end belief to generate an extrinsic desire to do what he believes to be a means to his children's faring well. So even though Bob's desire not to take heroin *should* be stronger than his desire to take heroin—'should' in the sense that it would be stronger if he were fully instrumentally rational—it might not be stronger in fact because he might not be fully instrumentally rational. When Bob deliberates and asks himself what he should do it is therefore a real possibility, a real possibility that we can imagine realised in his particular case, that he will come to the conclusion that he should act in a way in which he has no inclination to act.

Once we see that this interpretation of the claim that an agent should act in a certain way is available, we can readily see that other interpretations are available as well. For, generalising on the basis of this interpretation, the claim that an agent should act in a certain way is plausibly thought to amount to the claim that she would desire that she acts in that way if she had a set of desires that was fully rational *simpliciter*, where being fully rational *simpliciter* is a matter of eluding *all* forms of rational criticism. For example, since we can rationally criticise an agent's desires on the grounds that they are based on inadequate information, so the desires an agent would have if he were fully rational *simpliciter* are those he would have if he were fully informed. And since we can rationally criticise an agent's desires on the grounds that they contribute incoherence to an otherwise coherent desire set, so the desires an agent would have if he were fully rational *simpliciter* are those he would have if his desire set was maximally coherent. (Indeed, having desires that conform to the principle of instrumental rationality is arguably one dimension along which the coherence of an agent's desire set is measured.) And so we might go on.[6]

An example might help us bring out the way in which these further grounds for rationally criticising the sets of desires that agents have make possible even more glaring cases in which agents deliberate and come to the conclusion that they should act in certain ways, even though they do not desire to act in those ways. Imagine a variation on the case we have been discussing. Bob has just one intrinsic desire: a desire for pleasure. However the reason he has only this one intrinsic desire is complicated. In the past he had another intrinsic desire as well, an intrinsic desire that his children fare well. But at a certain point he fell in with a group of friends who dabbled in drugs for fun and recreation. Though it all began as harmless fun, over a period of time he found his own craving for drugs increased, and as his craving increased he found that he started leaving his children to their own devices more and more so that he could indulge himself. He initially hated himself for neglecting them, but as the neglect increased he managed to decrease the dissonance he felt by telling himself various lies: that he was useless; that his children would be better off without him; that they wouldn't understand his predicament if he told them about it; that they hate him anyway; and so on. The strategy was so successful that in the end he found himself believing the lies that he had told himself. As a result, he simply didn't care as much for his children as he used to. Finally he lost his desire that they fare well altogether.

Given this background, let's now ask what Bob should do in the circumstances he faces, where this is interpreted as his asking himself what he would want himself to do, in his present circumstances, if he were fully rational *simpliciter*, that is, abstracting away from any other requirements that there might happen to be, if he had a desire set that was maximally informed and coherent (where the coherence of a desire set includes conformity to the means-end principle). Taking the story as told at face value it seems to me quite plausible to suppose that the answer to this question is the same as before. On the one hand, even if Bob were fully informed he would still have his intrinsic desire for pleasure, so if he were also fully instrumentally rational then he would also have an extrinsic desire to take heroin as a means to pleasure. But, on the other hand, it is also plausible to suppose that he would regain his stronger desire that his

6   Michael Smith, *The Moral Problem* (1994) ch 5.

children fare well if he were to stop believing all of the lies that he has told himself and immerse himself fully in all of the facts—that he isn't useless; that his children aren't better off without him; that they would understand his predicament if he told them about it; that they still love him; and so on—and, having regained this stronger intrinsic desire that his children fare well, if he were fully instrumentally rational then he would also have a stronger extrinsic desire not to take heroin as a means to preventing his children's being neglected. What Bob would most want himself to do if he had a maximally informed and coherent desire set is thus to refrain from taking heroin. This is what he would most want himself to do if he were fully rational *simpliciter*.

Moreover, note that Bob might well even come to believe this to be so as the result of deliberation. He might, for example, become convinced that he would most want to refrain from taking heroin if he were fully rational *simpliciter* by talking with a trusted counsellor, or a friend. But since being convinced that he would most desire to refrain from taking heroin if he had a maximally informed and coherent desire set is one thing, and knowing what those relevant facts are and being maximally coherent (where this includes being fully instrumentally rational) is quite another, it follows that, notwithstanding his belief, Bob's desire not to take heroin might well not be stronger than his desire to take heroin in fact. When Bob deliberates and asks himself what he should do it is therefore once again a real possibility, one that we can imagine realised in his case, that he will come to the conclusion that he should act in a way in which he has no desire whatsoever to act.

Until now we have been focusing on the first of the two questions distinguished earlier: what is the content of the beliefs an agent forms when, as part of a process of deliberation, she asks herself what it would be good to do, or what she should do, or what it would be rationally justifiable for her to do? The answer we have come up with is that she thereby attempts to form beliefs about what she would want herself to do if she had a set of desires that was fully rational *simpliciter*, where this is a matter of having a set of desires that is maximally informed and coherent (where being coherent includes having desires that conform to the means-end principle). With this conception of the content of the beliefs agents form when they deliberate firmly before our minds, it seems to me that we are now in a position to answer the second question. What is it about the content of these beliefs that enables them to explain the agent's acquisition of corresponding desires?

In order to make matters more concrete, let's ask this question with respect to one of the two scenarios we have been considering. Let's suppose once again that Bob has just one intrinsic desire, a desire to experience pleasure, but that he used to have a stronger intrinsic desire that his children fare well in the past before he began telling himself all of those lies. In this context let's suppose that Bob deliberates. He consults widely and becomes convinced, after talking with a trusted friend, that he would desire that he stops taking heroin if he had a maximally informed and coherent set of desires. However, to make matters more straightforward, let's suppose that the friend has given Bob no grounds whatsoever for supposing this to be so. He has simply asked Bob to take his word for it, and Bob, trusting his friend as he does, has done just that.

We are thus to imagine that Bob finds himself with the belief that he would desire that he stops taking heroin if he had a maximally informed and coherent set of desires, and the question we must ask ourselves is how this particular belief is supposed to be capable of explaining his acquisition of a desire not to take heroin. What is the mechanism of acquisition supposed to be? The answer I propose is that Bob's belief can explain his acquisition of a desire not to take heroin because considerations of coherence augur in favour of his acquisition of this desire, given that he has the belief he has. The mechanism of acquisition would thus be Bob's quite general non-desiderative capacity to acquire and lose psychological states in accordance with norms of coherence.[7]

To see why considerations of coherence look to be the key, consider the following two rather simplified psychologies. One comprises both an agent's belief that she would want herself, in her present circumstances, to act in a certain way if she had a maximally informed and coherent set of desires and, in addition, a desire of hers to act in that way. The other psychology comprises her belief that she would want herself, in her present circumstances, to act in a certain way if she had a maximally informed and coherent set of desires, but does not comprise, in addition, a desire of hers to act in that way. Perhaps it comprises indifference, or aversion to acting in that way. What can we say about these two psychologies, from what we have said about them so far?

The answer seems to me to be plain enough. What we can say is that the first psychology exhibits much more in the way of coherence than the second. For the mere fact that agents fail to have desires, as regards what to do in their present circumstances, that they believe they would have if they had a maximally informed and coherent set of desires, would itself seem to *constitute* a kind of incoherence, or disequilibrium, in their

---

7   Michael Smith, 'The Coherence Argument: A Reply to Shafer-Landau' *Analysis* (forthcoming).

psychology. The mismatch between such agents' desires about what they are to do in their present circumstances and their beliefs about what they would want themselves to do, in these circumstances, if they had a maximally informed and coherent set of desires bears a striking family resemblance to paradigm cases of incoherence in a psychological state, a family resemblance so striking that we should simply admit that this is a case of incoherence too.

Moreover the fact that this is so is in turn significant. For it is plausible to suppose that rational agents possess a quite general non-desiderative capacity to acquire and lose psychological states in accordance with norms of coherence.[8] It is, after all, rational agents' possession of this capacity that explains why they tend to acquire beliefs that conform to the evidence available to them. Moreover it also explains why, when they do not acquire such beliefs, they take themselves to be liable to censure and rebuke. Rational agents quite rightly feel shame when they fail to believe in accordance with the evidence available to them because, given that the evidence dictates that belief, norms of coherence entail that they should have acquired the belief, and because, in the light of the fact that they possess the capacity to acquire the belief, they could have acquired it. They therefore rightly feel shame because they failed to acquire a belief that they should and could have acquired.

Similarly, rational agents' possession of the quite general non-desiderative capacity to acquire and lose psychological states in accordance with norms of coherence explains why they tend to acquire desires for the believed means to their desired ends and why, when they do not acquire such desires, they likewise take themselves to be liable to censure and rebuke. Rational agents quite rightly feel shame when they fail to desire the believed means to their desired ends because, given that coherence augurs in favour of the acquisition of such desires, they should have acquired them, and because, in the light of the fact that they possess the capacity to acquire these desires, they could have acquired them. They therefore rightly feel shame because they failed to acquire desires that they should and could have acquired.

It therefore follows that, if I am right that agents who believe that they would desire themselves to act in a certain way, in their present circumstances, if they had a maximally informed and coherent psychology, but then fail to have a corresponding desire, display a lack of coherence in their psychology as well, then the capacity that rational agents possess to

---

8   Michael Smith, 'A Theory of Freedom and Responsibility' in Garrett Cullity and Berys Gaut (eds), *Ethics and Practical Reason* (1997) 293–319.

acquire and lose psychological states in accordance with norms of coherence has the potential to explain not just why their beliefs tend to evolve in conformity to evidence, and their desires in conformity to their desires for ends and beliefs about means, but also why their desires as regards what they are to do in their present circumstances tend to evolve in conformity to their beliefs about what they would want themselves to do, in their present circumstances, if they had a maximally informed and coherent set of desires.

The question we have been attempting to answer is in what sense we are to suppose that Bob's belief that he would desire that he not take heroin, in his current circumstances, if he had a maximally informed and coherent set of desires, a belief he might form when he deliberates, is capable of explaining his acquisition of a desire not to take heroin in his current circumstances. We now have our answer. Bob's belief is capable of explaining his acquisition of a desire not to take heroin to the extent that Bob is someone who has the non-desiderative capacity to acquire and lose psychological states in accordance with norms of coherence. Contrary to the standard Humean dogma, it should therefore be no more puzzling that agents can acquire corresponding desires in the light of their beliefs about what they would desire if they had a maximally informed and coherent set of desires, than it is to suppose that they can acquire beliefs in the light of their appreciation of the evidence for those beliefs, or that they can acquire desires for the believed means to their desired ends in the light of their desires for those ends and their beliefs that the means are means to those ends. The mechanism of acquisition is the same in each case.

The picture we have is thus one according to which agents who are capable of deliberating—that is, capable of having not just desires and means-end beliefs, but of forming beliefs about what they would desire themselves to do if they had a maximally informed and coherent set of desires—and who, in addition, have a quite general non-desiderative capacity to acquire and lose psychological states in accordance with norms of coherence, are capable of controlling their behaviour in a further sense. It suffices for an agent to be in control of what she does in this further sense that her body moves in a certain way; that her bodily movement is caused by a relevant desire and means-end belief she possesses; that her bodily movement is counterfactually sensitive to small changes in her desires and means-end beliefs; that her desire is caused by her belief that she would want herself to act in that way in her present circumstances if she had a maximally informed and coherent set of desires; and that her desire is counterfactually sensitive to small changes in her beliefs about what she would want herself to do if she had a maximally informed and coherent set of desires. (The last condition simply rules out the possibility that the agent desires to do what she believes she would want herself to do in her present circumstances if she had a maximally informed and coherent set of desires as a matter of luck.)

With this further story of control of an agent's desires by his deliberations in the background, we are now in a position to say what it might mean to say that an agent has an irresistible impulse. We are also in a position to clarify the sense in which agents possess the capacity for self-control.

What is an Irresistible Impulse (Again)?

An initial thought might be this. An irresistible impulse is simply any impulse which causes an agent to act, but which isn't caused by her belief about what she would want herself to do in her present circumstances if she had a maximally informed and coherent set of desires; or which, though caused by her beliefs, isn't counterfactually sensitive to small changes in her beliefs about what she would want herself to do if she had a maximally informed and coherent set of desires.

However this can't be quite right. For an agent might well have, and act on, a desire which (say) is not caused by her belief about what she would want herself to do in her present circumstances if she had a maximally informed and coherent set of desires, and yet still have the *capacity* to have and act on the desire that is so caused: 'is not in a state that was so caused' does not imply 'could not have been in a state that was so caused'. Since such a desire would plainly be *resistible*, albeit not *resisted*, it follows that this initial thought does not adequately capture the nature of an irresistible impulse.

More plausibly, then, an irresistible impulse might be characterised as any impulse which causes an agent to act when that impulse is of a kind such that the agent lacks the capacity to have desires of that kind that accord with her beliefs about what she would want herself to do in her present circumstances if she had a maximally informed and coherent set of desires. The idea behind this condition is that an agent might be perfectly capable of desiring in accordance with her beliefs about what she would want herself to do in her present circumstances if she had a maximally informed and coherent set of desires so long as her beliefs are about desires with certain restricted subject matters, while being quite incapable of so desiring when her beliefs are about desires that concern other subject matters: say, drugs, alcohol or gambling.

Note how different this conception of an irresistible impulse is to the conception that was considered, and rejected, earlier. What matters in ascertaining whether an impulse is or is not resistible is not whether the agent could have had some alternative desire that would have outweighed the impulse in question. What matters is rather whether the agent has the capacity, in the circumstances of action she faces, to desire in accordance with her beliefs about what she would want herself to do in these circumstances if she had a maximally informed and coherent set of desires. The mere fact that, if her circumstances were completely different—say, because she had a much stronger competing desire not to be stung repeatedly by a swarm of bees—then she would desire and behave differently is thus neither here nor there.

Are there any irresistible impulses, as just characterised? The question is largely empirical, but it certainly seems to me that we are ordinarily prepared to recognise that there are at least some such impulses as we go about our everyday lives. Addictions are, after all, a common feature of the contemporary world, and what makes a desire into an addiction would seem to be precisely that it meets the condition just characterised: addictions are impervious to deliberative control. This is not, of course, to say that it is easy to prove, either beyond reasonable doubt or according to the balance of probabilities, that some particular impulse is irresistible. But I will leave it to others to determine what evidence might be adduced in support of any particular claim to the effect that some impulse is or is not resistible. My goal here has been more strictly conceptual rather than epistemological.

The Story of Self-Control

It might be thought that the existence of irresistible impulses would provide a rich source of excuses for bad behaviour. In the space that remains, however, I want to voice a note of caution about supposing this to be so. To anticipate, the reason is that, somewhat surprisingly, the mere fact that an impulse is irresistible does not imply that the agent lacks all capacity for self-control.

In deciding whether the existence of an irresistible impulse provides grounds for an excuse, the important point to remember is that there are, for the most part, two quite distinct moments at which agents can exercise such capacity as they have to desire in accordance with their beliefs about what they would want themselves to do if they had a maximally informed and coherent set of desires, or, as this capacity is more colloquially called, their capacity for self-control. And while it might well be true that agents are often incapable of exercising their capacity for self-control at one of these moments, it is much harder to believe that they so frequently lack the capacity to exercise the capacity at the other moment as well.

In order to see that this is so, note that there are two distinct moments at which we can come to realise that we have the potential to lose control of what we do. Suppose we envisage the possibility, at time t_1, that we will be out of control at time t_2. In other words, suppose we believe, at t_1, that we would want ourselves to act in a certain way at t_2 if we had a maximally informed and coherent set of desires, and believe as well that there is a good chance that at t_2 we lack that desire. The two distinct moments then reflect the possibility that t_1 and t_2 are the *same* time, and the alternative possibility is that they are *different* times.

Let's focus initially on the case in which t_1 and t_2 are the *same* time. To fix ideas, let's consider the particular situation in which Bob has two intrinsic desires, a stronger desire that his children fare well and a weaker desire to experience pleasure, and various means-end beliefs, and on the basis of all these let's suppose that he comes to the conclusion that, if he had a maximally informed and coherent set of desires, then he would have a weaker extrinsic desire to take heroin and a stronger extrinsic desire that he refrain. However, let's also suppose that, faced as he is with availability of heroin right before him, and encouraged as he is by his friends who remind him what great fun he would be missing out on if he refused, Bob becomes instrumentally irrational. His stronger intrinsic desire that his children fare well thus does not transfer its force across the means-end relation, only his weaker desire to experience pleasure does that, and, hence, he finds himself with a stronger extrinsic desire to take heroin rather than refrain.

Now, of course, the mere fact that Bob's extrinsic desire to take heroin is stronger than his extrinsic desire to refrain is no proof that he lacks any *capacity* to have a stronger extrinsic desire to refrain from taking heroin. We therefore need to address the question of his capacity on its own merits. One obvious question to ask, in this regard, is whether any strategy of self-control was available to him. For example, is there something Bob could have thought, or something he could have imagined, such that, if he had thought or imagined that thing then his desire that his children fare well would have transmitted its force across the means-end relation, in which case his extrinsic desire to refrain from taking heroin would have been stronger? Could he, say, have dwelled on the thought that his children depend entirely on him for their well-being, or could he have pictured the disappointment that would appear on their faces if they were watching him take heroin yet again, and, if he had had that thought, or pictured that scene, would this have had the effect of ensuring that his intrinsic desire that his children fare well transmitted its force across the means-end relation?

If we can answer 'yes' to some such question then it seems to me that Bob does, at that time, have the capacity to desire in accordance with his belief about what he would want himself to do if he had a maximally informed and coherent set of desires. If not, then it seems to me that Bob does not have that capacity. In the former case he fails to exercise self-control when the needed exercise of self-control was available to him. In the latter case he fails to exercise self-control, but no such exercise of self-control was available to him in the first place. Accordingly, in the former case we would not suppose that Bob is a candidate for being excused for what he does, whereas in the latter we might well suppose that he is.

In reality, of course, the difference that is being highlighted here will be one of degree. There will be cases in which it is as obvious as can be that there is something that Bob could have thought, or something that he could have imagined, which is such that, if he had thought or imagined that then his desire that his children fare well would have transmitted its force across the means-end relation. In those cases it will no doubt seem too weak to say that it was *merely possible* for Bob to have such a thought, or to engage in such an episode of the imagination, for it will be *astonishing* that he didn't *in fact* have the required thought, or engage in the required episode of the imagination. For example, if in the past Bob has always succeeded in having such thoughts, or in engaging in such episodes of the imagination, then, barring something special about this case, we will think that the possibility of his having the required thought, or engaging in the necessary episode of the imagination, in this case was, as we might say, a *real live possibility*. In other cases, however, though still possible, it will be a far more remote possibility for Bob to have the required thought, or to engage in the required episode of the imagination. For example, if he only very occasionally succeeds in having such thoughts, or engaging in such episodes of the imagination, then we will not be at all surprised that he failed (yet again) on this occasion to have the required thought, or to engage in the required episode of the imagination.

What all of this reflects, of course, is the fact that, in reality, an agent's capacity for self-control *comes in degrees*. What we should really say is thus that an agent, like Bob, might well be excused for doing what he does to the extent that his doing otherwise would have required an exercise of self-control that was beyond him. Even those who have a diminished capacity for self-control are required to exercise such capacity as they have. But they, too, might be excused when the needed exercise of self-control was beyond their capacity.

But now note that 'might'. So far we have focused on the capacity agents have for *synchronic self-control*. But the mere fact that an agent, like Bob, couldn't have exercised self-control at the moment at which he was vulnerable—the mere fact that he lacked the capacity for synchronic self-control—does nothing to show that he couldn't have exercised self-control at *some other time*. Let's therefore consider Bob's situation once again, but this time let's pull back to an earlier time at which Bob is at home with his children, fixing their dinner, suffering from no instrumental irrationality. Indeed, let's suppose that he has recently thought through his situation and has resolved to give up taking heroin, because he has foreseen the terrible effect that his heroin use will have upon his children's lives. At that very instant, however, his friends call him on the telephone and invite him over. They tell him that they have just purchased some heroin and that they would like him to join them for an evening of fun and recreation. Suppose they say that even if he doesn't want to take heroin, he should come over anyway just to have a few beers and a chat. What should Bob do?

The crucial point to note is that, at this moment, Bob has available both of the following beliefs. First, he has available the belief that, if he had a maximally informed and coherent set of desires then he would want himself, at the later time, to refrain from taking drugs. Second, he also has available the belief that, if he were to go along to his friends' house, resolving only to have a few beers and a chat, the prospect of taking heroin would make him instrumentally irrational and he would end up taking heroin despite his resolve: this, after all, is what has happened to him time and time again.

We are therefore quite within our rights to suppose that, at the earlier time, Bob can well envisage the prospect of his losing control of himself at the later time, and so, given that he desires more strongly that his children fare well, at that earlier time, and only less strongly that he experiences pleasure, it follows that, if Bob had envisaged that prospect, then, given that he is instrumentally rational, he would have extrinsically desired not to join his friends that evening. Moreover, in acting on this desire he would have been exercising a distinct kind of self-control: *diachronic self-control*. Bob possesses the capacity to exercise diachronic self-control at the earlier time because, being able to foresee that he would lose control in the future if he allowed certain circumstances to obtain, he is able to so construct his future circumstances as to ensure that those circumstances do not obtain.

The upshot is thus that, even if Bob is unable to exercise synchronic self-control—that is, even if he is not able to think or picture anything that would ensure that he doesn't suffer from instrumental irrationality and the desire to take heroin, when faced with the prospect of actually doing so—he might still not be excusable. He might not be excusable because, to be excusable, it would have to be the case that there was no prior moment at which Bob could have exercised diachronic self-control.

Conclusion

I said at the outset that my aim in this paper was to examine two ideas crucial to a proper interpretation of the McNaghten Rules: the idea of an irresistible impulse and the correlative idea of an agent's lacking self-control. The main findings can now be summed up as follows.

Though possession of desires and means-end beliefs that cause and differentially explain an agent's bodily movements suffices for agents to be in control of what they do in one sense, it does not suffice for their being in control in another, and more important, sense. For agents are in control in this more important sense when their desires are suitably responsive to their deliberations, that is, to their reflectively formed beliefs about what they would want themselves to do if they had a maximally informed and coherent set of desires. The capacity for self-control is one aspect of this responsiveness. It is the capacity rational agents possess to have desires corresponding to those they believe they would have if they had a maximally informed and coherent set of desires, a capacity which, in turn, is an instance of a more general capacity they have to acquire and lose psychological states in accordance with norms of coherence.

Armed with this definition of the capacity for self-control we can define the idea of an irresistible impulse. An irresistible impulse is an impulse which eludes an agent's exercise of his capacity for self-control. The distinction between synchronic and diachronic exercises of self-control is, however, crucial at this point. For to be completely irresistible an impulse must be more than one which an agent is unable to conquer synchronically: in other words, more must be true than that no feat of the imagination or thought which was within the agent's reach at the time could have stopped the impulse from having its effect at the moment at which he suffers it. An agent who could have foreseen that he would be out of control if he were to find himself in certain circumstances in the future, and who failed to take such steps as were available to him to ensure that those circumstances did not arise, though he may well suffer from a synchronically irresistible impulse, does not suffer from an impulse which is diachronically irresistible. Such an agent is not excusable for doing what he does, notwithstanding the fact that he acts on a desire that is, in a sense, irresistible.

4 Intention and Agency

GRANT GILLETT

In what way does the nature of intention reveal more than a physical description of bodily movements and engage our thought with the character of the agent who acts upon that intention? I will argue that to answer this question we have to achieve some clarity on four holistically related concepts. First we have to speak of the *person as an integrated rule follower* to understand the way the agent forms mental content. Second we have to speak of *mental content* to understand *the identity of an action* (a third key concept) and fourth we have to consider the individual who composes *a lived narrative* which is more or less coherent to understand the agentic origins of intentional action.

What is an Intention?

There is clearly a difference between that casual Mediterranean shrug of the shoulders and out-turning of the hands that *betrays* or inadvertently reveals the fact that one's body has been inscribed by a particular discursive context and the self-conscious production of that same gesture for effect. The difference is one of intent. If we were tempted by a certain philosophical view, we might say that in the latter case the gesture was caused by an explicit intention in service of a motive or project of conveying to one's audience that one's character has been infected by a kind of Mediterranean ambience or colouring to the soul. But this view seems too deliberative to do justice to the more spontaneous version in that such a reading would threaten the authenticity of the performance it is trying to explain. So this leads us to another question.

What is the relation between a particular intention and the act which it informs? Since John Stuart Mill, the relation has been conceived to be one of causal antecedent and consequent.[1] This is then related to the mental configuration of the subject. The intention tends to be conceptualised as a mental state produced by a combination of belief and desire and itself causally productive of the bodily movement which is the action.

My account (developed in several places[2]) portrays an action as the outworking through the body of an intentional content conceived in relation to the world. It is in fact close to the view, developed by Vallacher and Wegner writing from the context of psychology, that an intention expresses the identity structure of an action.[3] On this view, one acts when one uses the body to exhibit mental content that relates one to the world in a certain kind of way. An intention is a mental construct but is not conceived as being a causal antecedent of the action. The suggestion is that we are engaged in a constant bodily interaction with the world, tracts of which are informed by mental content—things like the belief that one is speaking too quickly, the conviction that a particular member of the audience is taking a keen interest in what one says, the thought that the moment is a special one to be shared in a special way with one's partner, and so on. At these particular points in one's lived conscious narrative, the accompanying thoughts guide and influence one's behaviour so that the stream of dynamic interaction between oneself and the world takes on a particular rhythm and character. This two-way interaction between the mind and the world is what we call intentional activity and is the proper context of action. Of course, when we look at actions we tend to focus on specific datable interventions in the domain to which we are adapted or even those interventions about which we deliberate before coming to a decision and, as a result, forget the seamless whole which is our normal run of conscious activity. It is by concentrating on a narrow range of examples at this deliberative end of the spectrum that we devise unrealistic philosophical doctrines about action. One such doctrine is that which I have attributed to Mill: an intentional action is a datable physical event preceded by a datable mental event called an intention. This is possibly the most popular philosophical view on the contemporary scene.

---

1   John Stuart Mill, *System of Logic, Ratiocinative and Inductive* (1874).
2   Rom Harre and Grant Gillett, *The Discursive Mind* (1994); Grant Gillett, 'Free Will and Mental Content' (1993) 6(2) *Ratio* 89; Grant Gillett, *The Mind and Its Discontents: An Essay in Discursive Psychiatry* (1999).
3   R R Vallacher and D M Wegner, 'What Do People Think They're Doing? Action Identification and Human Behaviour' (1987) 94 *Psychological Review* 3.

The Causal View

On the dominant view, the beliefs and desires of the agent causally produce an intention which is expressed in, or causally produces, an action. In this account, as Mill clearly notes, actions become no more problematic than other causally produced events in the world. This is attractive to those who want a certain kind of naturalism to prevail in metaphysics and the explanation of human affairs. The major problem for this view is that, although a correctly causally configured and relevant or even active set of beliefs and desires may exhaust the story of intentional action, it does not account for distinctions we are perfectly capable of making between actions and other things we do. Numerous examples have been produced to illustrate this point, one of the most memorable being Davidson's nervous mountaineer.[4] In this case there are two mountaineers, one of whom slips and is being saved from plunging to his death by his companion's steely grip on a rope. Unfortunately the companion has a streak of the Woody Allen in him and the fear that he might fall, his desire not to fall, and his further fear that he might let go and let his friend fall to his death so unnerves him that he lets go and his friend falls.

The nervous mountaineer is a typical deviant causal chain case in which it is true that his fear of death and his belief that his friend might cause him to fall to his death did cause him to let go of the rope but we would not say that his letting go was an intentional act done for those reasons. Such problem cases have led philosophers to the idea that an intentional action must be caused by the relevant beliefs and desires *in the right kind of way*—a way required by reason-giving explanation and not just causal explanation. This metaphysical requirement has proven somewhat difficult to fulfil in that it leads to us factoring into the account something like *the decision of the agent* or *her resolve to do what she envisaged* or something that is not just belief and desire but that which we might call a final *agent-involving intent*. It is this factor that allows us to conclude that it was, in a very real sense, up to him whether the act occurred and therefore he can and should take responsibility for it or otherwise as the case might be.

I think we can get nearer to understanding this extra agent-involving factor if we focus on the character and integrity of an agent as a minded

---

4   Donald Davidson, *Essays on Actions and Events* (1980) 79.

being who normally operates by deploying mental content in structuring his actions.

Intention Rules and Narrative

Daniel Dennett has developed a theory of consciousness which construes conscious mental life as a narrative 'take' on a continual stream of neural activity arising from the interaction between body and world.[5] His theory definitely accords with what we see in the brain and solves a number of problems in explaining perceptual, cognitive, emotive, and voluntary behaviour. (I have discussed these issues elsewhere.[6]) If Dennett is correct, then it is a universal feature of human behaviour and conscious experience that we make the best story we can out of a fairly seamless flow of activity which does not in itself determine what form that story will take. The form of the story of our lived conscious experience depends on two things:

1. the concepts and meanings that we have available to deploy in making sense of our own activity; and
2. the concepts we use on a given occasion.

Thus the narrative that is lived human experience is shaped by the meaning-giving skills which constitute the human subject considered as a situated narrator and itself forms the context within which intentions emerge. What we still have not got, however, is a sense in which our conscious thought life determines what actually happens with our bodies rather than just the way that we experience those events. We need this to be secure in order to have a chance of formulating an account of freedom of the will and genuine responsibility for intentional action such that the character of the agent as a moral agent is crucially involved.

Behaviour for Which We are Not Responsible

The nature of automatism (or partial complex epilepsy) as a cause of coordinated patterns of human behaviour gives us a clue we can follow in

---

5   Daniel Dennett, *Consciousness Explained* (1991).
6   Grant Gillett, 'Consciousness and Lesser States: The Evolutionary Foothills of the Mind' (1999) 74 *Philosophy* 331; and see Grant Gillett, *The Mind and Its Discontents* (1999).

the quest for an account of agent-involving intention. An automatism is a causal product of a state of electrical excitement in the brain. But so, on the monist account, is an action. Thus we need a philosophical account of the essential (or metaphysical) difference between the two, given that both are causal products of the activity in the same brain. To make this question vivid, we might ask ourselves, in the case of a voluntary action, 'why is this particular tract of electrical stuff even a candidate as a proper cause for an action and not some other kind of bodily manifestation of what is going on in the brain?' I will argue that the key lies in the way that the content of the action arises as a psychologically explicable part of a person's narrative. This answer returns us to Davidson's nervous mountaineer case in which it is clear that a genuine voluntary action has to take its place in the psychic economy in the right kind of way. When we examine 'the right kind of way' concerned, it is clearly not just a matter of causation by beliefs and desires. As Davidson so elegantly showed, it is a matter of the critical propositional attitudes being the ones the agent was acting on as the action was produced. We could say that the thoughts (or propositional attitudes) concerned appropriately relate the agent's behaviour at this particular point in time to the ongoing projects and character of the agent. Such relations, in a manner of speaking, map the agent as an agent onto the world via his or her constructions of the world and interests in it. Given our earlier thoughts about extended actions and tracts of behaviour, this feature does not sit well with the event-causing-event theory of human causation and is most realistically conceived of through a different model called the 'identity structure' model.[7]

The Identity Structure Model of Action

According to the identity structure model, an action occurs when a conscious conception takes control of my behaviour so that the behaviour becomes explicable as an expression of that content. 'I am shaking my head in a way that I was taken by in India' is a tract of my activity structured, or given form, by my thought that I want to imitate that action. This is a very sensitive and realistic way to understand the relationship between ideas (or mental content) and action. It is realistic because it analyses actions in their natural context—a lived human life. It is sensitive

---

7   See the sources cited above n 2.

because it tracks the crucial conscious states which actually or currently inform the behaviour being explained. Consider the action of walking to the door to go out: if on the way to the door I realise that the day outside is a lot colder than I originally thought it was, I might stop and take an extra waistcoat. As I turn aside to the closet to get the waistcoat, I am not doing anything explicable under the background 'going to the door to go out' but rather am getting a waistcoat to put on. The original plan and the mental content informing it (going to the door to go outside) is not on hold but rather it is not detailed enough to explain that bit of my behaviour. The way I capture that fact is to mention the new bit of content (it strikes me that it is sufficiently cold for me to need more clothes). This is even clearer if, say, I were walking into the office thinking about the day's work and then recalled the poorly laid flooring tile that I often trip over as I go in. The relatively automatic pursuit of my overall plan of walking into the office has now got a new subplot to be worked into it—scanning the ground for that pesky tile. If somebody approaches me and asks me to explain what I am doing, an adequate answer should include both elements. Because this type of explanation focuses on the content that is currently consciously directing and giving form to my activity, it is both *sensitive*—it can cope with the subtle shifts—and *realistic* in that it does not have me generating discrete mental causes or intentions for each chunk of my activity. What is more, it fits perfectly with a Dennett-type view of consciousness but it does not fit with any causally-detailed identity or supervenience theory that I know of.

The identity structure approach to action explanation is a theory based on content, so we must now devote a moment's thought to the idea of mental content (such as <shaking my head> or <the door>). Mental content is what appears in thoughts, desires, intentions, expectations and so on. For most philosophers, mental content has intrinsic semantic properties such that to spell out the content of the thought you have to say the way things would be in the world to make that thought true (we could call this set of conditions the truth conditions for the thought concerned). What is more, most people realise that mental content is an essentially normative notion.[8] I have argued in a number of places that mental content is structured by concepts and concepts are based on rules.[9] The rules govern the application

---

8   See Davidson, above n 4; and Grant Gillett, *Representation, Meaning and Thought* (1992); Ruth Millikan, *White Queen Psychology and other Essays for Alice* (1993).

9   Grant Gillett, 'Husserl, Wittgenstein and the Snark' (1997) 57 *Philosophy and Phenomenological Research* 331.

of a particular concept to the world and its internal or cognitive significance in relation to other concepts; thus <newt> is an item of content only properly applied to little critters of a certain kind and it is properly linked to concepts like <vertebrate>, <lizard> (though only in appearance), <amphibian>, and so on. I have also argued that rules carry an embedded metaphysical assumption of agency in a way that rule-governed transactions do not. Thus if you teach me the rule governing the concept <newt> it is up to me whether I learn it and follow it and come to grasp the concept or whether I do not choose to fit in to your practice. Of course, we work on our cognitive novices so that they are disposed to follow the rules, but we cannot causally compel them to (as anybody who has raised children knows). It isn't a *done deal* unless they go along with us. In fact nature itself is our accomplice in this task because it equips children with primitive tendencies to lock into relationships with other human beings but from that natural foundation we shape up what McDowell calls 'second nature'.[10] The notion of second nature captures the fact that our children find it natural to do certain things which we have trained them to do whereas, by and large, the repertoire of most animals means that what they find natural to do is given to them by biology and individual experience. Thus we are mind makers for our children and we transform their natural tendencies so that they exhibit the tricks of adaptation that our socio-cultural group has developed.[11]

But we need a little more here in relation to the *sense* attaching to the term 'agent' and therefore what follows from it (another, not totally satisfactory, name for *sense* is *cognitive significance*). The sense of a term tells me where in language the term is stationed and thus reveals its entailments and presuppositions. In fact the logical basis and implications of agency will get us to a point of clarity about intention.

To recap: human beings use mental content to structure actions. Mental content is shaped by following rules (even automatically). A rule follower can control behaviour in response to prescriptions. Thus, in manufacturing a creature who can deal with human mental content, we take an organism of the right kind (who is preprogrammed to learn from other human beings but who may or may not wish to fit in with our usage) and we train them. In fact, over a vast range of life situations, we take someone (whose nature disposes them to learn from us and gives them some of the same physical dispositions), we impose prescriptions and they change. We

---

10   John McDowell, *Mind and World* (1994).
11   Grant Gillett, *The Mind and Its Discontents* (1999).

all do this all the time and, by and large, it results in patterns of action exhibiting second nature provided only that the individual plays along and then wants to go on making use of the rule-governed techniques in which we have instructed her. In fact this is remarkably close to a passage in Kant's discussion of freedom. He notices that the moral law is such that it can impose a requirement on action which is not conditioned by the prior nature of the agent. For an Aristotelian it is to be expected that the norms shaping thought (and therefore knowledge) and action (therefore morality) should make maximal use of the 'natural' (in the sense of natural science) equipment with which we are endowed.

The implication of the rule-governed structure of cognition is that it comes about as a result of training and that a precondition is that the thinking subject is cognitively integrated over time. The precondition is evident because of the fact that training cannot be instantaneous. Kant realised the need for training and he realised that this implied an intersubjective standard of truth whereby each epistemic agent made use of skills honed in those (informal) prescriptive interactions where they learned to use the concepts that others use to structure their current experience and, as a result, master the actions that others exhibit.

The fact that it is skills of perceiving, thinking and acting that are cognitively shaped and refined over time now allows us to address the issue of intention and the responsibility of the agent. Think for a moment of the rules of chess. Before I have been disciplined by the rules and have developed any mastery of them, I am relatively helpless if you sit me down at a chess board with a set of pieces. I have not, as it were, any power to act in the domain cognitively structured by the rules of chess. The more I acquire a working knowledge of the rules, the more strength to my cognitive arm, as it were. I become empowered or able to act more and more in a way structured by my own strategies and reasoning, rather than just reacting responsively to the moves made by my opponent. Notice that our acts have to be referred to the same interactive domain—an actual singular (even if hypothetical) chessboard. It is the same with thought and action. The more I master the rule-governed skills the more empowered I am to devise and pursue my own projects for my own reasons. Thus 'the truth shall make you free', or at least the mastery of the rule-governed relationship between thought content and truth conditions will make you able to understand and act according to the dictates of your own reasoning in the domain where those thoughts have taken shape. A further consideration arising directly from the fact that rules do not causally compel my compliance with them also leads us directly to the topic of identity and character.

Identity, Character and Intention

Whether I follow the rules or not on a given occasion may or may not be a chance occurrence. If I am cognitively malfunctioning my not doing so is (in a forensic sense) a chance occurrence, but if I am functioning normally, my behaviour should, in principle, be explicable on the basis of my formed character or personal narrative. I could be expected, if I am well functioning, to have a reason for not following a rule that would otherwise give me an advantage. in life. If I decide not to learn number facts like 5+7=12, there is usually a reason and a school counsellor will set out to find that reason. It may be, as I have noted, that I do not have the properly functioning cognitive equipment to be able to do the task or it may be that I do not want to learn. This rational exploitation of, but not compulsion by, the rules goes on throughout life. Sometimes perfectly competent thinkers violate the rules of thought and they usually do so for effect: they coin a metaphor, have a creative and original thought, say something outrageous, or make a political statement. In each case the deliberate violation of the rules makes sense within a suitably sensitive life history of the person involved. It is the fact that the rules do not causally necessitate rule-following performances that allows this to happen and the fact that thought content is woven into (more or less) integrated narratives by the whole concept-using individual that explains its happening. The ability to call upon concepts and apply them to whatever is going on between oneself and the world at will is so basic to human consciousness that we take it for granted. This means that we do not realise the profound implications of this fact for longitudinal mental integrity (that is the integrity of personal identity over time) when somebody like Parfit formulates his claims about personal identity.[12]

Parfit's argument runs as follows:

1. The conscious experiences of any individual are linked together by various relations.

---

12   Derek Parfit, *Reasons and Persons* (1986).

2. These relations are only secured by the common causal substrate of the experiences.
3. A cause is metaphysically independent of its effects (even though descriptions may hide the fact).
4. The substrate has no intrinsic metaphysical connection to the stream of experience.
5. We can imagine the two diverging in various ways.
6. Identity is no more than a matter of degree of connectedness dependent on nothing intrinsically mental.
7. There is no intrinsic mental unity to conscious experience.

The present arguments have undermined 2 and substituted 2a and 2b.

2a. The relations depend also on the identity of the narrator who edits and binds them together.
2b. Narration is a conceptual or mental activity.

Taken together 2a and 2b imply the failure of 4 and the argument does not go through. What is more, the longitudinal and temporal implications of 2a and 2b are strengthened if we add 2c.

2c. Mental activity involving the competent use of concepts comes about as a result of training.

Thus there is a subjective and objective integrity in a life of thought and action such that we can properly think of a human being as an intentional agent who has an essential longitudinal continuity over the span of life.

The Role of the Agent

We now have our four holistically connected conceptions in play in understanding a human agent. First we have to speak of the *person as an integrated rule follower* to understand the way he or she forms mental content. Second we have to speak of *mental content* to understand *action* and lastly we have to speak of the individual who composes *a lived narrative* which is more or less coherent to understand conscious mental content and the process whereby it is woven together into an identity.

These four conceptions, taken together, imply that any action is only explained by relating it to the life history in which it arises in a way that essentially depends on regarding the agent as a rule follower and not merely a causally compelled device. Thus the conceptual basis of intention talk is a subject with an identity as a temporally integrated rule follower. I have noted that rule following is a prescriptively governed activity for a human being and whether or not the rules are followed depends on the interests of the person concerned and on their free choice to use a certain skill on a certain occasion. What rules are followed and the way that they are applied to the ongoing stream of interaction between the body and the world determines the intention which informs an action. Intention is, of course, crucial in law in that it often determines the culpability for an act that produces harm (through the doctrine of *mens rea*). Also important, but less immediately relevant to the nature of the act itself, the narrative of the individual gives rise to the motives for which an act is done. Motives are also structured inclinations or dispositions to attain certain ends and therefore also embody mental content but motives are only of evidential or explanatory weight in law and psychology and not constitutive of *mens rea*. Thus intentions are rational, inner (in the sense of intrinsic to an individual lived psychology) determinations of agents, as Kant so clearly noted, and they are formed to pursue a certain segment of the life trajectory of the agent. To be able to form a certain intent you must command a certain fragment of the mental content made available to you by the discourse around you and you must deploy it to structure your action in a certain way.

Intent is explicable when it can be related to the ongoing projects and therefore the character of the agent. Thus imputing an intent is generally a matter of laying out the ways in which the person concerned is currently relating him or herself to the human domain of activity in which he or she is operating. The internal self-determinations constituting the intention situate the person and the items in that domain according to the person's interests. The ongoing or unfolding complexes formed by situations, interests and activity all fit together as a lived narrative within which the person determines to do this or that. Determinations such as these evince one's character and thus there is a persuasive case to be made for a fairly direct connection between the moral character of an agent and the intentions upon which that agent acts.

Why the Judgment We Pass on an Act is a Judgment about a Moral Agent

When we decide, on the basis of evidence, that a given agent acted in a way that exhibited a given intention, we comment on the way that a tract of behaviour is to be nested into an understanding of that agent's narrative. This narrative, through its internal coherence and the activity it illuminates, explains the individual's relations to their environment and a particular action explanation is an important part of that narrative at the relevant point. The action explanation functions, we might say, analogously to the way that explanation of a move in chess functions to locate a physical displacement of a small artefact in a hodological (or purpose-ridden) space. When we say, for instance, 'she has moved her bishop out to the second row', we locate a tract of physical goings on within a structure of rules and strategies that engage us with the individual whom we are playing or observing. Her hopes, future intentions and schemes are unlikely to be transparent through the one act, if she is a player of any sophistication (and therefore potency), but the fact that she has moved her bishop, rather than idly shuffled a piece, such that the result coincides with that move, does the job of telling us, in part at least, what she is about. The unfolding pattern of her moves will tell us about her strategy and something of her character as a player.

If we broaden our gaze to the game of life in all its complex sweep, then the medium in which we engage with each other is far less bounded. It is, however, structured by rules of immense complexity and subtlety. It is fraught with real hazard, and carries the promise of joy, fulfilment, quiet satisfaction and moral challenge. We make moves in this domain and those moves engage us with others, with our mutually crafted artefacts, and with the natural world (which, insofar as it is untouched by the former, is shrinking by the day). In this domain we act by structuring our behaviour according to the meanings we consciously deploy and, by so doing, we reveal ourselves as persons with an identity that evinces a certain character.

When we discern the intention with which an agent acts, we discern, in some small measure, the narrative and therefore the moral character of the agent. We understand more when we discern the motives, vulnerabilities, needs, hopes and expectations that led to the formation of that intention. Such understanding ultimately makes us privy to the lived autobiographical narrative of another person. Thus the entire activity of action explanation is an exercise of gaining glimpses into the moral life of another. Faced with a comprehensive dossier of actions (and therefore of the intentions that have, from time to time, structured the person's behaviour), we have a comprehensive surview of the moral character of the individual with whom we are dealing (as Sartre so clearly noticed[13]). Every action I do is in its own way both formative of, and expressive of, my character as an agent although, of course, none of my actions exhausts my character as an agent.

---

13   Jean Paul Sartre, *Being and Nothingness* (H Barnes (trans)) (1958).

PART II:
INTENTION AND
INDIVIDUAL
RESPONSIBILITY

PART II

5 Negotiating Intentions in Trials of Guilt and Punishment

IAN D LEADER-ELLIOTT

Prologue

Elizabeth Anscombe, in her monograph on intention, relates the parable of the man at the poison pump.[1] He is a haunting, alienated figure, never fully articulated or human. His strangeness sticks in the memory. That and the jarring insouciance of this presentation of a Holocaust story. Here is the story, as Anscombe told it:

> A man is pumping water into the cistern which supplies the drinking water of a house. Someone has found a way of systematically contaminating the source with a deadly cumulative poison whose effects are unnoticeable until they can no longer be cured. The house is regularly inhabited by a small group of party chiefs, with their immediate families, who are in control of a great state; they are engaged in exterminating the Jews and perhaps plan a world war.[2]

The man who contaminated the source wanted to save the world from the threatened Holocaust. He believed, perhaps with good reason, that the death of the party chiefs would open the way for peace. He revealed all this to the man at the pump, who is the real subject of the parable.

Imagine now that the party chiefs were poisoned and the Holocaust was averted.[3] You are interrogating the man who worked the pump. You

---

1   Gertrude Elizabeth Anscombe, *Intention* (2nd ed, 1963).
2   Ibid para 23.
3   In each of the variations played on the story, Anscombe imagines a dialogue with the man as he operates the pump. Though he is *poisoning* the party chiefs, they have not yet consumed sufficient of the cumulative poison to die. If he ceases to pump, they might perhaps live. My account, which shifts the tense to the past, ignores significant differences between dialogues concerning present and past intentions. When criminal responsibility is in issue, it is the ascription of intentions for past conduct that counts.

ask him, 'Why did you replenish the house water supply with poisoned water?' His reply is not, 'To polish them off', but 'I didn't care about that, I wanted my pay and just did my usual job'.[4] He denies that he intended to kill and, in doing so, seeks to avoid or disclaim responsibility. For Anscombe, intentional actions are characterised by the fact that one can ask the agent *why* the action was done.[5] But this man says he had no reason at all to kill the party chiefs. He pumped the water for another reason entirely and so, it seems, did not intend to kill.

The poison pumper is close kin to a small band of archetypal figures who make recurrent appearances in criminal law texts.[6] The best known of them is Glanville Williams' airplane saboteur, who places a bomb on a passenger plane in the certain knowledge that passengers and crew will be killed, for the bomb is timed to explode in mid-flight. The airplane saboteur denies any intention to harm the people on the plane. He says that his sole intention was to destroy his baggage and claim the insurance money.[7] The story is supposed to illustrate the contention that there is no distinction worth making between one who intends to kill and one who acts in the knowledge that death will result: the saboteur is just as blameworthy as if he had meant to kill the passengers.

The remarkable thing about the way Glanville Williams tells the story of the airplane saboteur is his bland absence of any sense of surprise or

---

4   Ibid para 25.
5   Gertrude Anscombe, *Intention* (1957) 11: 'Intentional actions are ones to which a certain sense of the question "why?" has application'.
6   The eccentric and amoral surgeon who removes his victim's heart because he needs that organ for his experiments: A Kenny, 'Intention and Purpose in Law' in Robert Summers (ed), *Essays in Legal Philosophy* (1968) 146, 149 (the example is attributed to Glanville Williams); the father who sets fire to his house in order to claim insurance money, though it is virtually certain that his son will die: R Cross, 'The Mental Element in Crime' (1967) 83 *Law Quarterly Review* 215, 216; the aircraft designer who places a bomb in the prototype of an airplane designed by a competitor, intending to cause the plane to crash during its test flight: Monrad Paulsen and Sanford Kadish, *Criminal Law and its Processes* (1962) 442 and Brent Fisse, *Howard's Criminal Law* (5th ed, 1990) 387. In the philosophical literature, see the much discussed case of Terror Bomber and Strategic Bomber. There is an early version in Jonathan Bennett, 'Morality and Consequences' in Sterling McMurrin (ed), *The Tanner Lectures on Human Values, Vol II* (1981) 45, 95.
7   The formulation of the example has varied over the years. It is usually said to have begun its career in Glanville Williams, *The Mental Element in Crime* (1965) 34–5 and recurs in the judgment of Lord Hailsham in *Hyam v DPP* [1975] AC 55, 74; and in Glanville Williams, *Textbook of Criminal Law* (2nd ed, 1983) para 3.5.

curiosity at what would be a truly extraordinary human response to the question of why the bomb was on the plane. So also, in other instances of the genre. There is a remarkable willingness to accept answers that should strain credulity to the utmost. For the moment I will let the question lie: why might the airplane saboteur answer in this way?

Perhaps this suspension of incredulity and bland acceptance of the denial of intention reflects the judgment that nothing much hangs on the fact that intention is denied. Does it matter what the airplane saboteur intended? Does it matter what the man at the pump intended, once we are sure that he knew the water was poisoned? Anscombe remarks that his answer is of 'no ethical or legal interest': if he pumped the water only because he was paid to pump water, 'that will not absolve him from guilt of murder'.[8] That may well be true, though it is hard to be sure of the application of the law of murder to conduct that averts a Holocaust.

Let the question whether the answer given by the man at the pump is of legal interest pass for the moment. It is curious that Anscombe should suggest that there is no ethical interest in knowing whether he intended to avert the Holocaust or merely earn his usual pay packet. Though she discounts the ethical interest of the inquiry, Anscombe draws explicitly on Wittgenstein to insist that we 'just are interested in what is true about a man in this kind of way'.[9] Curiosity is hardly satisfied, however, by the man's response. At first impression, his answer to her question—'I wanted my pay and just did my usual job'—is the answer of a moral imbecile. And if that were all we could take from the parable we should have advanced very little. It is a presupposition of a dialogue of this nature that it is *not* conducted with a mute or imbecile and that there is something more that *can* be said.

Before going further, it is necessary to clarify the nature of these imagined dialogues. They begin with an assertion—usually an accusation—that the person has killed intentionally. The assertion is denied, but not on the ground that death was unforeseen or the consequence of an accident, mistake, slip or failure of coordination. Instead, the person denies that they intended to kill by asserting that they intended to do something different. They claim that the action was not intended to kill—it was meant for another purpose. The conjunction

---

8   Anscombe, above n 1, para 25.
9   Ibid.

between meaning and intending is significant, for the denial of intention is, at the same time, a claim, by the agent, that it is for them to say what they meant by their actions.

Wittgenstein, whose influence is very apparent in Anscombe's account of the poison pump, asked a more general question concerning these dialogues: 'Why do I want to tell him about an intention too, as well as telling him what I did?' This question presupposes that there is something more that *could* be said. Wittgenstein answers it in a way that seems to me potentially significant for understanding the role of dialogues about intention in criminal trials. He answers it thus (the emphasis is his): 'I want to tell him something about *myself*, which goes beyond what happened at that time.'[10] If the dialogue concerning his intentions provides the man at the pump with a vehicle for an explanation of himself, it is likely that his explanation will be of some ethical interest. If the explanation is of ethical interest, it is likely that it will be of legal interest as well.

If you spoke with the man at the pump you would not simply accept, at face value, his denial that he intended to kill the party chiefs. It is not difficult to imagine an explanation of his intentions that would place them in a more illuminating and humanly credible account if the dialogue were to continue. Before sketching that account, however, it is worth noting some of the constraints imposed by the requirement that the answer be credible or illuminating. Suppose, instead of slow poison in the water supply, the pump handle was wired to a bomb in the party chiefs' headquarters, so that the first downstroke of the handle detonated the bomb and killed them as they sat in the war room.[11] Or suppose the political assassin handed twice the usual wage to the man at the pump. If the external circumstances were to change in these or other ways that can be readily imagined, it will be very much harder, and perhaps impossible, for the man at the pump to deny that he intended to kill.

The intentions we can have are more or less constrained by the facts, circumstances and conventions of the world we inhabit. It is true, as Wittgenstein remarks, that there are occasions when a dialogue concerning intention will 'reach a point where a man can say "This is my intention",

---

10 Ludwig Wittgenstein, *Philosophical Investigations* (Gertrude Anscombe (trans)) (3rd ed, 1968) para 659, quoted in Anscombe, above n 5, para 25.

11 Anscombe, ibid para 24.

and no one else can contribute anything to settle the matter'.[12] His examples are of fleeting intentions,[13] what one might describe as internal movements of the mind.[14] When responsibility for objective physical harms is in question, however, the occasions when the subject can speak with such authority of their intentions will be infrequent. One reason for the exotic nature of so many of the imaginary scenarios in legal texts is that the space for disputes about intentions is so very limited, once it is clear that an act done with full knowledge of the consequences has brought about some injury to person or property.[15]

The story told by the man at the poison pump invites scepticism. He says that he pumped the poisoned water because he was paid to pump water. It is unlikely that one would concede, from the outset, that this was his final word on the question of his intentions. His response invites the obvious response: 'You pumped the water knowing that it would kill them. Unless you can provide a better explanation, I shall have to conclude that you *meant* to kill them.' The threat that one will make a presumptive judgement of this kind is a natural step in the dialogue with someone who denies intention where an imputation of intention seems warranted. Presumptions of this nature are natural enough: they are not borrowed from the law.[16] On the contrary, law borrows in this respect from ordinary usage and it often does so with unnecessary restraint, allowing the accused the benefit of the doubt.

Here is an outline of one possible explanation that might be given by the man at the poison pump. He says that he is a humble man. The war has passed him by. The village where he lives is poor, bleak and miserable and he, like the other inhabitants, survives only by unremitting toil. The events in the world that the political assassin described to him have no effect on

---

12 Ibid para 27.

13 Peter Cane, 'Fleeting Mental States' (2000) 59 *Cambridge Law Journal* 273.

14 Wittgenstein, above n 10, para 639 ff: 'Think of disputes about what I *meant* when I said ... How can you be certain that for the space of a moment you were going to deceive him? Weren't your intentions and thoughts much too rudimentary?' Compare Anscombe, above n 5, para 27: 'A contemptuous thought might enter a man's mind so that he meant his polite and affectionate behaviour to someone on a particular occasion only ironically, without any outward sign of this.'

15 Wittgenstein, ibid 337: 'An intention is embedded in its situation, in human customs and institutions. If the technique of the game of chess did not exist, I could not intend to play a game of chess.' Anscombe, ibid para 25: 'Up to a point there is a check on his truthfulness.'

16 Michael Bratman, *Intention, Plans and Practical Reason* (1987) 155–63.

life in his village. There are no Jews there. He never saw the party chiefs. They used to come and go in helicopters. Like the events in which they played such leading roles, the party chiefs were remote and unreal to him. They seemed like inhabitants of a different, peripheral world. The man at the pump could, in this way, elaborate his denial that he intended to kill them. He asserts or claims a limit to his moral responsibility and resists imputations of heroism and blame alike. Once he begins to speak in this way however—once the dialogue begins—it is not entirely for him to say what he intended and what he did not intend. For it is far from certain that I am bound to accept this denial. And it is far from certain that the man at the pump will persist in it. There is, in this example and others to be discussed, the possibility that a dispute over intention may be resolved by capitulation and acquiescence in the charge that death was intended.[17] In this respect, the ascription of intention may resemble the outcome of a negotiation in which the person whose intentions are the subject of inquiry discovers that they don't have the final say.

   Suppose I accept that he did not intend to kill. Though the inquiry concerned his intentions when he continued to pump the water after it was poisoned, the point of the dialogue was the revelation of a radical divergence between his values and mine. Acceptance of his claim that the death of the party chiefs was a mere unintended side effect of his intended activity of earning his wage required me to make a concession, perhaps unwillingly, that these are indeed his values and that this is indeed a possible way of describing his intentions. If killing the party chiefs is a good thing in this ambiguous example, he gets no credit for it. If it is taken to be a bad thing, however, his account does seem to palliate or mitigate the crime. It seems to do so because his reasons for doing what he did

---

17   In *Lang v Lang* [1955] AC 402, 431, the Privy Council held that a husband who retained a mistress in spite of his wife's protests betrayed an 'intention to break up the married life.' Consider the negotiations about intention that will follow a wife's accusation that her husband's infidelity was *meant* to put an end to their relationship. Her accusation may, for all his protests, be true. And it may be that he did not comprehend that this was his intention, until she made him admit to it. It is equally possible, of course, that he may persist in his denial and that his wife will accept his denial. Perhaps he meant to secure the pleasures of infidelity and the benefits of married life: the breakdown of the relationship with his wife may have been the last thing he intended. Glanville Williams remarked that the decision in *Lang v Lang* transformed a psychological insight, true of some cases, into a constructive rule for all cases.

dissociate him, to some extent, from worst case scenarios of murder. It is no defence, but the dialogue between prosecutor and defendant does not end if he is convicted of murder. His account of what mattered to him in the circumstances requires him to provide, at the same time, an account of the kind of person he is. From the interlocutor's point of view, 'the kind of person he is' provides the ground for both accepting his denial of intention[18] and, it would seem, for mitigating his sentence.

By comparison, the airplane saboteur remains opaque and lacking in intelligible human motivation. The saboteur is meant to exemplify a poised ambiguity of circumstance in which *he* can have the final say on the issue of intention. Why does he give the answer he does? It cannot be to excuse, mitigate or palliate his act of killing the passengers and crew. If he thought to excuse himself in this way, that would be cogent evidence that he is incapable of engaging in a moral dialogue. We do not have to assume, however, that a denial of intention to do harm is always offered as an excuse. Perhaps he *wants* his interlocutor to understand how little the destruction of human life matters to him. He is, let us say, being questioned by a recruiter for a terrorist organisation. His answer begins to make sense if it is taken as an expression of his wish to display contempt or cool disregard for human life.[19] Once again, his account of his intentions allows him to reveal 'the kind of person he is'. But it is not a kind of answer one would expect him to give in a criminal trial.

The story of the airplane saboteur was meant to suggest the conclusion that proof of an intention to kill should not be required for conviction of murder, if the crew and passengers are killed, or attempted murder, if the catastrophe is somehow averted.[20] The story was supposed to clinch the argument that there is nothing to choose, in terms of moral depravity, between an agent who intends harm and another who does not intend the harm, but knows it to be a certain consequence. Yet the example seems to

---

18 Compare Wittgenstein, above n 10, para 638 on momentary intentions: '[C]an't the evidence be too scanty? Yes, when one follows it up it seems extraordinarily scanty; but isn't this because one is taking no account of the history of this evidence? Certain antecedents were necessary.'

19 Compare the accusation: 'You meant to hurt me' and the response 'You think so? Don't flatter yourself. (Your hurt was the least of my concerns.)'

20 In Glanville Williams' account, the example was restricted in its application to the question whether the saboteur would be guilty of attempted murder. At that time, recklessness as to death was sufficient fault for a conviction of murder in English law: Williams, *Textbook of Criminal Law*, above n 7, 85.

prove too much. Who in their right mind would choose this way of making a fraudulent insurance claim for a lost suitcase? Daniel Dennett's question seems particularly appropriate: 'How can we intelligibly describe the relevant mental history of the truly culpable agent—the villain or rational cheat with no excuses?'[21] He would be more intelligible if he *had* intended to kill the passengers and crew. The airplane saboteur's claim that their deaths were a mere side effect of a projected fraud seems, more than anything else, to suggest that he is beyond dialogue, incapable of moral agency.[22]

If incredulity is suspended, the story of the airplane saboteur does suggest that a denial that harm was intended will sometimes inculpate rather than exculpate. Though the example is meant to demonstrate that there is no difference in culpability between intending a consequence and foreseeing it as a certainty, the implications seem more general. It is not immediately apparent why it should make any difference if the airline saboteur distrusted the explosive device and thought it no more than probable that it would explode. He might display precisely the same attitude of contemptuous disregard for the anticipated death of the passengers and crew. In conventional legal terms, what grounds can there be for distinguishing 'recklessness' from realisation of a certainty, where both express an attitude of utter indifference to the anticipated death of another? I will return to the recklessness issue later in this essay.

The question of whether courts and legislatures should take a person to intend a harm if it was known to be an inevitable side effect of the pursuit of an intended objective is taken up in a recent essay by Antony Duff.[23] He argues that it is an essential requirement for criminal responsibility, that the language of imputation in criminal trials be capable of use by the accused in 'authentic first person speech'.[24] He means by this

---

21 Daniel Dennett, *Brainstorms: Philosophical Essays on Mind and Psychology* (1979) 286–7.

22 Ibid 285. A matter of degree, no doubt: '[O]ur assumption that an entity is a person is shaken precisely in those cases where it matters: when wrong has been done and the question of responsibility arises. For in these cases the grounds for saying that person is culpable (the evidence that he did wrong, was aware he was doing wrong, and did wrong of his own free will) are in themselves grounds for doubting that it is a person we are dealing with at all.'

23 Antony Duff, 'Law, Language and Community' (1998) 18 *Oxford Journal of Legal Studies* 189.

24 Ibid 199.

that the language of condemnation must coincide with language that the guilty might use of themselves, reflecting a shared sense of understanding of right and wrong with those who make the accusation. If a crime requires proof of intention, that possibility of shared understanding is imperilled if courts ascribe intention in circumstances in which an offender could not avow that intention in the first person.

There is an evident link between Duff's expression of this requirement of mutuality of understanding with Wittgenstein's account of the reasons that induce a person to respond to inquiry and speak of their intentions: 'I wanted to tell him something of *myself.*' Duff is writing, however, from the other side of an inquisitorial divide, from the point of view of one who puts the question to the man at the pump or to the airplane saboteur with a view to making a judgment of their criminal liability.

Intending to do Harm

Criminal law allocates, with varying degrees of precision, proportionate punishments to particularly defined offences. The line between the issues of guilt and punishment is drawn with a degree of precision that is not matched outside the criminal law, where the denial that one *meant* to cause harm will usually possess a more flexible set of exculpatory applications than it does in criminal trials. Duff writes of a trial process that aspires to be a 'rational process of communication in which the defendant is actively involved'.[25] But communication will take place across a divide in which defendants' explanations of what they intended to do are frequently dissected and redeployed through the processes of accusation, justification, exculpation and mitigation of punishment.

The Meaning of Intention in Australian Criminal Law

Though courts and academic opinion are far from unanimous about the meaning of intention in criminal law, the formulation proposed in Chapter 2 of the Australian *Model Criminal Code 1992*[26] is relatively

---

25   Ibid 194.
26   Australia, Criminal Law Officers Committee of the Standing Committee of Attorneys-General, *Model Criminal Code—Chapter 2: General Principles of Criminal Liability,*

uncontroversial. The definition opens with the declaration that a 'person has intention with respect to conduct if he or she means to engage in that conduct'[27] and intention 'with respect to a result if he or she means to bring it about'.[28]

This first part of the definition does not take us very far. Indeed, it is not meant to take us anywhere at all. The equation of what one *intends* to do with what one *means* to do was meant to emphasise the point that there is a very substantial common ground where legal usage and ordinary usage coincide. The code goes on, however, to extend the meaning of intention to include a category of cases in which one would not say, as a matter of ordinary usage, that conduct was intended or intentional. A result is also intended or intentional when a person is 'aware that it will occur in the ordinary course of events', as a consequence of their conduct.[29] That the extension goes beyond ordinary meaning is immediately apparent. Though my dentist is aware that a particular procedure will cause me pain in the ordinary course of events, she does not, in any ordinary sense of the words, 'intend to cause pain'. Were I to accuse her of hurting me intentionally, she would deny it indignantly. If I persisted in the accusation, our relationship would quickly come to an end. For both of us, my pain is an unintended and unwanted side effect of her intentional activity. The extended legal sense of the concept, which would characterise her conduct as an intentional infliction of pain, is a particular and striking instance of departure from the principle advanced by Duff, that imputations of guilt should be made in the first person voice.

Discussion Draft (1992). Chapter 2 has been enacted by the Commonwealth as the *Criminal Code Act 1995*. The Act is due to take effect on 15 December 2001, when all Commonwealth criminal offences have been revised to harmonise with the general fault provisions of the code.

27 *Criminal Code Act 1995* (Cth) s 5.2(1).

28 *Criminal Code Act 1995* (Cth) s 5.2(3).

29 *Criminal Code Act 1995* (Cth) s 5.2(3); Draft Criminal Law Bill s 2(a), UK Law Commission, *Legislating the Criminal Code: Offences Against the Person and General Principles*, (Consultation Paper No 122, 1992). Compare the American *Model Penal Code 1962*, s 2.02(2), which displaces 'intention' in favour of 'purpose' in its formulation of fault elements: A person acts purposely with respect to a material element of an offence when: (i) if the element involves the nature of his conduct or a result thereof, it is his conscious object to engage in conduct of that nature or to cause such a result; and (ii) if the element involves the attendant circumstances, he is aware of the existence of such circumstances or he believes or hopes that they exist.

This extended sense of intention broadens the application of offences in which nothing short of proof of intention will suffice for guilt. In jurisdictions where murder requires proof of an intention to kill or cause serious injury, the extended definition is meant to ensure that Glanville Williams' airplane saboteur is convicted of that offence. Over a very large range of offences, however, where recklessness is an alternative ground for conviction, recourse to the extended definition is unnecessary. More needs to be said about intention, however, before the relationship between intention and recklessness can be clarified.

Intentions Translated, Transformed and Traduced

Most criminal prohibitions are aimed at things people do. There are exceptions, of course, when liability is imposed for a state of affairs, such as 'being without lawful means of support', but these are comparatively rare. In Australian law, most offences that impose liability for an intentional act of wrongdoing extend the scope of prohibition to include reckless commission of the act. But suppose, for the moment, recklessness is put to one side. Conviction of the offender will require proof that the proscribed act was intentional under a particular description required in the statement of the offence. An accused who denies guilt may do so by asserting that the act was done (intentionally) under another description, which displaces the description of a legally forbidden act. The man at the poison pump who asserted that he was merely earning his wages sought, in this way, to displace the assertion that he was (intentionally) poisoning the party chiefs.

Frequently, however, defendants' descriptions of their intentions do not prevail. Offenders who are convicted of theft as a consequence of 'borrowing' another's property must be surprised, on occasion, to discover that what they intended was a permanent deprivation of their victim's property. The *legal* meaning of 'intention to deprive permanently' goes far wider than ordinary language. Here, as at other critical points in the determination of criminal liability, there are potential constraints on the use of the first person voice. I should emphasise again that these constraints are not peculiar to legal processes. They are equally characteristic of extra-legal discourse, though legal constraints are less subtle and more arbitrary, particularly in cases close to the margin.[30] There is little consistency or system in these constraints: they are a mosaic of particularities. There is, however, a general tendency in the criminal law to translate a denial of intention to do harm into a claim that there was justification or excuse for what was done. The effect is similar to the rule that a person is taken to have intended a consequence that was known to be certain. In this instance, however, the trick is done by re-characterising the object of the person's intention.

Take a relatively clear example first. Women who kill violent husbands or partners in self defence frequently deny that the fatal wound was inflicted with intention to kill or cause serious injury. The claim that the act was done in self defence is expressed as an assertion that it was not done to kill or cause injury, but to stop an attack. There is nothing illogical or incomprehensible about the battered woman's denial of intention to kill.[31] Anyone who listens to her will know exactly what she means and it would be obtuse to suggest that she is somehow mistaken about appropriate applications of the concept of intention. A court might be expected, however, to bar her attempt to deny intention in this way. To permit liability for a murder to be defeated by her denial of intention would open the possibility of an escape from the requirements of reasonableness that constrain the plea of self defence.

The same tendency towards conclusive characterisation of intention, which overrides the defendant's own avowals, is apparent, in more subtle

---

30   For an extended treatment of the issue, see E D'Arcy, *Human Acts: An Essay in Their Moral Evaluation* (1963) 18–39. The requirements of dialogue constrain the ways in which we can describe acts that are of particular human significance or interest: ibid 29: 'For instance, 'killing B' may be given as a description of A's act, a description that may not be elided into such descriptions as 'succeeding to B's title', or 'inheriting B's fortune'.

31   It has, indeed, significant jurisprudential support. For a recent discussion, see Suzanne Uniacke, *Permissible Killing* (1994) ch 4. Quite apart from jurisprudential dispute over the issue, it is apparent that there will be divergent ethical dialects in a pluralistic community. Some years ago, in a television interview, a weapons instructor employed by the Los Angeles Police Department emphasised that recruits were trained to 'shoot to stop, but not to kill'. As the interview progressed it became apparent from the description of the ammunition used and the areas of the body targeted, that death was certain to follow if a shot was fired in accordance with instructions. When pressed by the interviewer the instructor maintained, with unperturbed gravity, that officers who obeyed their instructions shot to stop and did not shoot with the intention of causing death.

form, in offences that require proof of an intention to inflict 'harm', 'injury' or 'damage'.[32] These are 'thick' concepts in the sense that they 'enable us to describe ... human actions, in terms of substantive and specific ethical values'.[33] The reference to the collective plural, 'us', in this passage obscures the possibility that the substantive and specific ethical values of the person who is the subject of inquiry may be very different from those who charge the offence. If the court determines that what was done amounts to a harm, the focus shifts from a 'subjective' inquiry into the values of the individual to one that will determine whether the actions of the accused meet the 'objective' standards of the court.[34]

In England, the Law Commission has variously described tattoos, cosmetic piercing, scarification and surgical operations on compliant subjects who seek these services as 'injury' or 'seriously disabling injury'.[35] In Australia, the Model Criminal Code Officer's Committee characterises these services as an infliction of 'harm' or 'serious harm'.[36] If a cosmetic service is characterised as a harm, it follows that it is, for the purposes of the law, a harm done intentionally. Even more surprising is the characterisation of operations by a surgeon, dentist or other medical practitioner, who cuts human tissue or removes organs or parts of the body in order to ameliorate illness or injury, as harm or serious harm to the patient. The proposition that tattooists, mohels and surgeons intend to

---

32 Consider, for example, *Fancy* [1980] *Criminal Law Review* 171; discussed in A T H Smith, *Property Offences: The Protection of Property through the Criminal Law* (1994) para 27-23.

33 Duff, above n 23, 200, drawing on Bernard Williams, *Ethics and the Limits of Philosophy* (1985). Compare D'Arcy, above n 30, 24–5 on 'moral-species-terms'.

34 For a striking example, see *Watson* [1987] 1 Qd R 440, in which the Queensland Court of Criminal Appeal refused to countenance the possibility that a Palm Island man who cut his wife with a knife did not intend to harm her because this was a form of punishment for disobedient wives that was usual and accepted behaviour in his community.

35 UK Law Commission, *Consent in the Criminal Law* (Law Com CP No 139, 1995) Part VIII 'Medical and Surgical Treatment' and Part IX 'Circumcision, Tattooing, Cosmetic Piercing, Branding and Scarification'. Circumcision, tattooing, cosmetic piercing, branding and scarification are described as instances of 'injury inflicted deliberately by consent': ibid para 9.1. Though many would have no hesitation in describing circumcision as an 'injury' or harm, it would be a significant departure from Duff's requirement of condemnation in the first person voice to ascribe to the mohel who performs a ritual circumcision an *intention* to injure or harm the child.

36 Australia, Model Criminal Code Officers Committee, *Model Criminal Code—Chapter 5: Non Fatal Offences Against the Person, Report* (1998) 119–29.

harm their subjects can only be sustained if prosecutors exercise caution before putting the proposition to the test.

The object, once again, of the re-characterisation of the defendant's intentions is to exchange the normative coin of intention for a codified defence of consent, which will incorporate criteria for determining whether or not consent was adequate in the circumstances. Though a tattooist who inscribes a design on a juvenile can claim, quite truthfully and in all sincerity, that the act was not intended to harm, that will not bar a conviction for an offence of causing harm intentionally. The Law Commission and Model Criminal Code Officers Committee propose a conclusive re-characterisation of the tattooist's intentions. There is substantial support, in recent academic comment, for these conclusive characterisations, coupled with the proposal that excuses and justifications should be clarified and articulated, so as to reduce the latent normative element in ascriptions of intention.[37]

These displacements of the normative role of intention presuppose that it is always practicable to formulate appropriate excuses and justifications. In reality, courts and legislatures are often constrained, if not prohibited, from doing so by competing structures of folk psychology and its offshoots in folk law. When medical treatment borders on permissible euthanasia, courts and legislatures display extreme reluctance to articulate the rules that determine when life may be terminated. Legal and lay opinion divide on the question of whether it is ever permissible to administer a treatment with the intention of killing the patient. Though there is evident movement of opinion on the issue, many doctors, lawyers and lay people might be expected to insist that the question whether the act was done with intention to kill is still determinative of the question whether the treatment can be justified. Legislatures are unlikely to articulate determinative rules for permissible termination of patients' lives in the existing climate of

---

37 Andrew Ashworth, 'Criminal Liability in a Medical Context: The Treatment of Good Intentions' in A P Simester and A T H Smith, *Harm and Culpability* (1996) 179–80; I H Dennis, 'The Critical Condition of Criminal Law' (1997) 50 *Current Legal Problems* 213, 225: 'The problem with allowing matters of justification and excuse to bear generally on the issue of intention is that any overt restrictions of policy or principle on their scope as defences may simply be bypassed.' Compare Kevin Flannery, 'Natural Law Mens Rea Versus the Benthamite Tradition' (1995) 40 *American Journal of Jurisprudence* 377, 391: '[It] is clearly wrong to identify legal surgery as in any sense wounding. Our linguistic intuitions tell us as much.'

unresolved controversy.[38] They are particularly unlikely to do so while division remains on the question whether acceptable treatment could ever be characterised as an intentional termination of the patient's life.[39]

In more exotic and less frequented areas of the law, the normative role of intention is more pronounced. Last year, in the course of land rights litigation, Australian federal government ministers and members of parliament were accused of genocide. The plaintiffs argued that government legislation that reduced Aboriginal land rights was actuated by an 'intention to destroy a racial or ethnic group as such'. The claim failed for many reasons, among them the court's conclusion that, even if it were to be shown that the policies in question 'may have that *effect*, it is another matter to say the Ministers were actuated by an *intent* to destroy the Arabunna people'.[40] Or consider the 'intention to cause detriment to a corporation' required in certain offences involving company directors.[41]

---

38   Consider the implications of the recent Court of Appeal decision that Siamese twins might be separated, sacrificing the life of one who had no chance of survival, to save the other from certain death: *A (Children)* Case No B1/2000/2969 per Ward LJ at para 4.1. 'Unpalatable though it may be ... to stigmatise the doctors with "murderous intent", that is what in law they will have if they perform the operation and Mary dies as a result.' But compare Brooke LJ at paras 14, 25 and Robert Walker LJ.

39   Linguistic pluralism appears to prevail here as elsewhere. A recent survey of physicians professionally engaged in treatment of the terminally ill found that a significant proportion described the measures that they take as intentional termination of the patient's life. See the account of a study by Dr Charles Rosen presented to the Annual Scientific Congress of the Royal Australia College of Surgeons, Melbourne, 12 May 2000: The survey, of more than 1000 physicians, found that 36% stated that they had administered a fatal dose of a sedative or analgesic drug with the intention of causing death: *The Age*, 13 May 2000 and personal communication.

40   *Nulyarimma v Thompson* (1999) 96 FCR 153, 161 per Wilcox J (emphasis original), with whom Whitlam J agreed on this point. Earlier, Wilcox J supplied a more concrete example: 'A squatter who shot at Aborigines in reprisal for them spearing his cattle must be taken to have intended to kill the *individuals* at whom he shot; it cannot necessarily be presumed he intended to destroy the *group* as such, even in part.' At 160 (emphasis original). An application to the High Court for special leave to appeal was denied: *Nulyarimma v Thompson* HCA C18/1999 (Unreported, High Court, 4 August 2000).

41   See *Companies Code* (WA) s 229(4), as interpreted in *Chew* (1992) 173 CLR 626; discussed in Matthew Goode and Ian Leader-Elliott, 'Criminal Law' in *An Annual Survey of Australian Law* (1992) 199, 240–5.

The director must intend detriment and liability is not incurred unless the director perceived the conduct *as* a detriment to the corporation.[42]

These fugitive cases suggest a role for intention in the ordinary sense of the word, which does not extend to consequences merely because they are known to be certain. The *Model Criminal Code* proposal for codification of the extended sense of intention risks inflexibility in those areas of law where, for one reason or another, articulation of defences or excuses is unlikely. Glanville Williams expressed the same reservation briefly and obliquely in his discussion of the question whether consequences known to be certain are to be counted as intended. Though courts should, as a general rule, treat known consequences as intended, he thought that the rule gives way when it would be 'contrary to the purpose of the law or contrary to justice'.[43] In a criminal code, however, such convenient dispensations from general principles are rarely available.

Intending to Kill for No Reason at All

If a person kills for no reason at all, that is a reason for doubting whether they really understand what killing is about. The latent normative element in ascriptions of intention might seem to suggest that such a person does not really intend to kill at all. In the airplane saboteur hypothetical, there is a similar sense that some fundamental element of human understanding of the nature of moral obligations to others has gone missing. There is a sense in which the question whether a person intended a particular harm can be a

---

42   *Chew* (1992) 173 CLR 626, 633–4, per Mason CJ, Brennan, Gaudron and McHugh JJ: 'Once one concludes that there is a purposive element in the offence, it is necessary to establish not merely that the accused intended that *a* result should ensue, but also that the accused believed that the intended result would be an advantage for himself or herself or for some other person or a detriment to the corporation.' (Emphasis original.)

43   Williams, *Textbook of Criminal Law*, above n 7, 86. Codification of Australian federal criminal law has introduced an undesirable degree of rigidity in this respect. Section 5.2(3) of the *Criminal Code Act 1995* (Cth) imposes the rule that known consequences are taken to be intentional without provision for exceptions. The range of available defences for intentional harms is too restricted to reflect the range of circumstances in which denial of intention plays an indispensable normative role. In particular, the necessity defence in s 10.3 is restricted in its applications to 'sudden or extraordinary emergency'. Compare the American Law Institute's *Model Penal Code*, Proposed Official Draft 1962, s 3.02, which permits a general defence of choice of evils.

matter of degree, depending on the agent's competence to understand the world in which the action takes place.

A child of five can certainly intend to hurt the cat. We might doubt, however, that a child of that age could be said to have intended to kill it. Or if we do not baulk at that, we might baulk at the idea that the same child could intend to kill a sibling or parent. Participation in a common universe of social or moral conventions is a matter of degree. In her interviews with Mary Bell, almost twenty years after she was tried for the murder of two small boys, Gitta Sereny asked her what she had understood of the trial process. Mary Bell was ten when she killed the first of the boys and eleven when she killed the second and was put on trial:

> 'Did the fact of their being dead mean anything to you?'
> 'No, nothing, because I hadn't intended ... Well—how can I say this now?' she said right away. 'But I didn't know I had intended for them to be dead ... dead for ever. Dead for me then wasn't forever'.[44]

In law, children are protected from the full rigours of the criminal process by rules that limit their criminal responsibility. In similar fashion, the insanity defence provides an excuse for individuals who can satisfy the court that they suffered a mental impairment that diminished or destroyed their capacity for moral agency. But attainment of a particular age and freedom from a legally recognised form of mental impairment are no guarantee of competence. One might plausibly suggest that there can be no intention to cause grievous bodily harm or death if the killer lacked some necessary minimum understanding of the value of life and the meaning of death at the time of the fatal act. So, one might say, a person who does not understand the meaning of life, at that critical moment, cannot intend to kill. The issue arises in Australian case law when criminal liability is contested on the ground that the defendant was intoxicated at the time of the act.

In trials for murder and the more serious offences against the person, Australian courts have often admitted evidence of gross intoxication in

---

44   Gitta Sereny, *Cries Unheard: The Story of Mary Bell* (1998) 124. Sereny pressed the question on a number of occasions: 'I had pointed out to Mary time and again that in the case of Brian [her second victim] she could no longer persuade herself that death did not mean for ever. It was a question I put to her over and over: if she understood that she had murdered Martin Brown, why had she continued with Brian Howe? And she would not, I had to conclude could not, answer it.' Ibid 353.

support of the claim that the accused was so drunk as to lack the 'capacity to form an intention to kill or cause serious injury'. It seems obvious, however, that this talk of capacity to form intentions is legal jargon, which obscures a more basic human reality.[45] It is almost always implausible for individuals who rely on intoxication to suggest that they are incapable of acting intentionally. Nor is it necessary for them to do so. The whole thrust of the inquiry is whether they lacked intention to *kill*. A case recently decided in Adelaide, in which the South Australian Court of Criminal Appeal quashed a conviction for murder, provides a rare instance of clarity on the point.[46] The facts were depressingly familiar. Two friends got drunk together, provoking words were said and the defendant, David Machin, battered the other to death with a rock. The attack was described as 'mindless and bizarre',[47] but there is no suggestion that Machin lacked the capacity to form intentions. The blows that caused death were struck intentionally. He made an attempt to conceal what he had done before fleeing the scene in his motor car. These acts also appear to have been intentional. The conviction was quashed, nonetheless, because the direction to the jury on intoxication was inadequate. The jury should have been invited to consider the possibility that anger coupled with intoxication might have deprived Machin of an appreciation of 'the practical effect and enormity of his conduct'.[48] It was possible, in such a case, to suggest that he struck the blows without any adequate realisation that what he was doing amounted to grievous bodily harm. Or, more to the point, he may have lacked the capacity to appreciate what it meant—the *enormity* of the act—to kill or inflict grievous bodily harm on his friend.

These defendants are quite capable of acting intentionally. They are quite capable of intentionally punching, stabbing or kicking others. Intoxication and anger rob them, however, of any depth of appreciation of the significance and meaning of their actions. The court's decision permits a jury to acquit on the ground that a person in that state of attenuated comprehension might not have intended to cause grievous bodily harm or

---

45 See *Coleman* (1990) 47 A Crim R 306, 323 per Hall J: jury directions that ask whether the accused was capable of forming intentions are 'unnecessary and productive of confusion'. See Roger Shiner, 'Intoxication and Responsibility' (1990) 13 *International Journal of Law and Psychiatry* 9 for a convincing refutation.
46 *Machin* (1996) 68 SASR 526.
47 Ibid 538.
48 Ibid 539.

death. There could be no escape from a conviction for manslaughter, however, for Machin certainly intended to do harm to his friend.

In a formal sense, *Machin* denies the fault element of intention, which is required for a murder conviction. But the denial of an intention to kill rests on the implicit claim to an excuse or partial excuse because his capacity, as a moral agent who can be blamed, was diminished.

Considered as an excuse, gross intoxication has close historical affinities with insanity and infancy.[49] The affinity is apparent in modern Australian common law, which similarly permits an accused to rely on evidence of mental illness or brain damage to support a denial of intention to cause injury or death.[50] A defendant who denies intention in this way does not rely on the insanity 'defence' or the partial defence of diminished responsibility. Nor need the denial of intention involve an assertion that the injury was done in a state of automatism, involuntarily, by accident or mistake. The common element in these appeals to intoxication and mental impairment is the premise that one cannot be said to intend to kill or grievously injure another person unless one has an adequate understanding of what it *means* to kill or cause grievous injury. What I referred to earlier as the 'thickness' of the concepts of killing or causing grievous bodily harm—their latent evaluative content—permits a defendant whose moral competence is permanently or temporarily impaired to deny that death or grievous bodily harm was intended.

At this point, another set of parallels, this time between the pleas of intoxication and provocation, becomes uncomfortably apparent. It seems probable that the defence of provocation, which reduces murder to manslaughter, was once rationalised in a similar fashion, as a form of denial of intention to kill or cause serious injury.[51]

---

49   See Jeremy Bentham, *Introduction to the Principles of Morals and Legislation* (W Harrison (ed)) (1960) 284. Bentham saw no difference in theory between infancy, insanity and gross intoxication: they were all characterised as conditions in which criminal liability was defeated because the threat of punishment must be inefficacious. He conceded, however, that theory might not be realised in practice because of difficulties of proof. See also Charles Mercier, *Crime and Insanity* (1911) 47, 51; James Stephen, *A History of the Criminal law of England, Vol II* (1883) 165; James Stephen, *A Digest of the Criminal Law* (Herbert Stephen and Harry Stephen (eds)) (5th ed, 1894) art 27.

50   *Hawkins* (1994) 179 CLR 500; noted in Ian Leader-Elliott, 'Criminal Cases in the High Court of Australia: *Hawkins*' (1994) 18 *Criminal Law Journal* 347.

51   Earlier cases, such as *Holmes* [1946] AC 588 and the original formulation of the provocation defence in *Crimes Act 1900* (NSW) s 23, assume that a plea of

Jeremy Horder has explored the fluctuations of judicial attitude on the question of why provocation excuses. Is the homicide partially justified because it was precipitated by a wrong doing to the offender or mitigated because the defendant lost self-control?[52] This issue is far too complex for discussion here, but the briefest comparison with provocation is sufficient to indicate the extreme vulnerability of the Australian common law cases on intoxication and intention.

Horder describes a tendency, from the late seventeenth century, for courts to emphasise loss of self-control as the central requirement of provocation. That emphasis suggested that individuals who kill because they are overwhelmed by anger *could* not be guilty of murder: 'if it is found as a matter of empirical fact that defendants genuinely lost self control before killing, the killing should be reduced to manslaughter'.[53] Such a rule would be intolerable, however, for it would confer a privilege on unrestrained brutality. In reality, loss of self-control was never sufficient, of itself, to reduce murder to manslaughter. The plea of provocation was contained at first by the fiction that utterly inexcusable violence was actuated by malice rather than loss of self-control[54] and, subsequently, by the development of objective tests of proportionate, reasonable or humanly understandable retaliation. In this way, the denial of intention to kill or do grievous bodily harm was translated into a partial defence, limited by the rule that a grossly disproportionate response would still amount to murder.

---

provocation involved a denial of intention to kill. Modern orthodoxy insists, to the contrary, that the partial defence does not come into play until the jury has first concluded that the defendant intended to kill or cause grievous bodily harm: see *Parker* (1963) 111 CLR 610, 653 per Windeyer J. The effect of that orthodoxy has been to obscure the fact that the defendant's anger may lead a jury to doubt that the fatal response to provocation was accompanied by an intention to kill or do serious injury. South African law was once explicit in its adoption of the principle that provocation had a dual operation, providing a basis for denial of intention and, if that failed, a partial excuse for intentional killing. See: *Tenganyika* [1958] 3 SA 7; discussed in E M Burchell and P M A Hunt, *South African Criminal Law and Procedure, Vol I* (1970) 245.

52   Jeremy Horder, *Provocation and Responsibility* (1992) ch 5.
53   Ibid 95, referring to the views of the Criminal Law Commissioners (1831–41: 233) .
54   Ibid 91: 'The more disproportionate defendants' responses, the greater the (presumed) evidence that they had not lost their self control and that reason was, in fact, in its seat at the time of the killing.'

In *Machin* there was nothing that the law would recognise as provocation to prompt the defendant's anger. The remarkable thing about the case is the way in which the limits imposed by the law of provocation on the exculpatory effects of loss of self-control were outflanked. The absence of any reason for Machin's attack and its utterly disproportionate savagery are taken to support the inference that he did not intend to kill his friend. In provocation, on the other hand, courts insist that the partial defence has no application *unless* the defendant intended to kill or cause grievous bodily harm.[55] Incongruity is apparent if one compares *Machin* and *Parker*,[56] the central decision on the modern Australian law of provocation.

Parker was driven by jealousy to kill Dan Kelly, who had taken his wife from him. Parker pursued Kelly in his motor car, ran him down, attacked him with a knuckleduster when he was helpless on the ground and then stabbed him twice in the throat. No-one ever doubted that he was overwhelmed by rage and grief when he killed Kelly. Like Machin, he denied that he intended to kill or do grievous bodily harm. Dixon CJ responded to this denial with blunt simplicity: 'no question of intent to do grievous bodily harm arose, so far as I can see. He actually did it, by the very act he consciously performed. That is to say, in itself it amounted to grievous bodily harm.'[57] But one might say exactly the same thing of Machin, who bashed his friend to death with a rock. One might, on the other hand, ask the question that led the South Australian court to conclude that there was room for doubt on the question whether Machin intended to kill or inflict grievous bodily harm. Did Parker comprehend the 'enormity' of his actions when he killed Dan Kelly? These two cases stand on either side of a fragile doctrinal divide between the 'defence' of provocation and a 'denial' of homicidal intention.[58] The fact that Machin's violence was

---

55 The classic exposition of the point is to be found in *Parker* (1963) 111 CLR 610, 653 (HC) per Windeyer J.

56 Ibid 665 (PC).

57 Ibid 624.

58 For representative indicators of that fragility, see Stephen Odgers' fascinating attempt to meld the two doctrines in 'Contemporary Provocation Law—Is Substantially Impaired Self-Control Enough?' in Stanley Yeo (ed), *Partial Excuses to Murder* (1990):

> If the criminal law recognises that volition or mens rea may be negated by intoxication, it is difficult to see why it would not also recognise that sufficiency of self control needed to rebut provocation may be negated by intoxication.

extreme and without adequate motive provided grounds for the inference that he did not intend to kill or cause grievous bodily harm. Yet the whole object of the elaboration of objective tests in the law of provocation is to ensure that those who kill without reason, when no ordinary person would kill, are convicted of murder.

I will not try to reconcile the law on intoxication and provocation. The interest of the comparison lies in the bifurcation of doctrine that permits Machin to deny intention to kill or do grievous bodily harm, but transmutes Parker's denial of intention to kill or cause injury into a defence, governed by objective tests to determine whether the degree of provocation was sufficient to reduce murder to manslaughter.

Problems of Recklessness and Indifference

In the stories of the man at the poison pump and the airline saboteur, the discussion was untrammelled by any consideration of the way in which the law might judge the issue of intention. In each case, the agent's description of the intention with which the acts were done displaced the accusation that they acted with the intention of causing death. In the examples that followed, involving dentists, doctors and tattooists, ordinary language permits the same displacement of any accusation that they intended harm. Within the law, however, these instances of therapeutic or cosmetic interference with the body of a compliant subject are *taken* to involve an intentional infliction of harm. The practitioner's denial of intention is transmuted into the claim that the harm, though intentional, was justified, excused or not deserving of severe punishment. So also when provocation is pleaded to a charge of murder. The defendant is taken to have intended grievous bodily harm, at the least, though an alternative answer to the question of intention may be open.

There is no logical reason for distinguishing these modes of reasoning. A similar analysis should hold good for an accused who is unusually pugnacious.

See in addition, Fisse, above n 6, 434:

Another unsatisfactory line of demarcation is between the principle of voluntariness and the doctrine of provocation ... once D has lost control of himself his conduct becomes ... involuntary. This ought to mean that he should be acquitted, not merely convicted of a lesser offence.

Compare Horder, above n 52, 96 on isolated instances of reliance on loss of self-control induced by drink in nineteenth-century case law.

The *Model Criminal Code* rule that knowledge that a harm will occur is equivalent to an intention that it should occur is similar in its effects. The airplane saboteur and others of his ilk are taken to have intended the known side effects of their intentional conduct. The inquiry into guilt is shifted to a consideration of the question whether the defendant is entitled to one of the limited range of justifications or excuses available to a person who inflicts harm intentionally. Quite obviously, the airplane saboteur has neither justification nor excuse.

Once this step is taken, it might seem a logical progression to extend the concept of intention still further and re-introduce the presumption that a person is taken to intend the natural and probable consequences of their acts. So long as it was clearly understood that the presumption required proof that the defendant knew the consequences to be probable, courts could keep faith with the Australian commitment to a subjective determination of the defendant's state of mind. Though there are traces of such a progression in Australian case law, the central line of development has avoided that course. By and large, courts and legislatures have insisted on the bifurcation of intention and recklessness as distinct grounds for criminal liability.

The Meaning of Recklessness in Australian Law

The articulation of the concept of recklessness, and its deployment as a ground for criminal liability, is probably the most significant development in Australian criminal jurisprudence over the last half century.[59] The development culminates with the judgment of Brennan CJ in *He Kaw Teh*[60] in 1985 and the substantial legislative paraphrase of that judgment in the general fault provisions of the Australian *Model Criminal Code* and the Commonwealth *Criminal Code Act 1995*.[61] Australian common law and

---

59   The salient points of that development begin with the dissenting judgment of Dixon CJ in *Vallance* (1961) 108 CLR 56 and the first edition of Colin Howard's *Australian Criminal Law*, as it was then known, which was published in 1965. Howard took the judgment as central to his analysis of criminal liability and buttressed that analysis by explicit reliance on the *Model Penal Code*, American Law Institute, Proposed Official Draft, 4 May 1962.

60   (1985) 157 CLR 523.

61   Australia, Criminal Law Officers Committee of the Standing Committee of Attorneys-General, *Model Criminal Code—Chapter 2: General Principles of Criminal*

codified definitions of recklessness approach unanimity, and Chapter 2 of the *Model Criminal Code* expresses the generally accepted meaning of the concept. Recklessness requires realisation of a substantial risk of a criminative circumstance or criminative consequence, coupled with absence of any justification for incurring that substantial risk.[62] The fact that a risk of causing harm was consciously taken is not conclusive of recklessness. In modern criminal codes and, it would seem, at common law, incurring a known risk cannot be taken to have been reckless if the risk was justified.[63]

At least two issues of principle remain unresolved. The first, which is only peripherally related to the concerns of this essay, is whether recklessness, rather than negligence or strict liability, should mark the general presumptive threshold of criminal liability. The second issue is whether intention retains any significant role, independent of recklessness, as a defining element of criminal liability. Wherever the threshold of liability is set, we might conclude that no offence requires proof of intention, as distinct from recklessness, with respect to criminative consequences or circumstances. A significant minority among criminal law theorists have advocated a merger of recklessness and intention as a basis for guilt over all or almost all offences. In Australia, Professor Colin Howard has been the most persistent advocate of that position.[64] The

---

Responsibility, Final Report (1993) 21–31. The code was enacted as federal law in *Criminal Code Act 1995* (Cth).

62 *Criminal Code Act 1995* (Cth) s 5.4(2): 'A person is reckless with respect to a result if: (a) he or she is aware of a substantial risk that the result will occur; and (b) having regard to the circumstances known to him or her, it is unjustifiable to take the risk.' The definition of recklessness as to circumstances follows the same pattern. Compare s 2 of the English draft code in UK Law Commission, *A Criminal Code for England and Wales* (No 177, 1989); American Law Institute, *Model Penal Code* 1962 s 2.02(c). The most significant difference between these formulations is to be found in the degree of departure from acceptable conduct required before risk taking becomes recklessness. The American formulation, which requires proof of a 'gross deviation' from ordinary standards, is far more conservative than the Australian requirement of a 'substantial' and 'unjustifiable' risk and the English requirement of (any) 'unreasonable' risk.

63 See *Model Penal Code*, Proposed Official Draft ALI 1962, s 2.02(2)(c) 'Recklessly'; Australia, Criminal Law Officers Committee of the Standing Committee of Attorneys-General, above n 61, s 5.4.1; *Criminal Code Act 1995* (Cth) s 5.4.1.

64 Professor Fisse's edition of *Howard's Criminal Law*, above n 6, like its predecessors, promotes the view that recklessness and intention are alternative grounds for criminal liability over the major offences and general doctrines of the criminal law. See, in

argument is almost certainly unsustainable in relation to the law of attempts and other preparatory crime and it is difficult to sustain in the law of complicity. In these areas of criminal liability, Thomas Nagel's point that 'action intentionally aimed at a goal is guided by that goal'[65] is peculiarly appropriate. When the defendant has not done the act or caused the harm that constitutes the crime, liability requires proof that his or her conduct, which may appear quite unexceptionable, was informed by criminal intention and adjusted to the pursuit of the forbidden harm. There are, in addition, particular offences in which a requirement of proof of bad intention sets a limit to liability, which would be otherwise indefinable in extent or unduly restrictive of normal human and business intercourse.[66] In the general offences of injury to the person however, there are compelling arguments for counting recklessness and intention as equivalent grounds for conviction.

In Australia, the law of murder extends to include reckless killing. All States and Territories accept that conclusion, though there are significant differences of detail among them. In lesser offences against the person, however, distinctions are drawn between intentional and reckless harms. In Victoria, for example, the offence of causing serious injury intentionally is a distinct offence that carries a heavier penalty than the offence of causing serious injury recklessly.[67] The incongruity is manifest. The law of homicide, which is governed for the most part by common law, requires conviction on proof of recklessness. That is in flat contradiction with the underlying assumptions of statute law relating to lesser offences against the person.

---

particular, the discussion of murder 57 ff; rape 170 ff; theft 240–249; complicity 340 ff; conspiracy 372 ff; attempt 387 ff.

65   Thomas Nagel, *The View From Nowhere* (1986) 181.

66   Examples are legion. See, for example, *Question of Law Reserved (No 2 of 1998)* (1998) 101 A Crim R 317: requirement that conduct evince a sole or dominant purpose of disguising the nature of a 'significant cash transaction'; or *R v NMP* (2000) 146 CCC 167: undercover police officer does not 'communicate for the purpose of engaging in prostitution' if he discusses prices with a prostitute.

67   *Crimes Act 1958* (Vic): s 16 intentionally cause serious injury: 20 years; s 17 recklessly cause serious injury: 15 years. Section 18, which follows, provides graded penalties of 10 years and 5 years respectively for intentional and reckless infliction of lesser injuries.

Mrs Hyam Tries to Tell the Truth but Mr Aiton Stands Mute

Australians might as well claim the House of Lords decision in *Hyam*[68] as their own. Mrs Hyam was convicted of murder on a jury direction that an Australian court would regard as an unexceptionable application of the concept of recklessness. From an Australian perspective the direction was, if anything, too favourable to her. The jury was told that they could convict only if they were convinced that Mrs Hyam realised that death or grievous bodily injury was 'highly likely'.[69] But the decision of the House of Lords, upholding her conviction, no longer represents English law which now requires proof of an intention to kill or cause grievous bodily harm before a murder verdict can be returned.[70] *Hyam's* case certainly presents a more convincing factual scenario for an application of the concept of recklessness than anything to be found in Australian case law. Few Australian cases on recklessness in murder match the scenario of poised ambiguity found in that case. Like the decision of the Victorian Court of Criminal Appeal in *Aiton*,[71] which will be used as a foil in this discussion of *Hyam*, the Australian cases on homicidal recklessness present a depressing parade of mundane, brutal and unconsidered killings.

Mrs Hyam set fire to a house where Mrs Booth was sleeping with her three children. Mrs Booth and her son escaped, but her daughters died in the fire. Mrs Hyam was motivated by jealousy over Mr Jones, who had abandoned her in favour of Mrs Booth.

Mrs Hyam and Mr Jones were lovers for a decade. He deceived her during the last years of their relationship and formed a relationship with Mrs Booth, to whom he proposed marriage. When Mrs Hyam learned of the impending marriage she resolved to take action. She went to Mrs Booth's house in the early hours of the morning, poured half a gallon of

---

68 *Hyam* [1973] 3 All ER 842 (CA); [1975] AC 55 (HL).
69 Australian High Court cases variously require proof that the accused realised that death or grievous bodily harm was 'likely' or 'probable' or a 'real risk'. See *Crabbe* (1985) 156 CLR 733; *Boughey* (1986) 162 CLR 10; *Simpson* (1997) 103 CLR 19.
70 *Hyam* [1975] AC 55, 80 per Vis Dilhorne. Ackner J instructed the jury that the prosecution was required to establish intention to kill or cause grievous bodily harm. He went on to say that the prosecution could 'establish the necessary intent' by proof that Mrs Hyam set the fire with the knowledge that it was highly likely to cause death or serious injury. The direction falls well short of the recent restatement of the fault element in *Woollin* [1999] 1 Crim App R 8.
71 (1993) 68 A Crim R 578.

petrol through the letterbox in the front door, stuffed paper into the aperture and lit the paper. The fire blazed up immediately and Mrs Hyam left the scene without raising the alarm. Mrs Booth's daughters were killed in the ensuing conflagration.

Mrs Hyam said she wanted to frighten Mrs Booth so much that she would leave the neighbourhood. She denied that she intended to cause death or serious harm to anyone. But she knew that Mrs Booth and her children would be endangered if she set fire to their house; she went to check Mr Jones' house before she set the fire to make sure he was home and out of danger. Though she realised the danger, she testified that she would not have set the fire if she had really thought that someone might die.[72] Two doctors testified on her behalf, expressing the view that she was trying to tell the truth.

The trial judge offered the jury a choice among three possible accounts of what happened. The second would be described in Australian law as a direction on reckless murder. If we assume that the jury followed the directions given by the trial judge, they must have been persuaded of the truth of the first or second of the following possibilities:

- *Mrs Hyam lit the fire intending to kill one or more of the people in the house.* Perhaps she did it in order to remove Mrs Booth as a rival or perhaps she did it for revenge.
- *Mrs Hyam lit the fire to frighten Mrs Booth away.* She realised that it was highly probable that one or more of the occupants would die in the fire, but that did not induce her to do anything to minimise the risk.
- *Mrs Hyam lit the fire to frighten Mrs Booth away.* She never really expected the fire to take hold in such a way or anticipated that one or more of the family would probably die. She knew there was some risk, but had no real appreciation of the magnitude of the risk.

As in the dialogue with the man at the poison pump, the allegation that Mrs Hyam intended to kill impelled her to provide an alternative description of the intention with which she acted. If the alternative were

---

72 *Hyam* (CA) [1973] 3 All ER 842, 845 per Cairns LJ. It is regrettable that Mrs Hyam's testimony is omitted from reports of the case. In the House of Lords, *Hyam* [1975] AC 55, 79 Viscount Dilhorne suggests that Mrs Hyam conceded that 'she realised that what she had done was tremendously dangerous' but this remark appears to relate to her state of mind *after* she lit the fire.

accepted, however, that would not be sufficient to save her from conviction if she realised that one or more of the Booth family might be caught in the fire. The allegation of recklessness, if I may call it that in this Australian appropriation of *Hyam*, required her to take a further step and ask the jury a crucial question. It can be paraphrased thus: If you are not convinced that I *meant* to kill Mrs Booth or her children, can you believe that I would have lit the fire *knowing* that one or more of them would probably die?[73] The jury convicted, of course. One might surmise that the hypothesis that she intended to kill is more likely to have been true than the alternative hypothesis that she acted recklessly. What I would like to draw from the case, however, is the way in which the allegation of recklessness required her to extend her account of what she intended in lighting the fire to include an account of her appreciation of the likely consequences. She was impelled, as well, to ask the jury to assess the kind of person she was.

Mrs Hyam had a great deal to say for herself. Paul Aiton,[74] who was convicted of the murder of the two-year-old son of his de facto wife, had very little to say. He stood mute at his trial. There were, however, admissions to police and an unsworn statement in earlier proceedings in which he said he lost self-control and hit the little boy to stop him crying. The jury convicted him of murder on a direction that he was guilty of that offence if he intended death or grievous bodily harm or if he realised that either of those consequences was probable. An appeal against conviction and sentence to the Victorian Court of Criminal Appeal failed. It is the decision on his sentence that is of primary interest. Witnesses described him as a sadist, who boasted to workmates of his cruelty to the child during the months that preceded the final attack. The evidence that Aiton took sadistic pleasure in the infliction of pain[75] appears to have led the trial judge to conclude that this was a case of murder by recklessness; Aiton perceived the probable risk of death or serious injury as a mere side effect of his brutality to the child.

Though sentencing regimes for murder are not uniform across Australian States and Territories, courts in most jurisdictions have power to impose a determinate period of imprisonment for the offence. Aiton was

73 Ibid 845 per Cairns LJ: 'if the jury had directed their minds to the risk of death they might well have thought it inconceivable that the appellant should knowingly risk killing four people'.
74 *Aiton* (1993) 68 A Crim R 578.
75 The prosecution argued at one point that Aiton 'played with pain': ibid 592.

sentenced to imprisonment for 22 years. It was a particularly severe sentence. In terms of current judicial appreciation of the degrees of iniquity, Aiton takes his place among the worst category of murderers.[76] The Court of Criminal Appeal rejected the suggestion that death caused recklessly should be distinguished, in terms of culpability, from death caused intentionally. The appropriate penalty in each case was to be determined on the facts.

Suppose the children had not died in *Hyam* or in *Aiton*, but had suffered severe injury. The law of most Australian jurisdictions would require distinctions to be drawn between intentional and reckless infliction of injury. When England reformed the law in the *Offences Against the Persons Act 1861*, most Australian States and Territories adopted versions of the reforming legislation.[77] All jurisdictions distinguish levels of culpability according to the seriousness of the injury inflicted. Most, if not all, now distinguish between a major offence that requires proof of an intention to cause serious injury[78] and lesser offences of malicious or reckless injury. In Victoria, which reformed its law in 1986, adapting the provisions of the English draft criminal code,[79] the contrast between liability for intentional and reckless harms is sharpened still further. Victorian legislation sets out a graded series of offences in which intentional infliction of serious injury carries a higher maximum penalty than reckless infliction of serious injury which, in turn, carries a higher maximum than negligent infliction of serious injury.[80] The Victorian distinction between injuries intentionally inflicted and injuries recklessly inflicted reappears in Chapter 5 of the *Model Criminal Code: Non Fatal*

---

76 *Lauritsen* [2000] WASCA 203 (unreported, Supreme Court of Western Australia, 4 Aug 2000), citing *Aiton*, ibid.

77 With the exception of South Australia, each State or Territory included an additional general offence of causing injury by one or another variety of blameworthy inadvertence, most commonly negligence.

78 On the requirement of intention rather than recklessness in these offences, see *Hoskin* (1974) 9 SASR 531; *Re Knight's Appeal* (1965) 12 FLR 81; *Belfon* [1976] 3 All ER 46.

79 UK Criminal Law Revision Committee, *Offences Against the Person* (Cmnd 7844, 1980); UK Law Commission, *Codification of the Criminal Law* (Law Com No 143, 1985).

80 Australia, Model Criminal Code Officers Committee of the Standing Committee of Attorneys-General, *Report* (1998); and see *Boxtel* (1994) 70 2 VR 98, 103.

Offences Against the Person,[81] as a model for other Australian jurisdictions to follow.

The elaboration of these distinctions is not intended as a guide to social behaviour. How many times do we need to be told that we must not injure our fellow citizens? The distinctions are meant to allocate maximum penalties according to the degree of seriousness of the conduct that caused the injury. The statutory scheme requires courts to accept the principle that the worst cases in which serious injury is inflicted recklessly can never match the iniquity of the worst cases in which serious injury is inflicted intentionally. The difference in penalties for intentional and reckless harm in worst case scenarios implies that the punishment for injuries caused recklessly rather than intentionally will be discounted over the entire range of offending behaviour. If the children killed by Mrs Hyam and Paul Aiton had suffered serious injury rather than death, Hyam and Aiton would have been shielded from the penalties imposed on those who inflict injury intentionally.

What possible justification could there be for these discrepancies? The fact that serious injury rather than death resulted cannot be a ground for distinction. No one seems to have doubted that instances of reckless killing could figure among the worst instances of murder.[82] That was, indeed, the point of Glanville Williams' story of the airplane saboteur. What is shocking in the worst cases is the killer's lack of compunction, whether the case is one of killing for its own sake, killing in pursuit of some further end or killing as an incidental side effect of some other project.

It is true that the lower limits of recklessness are uncertain. The problems involved in distinguishing recklessness from negligence or other lesser forms of culpability are fundamental and far from resolution.[83] Uncertainty over the lower boundary of the concept of recklessness might justify a distinction between liability for intentional and reckless infliction of injury if mandatory minimum penalties were imposed. In the absence of

---

81   Australia, Model Criminal Code Officers Committee of the Standing Committee of Attorneys-General, ibid Division 5: 'Causing Harm'.

82   A conclusion expressed with cogent brevity by Lord Kilbrandon in *Hyam* [1975] AC 55, 98 (HL).

83   Consider, for example, current controversies over the meaning of recklessness as a fault element in rape: see Australia, Model Criminal Code Officers Committee, *Model Criminal Code—Chapter 5: Sexual Offences Against the Person, Report* (1999) 87–91. Alan Michaels, 'Acceptance: The Missing Mental State' (1998) 71 *Southern California Law Review* 953 provides an insightful discussion of the general issue.

mandatory minimum penalties, however, the fuzziness of the concept at the lower end of the range of culpability provides no reason to allow a sentence discount for indifference in the worst cases.

Conclusions

'What is within an agent's intention?' asks Kevin Flannery SJ, in an essay on the guilty mind.[84] Like Duff, he addresses the question whether an agent intends only those consequences that he aims to bring about; or also those that he foresees as being 'virtually certain',[85] though the answer Duff provides is very different.[86] What both authors seem to share, however, is the assumption that the concept of intention must play a significant role in the formulation of criminal prohibitions. I have attempted, in various ways, to suggest that there is a far more significant role for the concept of intention in the explanations that the defendant may provide when charged with an offence. The question, in other words, is not whether the forbidden harm was intentional, in cases where there is doubt on that score, but whether it was *excusable*. Inquiry into what the defendant intended is important because we commonly express our justifications, excuses and pleas in mitigation of harm in terms of what we *meant* to do. This is the way in which we explain ourselves, if we are so minded.

Acceptance of a denial that injury was intended does not necessarily excuse it. Indifference to the likelihood that another would suffer injury might even exacerbate blameworthiness. Flannery would force the concept of intention to carry the entire burden of moral judgment, arguing that the airplane saboteur *did* intend to kill.[87] If we can suspend incredulity, however, and take the story told by the airplane saboteur seriously, as an expression of his values, there is no reason to impute to him an intention that he denies. He is guilty of murder because he has nothing to say that can justify, excuse or mitigate his offence. His denial of intention is without exculpatory force.

The shift from the question of whether harm was intended to whether it was excusable is fundamental to the dialogue of the criminal trial. It is

---

84   Flannery, above n 37, 378, 392.
85   Duff, above n 23, 189.
86   Antony Duff, *Intention, Agency and Criminal Liability* (1990) 88–92.
87   Flannery, above n 37, 396.

easy to understand the pressures to extend the meaning of intention, if liability were to be limited to cases of intentional infliction of harm. The airplane saboteur, like Paul Aiton, could maintain silence in the face of the accusation and challenge the prosecution to prove intention rather than indifference with respect to the anticipated deaths. In theory, such a defendant could benefit from the presumption that harm was not intended and escape conviction for murder. In practice, juries are told to 'infer' intention. An allegation in the alternative, that the defendant meant to cause the harm or anticipated that it would occur, deprives the defendant of the tactical advantage of silence. If we are concerned to ensure that criminal trials encourage dialogue in a language embodying common values, there is no reason why the defendant *should* enjoy that tactical advantage. An inquiry concerning the intention with which a person acted is a collaborative engagement, involving elements of mutuality and negotiation over values. It is, in that sense, unlike a dispute about identification or a wrangle over who did what.[88]

In various ways existing law recognises this shift from the preoccupation with intention as a defining element of the prohibition to a concern with the question of whether there is a justification, excuse or mitigation for the defendant's conduct. Re-characterisation of the defendant's intentions in prohibitions against causing 'harm', 'injury', 'damage' or other undesirable consequences provides instances of unself-conscious reliance on the technique by courts and legislators. Similar in its effects is the characterisation of unconsidered and impulsive violence as an intentional infliction of serious injury or death. The extension of intention to include consequences known to be certain achieves the same effect. So, also, when recklessness and intention are alternative grounds for conviction. In all of these instances, the inquiry is shifted from concern with the question whether the harm was intended to consideration of the possibility of justification, excuse or mitigation. It may be that there is nothing the defendant can say to justify or palliate the offence. If there is,

---

88   Compare Alasdair McIntyre, *The Unconscious: A Conceptual Analysis* (1958) 56, on the discovery of intention in therapeutic relationships: 'What matters is what would happen *if* the agent were to be pressed on the matter ... [I]n the end an intention is something that must be capable of being avowed.' And subsequently, at 59–60: '[U]nless the patient will in the end avow his intention the analyst's interpretation of his behaviour is held to be mistaken. "In the end" is a phrase that covers the multitude of almost interminable turnings and twistings of which an analysis may consist.'

however, the defendant's account of what was intended provides a means of expression for that justification, excuse or mitigation.

6 Intention in the Law of Murder

SIR ANTHONY MASON

Introduction

For an unstated but obvious reason, this essay is written from a legal perspective. For this I make no apology. An apology would be in order if I were to offer an essay presenting a philosophical perspective. In presenting a legal perspective, I shall draw attention to the confusion which surrounds the law's treatment of intention and to the range of mental states that form elements of legal principle in criminal law, with particular reference to the crime of murder.

Lawyers are interested in intention as a central element in criminal liability. Philosophers, on the other hand, are interested in intention 'as a central feature of human action, and as a key determinant of moral liability'.[1] These related interests might have led to co-operative collaboration. But it was not to be. The result was that in 1987 Professor Glanville Williams concluded that philosophers had offered the lawyers 'only limited assistance'.[2]

Since then more work has been done with a view to analysing intention, particularly by A P Simester, Antony Duff and A W Norrie, on whose writings I have drawn liberally. My review of their analysis reveals that it has cast doubt on certain aspects of the past approach taken by the courts and has clarified some problems, though much of the discussion, being theoretical, is somewhat removed from the problem of giving practical directions to juries. In *Attorney-General's Reference (No 3 of 1994)*,[3] Lord Mustill acknowledged the extensive citation of passages from

---

1   Antony Duff, 'Intentions Legal and Philosophical' (1989) *Oxford Journal of Legal Studies* 76.
2   Glanville Williams, 'Oblique Intention' (1987) 46 *Criminal Law Journal* 417.
3   [1998] AC 245.

learned writers, present and past, and the use of other sources, stating '[a]ll have proved valuable'.[4] His Lordship went on to say:

> Notwithstanding the strong practical character of the criminal law it has over the years gained immeasurably from systematic analysis by scholars who have had an opportunity for research and reflection denied to those immersed in the daily life of the courts.[5]

Ascertainment of the criminal law's approach to intention in the context of murder is complicated by the circumstance that the law's approach to intention and *mens rea* has emerged out of the common law concept of malice, notably malice aforethought, loosely translated as wicked intent. Lord Mustill's speech, to which reference has just been made, illustrates the problems that this history causes for the modern development of the criminal law of intent.[6] His Lordship's example of the terrorist bomber who hides a bomb in an aircraft is an example of how traditional legal thinking must be converted into thinking about intention. His Lordship said:

> This is not a case of 'general malice' where under the old law any wrongful act sufficed to prove the evil disposition which was taken to supply the necessary intent for homicide. Nor is it transferred malice ... The intention is already aimed directly at the class of potential victims of which the actual victim forms part. The intent and the *actus reus* already completed by the explosion are joined from the start, even though the identity of the ultimate victim is not yet fixed. So also with the shots fired indiscriminately into a crowd. No ancient fictions are needed to make these cases of murder.[7]

A second difficulty in reaching a conjunction between law and philosophy has arisen from the concern in the criminal law with different degrees of fault and with the confusion that has arisen from the terminology which has been employed to describe these different degrees of fault. Another difficulty has been the tendency of the judges to extend the legal concept of intention to include the lesser mental state of foresight

---

4   Ibid 262.
5   Ibid. (His Lordship's Arcadian view of the modern world of academic scholarship may
      be open to question.)
6   Ibid 256–261.
7   Ibid 261.

of consequences. This is done to ensure that offences defined by reference to intention comprehend facts and incidents which lead the public to expect a conviction and to be outraged if an acquittal occurred simply because intention did not comprehend foresight of a high degree of probability. In this respect, judges have given effect to their sense of community moral responsibility and what is necessary for state control and security, without deserting the requirements of subjectivity and *mens rea* which form part of the liberal legacy. There have been some aberrations, when courts in England and, to a lesser extent, in Australia, have flirted with foreseeability and an objective standard.

To the extent that judges have given effect to their sense of community moral sensibility and what is necessary for state control and security, their task and their perspective differ from that of philosophers. There is a dimension to the judicial role which some would call 'social' or 'political', a description which most judges and lawyers would vigorously reject. That dimension involves the judge in interpreting the community sense of moral responsibility, knowing that, if the courts stray too far from community standards, there will be an erosion of public confidence in the administration of justice. The High Court of Australia has explicitly taken this factor into account in a number of cases.[8] The concern of the judges with community moral sensibility has led to the comment that the real source of uncertainty in the application of criminal law concepts such as intention is not to do with the concept itself but with 'practical, moral and political issues'.[9]

The Tension between the 'Ordinary Language' Approach and Conceptual Analysis

A separate source of uncertainty has been the dual approach of judges to intention arising from the use of both 'the ordinary language' notion of intention and conceptual analysis. The ordinary language notion of intention is bound to lead to some uncertainty, because the popular understanding of a word such as 'intention' is not sufficiently precise as to

---

8   *Jago v District Court of* NSW (1989) 168 CLR 23; *Grollo v Palmer* (1995) 184 CLR 348; *Kable v Director of Public Prosecutions (NSW)* (1997) 189 CLR 51.
9   Nicola Lacey, 'A Clear Concept of Intention: Elusive or Illusory' (1993) 56 *Modern Law Review* 621, 626.

be definitive and this is inevitably so when questions are left to a jury to be resolved according to the jury's understanding of what is involved in the concept. To some extent, a dual approach cannot be avoided. Conceptual analysis must take account of the ordinary meaning of words. The problem perhaps is that the law has failed to supplement the gaps in ordinary meaning by resorting to conceptual analysis.

In England, though not so much in Australia, the courts went a long way in adopting the ordinary language approach. That approach had attractions for judges. It offered a flexibility which conceptual analysis lacks and it enabled the jury to apply its own 'commonsense' understanding of the term. In this way, the recourse to ordinary language assisted in depicting the criminal law as non-authoritarian and as popularly based, thereby conforming to a rule of law ideal.[10] Recourse to ordinary language also contributes to the notion that the jury is a democratic institution. Indeed, in some modern English cases, the judgments emphasise the jury's use of good sense to decide whether the accused intended to kill or inflict serious harm, rather than the formulation of a clear definition of intention which the jury must apply.[11] This, as Jeremy Horder noted, leaves the jury with a small amount of moral 'elbow room' within which to decide whether the defendant's indifference to the death of the victim is sufficient to warrant conviction for murder.[12] Horder suggests that 'this is the point of stressing that the jury may, but not must, infer that [the accused] intended to kill when he foresaw an unlawful killing as a virtually certain product of his action'.[13]

Conceptual analysis can supply a framework for such an approach. In England, however, until very recently resort to conceptual analysis was not availed of to any great extent. The English Court of Appeal decision in *Scalley*[14] made this very clear. It held that the finding that the defendant foresaw death or really serious bodily harm could not be equated to a finding that he intended to kill or cause really serious bodily harm. Foresight in these circumstances, it was said, is no more than evidence of intent, to be weighed along with other evidence. There was no description

10   Ibid 635–636.

11   See especially *Moloney v DPP* [1985] 1 AC 905.

12   Jeremy Horder, 'Intention in the Criminal Law: A Rejoinder' (1995) 58 *Modern Law Review* 678, 687.

13   Ibid; and see *Moloney v DPP* [1985] 1 AC 905 per Lord Hailsham LC.

14   [1985] *Criminal Law Review* 504.

of the further state of mind that the defendant needs to have in order to constitute intention. It was simply for the jury to decide whether the defendant is a murderer on the basis of an oblique intention. This approach is a traditional technique employed by the law to avoid the need for clearer definition.

Here I should point out that the English law relating to murder differs from the Australian law on the subject. Australian law, whether stemming from the Criminal Codes or the statutory definition in s 18 of the *Crimes Act 1900* (NSW), still reflects, though not explicitly, the common law conception of malice aforethought. That conception consisted in three kinds of malice: express malice (intention to kill), implied malice (intention to cause grievous bodily harm) and constructive malice (where the killing takes place in the course of commission of a felony or in resisting lawful arrest or in assisting an escape from legal custody).[15] But malice aforethought also embraced knowledge of the probability of the occurrence of death or grievous bodily harm, which is sometimes referred to as 'recklessness'.

Constructive malice was abolished in England by s 1 of the *Homicide Act 1957*. In the course of judicial interpretation of the *Homicide Act*, beginning with *R v Vickers*,[16] the mental element in murder was confined to an intention to kill or an intention to cause grievous bodily harm. This interpretation, which ignored the element of knowledge of probability of consequences in malice aforethought, resulted in the vast difficulties experienced by English courts in fitting that class of case within murder. Fortunately, in Australia, we have not suffered from this self-inflicted wound.

Another difference between English and Australian law was the inability of English courts to order a new trial when an error of law vitiated the conviction. It was otherwise in Australia. The prospect that a guilty person might be acquitted as a result of an error of law, without the necessity of undergoing a new trial, may well have contributed to a willingness to uphold convictions based on a broad view of intention.

The approach adopted in England could scarcely commend itself to philosophers, who would have seen it as an unprincipled blurring of the crucial issue. Needless to say, if philosophers think about a legal

---

15   See Lord Goff of Chieveley, 'The Mental Element in Murder' (1988) 104 *Law Quarterly Review* 30, 33.
16   [1957] 2 QB 664, 672.

perspective on intention, they would, in all probability, not distinguish between legal analysis and conceptual analysis.

Mental States and Criminal Law

Of the mental states with which the law is concerned there are, apart from intention, a considerable number. It is enough to mention some of them: purpose, motive, foreseeability, knowledge (whether of the wrongfulness of the act or of the facts constituting the offence), recklessness, as well as the will and voluntariness. The law also employs other expressions, such as 'willfully', which imply knowledge.

Voluntariness connotes a number of different mental states.[17] It includes a conscious control of bodily movement.[18] Voluntariness may become an issue when the defendant is intoxicated. Otherwise, it does not feature in this discussion.

Much of the confusion that surrounds intention, as it is understood in law, arises from the imprecise use of the expression *mens rea* (guilty mind) in the criminal law. Over a century ago, in one of the classic statements in the law, which has been adopted and applied frequently, it was asserted that:

> There is a presumption that *mens rea*, an evil intention, or a knowledge of the wrongfulness of the act, is an essential ingredient in every offence; but that it is liable to be displaced either by the words of the statute creating the offence or by the subject matter with which it deals, and both must be considered.[19]

Subsequently it became clear that what was referred to as 'an evil intention' was to be equated to knowledge on the part of the accused 'that he was doing the criminal act which is charged against him, that is, that he knew that all the facts constituting the ingredients [of the offence] necessary to make the act criminal were involved in what he was doing'.[20] In other words, a person should not be found guilty of a criminal offence

---

17 *Ryan v The Queen* (1967) 121 CLR 205, 244 per Windeyer J.

18 *He Kaw Teh v The Queen* (1985) 157 CLR 523, 569 per Brennan J.

19 *Sherras v De Rutzen* [1895] 1 QB 918, 921; see also *He Kaw Teh v The Queen* (1985) 157 CLR 523, 528, 549, 553, 566, 591.

20 *R v Turnbull* (1943) 44 SR(NSW) 108, 109.

unless that person has a guilty mind defined in terms of subjective intention or knowledge.

Part of the problem is that the requirement for a mental element as an ingredient of an offence may relate not to an act or omission, but to the consequences of an act. While knowledge of the circumstances in which the act or omission takes place may be sufficient in the case of the act or omission, where a mental state is applicable to consequences it may entail the foresight of the possibility of their occurrence (if recklessness is an element) or knowledge of the probability (or likelihood) of their occurrence or (if a specific intent is an element) an intention to cause them.[21] In relation to consequences, knowledge of their probability, or likelihood, which is a species of foreseeability, will be a sufficient mental state, unless a specific intent is stipulated in the definition of the offence, in which event an intention to cause the consequences may be required. The species of foreseeability just referred to, that is knowledge of the probability (or likelihood) of the occurrence of the consequences, is applicable to cases of what the law confusingly calls 'general intent'. It is in relation to consequences, rather than in relation to the doing of the act that produces the consequences, that the nuances of intention are most likely to be revealed.

Before I turn to consider the relationship between intention, on the one hand, and, on the other hand, purpose and foreseeability (particularly foreseeability with reference to consequences), it is convenient to discuss the suggestion that intention can be defined in terms of desire. Although this suggestion has the powerful support of Glanville Williams, it is difficult to accept.

Is Intention to be Equated to Desire?

Glanville Williams considered that intention, at least direct intention as distinct from oblique intention, should be defined in terms of 'desire'.[22] This view has the support of Brennan J in *He Kaw Teh*.[23] But there are

---

21   *He Kaw Teh v The Queen* (1985) 157 CLR 523, 568 per Brennan J.
22   Williams, above n 2, 418.
23   *He Kaw Teh v The Queen* (1985) 157 CLR 523, 569:
         Intent, in one form, connotes a decision to bring about a situation so far as it is
         possible to do so—to bring about an act of a particular kind or a particular result.

strong arguments against this equation. First, as a matter of language, 'desire' and 'intend' are not equivalents. A person may desire a particular outcome without intending to bring it about. And a person may intend an outcome that one does not desire.[24] To equate the two is to assume that a decision to bring about the outcome has been made. To define 'intention' in terms of 'desire' is to give the word a special meaning which would call for an explanation when giving instructions to a jury. Further, Lord Bridge in *Moloney v DPP*[25] stated that intention is 'quite distinct from desire'[26] and *R v Crabbe*[27] seems to agree.

This view also accords with that of Stephen in his *Digest of Criminal Law* where, dealing with the concept of 'malice aforethought' as an element in his definition of murder at common law, he refers to category (b) murder (based on knowledge that the act which causes death will probably cause death or grievous bodily harm). Stephen says that knowledge of such consequences is a sufficient mental element to constitute murder 'although such knowledge is accompanied by indifference whether death or grievous bodily harm is caused or not, or by a wish that it may not be caused'.[28] Stephen's view was adopted by the High Court of Australia in *R v Crabbe*.[29]

If intention were to be defined in terms of desire, it would have provided a cogent answer to the argument in *Gillick v West Norfolk and Wisbech Area Health Authority*[30] that the doctor who provided the young girl with contraceptive advice and treatment was an accessory to illegal sexual intercourse. The answer given was not that the doctor did not wish to bring that about, but that bona fide clinical judgment could not found the requisite intent. Desire may constitute strong evidence of intent in various

---

Such a decision implies a desire or wish to do such an act or bring about such a result. Thus when A strikes B (the act), having decided or wishing to strike him, it can be said that he intends to strike B.

24   *Nedrick v DPP* [1985] 1 WLR 1025, 1027 per Lord Lane.
25   [1985] AC 905.
26   Ibid, 929. See also *R v Hyam* [1975] AC 55, 74; and *Mahan v DPP* [1976] 1 QB 1, 11: intention means 'a decision to bring about the commission of the offence ... no matter whether the accused desired that consequence of his act or not'.
27   (1985) 156 CLR 464.
28   James Stephen, *A Digest of the Criminal Law* (1877) article 233.
29   (1985) 156 CLR 464, 467–70.
30   [1986] AC 112.

circumstances, but it is not easy to conclude that desire is a necessary element in intention.

Is Intention to be Equated to Purpose?

English courts developed a classification of crimes of specific and ulterior intent which are concerned with the accused's mental attitude towards consequences in the world caused or to be caused by his own actions. It is the combination of these two considerations that induced Lord Simon of Glaisdale in *DPP v Majewski*[31] to discuss both specific and ulterior intent in terms of purpose. Majewski was convicted of assaults occasioning actual bodily harm and of assaults of a police officer in the execution of his duty. There was evidence that Majewski, as a result of taking drugs and alcohol, did not know what he was doing at the relevant time and had no recollection of events. Majewski was convicted on a direction to the jury that the offences charged, not being crimes of specific intent, did not require proof of any specific intention, so that it was no defence that he was self-intoxicated. This direction was upheld by the House of Lords where Lord Simon treated the *purpose* of a crime of specific intent as part of the *actus reus*.[32] The decision in *Majewski* relied heavily on the distinction between crimes of specific and basic intent in order to hold that intoxication is irrelevant to crimes of basic intent. The decision rested also on the public policy of safeguarding the citizen and of maintaining social order. In expressly taking account of that policy, *Majewski* reveals how social considerations can induce a court to depart from a conceptual analysis. Subsequently, in *R v O'Connor*,[33] the High Court of Australia declined to follow *Majewski*, holding that intoxication is relevant in ascertaining whether there is a guilty mind. *O'Connor*, by introducing voluntariness of the act of an intoxicated actor into the discussion, raised the additional element of will, which is distinct from intent. Different levels of intoxication affect the mind in different ways and 'partial intoxication at a particular level may be relevant to the existence of one mental state but not to the existence of another'.[34]

---

31 [1977] AC 443, 479–80.
32 Ibid 216-217 (note the use of the word 'ulterior').
33 (1980) 146 CLR 64.
34 *He Kaw Teh v The Queen* (1985) 157 CLR 523, 571 per Brennan J.

A man's purpose is essentially bound up with his actions; it is his reason for acting as he does,[35] or 'the result that he acted in order to bring it about'.[36] So the language of purpose is appropriate because it relates to the agent's mental state in relation to his own actions.[37]

Glanville Williams argues that purpose is not superior to desire as a synonym of intention because purpose implies desire: 'one can have an undeclared purpose, but not an undesired purpose'. That is true, at least in the weaker sense of the word 'desire'. But it does not follow from the proposition that all purposes must be desired that purpose and desire have the same meaning. What purpose adds to desire is recognition of the fact, stressed by Glanville Williams, that 'intention, for the lawyer, is not a bare wish; it is a combination of wish and act (or other external element)'.[38]

Purpose may be destined to play a larger part in the law governing criminal intent in its application to medical treatment.[39] Medical treatment may be undertaken in the knowledge that it will almost certainly or probably result in the death of the patient. In such a situation it is necessary to exclude from the concept of criminal intent a bona fide purpose of administering clinical or surgical treatment. Such an exception appears to have been recognised.[40] Whether the exception would extend to the administration of a lethal injection of a pain-killing drug is another question. If this action is to be legitimate, it must be on the footing that the purpose of injecting a drug is 'the care of the living patient, in his best

---

35   Antony Duff, 'Codifying Criminal Law: Conceptual Problems and Presuppositions' in I H Dennis (ed), *Criminal Law and Justice: Essays from the W G Hart Workshop, 1986* (1987) 95.

36   I H Dennis, 'The Mental Element for Accessories' in Peter Smith (ed), *Criminal Law: Essays in Honour of J C Smith* (1987) 40, 54.

37   Even in relation to accessory liability which is discussed (ibid) in the context of *Gillick v West Norfolk and Wisbech Area Health Authority* [1986] AC 112 (where the giving of contraceptive advice or treatment to a young girl lacked the necessary intent to ground liability). The exercise by a doctor of bona fide clinical judgment negated an intention to bring about consequential unlawful sexual intercourse: *R v Powell* [1999] 1 AC 1, 25 per Lord Hutton.

38   Williams, above n 2, 418.

39   The law relating to medical treatment of a patient unable to consent to treatment has been revolutionised by the recognition of the doctrine of necessity: see *R v Bournewood Community and Mental Health NHS Trust; ex parte L* [1999] 1 AC 458.

40   *R v Crabbe* (1985) 156 CLR 464, 470; *Gillick v West Norfolk ALIA* [1986] AC 112; see also *Re A (the Siamese Twins Case)* (unreported, Court of Appeal, 22 Sep 2000).

interests', to use the words of Lord Goff of Chieveley.[41] If the purpose is to terminate life, the treatment is unlawful.[42] The celebrated decision in *R v Adams*[43] is to be explained on this footing, rather than by reference to the so-called doctrine of 'double effect'.

Is Intention to be Equated to Motive?

Motive is the circumstance or thing which induces a person to act. Although in some circumstances motive may have the same meaning as intention, it has a different legal significance. In the absence of a statutory provision to the contrary, motive, unlike intention, is not an element in criminal responsibility. However, evidence of motive may be relevant to the establishment of intention.[44] In *Mutual Life Insurance Co of New York v Moss*,[45] Griffith CJ said: 'The existence of a motive may tend to show either that the person in question did the act *simpliciter*, or that he did it intentionally.'[46]

Intention, Foresight and Foreseeability

In general, mere foreseeability cannot give rise to criminal responsibility. Although willful blindness is sometimes equated to knowledge, willful blindness can only be found where it verges on actual knowledge. One cannot close one's mind to a risk unless one first realises that there is a risk.[47] The English decisions to the contrary, *Caldwell v DPP*,[48] and *Elliott v C*,[49] which held that a person who fails to advert to a risk which is obvious to a reasonable person is reckless, expounded a pernicious heresy.

---

41 *Airedale National Health Service Trust v Bland* [1993] AC 789, 867.
42 Ibid 865. But see the discussion in *Re A (the Siamese Twins Case)* (unreported, Court of Appeal, 22 Sep 2000).
43 [1957] *Criminal Law Review* 365.
44 *Plomp v The Queen* (1963) 110 CLR 234.
45 (1906) 4 CLR 311.
46 Ibid 317.
47 Glanville Williams, *Textbook of Criminal Law* (1978) 79, approved in *R v Crabbe* (1985) 156 CLR 464, 470–1.
48 [1982] AC 341.
49 [1983] 1 WLR 939.

Both language and philosophy maintain a distinction between intended actions and foreseen actions.[50] English law has not always clearly acknowledged this distinction. In *Hardy v Motor Insurers' Bureau*,[51] Pearson LJ said of the accused that 'he must have foreseen, when he did the act, that it would in all probability injure the other person. Therefore he had the intention to injure the other person'.[52] Lord Denning MR expressed a similar view.[53]

The basis of this view rests upon a legal presumption. The Supreme Court of Victoria explained the presumption by saying that, if the defendant 'knew what the consequences were likely to be, and with that knowledge he deliberately did the act and if the consequences did in fact follow, he must be taken to intend them'.[54] The thinking behind this statement is that a person who foresees a result as following from a deliberate act on his or her part may be said to intend that result, whether desired or not, for the reason that every person is presumed to intend the natural consequences of their own actions.[55] In the same year, in *DPP v Smith*, Viscount Kilmuir LC went even further, discussing 'the test of what a reasonable man would contemplate as the probable result of his acts, and therefore would intend'.[56] His Lordship attributed intention to the wrongdoer simply by reference to what a reasonable man would contemplate in the circumstances, thereby sacrificing subjectivity to an objective standard.[57]

A decade earlier this presumption had come under strong criticism in Australia. In *Stapleton v The Queen*,[58] the High Court said: 'The introduction of the maxim or statement that a man is presumed to intend the consequences of his act is seldom helpful and always dangerous.'[59] In

---

50   A P Simester, 'Moral Certainty and the Boundaries of Intention' (1996) 16 *Oxford Journal of Legal Studies* 445.
51   [1964] 2 QB 745.
52   Ibid 764.
53   Ibid 258.
54   *R v Jakac* [1961] VR 367, 371.
55   *Stapleton v The* Queen (1952) 86 CLR 358, 365.
56   [1961] AC 290, 326.
57   The *Criminal Justice Act 1967* (UK) reversed the effect of *Smith*, since when it has been recognised in England that the mental element has been concerned with the subjective question of what was in the mind of the person accused of murder: *R v Hyam* [1975] AC 55; *R v Woollin* [1999] 1 AC 82.
58   (1952) 86 CLR 358, 365.
59   Ibid 365.

Parker v The Queen,[60] the re-statement in *DPP v Smith* of the presumption caused Dixon CJ, with the concurrence of his colleagues, to make his celebrated observation that the court would depart from its policy of following House of Lords decisions. The Chief Justice said:

> There are propositions laid down in the judgment which I believe to be misconceived and wrong. They are fundamental and they are propositions which I could never bring myself to accept.[61]

The English courts moved more slowly to a similar conclusion, which found expression in the decision of the Privy Council in *Frankland & Moore v R,*[62] which overruled *DPP v Smith*. Lord Goff of Chieveley has observed: 'Foresight of consequences is not the same as intent, but is material from which the jury may, having regard to the circumstances of the case, infer that the defendant really had the relevant intent.'[63]

English acceptance of this position is largely associated with Lord Asquith's view that intention 'connotes a state of affairs which the party "intending" ... does more than merely contemplate: it connotes a state of affairs which, on the contrary, he decides, so far as in him lies, to bring about'.[64] On this view, mere foresight of consequences, as a matter of language and analysis, cannot amount to intention, though it was conceded by Lord Hailsham that intention includes not only those things done as ends and means, but also 'the inseparable consequences of the end as well as the means'.[65] The example given by Glanville Williams is:

> A villain of the deepest dye blows up an aircraft in flight with a time-bomb, merely for the purpose of collecting an insurance. It is not his aim to cause the people on board to perish, but he knows that success in his scheme will inevitably involve their deaths as a side-effect. [66]

---

60   (1963) 111 CLR 610.
61   Ibid 632.
62   [1987] 2 WLR 1251.
63   Goff of Chieveley, above n 15, 41. See also *R v Moloney* [1985] AC 905, 928 per Lord Bridge; *R v Hancock & Shankland* [1986] 1 AC 455, 473 per Lord Scarman.
64   *Cunliffe v Goodman* [1950] 2 KB 237, 253.
65   *R v Hyam* [1975] AC 55, 77; see also *Moloney v DPP* [1985] AC 905, 926 per Lord Bridge.
66   Williams, above n 47, 59.

Lord Hailsham considered that the death of passengers will result in a conviction for murder 'as their death will be a moral certainty if he carries out his intention'.[67]

Lord Goff[68] and Antony Duff[69] have challenged the proposition that knowledge of that which is morally certain to occur is equivalent to intention. Their contention is that, as a matter of ordinary language, I intend only those effects which I act in order to bring about.

Lying behind these conflicting opinions is a judicial conviction that criminal responsibility for serious or very serious offences should extend not only to that which is intended, but also to consequences of which there is knowledge of the probability, or a high degree of probability, of their occurrence. Lord Hailsham sought to justify this extension on the basis that knowledge of moral certainty is the equivalent of intention. On the other hand, Lord Diplock considered that, where intention to produce a particular result is an element in an offence, the law makes no distinction between intention and knowledge of probability of consequences.[70] Lord Diplock's approach is closer to that taken by the High Court of Australia in *R v Crabbe*,[71] where the court insisted on foresight of *probable* consequences, without requiring a high degree of probability. The High Court's approach was based on the common law understanding of the expression 'malice aforethought', which is a larger concept than intention.

Indeed, it is significant that in an earlier case, *Pemble v The Queen*,[72] the High Court, drawing upon the concept of malice aforethought, distinguished between intention and recklessness as a basis for conviction of murder. In doing so, the court, notably Barwick CJ (with whom Windeyer J concurred), treated foresight of *possible* consequences, namely

---

67   *R v Hyam* [1975] at 74.
68   Goff of Chieveley, above n 15, 59.
69   Antony Duff, *Intention, Agency and Criminal Liability* (1990) 80.
70   *R v Lawson* [1979] AC 617, 638:
> no distinction is to be drawn ... between the state of mind of one who does an act because he desires it to produce a particular evil consequence, and the state of mind of one who does the act knowing full well that it is likely to produce that consequence though it may not be the object he was seeking to achieve by doing the act. What is common to both these states of mind is willingness to produce the evil consequences.
71   (1985) 156 CLR 464.
72   (1971) 124 CLR 107.

death or grievous bodily harm, as giving rise to recklessness, not intended murder.[73] That view was displaced in *Crabbe*.

But, in insisting only on foresight of probable consequences in *Crabbe*, the High Court of Australia has settled for a lower level of intent[74] than that now required in England. In *R v Woollin*,[75] the House of Lords, affirming the test stated in *Nedrick*, held that, where it was not enough to direct the jury that it was for them to decide whether the defendant intended to kill or do grievous bodily harm, they should be directed that they were *not* entitled to find the necessary intention to convict for murder *unless* death or grievous bodily harm had been a virtual certainty (barring some unforeseen intervention) as a result of the defendant's actions and that the defendant had appreciated such was the case. The use of the phrase 'substantial risk' by the trial judge was a material misdirection because it enlarged the scope of the mental element required in England for murder, that is, intention. Because intention represents the mental element in murder in England and malice aforethought has been excluded, the mental element in murder in England differs from that in Australia.[76] The presence of the malice aforethought element in Australia means that there is little, if any, necessity to adopt the virtual certainty approach.

Knowledge of virtually certain consequences is a stronger requirement than foresight of probable consequences and can be characterised as an instance of intention. Take the example given in *Crabbe*[77] of the surgeon who operates to save the patient's life, appreciating that death is probable, though not inevitable. The stronger requirement would reduce, but may not eliminate, the problem.[78]

---

73 Ibid 119–21; but cf 127 per McTiernan J; 135 per Menzies J. Both McTiernan and Menzies JJ considered that foresight of probable consequences was required to sustain a conviction for murder. Their view was upheld in *Crabbe*.

74 Here I use the word 'intent', as distinct from 'specific intent' or 'intention', in a broad sense to refer to any mental element forming an essential part of the case for the prosecution.

75 [1999] 1 AC 82.

76   See the discussion in A P Simester, 'Murder, Mens Rea and the House of Lords— Again' (1999) 115 *Law Quarterly Review* 17, 20–1.

77 (1985) 156 CLR 464, 470 (where the court concluded that the act was 'justified or excused by law').

78 See also *Re A (the Siamese Twins Case)* (unreported, Court of Appeal, 22 September 2000), where it was known that the operation would result in the death of one of the twins. The Court of Appeal was divided on the question of intention to kill. Walker LJ

In the case of secondary or accessory liability, a lesser degree of knowledge will be a sufficient ingredient of liability. In what is known as joint enterprise criminal liability, it is sufficient to found a conviction for murder for a secondary party to have realised that, in the course of carrying out the planned (intended) joint enterprise, the primary party might possibly kill with the requisite intent to do so or to cause grievous bodily harm, even though the killing is outside the scope of that planned enterprise.[79] It will be enough to participate in the enterprise and to have a shared common intention to kill or an individual contemplation of the intentional infliction of grievous bodily harm as a possible incident of the venture.[80] In this respect, knowledge of possible consequences may suffice in the case of the secondary party, though it does not in the case of the primary offender. Yet both are guilty of murder. The rationalisation of this supposed anomaly lies in practical and policy considerations. If the law required proof of specific intent on the part of the secondary party, the utility of the accessory principle would be gravely undermined. The secondary party ought to be criminally liable for harm which he foresaw and which in fact resulted from the crime which he assisted and encouraged.[81]

The treatment of the mental element in the law of murder by the United States courts reflects a number of the difficulties presented by Anglo-Australian law. Specifically there is the complication arising from the different degrees of homicide and the continuing link with malice aforethought, malice being the element which distinguishes murder from manslaughter. Malice connotes an intentional killing. Malice may be expressed or implied. Implied malice requires a subjective awareness of a high probability of death, with wanton disregard thereof. It is to be distinguished from gross negligence by both the higher degree of risk involved and by the requirement that risk be subjectively appreciated rather than merely objectively apparent.[82]

---

seems to have thought that there was no such intention, but Ward LJ and Brooke LJ thought otherwise.

79   *McAuliffe v The Queen* (1995) 183 CLR 108; *R v Powell* [1999] 1 AC 1.
80   *McAuliffe v The Queen* ibid 118. Although judges speak of 'intention' in this context, there is no reason in principle why 'intent' signifying knowledge of probable consequences would not suffice for a conviction of the primary party for murder.
81   *R v Powell* [1999] 1 AC 1, 14 per Lord Steyn.
82   40 Am Jur 2d para 38.

The Distinction Between Foresight and Intention

The fundamental distinction between foresight and intention, as understood by philosophers, can be illustrated by Bennett's[83] example: Terror Bomber and Strategic Bomber both have as their goal promoting the war effort against Enemy by dropping bombs. TB's plan is to bomb the school in E's territory, killing children of E, terrorising E's population and forcing E to surrender. Strategic Bomber's plan is to bomb E's munitions plant, thereby undermining E's war effort. However, SB also knows that next to the munitions plant is a school and that when he bombs the plant he will also kill the children inside the school. Does SB intend the children's death? There are arguments for a negative answer. SB does not desire the deaths, either for their own sake or as a means to destroying the munitions plant. Further, he does not bomb the plant in order to bring their deaths about. So Lord Asquith's test is not satisfied.

If we define 'a part of what he intends' as any state of affairs *he* thinks he will bring about in bringing about what he intends, then the children's death forms part of the phrase.[84] This approach is similar to the virtual certainty test approved in *R v Woollin*.[85] Sidgwick goes further, saying all foreseen consequences are intended,[86] while Bentham would consider the deaths *obliquely* (as opposed to *directly*) intended.[87]

Cross rejects these claims with the following example:

> Intending to make a claim against his insurance company, A sets fire to his house knowing that it is virtually certain that his baby son who is alone in the house will be burned to death. Popular speech, morals and the law begin to part company. If the baby is burned to death, A would not, in ordinary language, be said to have killed him or to have caused his death intentionally.[88]

---

83 Jonathan Bennett, 'Morality and Consequences' in Sterling McMurrin (ed), *The Tanner Lectures on Human Values* (1981) 45, 95.

84 Simester, above n 50, 449.

85 [1999] 1 AC 82.

86 H Sidgwick, *The Methods of Ethics* (1901) 60, 202.

87 Jeremy Bentham, *An Introduction to the Principles of Morals and Legislation* (W Harrison (ed)) (1960) VIII, VI.

88 R Cross, 'The Mental Element in Crime' (1967) 83 *Law Quarterly Review* 215, 216

The view of Cross is at least debatable, certainly as a matter of ordinary language. Most people would say A killed the baby and many would say he intended to kill the baby, killing the baby being a foreseen consequence inseparable from that which was intended. *R v Woollin* would treat this as a case of intentional killing. *Crabbe* would treat it as murder, though not perhaps as intentional killing.

Simester rightly notes that the essential distinction between TB and SB is the lack of a consequential connection between SB's desiring the outcome (as either end or means) and his behaviour. Simester does not disagree with Lord Lane's view in *Nedrick*[89] that one may intend something one does not desire. TB wants to kill the children in order to win the war, but only for that end. He adopts their deaths as an element in achieving the aims which motivate his behaviour. The children's death is not a reason for his conduct. For SB, the deaths are a side effect.

Philosophers have emphasised the motivational insignificance of side effects, pointing out the corresponding absence of features which normally accompany a motivational connection. TB would regard his conduct as having failed if he were not to kill the children, whereas SB would not do so.[90] Cross makes the additional point that, as a matter of ordinary language, we cannot say that SB behaves 'with the intention' of killing the children.[91] This point is at least debatable and, in any event, it may depend upon shades of difference in meaning between 'SB intends to kill the children', 'SB kills the children intentionally' and 'SB acts with the intention of killing the children'.

Cross also suggests another departure.[92] The actor may desire that a side effect not occur, and indeed may hope it does not occur. Can it then be intended? A means or a consequence may be regretted or unwanted if it is desired only for the sake of something else. This brings us back to the relationship between desire and intention. Given SB's beliefs, he cannot rationally hope to achieve his end while the children survive any more than TB.[93]

---

89   [1986] 1 WLR 1025, 1027.
90   Duff, above n 69, 61–63; Simester, above n 50, 451.
91   Cross, above n 88, 216.
92   Ibid.
93   Simester, above n 50, 451.

Chisholm suggests a different means by which we might blur the intention–foresight division. He proposed a principle of 'the diffusiveness of intention':

> If (i) a man acts with the intention of bringing it about that p occurs and if (ii) he knows or believes that if p occurs then the conjunctive state of affairs, p and q, also occurs, then (iii) he acts with the intention of bringing it about that the conjunctive state of affairs, p and q, occurs.[94]

The principle is similar to Aune's assumption that whatever one chooses one thereby intends.[95]

Simester doubts that the diffusiveness principle is correct. While we have a reason to think of p and q as intended, it is not as conclusive as Chisholm's principle suggests. There are countervailing considerations, notably the point that intention includes motivation beyond belief. Certainty is neither a necessary nor sufficient element. The judge who finds for the plaintiff in some case may know that the damages will bankrupt the defendant; yet the judge does not intend her bankruptcy. So SB accepts the children's deaths, but he does not intend to bomb the plant and (thereby) kill the children. He intends to bomb the plant irrespective of the fact that he will thereby kill the children.[96] The bankruptcy illustration gives force to the claim that neither certainty nor knowledge of certainty is sufficient to found intention. This challenges the correctness of the approach now taken by the courts.

The connection seen by Chisholm and Aune underlies Lord Diplock's analysis in *Hyam*[97] already quoted. According to Simester, while Lord Diplock would be correct to say that both bombers are willing to cause death, he neglects the important further sense in which it is solely TB whose *will* is that the children should die.[98]

There is a moral feature which accompanies intended actions: that an agent is fully exposed to moral assessment of his or her action whenever it is intended. An agent who intends X warrants moral judgment for his or her behaviour simply according to the moral quality of X itself, though that

94 Roderick Chisholm, 'The Structure of Intention' (1970) *Journal of Philosophy* 633, 640.
95 Bruce Aune, *Reasons and Action* (1977) 115.
96 Simester, above n 50, 453.
97 [1975] AC 55, 85.
98 Simester, above n 50, 454.

judgment may be offset by moral assessment of the other ramifications of the actor's behaviour and also by excuses. Even when an agent is culpable for inadvertent action, the moral assessment of that action does not usually attach to quite the extent that it would, were the action intended. Hence the claim 'I did X unintentionally' may be proffered as an excuse; although, depending upon the circumstances, that claim may not deny culpability in respect of X altogether, it reduces such culpability to a lower level. On the other hand, in most cases, the claim 'I foresaw but did not intend X' is not an excuse. And in many situations it will not justify reducing culpability to a lower level.

Hence Audi's example of killing the stag and the king: X did not want to kill the king, but fired a bullet which would pass through the stag and, to X's knowledge, lodge in the king's heart. The killing of the king would not be *unintentional*, for this suggests that X made a mistake or acted in ignorance. 'I didn't intend to' would not be accepted as an excuse, nor as a factor reducing culpability, because X intended to bring about the king's death, although he did not wish to do so.[99]

Moral culpability for advertent action attaches to SB as well as to X. Although the presence of moral culpability makes us the more willing to treat these instances as intention, Simester rightly argues that a purely cognitive state is simply an insufficient basis upon which to ascribe intention.[100] The law now appears to recognise this insufficiency as a matter of language and analysis. In any event, in terms of criminal responsibility and moral assessment, there is a case for saying that no distinction should be drawn between them for the purposes of punishment. That is why Australian law treats the mental element as extending not only to cases of direct intention but also to knowledge or foresight of probable consequences, going beyond cases of 'virtual certainty'.

Inseparability

Earlier I adverted to the question whether the inseparable consequences of an intended act can be regarded as intended, suggesting that the question can be answered in the affirmative. The question has been the subject of

---

99 Robert Audi, 'Intending' (1973) 70 *Journal of Philosophy* 387, 397.
100 Simester, above n 50, 455.

considerable discussion by Glanville Williams,[101] Kenny[102] and Cross.[103] Many jurists, including Glanville Williams, Kenny and Cross, consider that there are effects which, though not sought, are so closely connected to an intended effect that they must also be regarded as intended. The problem is to determine when the consequences are sufficiently close. It is difficult to identify any bright line, principle or criteria which will advance the ascertainment of the necessary degree of connection. So much depends upon the particular situation under examination and what can be extracted from it.

Duff[104] thinks that empirical certainty is insufficient and Simester[105] agrees with him. Duff considers that the connection is one of logical entailment, as does Simester, though he does not accept the validity of Duff's approach to logical entailment. Whether criteria can be identified remains to be seen. The ascription of intention on the basis of appreciation of virtual certainty, or foresight of probable consequences, in England and Australia respectively seemingly reduces the search for criteria to the level of a theoretical exercise.

Conclusion

The discussion of intention by philosophers can certainly aid legal understanding of the topic. The divide between philosophers and lawyers is not as wide as it was in England. However, having regard to the wider purposes which the law, notably the criminal law, serves, there is bound to be a difference between legal and philosophical approaches to the subject. Further, the need to fashion directions in practical comprehensive terms for juries makes it difficult to reflect in detail the distinctions which philosophers draw in the process of conceptual analysis.

---

101 Glanville Williams, *Criminal Law* (2nd ed, 1961) para 18.
102 A Kenny, 'Intention and Purpose in Law' in Robert Summers (ed), *Essays in Legal Philosophy* (1968) 146.
103 Cross, above n 88, 224.
104 Duff, above n 69, 89–90.
105 Simester, above n 50, 457.

7 *Mens Rea* in Tort Law

PETER CANE*

In ethical terms, intention is widely felt to be the clearest and strongest basis for the attribution of personal responsibility for conduct and outcomes. In the law, this view is reflected in the importance of intention as a ground of criminal liability. By contrast, in tort law intention is a much less important ground of liability than negligence. Indeed, it is no exaggeration to say that, while responsibility for what one does and brings about intentionally is the paradigm in the moral sphere,[1] liability for negligence is the paradigm in tort law. Later in this essay I offer an explanation for the relative unimportance of intention as a basis of tort liability, given its supposed centrality in the making of ethical judgments. That explanation rests on the observation that, whereas intention is an agent-focused ground of responsibility, tort law is concerned not only with agents but also with victims and with society more generally. But, before giving this explanation, it is necessary to analyse what is meant by 'intention' in tort law. In general, tort lawyers have not given much attention to this issue,[2] and the discussion in the first section of the essay goes some way to making good this omission. The following section maps the place of intention in tort law and provides support for the proposition that its role is a minor one. My aim in this essay is essentially descriptive

*   This essay was originally published in (2000) 20 *Oxford Journal of Legal Studies* 533, and is reproduced by permission of Oxford University Press. Sincere thanks to Ngaire Naffine for asking me to write on this topic; to the participants in her 1999 Adelaide seminar series for provocative questions; and to John Eekelaar, Claire Finkelstein, Niki Lacey, Declan Roche and Jane Stapleton for penetrating comments on earlier versions.
1   Consider, for example, John Mackie's 'straight rule of responsibility: an agent is responsible for all and only his intentional actions': John Mackie, *Ethics: Inventing Right and Wrong* (1977) 208.
2   For a possible explanation of this reticence see W V H Rogers, *The Law of Tort* (2nd ed, 1994) 15; W V H Rogers (ed), *Winfield and Jolowicz on Tort* (14th ed, 1994) 48. An exception is Francis Trindade: Francis Trindade and Peter Cane, *The Law of Torts in Australia* (3rd ed, 1999) 30–6, 111–13, 146–8, 178–9, 216–18, 224, 230–3, 243–4, 247–8.

and explanatory. I offer no view about the proper role of intention in tort law. Before tackling that issue, we need a clearer understanding of the nature of 'tortious intention' and its place in the conceptual structure of tort law.

What is Intention?

The Core of Intention

What do we mean by 'intention'? As I have said, this is an issue to which tort lawyers have given relatively little attention. Because of the importance of *mens rea* in criminal law, the meaning of intention has been more discussed in that context;[3] but it is not safe to assume that 'intention' is used in the same way in tort law as it is in criminal law. There is also a large philosophical literature about intention, but there are several reasons why that literature is not of much help for my project. For one thing, philosophers tend to analyse intention primarily in terms of 'purpose'; but as we will see, tort law takes a broader approach. Secondly, most philosophers do not discuss legal meanings of intention; and those who do tend to focus on criminal law. Thirdly, philosophers are by no means agreed amongst themselves about what we mean by 'intention'. While the philosophical and criminal law literature can provide a useful starting point, it needs to be supplemented by careful analysis of tort law. So what is 'tortious intention'?

As a preliminary to answering this question it is important to distinguish between conduct and consequences, because, even in cases where tort liability rests on having done something with the intention of producing certain consequences, liability for the consequences of that conduct may not depend on their having been intended. This is true of the tort of deceit, for instance: a person can be liable for deceit only if they made a false statement, which they did not believe to be true, with the intention that the addressee of the statement should rely on it. But liability for deceit extends beyond intended and foreseeable harm to all harm directly caused by the tortious conduct.

---

3   Eg Antony Duff, *Intention, Agency and Criminal Liability: Philosophy of Action and the Criminal Law* (1990).

In both philosophical and legal literature, the most widely accepted account of the 'core' of the concept of intention in relation to conduct is based on the idea of choice; and in relation to consequences, on the concepts of aim, purpose and objective. What one chooses (not) to do, one intends (not) to do; and events which one aims to bring about (or avoid), one intends to bring about (or avoid). Many legal accounts of intention also give a prominent place to desire. But the word 'desire' is ambiguous. In one sense (which John Finnis dubs 'volitionally desiring'[4]) what one chooses to do, one desires to do; and events which one aims to bring about, one desires to bring about. In this sense, 'desire' is synonymous with choosing or aiming at, as the case may be. But in another sense (which Finnis dubs 'emotional desire'[5]), one may choose to do what one would rather not do, and may aim to bring about events which one would rather avoid. Intending is also to be distinguished from trying. Whereas, in relation to actions, doing something intentionally involves trying to do it, this is not so in relation to omissions. A person can intentionally refrain from action without trying to do so.

Intention, Recklessness and Negligence

Defined in terms of purpose, intention is clearly distinguishable from recklessness. Recklessness in its core sense is commonly conceptualised in terms of awareness of a risk that certain consequences will result from conduct, and indifference to that risk.[6] A person intends a particular consequence of their conduct if their purpose is to produce that consequence by their conduct. A person is reckless in relation to a particular consequence of their conduct if they realise that their conduct may have that consequence, but go ahead anyway. The risk must have been an unreasonable one to take: a surgeon is not reckless simply by virtue of being aware of the risk that the patient may die on the operating table. While the frame of mind of the intentional agent is different from that of the reckless agent in relation to the consequences of their conduct, their frame of mind in relation to the conduct itself is the same: both set out to engage in the conduct, the reckless person regardless of the risk of the

---

4   John Finnis, 'Intention and Side-Effects' in R G Frey and C W Morris (ed), *Liability and Responsibility: Essays in Law and Morals* (1991) 37.
5   Ibid.
6   Andrew Ashworth, *Principles of Criminal Law* (3rd ed, 1999) 184–5.

consequence, and the intentional person in order to produce that consequence. In relation to their conduct both, we might say, engage in it deliberately.

Some people are willing to extend the concept of intention to consequences that the agent realises will almost certainly, or at least very probably, result from deliberate conduct but that it was not the agent's purpose to bring about.[7] This extension is referred to as 'oblique intention', and its effect is to blur the distinction, or at least to move the boundary, between intention and recklessness. The precise location of this boundary is of less importance in tort law than in criminal law. Although it appears that there may be[8] some circumstances in which a person can be liable in tort for harm done to another only if the person aimed to do harm to the other, in many situations it appears that recklessness is sufficient to satisfy a requirement of intention.[9] An explanation for this, I think, is (as I have just said) that the person who intends that their conduct should produce a particular consequence, and the person who is reckless as to whether their conduct will produce a particular consequence, both engage in the conduct deliberately. It is this element of deliberateness[10] in relation to conduct that links intention and recklessness and leads to their assimilation in tort law. Deliberately doing something of which the law disapproves is worse than doing it without deliberateness; and it is this line between deliberate and non-deliberate conduct to which tort law gives prime significance.

---

7   Eg ibid 178–9.
8   This exceedingly non-committal form of words is made necessary by the lack of clarity in and consistency between judicial discussions of intention in tort law. The secondary literature is equally confused and confusing.
9   See, eg, American Law Institute, *Restatement of Torts 2d*, §8A. In a recent article, Philip Sales and Daniel Stilitz have argued that liability for inflicting harm by unlawful means will arise only if it was D's aim or purpose to harm P either as an end in itself or as a means to some further end: 'Intentional Infliction of Harm by Unlawful Means' (1999) 115 *Law Quarterly Review* 411, 425–30. In their view, there can be no liability if D merely foresaw the risk of harm to P as a side effect of what they intended, even if it was nearly certain to materialise. However, their discussion wavers uneasily between the descriptive and the prescriptive.
10 I use this somewhat infelicitous term, instead of 'deliberation', so as not to beg the question of whether a person's conduct can be deliberate even though not preceded by conscious deliberation. An analogous issue arises in relation to intention: can a person's conduct be intentional even though not preceded by the conscious formation of a 'plan of action'? See Peter Cane, 'Fleeting Mental States' (2000) 59 *Cambridge Law Journal* 273.

Because liability for 'intentional torts' can sometimes be attracted by recklessness, it is important to map the boundaries of tortious recklessness, and in particular to map the boundary between recklessness and negligence. The starting point must be to understand the nature of tortious negligence. Negligence in tort law is failure to comply with a legally specified standard of conduct, pure and simple. It has no mental element. On the one hand, the plaintiff in a tort action for negligence does not have to prove inattention or inadvertence on the part of the defendant.[11] Inadvertence is not a precondition of tort liability for negligence (or under any other head). On the other hand, if a driver intentionally rams a pedestrian with their car in order to injure, and emotionally desiring to injure, the pedestrian, the driver could be held liable in tort for negligence on the ground that a person who does that fails to take reasonable care for the safety of another.[12] Similarly, a driver who injures a pedestrian as a result of speeding, having adverted to the possibility of harm and being consciously indifferent to the risk, could be held liable in tort for negligence.

These examples illustrate a more general point. The elements of the various heads of liability we call torts do not describe the conduct that falls within the relevant head of liability. Rather they specify conditions for the imposition of liability. Conduct may satisfy those conditions even if we would not 'naturally' describe it in terms of those conditions. This is obvious in the case of strict liability. Absence of fault is not a condition of strict liability. Conduct may attract strict liability even if it is negligent, or even reckless or intentional. Indeed, an important justification for strict liability, first put forward by Justice Oliver Wendell Holmes and taken over by modern economic analysts of law,[13] is that it increases the chance

---

11   It is true, of course, that inadvertence and inattention are features of the typical negligence case. But it is not the inadvertence or the inattention that constitutes the negligence.

12   In *Reeves v Commissioner of Police of the Metropolis* [2000] 1 AC 360 the House of Lords held that a prisoner who committed suicide while of sound mind could be held guilty of contributory negligence for failing to take reasonable care for his own safety. Conscious risk taking, for instance by employers in the design of working systems, and by manufacturers in the design of products, may attract liability for negligence. It is often pointed out that the deterrence function of liability for negligence is more likely to be achieved in relation to consciously risky behaviour than in relation to inadvertently risky behaviour.

13   See David Rosenberg, *The Hidden Holmes* (1995) 126, 138–40; Steven Shavell, *Economic Analysis of Accident Law* (1987) 26–32, 264–5.

that those guilty of fault will be held liable in circumstances where proof of fault is difficult, albeit at the possible cost of imposing liability in some cases in the absence of fault. It follows that, in principle, conduct may attract liability under more than one head. For instance, intentional conduct may attract liability for negligence and also under some other head of liability for which proof of intention is a condition. Thus, a fraudulent misstatement may attract liability for negligence or for deceit. The plaintiff would have a choice whether to sue for negligence or deceit, knowing that any advantages of liability for deceit over negligence liability could be obtained only at the expense of undertaking the difficult task of proving fraud.

Since tortious negligence involves no mental state, the line between it and 'conscious' recklessness (which entails actual awareness of risk) is clear enough. In order to be consciously reckless a person must take an unreasonable risk of which they were actually aware, whereas a person can be negligent even if they were not aware of the unreasonably risky nature of their conduct, provided they should have been. But, in the context of criminal law, Antony Duff has argued that a person can be indifferent to a risk of which they are unaware, and that indifference need not be conscious but need only be 'manifested in' conduct.[14] It might seem very difficult to distinguish recklessness so understood[15] from failure to comply with a legally specified standard of conduct. As Duff puts it (speaking of recklessness):

> [We] could usefully ask this question: 'how else could a person who acted thus have failed to notice that risk if not because he did not care about it?'[16]

In other words, whereas negligence is failure to take reasonable care to avoid causing harm to others, recklessness is failure to care, as the normal person would, about the risk that others may suffer harm as a result of one's conduct. For Duff, what distinguishes recklessness from negligence is not that the latter is failure to comply with a legally defined standard of

---

14   Duff, above n 3, ch 7.
15   Which Duff calls 'practical indifference'.
16   Duff, above n 3, 166. In some cases, the test of negligence is not 'did D behave unreasonably?', but 'was D's behaviour such as no reasonable person could have engaged in?' In such cases, the line between negligence and recklessness (as understood by Duff) might be very fine indeed.

conduct while the former is a frame or state of mind, but rather that recklessness and negligence consist of failure to comply with different legally specified standards of conduct.[17] Recklessness is unreasonable failure to care for the welfare of others, and negligence is unreasonable failure to take care (ie precautions) to prevent harm to others. Of course, a person who fails to meet the legal standard of caring for the welfare of others may, in fact, have been aware of the risk. But, just as intentional conduct may amount to tortious negligence, so too, applying Duff's view, 'conscious' recklessness could constitute recklessness defined as unreasonable failure to care for the welfare of others. This does not, however, alter the nature of the legal tests of negligence or recklessness respectively.

Duff's approach to recklessness was developed in support of certain leading decisions in English criminal law; and, whatever one thinks of it in that context, I am not aware of any evidence to support its applicability to tort law. From now on, therefore, I shall assume that recklessness in tort law means conscious recklessness. Because recklessness may satisfy a requirement of intention in tort law, I shall use the term 'tortious intention' to refer to this composite of intention and conscious recklessness, and 'intention' by itself to distinguish intention from recklessness. For the sake of simplicity, parts of the discussion that follows will refer only to intention. However, in most instances, something very similar to what I say about intention could, I think, be said about conscious recklessness as well.

Intention, Knowledge and Belief

Intention is related to belief. Normally, saying that a person intended some conduct or event X involves saying that they believed X not to be impossible. Similarly, to say that a person was consciously reckless in relation to a particular outcome involves saying that they believed the outcome not to be impossible. In some torts, the mental element may be expressed in terms of 'lack of honest belief': for instance, lack of honest

---

17 Ibid 165. Notice that the view we are considering here does not concern how one would prove whether a person was aware of a risk, but rather whether it is necessary to prove awareness. Duff's position appears to be that it is only when the risk in question was very obvious and serious that unawareness will manifest indifference. In cases in which the risk could not be so described, it would be necessary to prove awareness in order to establish recklessness.

belief in the truth of a statement in deceit, and lack of honest belief that what one did was *intra vires* in misfeasance in a public office. Lack of honest belief in X implies awareness of the risk that not-X.[18] To make a statement, aware of the risk that it might be false, is to make a false statement recklessly.

Secondary tort liability for inducing and authorising the tortious conduct of another will arise only if the defendant knew of the circumstances which made the conduct tortious (although, of course, they need not have appreciated that it was tortious). In other words, the 'secondary party' must have acted with deliberation in furthering the tortious conduct.

Motives in Tort Law

Intention and motive
In tort law it is important to distinguish between intention and motive. In relation to intentional conduct, one's motive is the reason why one engages in the conduct or intends its consequences. In any particular case, intention and motive may coincide: a person may aim to produce a particular outcome because they desire it.[19] But equally, they may diverge: a person may intentionally do X not because they desire to do X but because, for

---

18 In deceit, the defendant must also have intended the statement to be relied upon by the plaintiff. But D need not have intended the harm suffered: the remoteness rule requires a direct causal link. It is unclear whether a person can be said to have intended reliance on their statement if they were merely reckless as to such reliance. The law governing liability for negligent exercise of public powers is complex and uncertain. Repeated attempts have been made to persuade courts in Australia and elsewhere to water down the mental element of misfeasance in a public office or to remove it entirely. It remains unclear, in Australia at least, whether D must have known that the exercise of power was *ultra vires* or whether awareness of a risk that it might have been *ultra vires* is sufficient; and it is unclear whether D must have intended to injure P or whether recklessness, or even negligence, in relation to injury will suffice. Leading recent Australian cases are *Northern Territory of Australia v Mengel* (1996) 185 CLR 307 and *Sanders v Snell* (1999) 196 CLR 329. Despite considerable terminological confusion, the decision of the House of Lords in *Three Rivers District Council v Bank of England* [2000] 2 WLR 1220 seems to support the sufficiency of recklessness in relation to both issues.
19 Here I am using 'desire' as a synonym for 'want'; ie for 'emotionally desire', to adopt Finnis's terminology, above n 4.

instance, they promised to do X;[20] indeed, the person's desire may be not to do X.

Bad motives

In tort law, bad motives are referred to as 'malice'. The concept of malice is important to an understanding of tortious intention because to say that a person's conduct was malicious implies that it was intentional or consciously reckless. Indeed, intention and conscious recklessness are sometimes themselves referred to as 'malice', but this confusing terminology is better avoided. A person can act intentionally or recklessly for good reasons. Confusing, too, and better avoided, is using the term 'malice' to describe the making of a statement without qualification, as if it were true, but with the belief that it might not be true. Such conduct is better described as recklessness. A person can make a statement, which they believe to be true, out of a bad motive.[21]

Malicious motives are of two types, which I shall refer to as 'intrinsic' and 'collateral'. Intrinsic malice is inherently reprehensible. Collateral malice need not be inherently reprehensible. For instance, malice defeats a defence of qualified privilege in defamation; and in this context, malice may consist in using an occasion of privilege for some purpose other than that for which the privilege is given, even if it is not inherently reprehensible. Furthering one's own interests is not regarded by the law as inherently reprehensible, but it can constitute collateral malice. Inherently reprehensible motives include 'spite or ill will', and emotionally (as opposed to volitionally) desiring to harm someone or to make a gain at their expense. People often have mixed motives, and tort law uses the concept of 'predominant motive' to measure, in a vague way, the relative strengths of mixed motives.

Malice plays a role in various contexts in justifying the imposition of tort liability. Malice, both intrinsic and collateral, can defeat certain defences to a prima facie case of defamation (as can conscious indifference to truth). Intrinsic malice is one basis of liability for injurious falsehood (the other is a belief that the statement might be false); and it is a

---

20   So we may say that, while they do not desire to do X, they do desire to fulfil their promise.

21   For an instance of both confusions see *Northern Territory of Australia v Mengel* (1995) 185 CLR 307, 370 (Deane J).

precondition of liability for abuse of legal process.[22] There can be no liability for lawful means conspiracy unless the conspirators' predominant motive was intrinsically malicious. There is authority for the proposition that malicious conduct can constitute an actionable nuisance even if it does not amount to an unreasonable interference with the use and enjoyment of land (which is the normal test of an actionable nuisance).[23] But care is needed here. The test of unreasonableness in nuisance operates as a standard of conduct, and it is similar to the ordinary concept of negligence in tort law. While maliciously causing someone harm can be 'negligent' within the meaning given to that term in tort law, harm-causing conduct cannot be negligent merely by virtue of being malicious. So how can malicious conduct attract liability for nuisance if it is not an unreasonable interference with the use and enjoyment of land?

The situation here is different from that in defamation or injurious falsehood. In those cases, malice justifies the imposition of liability for conduct which is prima facie wrongful: in the case of injurious falsehood the making of a false statement and in the case of defamation the making of a (false) defamatory statement. But in the case of nuisance the supposed effect of malice is to justify the imposition of liability for conduct which is prima facie lawful. This would not create a problem if, as in the case of lawful means conspiracy, intrinsic malice were a precondition of liability in every case; but malice is not an element of the basic test of nuisance. John Finnis says

> the claim that ... bad motives cannot delegitimate lawful means ... sophistically ignore[s] one of morality's most elementary principles and one of moral philosophy's most strategic themes ... One's conduct will be right only if *both* one's means *and* one's end(s) are right ... *all* the aspects of one's act must be rightful for the act to be right.[24]

In this passage, and throughout the section from which it comes, there is an equivocation between intention and motive. But Finnis's basic point seems to be that where harm is done out of a bad motive (immorally) there

22   See Peter Cane, *Tort Law and Economic Interests* (2nd ed, 1996) 266–8.
23   See Trindade and Cane, above n 2, 634–5; J G Fleming, *The Law of Torts* (9th ed, 1998) 472.
24   John Finnis, 'Intention in Tort Law' in David Owen (ed), *Philosophical Foundations of Tort Law* (1995) 238 (emphasis original). Finnis's specific comment on nuisance is at 241, n 51.

should be liability unless, for instance, D inflicted the harm on P in response to a refusal by P to do or to abstain from doing something which it was already P's legal duty to do or not to do; or D enjoyed legal privilege;[25] or where D's conduct was an omission in circumstances where D had no (legal?) duty to act.[26] The thrust of Finnis's argument is against the English law, established in *Allen v Flood*,[27] that, in the absence of combination, intentional harm causing will attract tort liability only if the conduct which caused the harm was intrinsically unlawful; and in favour of the American prima facie tort doctrine, under which intentional infliction of harm is actionable unless 'justified', that is, done for a good motive or proper reason.

By recognising exceptions to his general rule, Finnis undercuts his position because the exceptions allow the defence that what was done, despite bad motive, was not unlawful.[28] Consistently with this concession we might argue, in relation to nuisance, that liability for doing with a bad motive that which would not be a nuisance (or any other legal wrong) if done for good reason is anomalous. On the other hand, an explanation which fits some (although not all) of the relevant nuisance cases in which liability was based on bad motive is that what the defendant did served no useful social purpose.[29] Furthermore, since the test of unreasonable user in nuisance is a utilitarian balancing test, this explanation would suggest that, in the 'malice' cases, the defendant's conduct was actually an unreasonable use of land precisely because it served no useful social purpose. Take *Christie v Davey*,[30] for instance. The defendant was held liable for making loud noises 'maliciously' and 'only for the purpose of annoyance' in order to interrupt a neighbour's music teaching even though, it was said, the offending conduct would not have amounted to a nuisance if it had been done 'perfectly innocent[ly]'. We might argue that the means chosen by the defendant to deal with the situation were likely to exacerbate conflict and,

---

25 Such as absolute privilege in defamation.
26 Finnis, above n 24, 240, n 44.
27 [1989] AC 1.
28 The source of the exceptions is J B Ames, 'How Far an Act May be a Tort Because of the Wrongful Motive of the Actor' (1905) 18 *Harvard Law Review* 411. Ames himself explains these cases as ones in which malice is irrelevant because the conduct was not unlawful.
29 Finnis, however, would not accept this explanation because it smacks of utilitarian balancing of conflicting personal and social interests: Finnis, above n 24, 242.
30 [1893] 1 Ch 316.

therefore, unreasonable (or, as the court put it, 'not legitimate'), regardless of D's motives. What is anomalous, we might think, is a rule under which a person whose conduct was reasonable should be held liable merely because it was not also sweet.

Good motives

In tort law, good motives find their place in the concept of 'justification', although not all justifications are good motives: some are legal powers or privileges. The most firmly established justifying motive in tort law is self-interest.[31] In the tort of lawful means conspiracy, a predominant motive of furthering one's financial interests can justify conduct which is also motivated by a desire to injure another; but self-interest cannot justify interference with rights under existing contracts, even if unlawful means have not been used. There is authority for the proposition that a desire to protect or further some moral or social principle of good conduct can justify interference with contractual rights, at least if unlawful means have not been used.[32] But the cases do not establish a general rule that unlawful means can never be justified, nor even a general rule that unlawful means can never be justified by pursuit of self-interest.[33]

Intention and Proof

So far I have been discussing the nature and content of the concepts of intention and recklessness. It is one thing to understand what mental states count as intention and recklessness, but quite another to prove that a person acted intentionally or recklessly. In practice, it may be very difficult to give effect to distinctions that are clear in theory. The classic legal approach to proof of intention starts with the proposition that intentions are not directly observable. From this it is concluded that, in order to determine whether a person's conduct was intentional and whether its consequences were intended, we must rely either on that person's account of their frame of

---

31   Note that, depending on the circumstances and the nature of the interest the law is protecting, self-interest can constitute collateral malice or a justification.

32   *Brimelow v Casson* [1924] 1 Ch 302. See generally Fleming, above n 23, 762–4; J D Heydon, *Economic Torts* (2nd ed, 1978) 42–4; also 19–22, 24–6 (re lawful means conspiracy).

33   For a range of views see Sales and Stilitz, above n 9, 481; Tony Weir, *Economic Torts* (1997) 76; J D Heydon, 'The Defence of Justification in Cases of Intentionally Caused Economic Loss' (1970) 20 *University of Toronto Law Journal* 131, 171–82.

mind at the relevant time, or on 'inferences' from their conduct and its surrounding circumstances.[34] This conclusion in turn has important implications for analysis of the legal concept of intention. Even leaving aside the possibility of lies, defects of memory and *ex post facto* rationalisations, and assuming truthfulness, the agent's own account of their mental state will inevitably be mediated through their understanding of the concept of intention. In other words, the account is unlikely to consist merely of 'raw' data about the agent's frame of mind. A skilled questioner might hope to be able to elicit useful information from the agent about their state of mind, but we should not, perhaps, be too sanguine about the 'accuracy' of self-reporting of past mental states even in response to skilled interrogation.

In the common case in which the subject's mental state has to be inferred from behaviour and surrounding circumstances, the position is much worse. In such cases, it seems to me, a judgment that a person's conduct was intentional will be underpinned by an assertion about the 'normal person', not about the agent. In relation to conduct, the reasoning will go something like this: the agent's conduct must have been intentional because what the agent did is not the sort of thing that people normally do unintentionally. And, in relation to consequences, the reasoning will go somewhat as follows: the agent must have intended these consequences because they are not the sort of thing that people normally bring about unintentionally. If I am right about this 'inferred intention', as we might call it, is not a frame of mind at all; rather it expresses a judgment about the way people normally (ought to) behave.

My argument is not that when a person is found, by inference, to have intended conduct or its consequences they did not so intend. They may or may not have had the intention that is attributed to them; and so they may or may not bear the responsibility that attaches to intentional conduct and intended consequences. Rather my point concerns the relationship between the meaning of intention and the criteria for the imposition of legal liability for intentional conduct. Consider strict liability: as was noted earlier, an important justification for strict liability is that it increases the chance that those guilty of fault will be held liable in circumstances in which proof of

---

34 For a contrary view see Duff, above n 3, 27–31: 'we can, in a perfectly ordinary sense observe, or look into, the mind of another; for we can see his mind *in* his actions' (emphasis original). But the problem is that different states of mind may precede precisely similar actions.

fault is difficult. Similarly, the 'normal person test of intention' is a concession to the difficulty of proving intention: a rebuttable presumption of intention, in other words. And, because it is rebuttable, the agent may escape liability by proving that in fact the conduct in question and its consequences were not intended. The truth remains, however, that for practical purposes this concession turns a finding of intention from a proposition about a person's (subjective) frame of mind into a statement about normal behaviour. It does not follow that the agent may not bear the responsibility of having acted intentionally. But it does follow that bearing this responsibility is not a necessary condition of incurring legal liability for having acted intentionally.

This startling conclusion might seem to open up an even larger gap than the one I identified at the beginning of this article between ideas of responsibility outside the law and responsibility in (tort) law. The gap I referred to initially is created by the fact that legal responsibility can arise even in the absence of intention. But here we find that legal liability for intentional conduct may arise even in the absence of intention! However, I think that the gap is not as large as it might appear at first sight. Most moral philosophers confine their attention to the *meaning* of concepts such as responsibility and intention, and ignore problems of proof. But the problems of proof that arise in legal contexts also arise in moral contexts as soon as we go beyond defining intention and concern ourselves with the practical matter of imposing sanctions (such as blaming and shaming) for intentional conduct. It does not follow, of course, that problems of proof are solved in the same way in extra-legal contexts as in legal contexts. But the problems arise in both places and need to be resolved in both places. We have no greater access to other minds in 'ordinary life' than in the courtroom. However, because heavy sanctions can attach to legal responsibility, problems of proof typically need to be addressed in legal contexts more urgently and carefully than in non-legal contexts.

Motives, too, may present problems of proof.[35] The problems and the possible solutions are, no doubt, similar in nature in relation to motives as in relation to intention; although we might think that proving why a person behaved as they did would be even harder than proving that their conduct executed a plan. It is one thing to say that a person's conduct manifested a

---

35 Indeed, this was one of the reasons given in *Allen v Flood* [1898] AC 1 for denying motive a place in tort law: R F V Heuston and R A Buckley (eds), *Salmond and Heuston on the Law of Torts* (21st ed, 1996) 19.

plan of action; or to say, 'given what you did, you must have intended it', or 'the reasonable person would not have done X without a plan'. It is quite another thing to say that a person's conduct reveals their reasons for action; or to say, 'given what you did, this rather than that must have been the reason for your conduct'; or that 'the reasonable person would not have done what you did for the reason you say motivated your conduct'.[36]

The Economic Account of Intention in Tort Law

The analysis so far has treated intention as a concept tied to ideas of individual agency and responsibility. There is an 'economic' account of intention that deserves some attention. I will focus on the discussion by Landes and Posner in their book *The Economic Structure of Tort Law*.[37] Their approach to intention is rather different from their approach to negligence. As is well known, the basic economic interpretation of negligence utilises the concept of efficiency: negligent conduct is inefficient conduct, understood in terms of the formula $C<pH$, where H stands for the harm suffered, C stands for what it would have cost to prevent the harm, and p stands for the antecedent probability of the harm occurring. If the cost of precautions is less than pH, it is negligent not to take those precautions. In other words, the formula $C<pH$ provides us with a *definition*, in economic terms, of the legal concept of negligence. By contrast, Landes and Posner define intention in terms of 'trying[38] to cause harm'. However, they do relate intention to the economic definition of negligence. Negligence, they say, occurs when C 'is less, but not dramatically so',[39] than pH. The paradigm case of intention occurs where p (and, hence, pH) is high (because D was trying to cause harm) and where C is negative (that is, where D has to expend resources to cause harm, for instance, by aiming a blow at P).[40]

---

36 But see Heydon, above n 32, 17–18: unusualness of conduct may be evidence of malice.

37 William Landes and Richard Posner, *The Economic Structure of Tort Law* (1987) 149–85.

38 Landes and Posner seem to use the word 'try' as a synonym for 'volitionally desire'.

39 Landes and Posner, above n 37, 159.

40 Cases of recklessness occur where C is negative and p is very low; and where C is positive, but very low, and p is high. In *Economic Analysis of Law* (4th ed, 1992) 208, Posner says that cases in which pH is very high and C is negative are *qualitatively* different from cases in which the difference between C and pH is small. However, the

In one place, Posner says that intention should be treated 'as a proxy for certain characteristics of the tortious act, notably a large gap between the cost of the act to the victim and the small or even negative cost to the injurer of not committing the act'. [41] On the other hand, Landes and Posner argue that

> [t]he inability to peer inside another person's head requires that inferences of intent be drawn from behaviour ... intent can ... be inferred from any combination of probability, severity, and cost of avoidance [of harm] that shows that the injury was not merely a by-product of lawful activity. [D] will not be heard to deny that he wanted to [cause the harm]; there is no other plausible interpretation of his motives. [42]

This passage suggests that the identified characteristics of the behaviour are a proxy for intention, not vice versa; or that they provide a criterion for proving intention. This latter view arguably fits better with the nature of negligence and intention respectively as grounds of legal liability. Legal negligence is defined in terms of a standard of conduct that is unrelated to the agent's state of mind. The tort of negligence has no mental element. It is possible, therefore, to define legal negligence purely in terms of conduct that possesses certain characteristics, and without reference to the agent's mental processes. But not even Posner believes that the concept of intention makes no reference to the agent's mental world. As he himself says: 'I deny not the existence of mental phenomena but the utility for law of the concept of mind in which intentions ... figure'. [43]

The account of intention (and recklessness) in terms of probability and cost of avoidance of harm seems to me to provide a helpful objective criterion for inferring intention in the absence of more direct evidence about the agent's frame of mind. On this interpretation, the economic account of intention does not require any fundamental reconsideration of the account based on concepts of agency and personal responsibility, and is not inconsistent with it.

---

difference is only quantitative. The qualitative difference resides in the distinction between 'trying to cause harm' and 'harming without trying'.

41 Richard Posner, *The Problems of Jurisprudence* (1990) 169–70.
42 Landes and Posner, above n 37, 152–3.
43 Posner, above n 41, 176.

Summary

In this section I have noted that in tort law intention often includes recklessness, and I have suggested that in this context recklessness means 'conscious indifference to risk'. I have argued that an essential difference between tortious intention and tortious negligence is that the latter does not have a mental element whereas the former does. However, I have also argued that the practical difficulty of proving the mental element of tortious intention may effectively blur this contrast with negligence. I have noted the importance of the distinction between conduct and consequences in tort law; and I have distinguished between tortious intention on the one hand and motive (or desire) on the other.

   With this theoretical groundwork in place, we are now in a position to analyse in more detail the role of intention in tort law.

The Functions and Role of Tortious Intention

The Functions of Tortious Intention

Tortious intention performs two juridical functions which we might respectively call its 'independent' function and its 'ancillary' function. The independent function of tortious intention is to justify the imposition of liability in relation to conduct and consequences which would not attract liability in the absence of tortious intention. Its ancillary function is to provide an alternative or additional ground of liability in respect of conduct and consequences which might attract liability even in the absence of tortious intention.

The independent function
Because tortious intention involves deliberateness and either aiming to do harm or conscious indifference to risk, it is a 'stronger' basis for responsibility than negligence or the mere causing of harm without 'fault'. Intention as to conduct and its consequences can justify the imposition of liability when there would be no liability in the absence of intention. For instance, secondary tort liability for inducing and authorising the

commission of a tort by another will arise only if the accessory conduct was deliberate.[44]

Tortious intention plays an important part in justifying liability for abuse of legal process;[45] and for inflicting harm by competitive market activity. To the extent that competition is a zero-sum game, one person's loss is another person's gain; and so the law does not impose tort liability for *negligently* harming a person by competing with them. But even liability for intentional harm might be thought to inhibit market activity unduly, and so the law requires, in addition, either unlawfulness (as in the case, for example, of intimidation) or combination plus a 'predominantly' bad motive[46] (as in the case of 'lawful means' conspiracy). Tortious intention plays an analogous role in justifying liability for harm inflicted by organised labour in furtherance of their economic interests *vis-à-vis* capital (and other labour organisations).

Another area in which tortious intention plays an independent role is that of causing harm to a person by interfering with the performance of a contract between that person and a third party.[47] The defendant must have known of, or been consciously indifferent to, the existence of the contract. Negligent interference with contract is not actionable in tort. There are two explanations for this. One is that interference with contracts is an almost inevitable concomitant of market competition and is a feature of much industrial action by organised labour. The other is that the imposition of tort liability for interference with contract involves giving an action for failure to comply with a contract to a person who is not a party to the contract. The interference may take the form of inducing a person not to perform a contractual obligation,[48] disabling a person from performing, or

---

44 There can be no accessory liability for tortious negligence. However, analogous issues arise in the context of liability for negligent failure to control third parties. Negligent failure to prevent another causing harm is less culpable than negligently causing harm. See generally Jane Stapleton, 'Duty of Care: Peripheral Parties and Alternative Opportunities for Deterrence' (1995) 111 *Law Quarterly Review* 301.

45 See Trindade and Cane, above n 2, 82–100, 241; Cane, above n 22, 266–8.

46 ie 'malice'.

47 See further Roderick Bagshaw, 'Inducing Breach of Contract' in Jeremy Horder (ed), *Oxford Essays in Jurisprudence, Fourth Series* (2000) 140–3.

48 This is a form of secondary liability; but see Weir, above n 33, 35. Analogous is assisting a breach of trust: *Royal Brunei Airlines v Philip Tan Kok Ming* [1995] 2 AC 378; but see Hazel Carty, 'Joint Tortfeasance and Assistance Liability' (1999) 19 *Legal Studies* 489.

intimidating a person into not performing. Some forms of this tort require unlawful means in addition to intention to injure the plaintiff.

Finally, tortious intention may serve to justify imposing tort liability for types of harm which would not otherwise be actionable. For example, preventing a person from making an advantageous contract may be tortious if done intentionally, but not if done negligently. Again, it has been argued that Australian law should recognise a tort of intentional infliction of mental distress which does not fall within the definition of 'nervous shock'.[49]

The ancillary function

The independent function of tortious intention is to justify causes of action where none would exist in the absence of intention. The ancillary function of tortious intention is to justify the awarding of remedies which would not be available in the absence of intention.[50] For instance, inflicting economic harm by negligently making a false statement on which another relies has been actionable in tort since the decision of the House of Lords in *Hedley Byrne & Co Ltd v Heller & Partners Ltd*.[51] Before then, liability for economic harm resulting from the making of a false statement depended on proof of 'deceit'. Since the decision in *Hedley Byrne*, the cause of action for deceit has survived mainly because the rule of remoteness of damage in deceit is more favourable to the plaintiff than that in negligence. In other words, prior to *Hedley Byrne* tortious intention performed its independent function in this area, whereas now it performs its ancillary function.

A more complex example of the ancillary function of tortious intention is provided by the tort of injurious (or 'malicious') falsehood. This tort provides remedies for the infliction of pecuniary harm, and in this respect it bears similarities to deceit. On the other hand, it has analogies with defamation: it effectively protects a person's financial interest in their

---

49 Trindade and Cane, above n 2, 71–82.
50 The ancillary function of tortious intention should be distinguished from concurrency of causes of action. Tortious intention performs its ancillary function by virtue of the fact that intentional conduct is 'more culpable' than unintentional conduct. By contrast two causes of action may lie concurrently even though the conduct which attracts liability under them is the same. Notably, it appears that a breach of contract will be actionable in tort only if it is negligent.
51 [1964] AC 465.

commercial reputation.[52] However, there are three important respects in which the analogy with defamation breaks down: damages for injury to (commercial) reputation are not available in an action for injurious falsehood, while they are in a defamation action; liability for defamation is basically strict (although some of the defences allow issues of fault to be raised); and the burden of proof on the issue of truth rests on the plaintiff in an action for injurious falsehood, but on the defendant in a defamation action.

In the common law world, there is a difference of judicial opinion about whether there should be tort liability for negligently causing a person financial loss by making a false (and defamatory) statement about them to a third party.[53] The main argument against is that negligence liability in such circumstances would outflank the defence of qualified privilege, which might be available in a defamation action. The argument in favour is that the action in negligence protects a different interest from that protected by the action in defamation: damages for injury to reputation are not available in the negligence action. In this latter respect, the tort of malicious falsehood is analogous to the tort of negligence; but the element of intention in injurious falsehood removes the outflanking objection: a person who intentionally defames another should not be allowed to plead qualified privilege. In the tort of defamation, this is recognised in the rule that a person who did not believe the defamatory statement to be true cannot plead qualified privilege.

Justifying the award of punitive damages is an ancillary function of tortious intention.[54] In *Lamb v Cotogno* the High Court of Australia said that 'in actions for tort exemplary damages may be awarded for conduct of a sufficiently reprehensible kind'.[55] The court did not define such conduct. However, punitive damages would probably be awarded only where the defendant's conduct and its consequences were intentional or where the defendant was reckless in the narrow sense of consciously indifferent;

---

52 The fact pattern underlying a claim for malicious falsehood is the same as that underlying a claim in defamation: D makes a false statement about P which X relies on (or believes) to P's detriment. Deceit covers cases where D makes a false statement to P on which P detrimentally relies.

53 Lord Cooke of Thorndon, 'The Right of Spring' in Peter Cane and Jane Stapleton (eds), *The Law of Obligations: Essays in Celebration of John Fleming* (1998) 37–57.

54 Intention also plays a part in justifying awards of disgorgement damages: Cane, above n 22, 300–1.

55 (1987) 164 CLR 1, 7.

although it is clear from *Lamb v Cotogno* that 'actual malice' is not required.[56]

What is the relationship between the independent function of tortious intention and its ancillary function of justifying awards of punitive damages? In cases where tortious intention performs its independent function, it is a precondition of the award of compensatory damages; and, therefore, it might be thought that in such cases some element of culpability more serious than intention would be needed to justify awarding punitive damages. On the basis of the holding in *Lamb v Cotogno* that 'actual malice'[57] is not required to justify an award of punitive damages, the presence of malice could provide a ground for such an award in cases where intention, but not malice, was a condition of an award of compensatory damages. Even in cases in which malice is a precondition of a compensatory award (as in malicious prosecution), an award of punitive damages could perhaps be justified by distinguishing between different categories of malice. For instance, if malice in the sense of a desire (ie an emotional desire) to injure, or of 'spite or ill will', could justify an award of compensatory damages, an additional motive of making a gain at the plaintiff's expense might justify an award of punitive damages.[58]

The Role of Tortious Intention

It will be noticed that many of the torts that are commonly classified as 'intentional' are absent from my account of the functions of tortious intention. The most important category of torts commonly thought of as torts of intention that find no place in my account are the 'trespass' torts: trespass to land; conversion, detinue and trespass to goods; and assault, battery and trespass to the person. In order to understand the role of these torts, it is important to distinguish between two distinct functions of tort liability: that of protecting property (and related) rights against unauthorised interference and exploitation, and that of protecting humans from bodily and mental harm and damage to their tangible property. As I

---

56   Ibid 13.

57   The court does not define this term. I shall assume that it refers to bad motives.

58   See *Mafo v Adams* [1970] 1 QB 548, 555 E–H (Sachs LJ). An awareness that what one is doing is a breach of *the law* may also provide an added element of culpability: ibid 559 B–C (Widgery LJ).

have explained elsewhere,[59] an important characteristic of torts that provide protection against interference and exploitation for property (and related) rights is strict liability. Far from being intentional torts, 'right-based torts' basically impose strict liability. On the other hand, 'harm-based' 'trespass' liability for personal injury and property damage has now been more or less effectively subsumed under the rubric of negligence. In theory, it is possible to sue for intentional harm to property and to the person, but the difficulties of proving intention and uncertainty about the benefits of doing so have largely robbed this avenue of practical importance.

A 'General Principle' of Tort Liability for Intention?

It is often said that, whereas tort law recognises a 'general principle' of liability for negligence, there is no 'general principle' of tort liability for intention. The first part of this statement rests, it seems to me, on several analytical inadequacies. First, it involves focusing on the conduct which attracts negligence liability and ignoring the interests which negligence liability protects. The second inadequacy is related to the first: the focus on conduct leads to a failure to notice that the duty of care concept in negligence operates to impose significant limitations on the supposed general principle. Some interests are better protected from negligent interference than others, and some interests are not protected at all. Thirdly, the statement wrongly suggests that there is a single test of negligent conduct in tort law. In fact, even within the tort of negligence there are two definitions of negligence, one in terms of what the reasonable person would do or omit to do, and the other in terms of what no reasonable person could do or omit to do.[60] Furthermore, the test of unreasonable user in nuisance is structurally very similar to the concept of unreasonableness in the tort of negligence: both are standards of conduct based on the balancing of personal and social interests. The fundamental

---

59   Cane, above n 22, ch 2.
60   In England, and to an uncertain extent in Australia, the second test is relevant to the liability of public authorities (in the guise of '*Wednesbury* unreasonableness') and certain professional groups, notably doctors (in the guise of 'the *Bolam* test'). See *Bolam v Friern Hospital Management Committee* [1957] 2 All ER 118; *Wednesbury Corporation v Ministry of Housing and Local Government* [1965] 1 All ER 186.

difference between them is that the negligence test takes account of the cost of precautions in a way that the nuisance test does not.[61]

Some people see the lack of a 'general principle' of tort liability for intention as involving an undesirable devaluing of the importance of intention as a ground of responsibility; and so they claim that tort law does, or at least that it should, recognise some such general principle. However, proponents do not all have the same general principle in mind, nor are they all similarly motivated. Heydon[62] and Weir[63] are concerned about the impact of tort liability on (competitive and productive) economic activity; and so their attempts at generality extend no further than the use in that context of the so-called 'economic torts'. By contrast, the explicit aim of Sales and Stilitz[64] is to generate a general principle of liability for intentional infliction of 'harm', not restricted to 'interference with trade or business'.

Within the first camp, Heydon and Weir are on opposite sides of the 'unlawfulness' fence. Heydon favours the American prima facie tort doctrine, which limits liability for intentional harm by reference to the idea of 'justifiability' or 'propriety'; while Weir favours the English rule, which (in the absence of combination)[65] uses the concept of '(independent) unlawfulness' as the limiting factor. However, standing in the way of Weir's analysis is *Lumley v Gye*,[66] which is commonly taken as authority for the proposition that persuading another to breach a contract with a third party is actionable even if the persuasion was not itself unlawful. Weir says of this case that '*[p]ersuading* your target's contractor to break his contract with the target constitutes wrongful means, the contractor's conduct being the means to the end'.[67] But what must be wrongful is what *you* do, not what the contractor does. So Weir also says that 'seducing' someone from the path of duty is in itself a wrong.[68] A critical question for Weir (which he does not answer) is whether 'seduction' is a legal wrong or a moral wrong because, as we have seen, Weir rejects the prima facie tort doctrine.

---

61   This is not to say that precautions are irrelevant to nuisance liability. See Trindade and Cane, above n 2, 633.
62   Heydon, above n 32.
63   Weir, above n 33.
64   Sales and Stilitz, above n 9.
65   Weir approves of this exception: Tony Weir, *A Casebook on Tort* (8ᵗʰ ed, 1996) 620.
66   (1853) 118 ER 749.
67   Weir, above n 33, 45.
68   Ibid 35.

At all events, it appears that Weir's objection to the traditional analysis of *Lumley v Gye* is pragmatic. In his view, concentration on the plaintiff's rights rather than the defendant's conduct has resulted in an undesirable watering down of the requirement of breach of contract to a lesser requirement of non-performance of a contract,[69] and in extension of the requirement of intention from planned to merely foreseen consequences.[70] The integrity of Weir's larger project could be preserved by attacking these developments as 'mistakes' in their own right while, at the same time, accepting combination and persuasion as justifying exceptions to a general requirement of unlawfulness (especially since Weir considers liability for persuasion of breach, on the one hand, and disablement of performance on the other, as resting on different principles, even though (in his view) they both require wrongful means).[71]

Weir's argument concerns the independent function of intention, and particularly intention's independent function of limiting the impact of tort liability on economic activity. In this respect, his ambition of generality is modest. Sales and Stilitz, by contrast, seek[72] a principle of liability for intentional conduct and its consequences which straddles the independent and the ancillary functions of intention. Under the principle they suggest, liability would arise for harm of any sort resulting from conduct by which the defendant intended to harm the plaintiff and that was unlawful. By 'unlawful' the authors refer to conduct 'forbidden by law'[73] regardless of whether it is intrinsically actionable by the plaintiff. Sales and Stilitz define 'intention' narrowly so as to exclude consequences that were not planned but merely foreseen. In the authors' view, the narrowness of this definition of intention counteracts their broad definition of unlawfulness. The recognition of such a principle would, they think, encourage the courts to view intention as a basis of tort liability in the same way as they view negligence, namely as a prima facie justification for the imposition of

---

69   *Torquay Hotel Co v Cousins* [1969] 1 All ER 522.

70   *Millar v Bassey* [1994] EMLR 44; reproduced in Weir, above n 33, 79–109.

71   Weir, above n 33, 46. See also Roderick Bagshaw, 'Can the Economic Torts be Unified?' (1998) 18 *Oxford Journal of Legal Studies* 729, 733–6.

72   At one point, the authors suggest that their principle provides 'a coherent account of the authorities': Sales and Stilitz, above n 9, 411; but parts of their analysis have a prescriptive tone.

73   Ibid 419. Unlawful means are means which the defendant was 'not, according to law, at liberty to employ': ibid 414. A person acts unlawfully if they do something which 'they were not entitled to do': ibid 419

liability subject to countervailing policy arguments against liability. The point of having a separate 'general' principle of liability for intentional harm is that, '[w]here harm is inflicted intentionally, more extensive recovery for loss suffered is justified by the more stringent criteria to be satisfied before imposing liability'.[74]

Several points deserve to be made about the approach of Sales and Stilitz. First, it is wrong to think that there is anything like a presumption in favour of the imposition of tort liability for negligently inflicted harm. This may be true in relation to personal injury and, perhaps, physical damage to tangible property, at least where either is caused by the defendant's positive act; but it is certainly not true in relation to purely economic harm. Secondly, the notion that intention justifies more extensive liability than negligence applies only to the ancillary function of intention. Where intention performs its independent function, it is perceived (relative to negligence) as a liability-restricting device, not a liability-expanding concept.

Thirdly, the policy-based exceptions to the proposed general principle of liability for intentional infliction of harm turn out to be numerous and complex. One of the most general is that liability should not be imposed under the 'intentional harm principle' where this would 'upset the balance' between the interests of the parties, 'carefully worked out' and given effect to under other applicable heads of liability.[75] What this seems to mean is that a plaintiff should not be allowed to avoid the operation of liability-negativing or liability-nullifying rules simply by proving intention and unlawfulness. However, the way Sales and Stilitz apply this non-avoidance principle lacks a discernible pattern. For instance, they argue that there should be no tort liability for intentional breach of the insurer's obligation of utmost good faith because negligent breach of this duty is not actionable. By contrast, they argue that liability for intentional breach of statutory duty should be allowed even if the breach of statutory duty would not be actionable according to the rules developed for the purposes of the tort of breach of statutory duty. Again, they argue that intentional breach of contract should not be actionable in their 'intentional harm tort', but that intentionally tortious behaviour should.

---

74   Ibid 436.
75   Ibid 420.

The search for 'general principles of liability' based on types of conduct is at best a waste of time, and at worst a potential source of serious confusion; and the broader the principle, the more is this so. Tort law is a complex interaction between protected interests, sanctioned conduct and sanctions;[76] and, although there *are* what might be called 'principles of tort liability', by and large they are not very 'general'. More importantly, they cannot be stated solely in terms of the sorts of conduct which will attract tort liability. Each principle must refer, as well, to some interest protected by tort law and some sanction provided by tort law. And, as I argue below, this is the key to understanding the role of intention in tort law.

The Relative Unimportance of Tortious Intention

Intention and recklessness play only a minor role in tort law. So far as the ancillary function of tortious intention is concerned, mental states are often difficult to prove; and the legal advantages to be gained by establishing tortious intention may not often be sufficient to justify the attempt. So far as concerns the independent function of tortious intention, it is of little practical importance outside the context of industrial disputes; and to the difficulties of proving intention or recklessness are often added other barriers to success such as the requirement of unlawfulness and the defence of justification.

It should be noted, too, that intention and recklessness play a part only in relation to torts of which harm is the gist (that is, in which there can be no liability without proof of harm resulting from the tort). Some torts (such as trespass to land) are actionable per se, that is, without proof of harm. These torts protect rights. Rights create protected spaces (both physical and metaphysical); and crossing a boundary into a protected space without the permission of the right holder is tortious in itself, regardless of whether it causes any harm to the right holder and regardless of whether the boundary crossing was negligent, reckless or intentional. Tort liability for boundary crossing is strict. The only requirement is that the boundary crossing should have been the agent's act; in other words, it must not have been involuntary. In tort law, 'intentional' is sometimes used in the sense of

---

76   See generally Peter Cane, *The Anatomy of Tort Law* (1997).

'voluntary', but this is misleading because involuntariness negatives agency while absence of intention does not.

Why are intention and recklessness of such little importance in tort law? And why is negligence the paradigm of tort liability while intention is the paradigm of criminal and moral responsibility? The key to answering these questions lies, I believe, in the fact that the concepts of intention and recklessness focus on the agent's conduct[77] and mental state at the expense of the interests of those directly and indirectly affected by the agent's conduct. Focus on agents is a central feature of many philosophical analyses of responsibility[78] and of the criminal law. Crimes are traditionally defined in terms of the agent's conduct (*actus reus*) and 'mental state' (*mens rea*). Consequences are not unimportant in criminal law; but there are inchoate offences and victimless crimes; and attempting a crime is itself a crime. The paradigm criminal sanctions (hard treatment and fines) are agent-focused. Victims also traditionally play little part in the criminal justice process. Relatively few crimes are prosecuted by victims; and when the state prosecutes victims are more or less passive observers.

Things are quite different in tort law. Tort litigation is initiated and conducted by victims. Tort remedies (even punitive damages) benefit victims. There are no inchoate or victimless torts, and attempting a tort is not itself a tort. Tort law is as much concerned with the interests of victims as with the conduct of tortfeasors. Tort law explicitly seeks to balance agent autonomy and victim security, while not ignoring wider social interests. Thus the legal definition of negligence refers to the interests of the victim (the harm done and its probability), the interests of the agent (the cost of precautions) and the wider interests of society (the value of the agent's activity).

Criminal law's focus on agency and on fairness to agents is partly a function of the greater degree of social stigma that typically attaches to criminal liability as opposed to civil liability, and of the severity of the archetypal criminal sanction: deprivation of personal liberty. By contrast, focusing on the interests of victims makes tortious intention appear unduly favourable to agents as a requirement of liability in many contexts. From this perspective we can better understand the dominance of negligence as a

---

77 I use the words 'agent' and 'conduct' to cover both acts and omissions.
78 Many philosophers start from the position that the meaning of responsibility is to be found in ideas of agency and free will.

basis of tort liability, and it is from this perspective that we should view the ancillary function of tortious intention: intentional conduct involves an assertion of one's autonomy which, if it produces harmful consequences, may justify more onerous liability than negligence, for instance. Taking account of victims helps to explain why negligence-based and strict criminal liability is more controversial than negligence-based and strict tort liability. Indeed, if one starts from the position that people should be criminally liable only for what they actually plan and choose to do, strict criminal liability is completely unjustifiable. By contrast, negligence-based and strict tort liability can be justified as a means of protecting the interests of victims. This may be one reason why, in tort law, recklessness often satisfies the requirement of intention: from the point of view of a harmed victim, the distinction between purpose and indifference may seem a fine and irrelevant one. Ironically, it may also account for the fact that recklessness in tort law is apparently confined to *conscious* indifference: as we saw earlier, proving a state of mind solely by interpreting behaviour gets very close to establishing liability by proving failure to comply with a standard of conduct. In other words, recklessness that does not involve *conscious* indifference is practically indistinguishable from negligence; and in tort law, where liability for negligence is uncontroversial, there is little reason to recognise a separate category of 'non-conscious' indifference. By contrast, since criminal law looks at matters predominantly from the agent's point of view, distinctions between purpose and indifference, and between conscious and 'unconscious' indifference loom much larger.

While focusing on the interests of victims helps to explain the ancillary function of intention and recklessness in tort law, focusing on the interests of society helps to explain its independent function. In some contexts (such as market competition and industrial disputes), the interests of harmed individuals must yield to wider social interests; and here, a requirement of intention or conscious recklessness helps to protect those social interests by protecting the autonomy interests of individual agents. When a harm-causing activity has high social value, a requirement of intention for tort liability helps to protect society's interest in the continuance of that activity. In an analogous way, judgments about the social value of activities play a part in the negligence calculus. From this perspective, we can also see why 'intention' in tort law might sometimes not include indifference but be limited to purpose: the greater society's interest in individual autonomy, the narrower the potential for incurring tort liability.

The concern of tort law with balancing victim security, agent autonomy and social value also helps to explain its approach to motives. Finnis's view, that a good motive cannot redeem wrongful conduct, and that a bad motive necessarily taints conduct which is not wrongful in itself, is based on an analysis which focuses on the agent and their 'moral standing' judged in terms of an austerely duty-based ethical system. The law takes a more pluralistic approach. Inducing breach of contract provides an excellent example. Contracts ought to be kept, and people's contractual rights respected. Inducing (or, as Weir would have it, 'seducing') a person not to keep their contract is wrong, prima facie at least. Merely promoting one's own financial interests is not a good reason to persuade another to breach a contract. But protecting one's own contractual rights, or promoting some public interest (such as the health and safety of workers, or protection of workers from sexual exploitation, or from racist practices) might be. Inducing a person to breach a contract may not be wrong if the contract is itself a vehicle of wrongdoing.

Ironically, while focusing on the interests of society can help explain why tort liability might be narrower than it would be if more weight were given to the interests of victims, focusing on the interests of society can help to explain why intention and recklessness are not the only bases of criminal liability, and why, in practice, intention plays a considerably lesser role in criminal law than its symbolic importance might suggest.[79] From a strongly agent-focused perspective, negligence-based and strict criminal liability are difficult, if not impossible, to explain. They would be easier to explain if the interests of victims were more central to criminal law than they have traditionally been. But, without introducing a focus on victims, we could understand negligence-based and strict criminal liability as designed to give society's interest in security and wellbeing greater protection than would be provided by a criminal law that only imposed liability for intention and recklessness. Even so, negligence-based and strict criminal liability remain more or less controversial. This suggests

---

79 Nicola Lacey, 'A Clear Concept of Intention: Elusive or Illusory' (1993) 56 *Modern Law Review* 621, 622; Andrew Ashworth and Meredith Blake, 'The Presumption of Innocence in English Criminal Law' [1996] *Criminal Law Review* 306. The interests of society also find a place in the stipulation that taking a foreseen risk is reckless only if the risk is 'unreasonable'.

that for some people the interests of society do not provide as good reasons for encroaching on the autonomy of agents as do the interests of victims. So long as the criminal law largely ignores victims, crimes that lack a mental element will probably remain controversial.

My argument, then, is that the relatively minor role of intention in tort law, as compared with criminal law (and philosophical analyses of 'moral' responsibility), can be explained by the fact that tort law is concerned with the interests of victims and of society to an extent that criminal law, and philosophical analyses of responsibility, are not. I would go further and suggest that criminal law and civil law (of which tort law is a part) reflect two different paradigms of, or approaches to, responsibility, one much more agent-focused than the other. These two different approaches in turn reflect a difference of functions. The dominant function of criminal law is the regulation of conduct by the imposition of penalties, whereas the dominant function of civil law is the prevention of rights violations and the repairing of harm by the award of remedies. Note my use of the word 'dominant': neither of these functions is necessarily exclusive to one area of the law or the other. There is no conceptual reason why reparation should not play a part in the criminal justice system, or why punishment should not play a role in civil law. My point is simply that the different functions reflect different paradigms of responsibility.

Conclusion

The concept of 'intention' is used loosely in tort law. Sometimes it appears as a synonym for 'voluntary'; sometimes it is described as a 'motive'; and it is often used to embrace recklessness. In this paper I have attempted to clarify the meaning and role of intention in tort law and the relationship between tortious intention and motive. I have argued that the minor practical and symbolic importance of tortious intention is a function of the fact that tort law is as much concerned with the interests of victims and of society as with those of agents. I have also argued that the normative pluralism of tort law makes the project of discovering or generating a general principle of liability for intention difficult and undesirable. These arguments support a broader thesis to the effect that the concept of 'responsibility' which underlies tort law in particular, and civil law in general, is 'relational' in the sense that it cannot be captured by focusing on the conduct of 'the responsible person' at the expense of the interests of the victim and of society more generally. Development of this broader thesis must await another occasion.

8 Tales of Intention: Storytelling and the Rhetoricity of Judgment

SANDRA BERNS

Introduction

Intention in the common law is a wondrous beast, at once illusory and monstrous. The distinction between intention as a formal device for assigning liability for particular consequences and intention as a mental state is critical. While Peter Cane suggests in his book *The Anatomy of Tort Law* that 'conduct is intentional if it is done with the intention (or "aim") of causing a particular consequence',[1] this misconceives the diverse roles intention plays in tort law. Although it is reasonably appropriate in the economic torts,[2] it is curiously inappropriate in trespass to the person, and bizarre in the action on the case for intentionally causing nervous shock. As Cane rightly notes,[3] however, intention neither is, nor purports to be, an interrogation of the mental state of the defendant. The defendant's mental state is unimportant, and malice and beneficence are equally irrelevant.[4] Particular acts in particular circumstances are legally assigned particular mental states, and these are characterised as 'intentions'.

---

1   Peter Cane, *The Anatomy of Tort Law* (1997) 32.
2   The High Court in *Northern Territory of Australia v Mengel* (1995) 129 ALR 1, 14 suggested that the 'economic torts' represented a 'template' for tort liability in the intentional torts.
3   Cane, above n 1, 32.
4   This is particularly true of those torts, such as trespass to the person, which are actionable per se.

This essay[5] explores two representative intentional torts: trespass to the person and the action on the case for intentionally causing nervous shock. I call these actions dignitary torts because they affirm the inviolability of the person. In dignitary torts, judicial understandings of intention become judicial stories of when the inviolability of the person must be affirmed and protected and when it may safely be disregarded. Intention is a fulcrum upon which conceptions of consent and dignity pivot and these torts have much to tell us, if only by indirection, about judicial understandings of human dignity and the characteristics of those whose dignity warrants protection. The dignatory torts also shed light on the role of intention in the common law and the ways in which readings of intention are grounded in particular contexts, and the genres and roles characteristic of those contexts.

Stories of gender and gendered expectations are fundamental to the way in which these stories are told and retold by judges. I do not mean that the gender of the parties plays a critical role, although it often surfaces in predictable ways. I am suggesting that certain legal stories are structurally 'male' in that they turn upon responses and reactions that are conventionally understood as masculine, while other legal stories are structurally 'female' or, still more ambiguously, 'other'. In masculine stories, stimulus and response are tightly linked, predictable, even fixed, in character. The genre is that of the thriller or action film. In 'female' stories, responses and reactions seem ambiguous, lacking in direct and obvious causal connection to the original act, and thus are more readily discounted or dismissed as an overreaction to a trivial incident. Here the genre is more closely aligned to the Victorian melodrama. When the stories before the court are difficult to reconcile with the genre exemplifying the cause of action, cognitive dissonance results, destabilising conceptions of intention, consent and dignity and setting the court adrift in uncharted territory.

---

5   It is part of a wider project seeking to develop a narrative theory of law suitable for a 'procedural republic'.

Figuring Intention in Trespass to the Person

In trespass, the nomenclature of intention is curious. Legally, it may exist where the act (or omission[6]) constituting the trespass is negligent or reckless or where all that can be made out is constructive intent. Thus intention is a matter of form, rather than substance. Its nature is more curious still. Because the act, rather than its consequences, must be intentional motive is irrelevant.[7] Motive emerges from the legal shadows only when aggravated or exemplary damages are sought. Intention thus becomes formal, coming only when summonsed by counsel. *Collins v Wilcock*[8] is an excellent example of the genre. The facts were these:

> On 22 July 1982 Woman Police Constable Wilcock and Police Sergeant Benjamin were on duty in a police vehicle and saw two women walking along the street, one of the two was a known prostitute, the other was the defendant. The officers observed the two women, both of whom appeared to them to be soliciting men in the street. The officers, without alighting from their vehicle, asked the two women to get into the police car so that they could have a word with them. One woman got into the car, the defendant refused to do so. The officers repeated their request to the defendant, who again refused and walked away, followed by the police car which then pulled up alongside her. She again walked away. The prosecutrix got out of the car and followed the defendant on foot, asking her why she didn't want to talk to the police and also for her name and address. The defendant again started to walk away. The prosecutrix told her that she had not finished talking to her and the defendant replied 'fuck off' and started to walk away yet again. The prosecutrix took hold of the defendant by the left arm to restrain her and the defendant shouted 'just fuck off copper' and scratched the prosecutrix's right forearm with her

---

6   Conceptually, the notion of an intentional omission is curious. One way of reading an intentional omission is in the sense of negligence or inadvertence, yet it is difficult to conceptualise these as intentional. Only where the omission is deliberate, in that the defendant omits a course of action that he or she would normally undertake and does so consciously and deliberately, does the nomenclature of intention seem obvious and appropriate.

7   While some cases suggest that the touching must be 'hostile', the 'hostility' required is as formal as intention. Hostility is not a state of mind pertaining to the defendant, but a contextual inference from the unlawfulness of the act. See *Wilson v Pringle* [1987] QB 237.

8   [1984] 1 WLR 1172.

finger nails. The defendant was then arrested for assaulting a police officer in the execution of her duty.[9]

Ms Collins countered the criminal charge of assaulting a police officer with an allegation of trespass. Legally, because she was not known to be a common prostitute, the police were, at most, entitled to caution her and to record her details. Because the attempted restraint by WPC Wilcock went beyond the 'generally acceptable conduct of touching a person to engage his or her attention', at common law it was a battery.

When the writ of trespass emerged as a discrete cause of action, hostility, described as the 'least touching in anger', was a kind of shorthand, a way of designating those unwanted and intentional touchings that seemed likely to lead to a violent response.[10] The structure of the typical trespass scenario was clear. Was the touching alleged of a kind likely to lead to a violent response? If so, the plaintiff had a good cause of action unless the touching could be shown to be lawful. 'Hostility' was determined from a particular perspective, the perspective of a hypothetical (male) victim subjected to unwanted physical contact.[11] If, from his perspective, the touching was likely to generate a violent response and was without lawful excuse, it was hostile. If it did not fall within these parameters, the action would fail either because the act was not 'hostile' or because the trespass was justified and therefore lawful. The scenario outlined above is archetypal. An attempted restraint, a clear desire to avoid physical contact, an angry and immediate response; these are the classical ingredients of trespass, ingredients that, I would argue, are securely located within masculine understandings of violence and reprisal.[12] The genre is

---

9   Ibid 1173.
10   Here it is well to remember that the original formulation, *trespass vi et armis contra pacem domini regis*, signified an intervention likely to lead to an affray or other serious breach of the 'King's Peace'.
11   A hypothetical female victim may respond very differently, as in the context of domestic violence, or refrain from responding out of fear, as in many cases of unwanted sexual attentions. The lingering 'pseudo-requirement' for hostility also explains why the common law has been tardy in allowing a remedy in trespass for unwanted sexual overtures. Sexual touchings are difficult to characterise as likely to lead to a violent response, at least directly, although they might well have led to a violent response by a kinsman of the victim.
12   That both protagonists are female does not alter the structural characteristics of the scenario. If we substitute an unwanted kiss or sexual overture, the only Anglo-Australian case of which I am aware is the unreported *Barker v Hobart City Council*

that of the action film or thriller, action replacing plot and character as the central motif.

The actual (and lawful) intention of WPC Wilcock, to caution Ms Collins in respect of soliciting for the purposes of prostitution, becomes irrelevant in this scenario.[13] The only relevant issue is whether the action of the police officer went beyond the 'generally acceptable means' of gaining Ms Collins' attention. Once the police officer's action was identified as unlawful, the alleged assault by Ms Collins became self-defence. Hostility was jettisoned, undoubtedly because it was rightly perceived to be superfluous in a context in which the key issue was an overreaching of authority.

Wilson v Pringle[14] reinstated hostility as the touchstone, insisting that the intentional touching must also be a 'hostile' touching. The facts involved another classically male scenario, a scuffle between schoolboys that got out of hand and resulted in injury. Here hostility, or its earlier formulation, touching in anger, seemingly had a role to play in differentiating schoolboy rough-housing from an actual fight, and thus delineating the parameters of an implied consent. Having reinstated hostility the court felt obliged to illuminate its character and universalise it.

> [T]he authorities lead one to the conclusion that in a battery there must be an intentional touching or contact in one form or another of the plaintiff by the defendant. That touching must be proved to be a hostile touching ... Hostility cannot be equated with ill-will or malevolence. It cannot be governed by the obvious intention shown in acts like punching, stabbing or shooting. It cannot be governed by an expressed intention, although that may be strong evidence ... It may be imported from the circumstances. Take the police officer in *Collins v Wilcock* ... She touched the woman deliberately, but without an

---

(unreported, Supreme Court of Tasmania, Slicer J, 6 May 1993). See Sandra Berns, 'The Hobart City Council Case: A Tort of Sexual Harassment for Tasmania?' (1994) 13 *University of Tasmania Law Review* 112. In that case, persistent and unwanted sexual overtures, including attempted sexual assault, were held to be actionable in trespass.

13 The relevant legislation provided that where a person, who was not known to be a common prostitute, was suspected of soliciting for the purposes of prostitution, that person was to be asked to provide their name and address and was to be cautioned in respect of soliciting.

14 [1987] QB 237, 253.

intention to do more than restrain her temporarily. Nevertheless she was acting unlawfully and *in that way was acting with hostility.*[15]

This clarification raises more questions than it answers. Hostility, often thought of as a mental state, becomes a surrogate for unlawfulness, an unlawful act being hostile. The mental element is detached from the defendant. We are told at length what hostility is not. It is not ill will. It is neither the motive behind an obviously violent act nor the expressed intention of the defendant. Instead, it is contextually determined. Within the frame of reference of an attempted caution for the purposes of soliciting, the unlawfulness of the restraint attains primacy. Within the frame of reference of a schoolboy scuffle, the question becomes whether the alleged contact went beyond the normal limits of schoolboy rough-housing and was thus without consent and unlawful. Once again, despite possible factual ambiguities, the paradigm is clear, involving both intention and whether the alleged contact went beyond that consented to. The limits of the consent involved in a schoolboy scuffle effectively determine the legality or otherwise of the contact. The gendered frame of reference remains intact, and, unsurprisingly, the underlying notion of human dignity is intimately bound to traditional liberal ideas of the security of the person. We might term it Hobbesian in character.

Consent affords further mysteries. As one explores the kinds of touchings to which consent is possible and the kinds to which it is not, its interaction with intention becomes fascinating. As a general rule, one cannot consent to serious bodily harm, whether in trespass or in the parallel criminal actions at common law. This position was recently reaffirmed in *R v Brown*,[16] a curious case (with an even more curious judgment[17]) involving sadomasochistic practices among consenting adults. Confronted by videotapes of a variety of consensual practices involving bondage the court saw no difficulty in holding that the consents were invalid, one not being entitled to consent to serious bodily harm despite the lack of evidence of any actual harm.[18] Yet, where, as in *Hegarty v Shine*,[19] the act is not of

---

15   Ibid (emphasis added).

16   [1993] 2 All ER 75.

17   It is tempting to describe the account of the practices contained in the recital of the facts as salacious.

18   In most bondage scenarios, the 'harms' inflicted by the 'top' are relatively minor, roughly comparable to those in a schoolboy scuffle and far less hazardous than those normally inflicted in a boxing match.

19   (1878) 14 Cox CC 145.

itself harmful, consent is given. Despite the plaintiff's assertion that she would not have consented had she been aware that the defendant suffered from a venereal disease, the court was preoccupied with the immorality of the plaintiff. The immorality of the defendant escaped the notice of the court. Despite the acute inequality of the parties (the case involved a master and his youthful servant), the plaintiff's status as a fallen woman dominated the judgments and disentitled her to relief.[20] Here, consent is as formal as intention. If one consents to the act, one has, in effect, consented to all of its consequences even if one is unaware of the possibility of a particular consequence at the time of consent. It does not even matter that one of the consequences is something that would ordinarily render the consent invalid, serious bodily harm.

The language of the case is redolent of the origins of trespass, the writ averring that the 'defendant assaulted and beat the plaintiff, whereby she became infected'. Counsel argued that her consent was obtained by fraud, the defendant having failed to inform her of his condition. This argument was dismissed out of hand. In the absence of a binding contract the defendant was under no legal obligation to inform her of his condition. The oscillation between tort and contract is remarkable, given the very different role of consent in contract and tort.[21] Once consent becomes a matter for contract rather than tort, the court washes its hands of the matter on the ground of immorality. After all, a contract to perform an immoral act is *contra bones mores*, and unenforceable. In tort, however, it seemingly remains possible to argue that any consent she might have given would have been invalidated by the defendant's undisclosed condition, no person being able to consent to serious bodily harm.[22] In *R v Clarence*,[23] on strikingly similar facts, the court lacked the convenient escape of immorality, the plaintiff being a respectable married woman. Here, the matter was complicated by marital privilege, the fact of the marriage

---

20 See the extended discussion of *Hegarty v Shine* and similar cases in Sandra Berns, *To Speak as a Judge: Difference, Voice and Power* (1999) 113 ff.

21 Conventionally, in contract consent is 'enabling'. Without consent, the contract cannot come into existence. In tort, however, consent operates as a defence, rendering lawful what would otherwise be unlawful.

22 This position was forcefully restated in *R v Brown* [1993] 2 All ER 75; however *Bain v Altoft* [1967] Qd R 32 suggested the position might be otherwise where the plaintiff was involved in a scuffle which he instigated.

23 (1888) 22 QBD 23 (CA).

providing evidence of consent, although the majority acknowledged that had her husband disclosed his condition she would have been entitled to reject his advances on medical grounds. Stephen J insisted:

> In this case there was no intention, and therefore no attempt to infect, and it seems anomalous to make a consequence which, though highly probable, was neither intended nor necessary, relate back on its occurrence in such a way as to turn an act not punishable in itself into a crime.[24]

Here, intention itself is transformed. Perhaps because the action was criminal rather than civil, a wife being unable to sue her husband in tort, intention was detached from the act and attached to its consequences. Effectively, the defendant intended to have sexual relations, not to infect his wife with a venereal disease, which was at that time an incurable condition. Since consent to sexual relations was given for all time by marriage, the only question was the content of the relevant intention and, according to the court, that intention was lawful. Had he intended to infect his wife, the act would, of course, have been criminal. The same argument was put in *R v Brown*,[25] that is, that the defendants intended to engage in fantasy practices for sexual gratification, not to cause serious bodily harm. Here the argument failed. The consent was unlawful despite the absence of evidence that serious bodily harm eventuated. Wherein lies the difference? In *Brown*,[26] it is plausible to argue that no dignitary harm was involved apart from that inflicted by the court. In *Clarence*, as in *Hegarty v Shine*,[27] the dignitary harm involved was far closer to that in case than to the masculinised conventions of trespass and criminal assault. While the harm was direct, rather than indirect, the defendant's culpability lay precisely in his refusal to treat his victim as an end in herself,[28] rather than a means to his own gratification, a fact noted by Hawkins J in dissent:

---

24   Ibid 45.
25   [1993] 2 All ER 75.
26   Ibid.
27   (1878) 14 Cox CC 145.
28   Kant understood marriage as a contract for the use of the parties' sexual organs. Marriage, however, avoided the force of the Kantian dictum by the fact that the use was mutual. If the proviso were to be read legally perhaps one might argue that the service provided was unfit for its purpose! The gloss supplied by Hawkins J in dissent comes close to capturing the spirit of the Kantian dictum.

Rape consists in a man having sexual intercourse with a woman without her consent, and the marital privilege being equivalent to consent given once for all at the time of marriage, it follows that the *mere act of sexual communion is lawful*; but there is a wide difference between a simple act of communion which *is lawful*, and an act of communion *combined with infectious contagion* endangering health and causing harm, which *is unlawful* ... If a person having a privilege of which he may avail himself or not at his will or pleasure, cannot exercise it without at the same time doing something not included in this privilege and which is unlawful and dangerous to another, he must either forego his privilege or take the consequences of his unlawful conduct.[29]

In such cases the genre is very different. The action thriller is replaced with *film noir*, the straightforward conventions of the thriller replaced by ambiguous relationships and even more ambiguous harms. The relationship between plot and character becomes tangled. The distasteful, but simultaneously alluring, practices associated with bondage, the fallen woman beloved of Victorian literature and the wronged and virtuous wife coalesce in a rich thematic brew. The straightforward resolutions typical of the action thriller give way to ambiguous endings and moralising by the court. One constant emerges. To be other is to be one whose dignity is fundamentally irrelevant, beneath the notice of others and of the court.

Other tales of touching and of consent, and its absence, also suggest ambiguous readings, and a clear grounding in respect for human dignity and the inviolability of the person. *Re F (Mental Patient: Sterilisation)*[30] reiterated the general principle that any touching is, in the absence of lawful excuse, a battery and a trespass. Whilst Lord Goff, too, emphasised the unlawfulness, unlawfulness was not a surrogate for hostility but the touchstone for distinguishing between touchings that are a normal part of everyday life and those that transcend those limits. Intention vanishes and the spotlight shifts to consent, emphasising the dignitary role of the tort. The inviolability of the person occupies centre stage. According to Lord Goff:

In the old days it used to be said that for a touching of another's person to amount to a battery, it had to be a touching 'in anger'; and it has recently been said that the touching must be 'hostile' to have that effect. I respectfully doubt whether that is correct. A prank that gets out of hand; an over-friendly slap on

---

29   *R v Clarence* (1888) 22 QBD 23, 54–5.
30   [1990] 2 AC 1, 72–3 (HL).

the back; surgical treatment by a surgeon who mistakenly thinks that the patient has consented to it—all these things may transcend the bounds of lawfulness, without being characterised as hostile. Indeed, the suggested qualification is difficult to reconcile with the principle that any touching of another's body is, in the absence of lawful excuse, capable of amounting to a battery and a trespass.[31]

Yet these stories, whether of intention, or hostility, or, more magically and elusively still, of normal touchings and everyday life, are strange. They are formal, disconnected from what you and I might think of as ordinary life, and imposed after the fact. They have nothing to do with the parties and their states of mind. Those present would, undoubtedly, have described the events very differently. They are law stories; stories that ring true within the procedural republic that is law, but are utterly disconnected from the life-worlds of the parties. While intention is, formally, one of the ingredients of trespass, it is almost never at issue because of law's understanding of what it means, in this context, to intend. Intention is not a mental state but a device for locating the onus of proof. Once the plaintiff has established the act complained of, the onus moves to the defendant to excuse the conduct if possible. Only in exceptional circumstances, for example where the defendant avers that the act was committed while sleepwalking or in a state of automatism, does intention move from the shadows into the foreground.[32] While the rhetoric of intention figures in legal analysis, in reality intention is irrelevant, simply a formula used while announcing a pre-ordained outcome.

The Action on the Case for Intentionally Causing Nervous Shock

If intention in trespass is typically formal and procedural, in the action on the case, the disjunction between intention-in-fact and intention-in-law is still more marked. The action originated late in the last century in *Wilkinson v Downton*.[33] The reported judgment tells us that the plaintiff

---

31   Ibid 73.
32   See *Morris v Marsden* [1952] 1 All ER 925, 925.
33   [1897] 2 QB 57. The case is a descendant of the slightly earlier *Bird v Holbrook* (1828) 4 Bing 628, differing principally in that the mechanism by which the injury was caused was 'mere words' rather than a spring gun loaded to go off when tripped by an intruder.

was a married woman in apparent good health. The defendant came to her home, and, as a practical joke, told her that her husband had been seriously injured in an accident and that she must go at once to fetch him home. She did so and, subsequently, suffered a psychiatric illness followed by lasting physical illness. The common law had, in the somewhat earlier *Victoria Railways Commissioners v Coultas*,[34] signalled its unwillingness to allow recovery for nervous shock in the nascent tort of negligence. Here, because of the interpolation of a physical injury and the intentional quality of the act, recovery was allowed. Still more bizarre was the cause of the injury, mere words, spoken as a practical joke. Undeniably, in *Wilkinson v Downton*, as in the somewhat later case of *Janiver v Sweeney*,[35] the required intention went simply to the utterance and not to its consequences, despite the apparent legal requirement for an act intended to cause harm to the plaintiff. Once the words and the attendant injury were made out, liability followed. The actual intention of the defendant, to play a sick practical joke at the plaintiff's expense, was irrelevant. In *Wilkinson v Downton*, as in trespass, intention is formal.[36]

The change of genre is fascinating. The classically male paradigm of trespass has vanished with its hallmarks of physical contact, a clear desire to avoid it, and an angry and immediate response. In its place, a very different genre emerges: the respectable woman firmly located within the security of her home, a bizarre and apparently pointless practical joke, and a serious physical illness. The facts are sharply distinguished from those in *Victoria Railways Commissioner v Coultas*[37] by the fact that here the plaintiff had not ventured beyond the security of her home until she was forced to do so by the defendant's practical joke. If the dominant motif in trespass was the action thriller, in case it is melodrama. Plot and character dominate; action is both stylised and minimal. In keeping with the change in genre, the wrong is 'Kantian' rather than 'Hobbesian'. The defendant embarks upon a course of conduct in which self-gratification is the central motif, the victim being nothing more than a means to its realisation. The

---

34   (1888) 13 App Cas 222.

35   [1919] 2 KB 316. In *Janiver v Sweeney*, the defendant told the plaintiff lady's maid that she was being watched by the secret service, hoping thereby to frighten her into betraying her mistress's trust and providing him with a letter.

36   While Wright J used the term 'calculated' the import of this is unclear. It could mean intended or likely. In any case, His Honour was clearly prepared to impute the relevant intention to the defendant. See *Wilkinson v Downton* [1897] 2 QB 57, 59.

37   (1888) 13 App Cas 222.

dignitary aspect shifts from the physical inviolability of the person to the right of the person to be treated as an end in herself, rather than simply as a means to the ends of another.

The leading Australian case, *Bunyan v Jordan*,[38] comes close to exemplifying the genre, although its disturbing twists of character and locale simultaneously destabilise it and signal a further shift. The defendant merchant, while inebriated, embarked upon a complex and theatrical charade shortly before closing. He brandished a bottle of poison, threatened to kill himself and retreated, loaded revolver in hand. Shots were heard and he then reappeared, only to rip the evening's takings in half and to remark that he would not be there to mend them in the morning. While the reason for his performance was obscure, the facts suggest that he may have wished to frighten his sons who also worked in his business. The Kantian flavour is unmistakable. Almost all of the ingredients of classical melodrama are present although some disturbing transpositions presage the tangles created by the High Court. An independent young working woman replaces the delicate maiden or virtuous wife, destabilising conventions at the core of melodrama. More disturbing still, the home, symbol of virtue, purity and delicacy, becomes a sub-text, replaced by the rough and tumble of commerce.

The court was divided as to the intention required, ostensibly because the performance was not directed at the plaintiff, although she witnessed the entire melodrama either directly or through a window. Three readings of intention were offered, only one of which fell within the prior conventions of the action on the case. According to Rich J:

> It would be unkind, perhaps, to assume that both her claim and her condition were more readily attributable to the loss of her employment. But whatever may have produced her nervous breakdown, I am unable to take the view that a reasonable person might antecedently expect that it would ensue from the emotions however creditable to the human heart which would be excited by the spectacle of an alcoholic storekeeper, pretending however realistically, that he was taking his own life. In fact there appears to have been but little realism. But perhaps a female clerk could not be expected to discover the incongruities of the respondent's behaviour and to discredit the theatrical threats of a man who produced first poison and then a revolver and after the

---

38   (1937) 57 CLR 1.

fullest advertisement of his suicidal purposes retreated with the revolver to the public thoroughfare.[39]

Acknowledging the genre, and its incongruity in the commercial setting before the court, Rich J introduces that wondrous character, the reasonable person, abruptly shifting the genre from melodrama to slapstick. He assures us that no reasonable person could possibly attribute the plaintiff's illness to the theatrical threats of an alcoholic shopkeeper, while conceding that a 'female clerk' might be misled. Intention and the antecedent expectations of a hypothetical reasonable person fuse, blurring the line between case and negligence and acknowledging the increasing hegemony of the latter. Once the reasonable person replaces the villain of melodrama, the focus shifts from intention to causation. The question becomes not whether the defendant acted intentionally but whether a reasonable person in the position of the defendant would expect illness on the part of the plaintiff to follow the constellation of acts alleged.

Yet this is puzzling, even bizarre. A reasonable person would be singularly unlikely to produce poison and a revolver and threaten suicide. A reasonable person would also be unlikely to indulge in practical jokes of the type alleged in *Wilkinson v Downton* or unlawful threats of the type in *Janiver v Sweeney*. To the extent that the reasonable person is a useful construct in the tort of negligence, the construct is useful precisely because the act that causes harm or loss is not deliberate or wilful, but inadvertent. It is for this reason, and this reason only, that it becomes useful to examine the act from the perspective of a reasonable person rather than that of the defendant.

Odder still is the implied contrast between the sophistication and resilience built into the antecedent expectations of a hypothetical reasonable person regarding the impact of such a charade on his audience and the categorisation of the plaintiff as a 'female clerk'. A female clerk, according to Rich J, was likely to lack both the experience and the acumen to recognise the defendant's charade for what it was, but this, of course, was no fault of the defendant. The judgment implies that the defendant is entitled to calculate the impact of his charade by reference to its effect upon an ordinary (male) person with sufficient experience to recognise the charade for what it was, a bit of drunken theatrics.

---

39   Ibid 15.

In case, as in trespass and the intentional torts generally, intention typically attends the act rather than its consequences. Why has this test been abandoned? After all, the defendant did intend his acts. They were carefully staged, the appropriate props obtained in advance. However disordered his mind, he did not act as an automaton or while sleepwalking. The performance was clearly directed at his audience and one presumes he sought gratification from its reaction. If, in the action on the case, it is the 'negligence test' which prevails, on the same test, the plaintiff in *Wilkinson v Downton* should also have failed. In the ordinary course of events, practical jokes are attended at most by minor consequences. The shift in genre provides the key. Once the female world of the melodrama, with its domestic setting and fragile heroine, is replaced by the masculine world of slapstick, with its public setting and farcical overtones, the plaintiff becomes a figure of fun, epitomised by the dumb blonde, rather than a woman who has been wronged.

The matter is clouded further in the judgment of Dixon J. Like Rich J, Dixon J links the required intention not to the act, but to its consequences. Here intention is elaborated, not as a legal construct for assigning liability, but as an ordinary language mechanism for connecting act and consequences. The question becomes, not whether the defendant intended the performance, but whether he intended the precise harm suffered by the plaintiff, a reading that makes a mockery of the Kantian underpinnings of the case.[40] The reasonable person is elaborated, becomes a person of ordinary nerves and normal sensibilities. The question becomes not what consequences a reasonable person in the position of the defendant might ascribe to his acts as in the tort of negligence, but what effect those acts would have on a 'person of ordinary nerves and normal sensibilities'[41] in the position of the plaintiff.

> If, however, the defendant did not intend the physical harm, but only a mild fright or mild nervous shock which would work no further harm in a person of ordinary nerves and normal sensibilities, the accepted rule seems to be that there should be no recovery ... It is, of course, quite clear that the defendant did not intend to bring upon the plaintiff a nervous breakdown or any physical harm. He may have intended to frighten those surrounding him, but, if so, it was only for the purpose of sensationalism. The shock he intended to give or

---

40   That such readings are usual in the economic torts underscores the shift in genre.
41   In short, a man!

the emotions he intended to arouse could not in a normal person be more than transient.[42]

Yet, as I read the earlier cases, what the defendant actually intended is irrelevant. In one, the intent was to observe the effect of a distasteful practical joke; while in the other the intent was to frighten a lady's maid into betraying her mistress's trust. While these intentions are unsavoury, it is untenable to suggest that actual harm was intended in either case. As in *Bunyan v Jordan*, the actual intention was very different, to realise the defendant's goals through the responses of others to the performance.

The literalist reading of the connection between act and consequences suggests that Dixon J was working within the conceptual structure of *Bird v Holbrook*[43] rather than that of *Wilkinson v Downton*, underlying the shift from melodrama to slapstick. If one sets a spring gun, one can quite reasonably be thought to intend to cause actual physical harm to any person sufficiently unfortunate to trip the wire. Legal intention and ordinary language intention fuse. The thematic structure in *Bunyan v Jordan* is very different, the defendant's intention being wholly self-regarding.

Only Evatt J, in dissent, banished both actual intention and the ordinary man:

> Where a person, whether for malicious motives or those of self-display, wilfully alarms or terrifies another by the unlawful act of threatening to commit suicide, and that condition of alarm or terror causes physical illness, an action lies; and it is no answer to such an action for the defendant to set up either (a) that he was threatening to kill or injure himself, and no other person, or (b) that the plaintiff did not apprehend physical danger to himself, or (c) that many persons, or even that especially formidable person 'the ordinary, normal human being' would not be alarmed or terrified, or have suffered illness as a result of the defendant's action.[44]

For Evatt J, clearly, formal intention sufficed. The defendant clearly intended (albeit through an alcoholic haze) the words and the actions that terrified the plaintiff and caused her illness. Given that was the case, it did not lie in the mouth of the defendant to suggest he intended something

---

42   *Bunyan v Jordan* (1937) 57 CLR 1, 7.
43   (1828) 4 Bing 628.
44   *Bunyan v Jordan* (1937) 57 CLR 1, 17–18.

else! In any case, what the defendant actually intended is, within the traditional scope of the action, irrelevant. In words that were powerfully evocative of trespass, Evatt J focused on intention and unlawfulness.[45] Even the fact that the words and actions of the defendant were not directed at the plaintiff was summarily dismissed as irrelevant. She was within earshot and that was sufficient. The reasonable person was banished to negligence from whence he came. Despite the evocation of trespass, the genre, for Evatt, remains melodrama. The focus becomes the performance of its central motif, the villain. Nothing further is required.

While *Wilkinson v Downton* is infrequently litigated in Commonwealth jurisdictions,[46] it has recently been mooted in the United Kingdom[47] and perhaps in Queensland.[48] The Queensland case, *Midwest Radio Ltd v Arnold*,[49] is interesting, not least because whether the matter is case or negligence is fundamentally ambiguous. While both *Wilkinson v Downton* and *Bunyan v Jordan* were cited with particular reference to the intentional conduct of the defendant's servant, suggesting case, *Jaensch v Coffey*[50] was also cited, and the cause of action framed within breach of an employer's duty of care, suggesting negligence.[51] The facts are set out in the joint judgment of MacPherson JA and Williams J:

---

45 David Gardner and Frances McGlone, *Outline of Torts* (2nd ed, 1998) suggest that in the UK *Bird v Holbrook* and *Wilkinson v Downton* have been assimilated into trespass, the directness rule having been abolished. In Australia, the directness rule remains firmly in place.

46 By contrast, in the United States it has been expanded into a tort of insult and outrage.

47 *Khorasandjian v Bush* [1993] QB 727 is particularly interesting, despite the fact that it was recently overruled by the House of Lords in *Hunter v Canary Wharf Ltd* [1997] AC 655. In *Khorasandjian*, the Court of Appeal suggested that, even though actual harm had not eventuated, the fact that the defendant had embarked upon a course of action likely to cause harm to an ordinary young woman in the position of the plaintiff was sufficient.

48 *Midwest Radio Ltd v Arnold* [1999] QCA 20 (unreported, Queensland Court of Appeal, 12 February 1999) <http://www.austlii.edu.au/do/disp.pl/au/cases/qld/QCA/1999/20.html> at 19 June 1998.

49 Ibid.

50 (1984) 155 CLR 549. In *Jaensch v Coffey* Deane J, at 611, treated both *Wilkinson v Downton* and *Bunyan v Jordan* as essentially special cases within overall negligence liability for nervous shock. Other members of the High Court did not comment on this point. Cf *Wodrow v Commonwealth* (1991) 105 FLR 278 where they were clearly recognised as separate causes of action.

51 The cause of action was variously described as breach of an employer's duty of care or breach of the *Workplace Health and Safety Act 1989* (Qld) s 9. Despite this, the facts suggest that this is surely a case where *Wilkinson v Downton* would have been a viable

In late August 1991, the plaintiff was re-appointed to the staff of the newspaper, this time as sales manager and features co-ordinator. She continued to be so employed until 6 December 1991, when she left the defendant's employment because of the condition she was in. Since that date, she has not worked again. Dr Green, a specialist psychiatrist, to whom the plaintiff was referred in January 1992, and whose evidence at the trial was accepted by his Honour, diagnosed her as suffering from a major depressive disorder or illness. It was Dr Green's opinion 'that it was the situation she found herself in when working in the office of the Independent Newspaper that was the major factor in precipitating the psychiatric disorder'.

The 'situation she found herself in' was the state of affairs that prevailed in the office of the defendant's newspaper in Townsville under the management of Mr Geoff Williams ... Stated generally, the plaintiff's complaint ... was that ... Williams 'engaged in conduct ... towards the plaintiff and others on a fairly frequent basis ... that could properly be described as aggressive, bullying, abusive, belittling and sarcastic', and which was 'often expressed in or accompanied by foul language'. Elsewhere his Honour remarked that the plaintiff's claim was primarily based upon Williams' conduct towards her, while she also claimed to have been adversely affected by his conduct towards other members of the staff as well. As to that, his Honour said that 'in a case like this, where the evidence establishes a course of conduct generally towards her and other members of the staff ... she is entitled to rely upon such incidents, even though they were not directed against her personally'. He added that if he was wrong about this, the plaintiff was still entitled to succeed because the conduct of Williams towards her, particularly at the regular weekly staff meetings, 'must be regarded as a substantive cause of her psychiatric condition'.[52]

A majority in the Court of Appeal rejected the approach adopted by the trial judge and the medical evidence and also rejected expert evidence that the workplace atmosphere was capable of causing psychiatric disturbance in ordinary people, saying:

Unforgivable as the conduct of Williams towards his staff is clearly shown to have been, it continued for only about three months at most, during which the plaintiff was one, but not the only one, of the principal targets of his

---

alternative, and arguably stronger than an action for breach of an employer's duty of care.

52   *Midwest Radio Ltd v Arnold* [1999] QCA 20 (Unreported, Queensland Court of Appeal, 12 February 1999) [4–5].

misanthropic attitude. Perhaps all of the other 10 or so employees were individuals of more than ordinary resilience; if not, it is not easy to understand why none of them appear to have complained of psychiatric disorders of the kind and extent predicated by Dr Green of average persons of normal fortitude placed in the same circumstances.[53]

Intention plays, at most, a subordinate role in the text. While the majority accepted without demur that the 'misanthropic attitude' of Williams towards his staff was wholly unforgivable, the focus lay elsewhere, and that elsewhere was causation. In contrast to *Bunyan v Jordan*,[54] in which intention was discussed obliquely in the majority judgments and dominated the dissent, here the only references are to William's 'misanthropic attitude' and to 'an overall course of conduct of an abusive and derogatory nature which was unremitting'. Unlike the earlier cases in Australia and elsewhere, where the incident or incidents relied upon were isolated one-off incidents, here the behaviour pattern was clearly deeply entrenched and ongoing. The pattern of conduct alleged is far closer to the typical factual scenario in the American tort of insult and outrage[55] than that in existing Australian case law.[56]

In *Midwest Radio v Arnold* the reading given to *Wilkinson v Downton* is almost perversely narrow. Faced with a deliberate and admittedly unacceptable course of conduct that persisted over more than three months,[57] the Court of Appeal was more concerned with the predisposition of the plaintiff to emotional injury than with intentional quality of the conduct. The case became one of negligence yet, even on a broad reading

---

53   Ibid [31].
54   (1937) 57 CLR 1.
55   In the United States, *Wilkinson v Downton* evolved into a general action for intentionally causing emotional distress. The action has been used in cases of racial abuse and name calling and appears frequently in the context of employer–employee relations. See *Alcorn v Ambrose Engineers Inc* 468 P2d 216, 218 (1970); *Molien v Kaiser Foundation Hospitals* 616 P2d 813 (1980); *State Rubbish Association v Siliznoff* 240 P2d 282, 285 (1952). The American (Second) Restatement provides that 'one who by extreme and outrageous conduct intentionally or recklessly causes severe emotional distress to another is subject to liability for such emotional distress, and if bodily harm results from it, for such bodily harm'.
56   The *Midwest Radio* scenario is a classical example of workplace bullying or harassment involving an abuse of power by a senior member of staff.
57   Arguably, the course of conduct was unlawful under the terms of the *Workplace Health and Safety Act 1989* (Qld) s 9.

of contemporary negligence cases,[58] the finding seems out of step. In *Jaensch v Coffey*,[59] faced with an acknowledged predisposition to emotional illness, the High Court was prepared to find that some form of psychiatric illness was foreseeable, even though that suffered by the plaintiff was extreme. Similarly, in *Mt Isa Mines v Pusey*[60] there was no evidence that any others who may have witnessed the event or its aftermath were affected; yet this went unremarked.[61] Why, then, in *Midwest Radio*, did the majority judgment place more weight on the failure of the plaintiff's co-workers to report symptoms of psychiatric illness than on the defendant's conduct? Like the cause of action, the genre is uncertain. If *Bunyan v Jordan* oscillated uneasily between melodrama and slapstick, *Midwest Radio* opts for farce, a reading underscored by the emphasis on whether the plaintiff's workmates were similarly affected. Within that genre, the fate of the plaintiff is unimportant. Attention focuses upon the defendant's conduct (simultaneously 'unforgivable' and legally irrelevant), and on the absence of symptoms among her co-workers.

Concluding Thoughts: Intention, Dignity and Consent

Midwest Radio represents yet another missed opportunity. Confronted by facts that represented a clear invitation to follow the US lead and allow further development within the framework of *Wilkinson v Downton*, the safe harbour of negligence was preferred over the chancier, but more appropriate, action on the case. The court's ambivalence remains interesting and suggestive, given that leading cases on the action on the case are treated as appropriate authorities within the overall framework of negligence. Clearly, the courts remain ill at ease in dealing with facts that fall outside the classical masculine paradigm of unwanted physical contact, an absence of consent, and an immediate and violent response. A Hobbesian reading of dignity prevails over a Kantian reading, a masculinised scenario over a feminised narrative. Where the act is

---

58 Eg *Jaensch v Coffey* (1984) 155 CLR 549 and *Mt Isa Mines Ltd v Pusey* (1970) 123 CLR 383.
59 Ibid.
60 (1970) 123 CLR 383.
61 Of course, given that the plaintiff in *Mt Isa Mines* was a rescuer, it may be that a different standard was adopted by the court.

unambiguously physically invasive and the response is immediate, negating actual or implied consent, the violation is unmistakable. Where psychic manipulation and invasion predominate, and no realistic physical response is available, the affront to dignity is trivialised and the victim's response becomes an overreaction, suggestive of hysteria. Here, too, the setting of the invasion becomes critical. Where the plaintiff remains securely within the private realm and the defendant has entered that realm, the reading of intention becomes formal, act-bound. Where the plaintiff has entered the world of commerce, the reading of intention focuses upon whether the defendant intended the consequences that ensued, rather than upon the intentional quality of the act. The parallels with readings of intention in the economic torts, a paradigmatically masculine domain, are unmistakable.

What have we learned about intention? First, and critically, intention is invoked (when it is) as a filter, a way of isolating those wrongs that are, for whatever reason, compensable, from those that are not. Whether the reading is, as in *Collins v Wilcock*,[62] *Wilkinson v Downton*,[63] *Janiver v Sweeney*[64] and *R v Clarence*,[65] purely formal, or whether, as in *Bunyan v Jordan*,[66] it is open-ended and fluid, depends upon whether the court is disposed to grant the remedy sought. To read intention otherwise is to ignore the stories the judges tell about what it means to intend. Intention becomes in that way a rhetorical justification for a decision made on other grounds. As reasonable persons slide in and out of argument in the action on the case, the artificiality of that construct and its role in obliterating the intentional quality of the conduct is transparent. If we look for parallels we find them, not as devices for assigning liability, but as defences, as in the defence of provocation. There the question is not whether a reasonable person in the position of the defendant would have anticipated particular outcomes, but whether a reasonable person with some of the defendant's characteristics would have reacted as did the defendant to the alleged provocation.

Clearly, intention has many guises. The formal intention of trespass to the person, where the only requirements are that the mind directs the act

---

62   [1984] 1 WLR 1172.
63   [1897] 2 QB 57.
64   [1919] 2 KB 316.
65   (1888) 22 QBD 23.
66   (1937) 57 CLR 1.

and that the act is unlawful, shifts the onus of proof to the defendant. Once the plaintiff has made out the act alleged to constitute a trespass, it remains for the defendant to justify or excuse the alleged trespass, for example by establishing that it was utterly without fault or that the plaintiff consented. Within the trespass paradigm, there is nothing more for intention to do, indeed, nothing more that it could possibly do. The absence of any requirement for harm or loss and the historical origins of trespass as an alternative to self-help remedies and violent reprisals circumscribe its role.

While intention figures prominently in trespass, it does so, not as a mechanism for linking a voluntary act to a set of concrete consequences, but as an affirmation of the importance of the inviolability of personal security from wrongful invasion. As figures of hostility surface, albeit ambiguously, only to be again banished, it is clear that the origins of trespass scar law's understandings of wrongfulness. Trespass is most at home where the act is unambiguously wrongful. It is only recently, and with the greatest reluctance, that trespass has been available for unwanted and unsolicited sexual attentions[67] and in cases of domestic violence. Here, the dignitary interests involved have only been recently acknowledged, and reluctantly at best.

When we move from trespass to the second of the dignitary torts we have examined, the action on the case for intentionally causing nervous shock, intention undergoes a profound transformation. Although the name by which the action is conventionally known suggests that intention has ceased to be formal and act-directed and is focused instead upon whether the consequences are intended, this is not unambiguously the case. In the early cases, the courts consistently adopted the position that to intend the act[68] was, in effect, to intend its consequences. Thus, a practical joke told to amuse the defendant at the plaintiff's expense becomes an act intended to cause nervous shock.

---

67   *Barker v Hobart City Council* (Unreported, Supreme Court of Tasmania, Slicer J, 6 May 1993).

68   Here, of course, matters were complicated because the 'act' I have disingenuously referred to was in fact wholly or partly a speech act. Given the infinitely varied character of speech acts, ranging from the practical joke of *Wilkinson v Downton* to the veiled threat of *Janiver v Sweeney* to complex charade, partly verbal and partly visual, in *Bunyan v Jordan*, and their equally varied consequences, the formality of our understanding of act is critical.

182 Intention in Law and Philosophy

Why then, in *Bunyan v Jordan*,[69] was intention subsumed into an inquiry indistinguishable from that in negligence cases? Reviewing the case law, I am drawn to the conclusion that the setting and the genres associated with the setting are critical. Where the plaintiff remains securely enclosed within the private sphere, the conventions of melodrama prevail. Where the plaintiff has abandoned the private sphere for the rough and tumble of commerce, other conventions prevail, those associated with the economic torts.

Once intention was linked to consequences, a further step was inevitable. The question then became whether a reasonable person in the position of the defendant would have foreseen that the consequences alleged might flow from that act. Here, too we find intense concern with the normality of the plaintiff rather than attention to the intentional and unjustified behaviour of the defendant. While it may be that the determining factor in the majority approach was the fact that the defendant's charade was not directed at the plaintiff, earlier decisions in both Canada[70] and New Zealand[71] suggested this was not an absolute requirement. The double indirection, however, may have been instrumental in the tacit decision of the majority to treat the matter as negligence rather than as case. Confronted with a situation in which not only was the harm indirect in that it flowed from largely verbal charade but also it was indirect in that it was not specifically aimed at the plaintiff, the negligence rule seemed a safe haven. The intentional quality of the defendant's conduct became immaterial.

In the dissent of Evatt J, the approach taken was very different. By emphasising the intentional quality of the defendant's conduct and its unlawful character, he subtly moved the action closer to trespass than to case. Having done so, he encountered no difficulty in dealing with intention formally and suggesting that it was not for the defendant to excuse himself by suggesting that he did not 'intend' to harm the plaintiff. I find it regrettable that Australian courts have not yet taken up the clear invitation implicit in Evatt J's dissent. His reasoning could, with only a little refinement, provide the foundation for something very similar to the US action for insult and outrage. Instead, in the recent case of *Midwest*

---

69   (1937) 57 CLR 1.
70   *Bielitzki v Obadisk* [1922] WWR 238.
71   *Stevenson v Basham* [1922] NZLR 225.

Radio,[72] almost no attention was paid to the intentional quality of the defendant's conduct. Attention was focused upon the plaintiff and, despite the evidence of an expert witness, the court concluded that the hypothetical 'ordinary person' would not have suffered psychiatric illness despite the defendant's abusive practices. While some of the reticence can surely be attributed to the weight of precedent, I do not believe that precedent alone can account for the inattention to the intentionally abusive and misanthropic behaviour of the defendant and the focus upon the vulnerabilities of the plaintiff. Rather, counsel resisted the clear invitation to test *Wilkinson v Downton*[73] as a platform for building a tort remedy for a hostile work environment along US lines and retreated to the safer and more familiar shores of negligence.

Perhaps *Wilkinson v Downton* is gradually being absorbed into negligence, as was the rule in *Rylands v Fletcher*.[74] Tort law generally is in a state of flux, both in Australia and elsewhere. The rule in *Rylands v Fletcher* is now dead, foreclosing the development of a potential environmental tort of some power. The adventurism of an earlier High Court in *Beaudesert Shire Council v Smith*[75] in recognising a new action on the case was rejected by a later High Court in *Northern Territory of Australia v Mengel*.[76] According to the majority,

> the recent trend of legal development, here and in other common law countries has been to the effect that liability in torts depends on either the intentional or the negligent infliction of harm.[77]

Their Honours subsequently referred to the developments in the 'economic torts' as something of a template for liability on the basis of the intentional infliction of harm. Yet intention in the economic torts is very different from intention in trespass and from intention in *Wilkinson v Downton* (as originally conceived). If intention is moving to the model suggested by the economic torts, one in which the focus is upon what the

---

72   *Midwest Radio Ltd v Arnold* [1999] QCA 20 (Unreported, Queensland Court of Appeal, 12 February 1999).
73   [1897] 2 QB 57.
74   *Rylands v Fletcher* [1861–73] All ER Rep 1, absorbed into negligence in *Burnie Port Authority v General Jones Pty Ltd* (1994) 179 CLR 520.
75   (1966) 120 CLR 145.
76   (1995) 129 ALR 1.
77   Ibid 14.

defendant actually intended and in which exploration of primary and secondary consequences is the norm, this suggests a much more demanding test.

How might such a model be realised in trespass and in the action on the case for intentionally causing nervous shock? In trespass, in place of the requirement that the act be intentional and without lawful justification or excuse, the requirement would be that the defendant intends the consequences which attended the act, whatever they might be. In a case of negligent trespass such as *McHale v Watson*[78] the plaintiff would be required to establish that the dart was thrown with the intention of injuring the plaintiff. Negligence, with all the difficulties posed by the construction of a reasonable twelve-year-old boy, would be the sole remaining option. The dignitary aspect of the tort would be lost. In cases such as *Collins v Wilcock*,[79] where the concept of consequences is bizarre, given that the plaintiff's personal space was violated but she suffered no injury other than dignitary harm, the outcome is clearer still. To succeed, she would be required to establish that WPC Wilcock intended to restrain her unlawfully. Throughout the law of trespass, the formal character of intention ensures that these actions are available for purely dignitary harms. If that is lost, the role of trespass in protecting the dignitary interests of the plaintiff vanishes as well.

Despite the purported requirement in a *Wilkinson v Downton* action for intention as regards the consequences rather than the act itself, in practice this has typically been imputed where the factual situation warrants it. Like trespass (and despite the requirement for actual injury), case is also fundamentally dignitary in character. It protects us against manipulative and abusive conduct by others in pursuit of their own ends. If we look at the decided cases, in each the conduct was aimed, not at causing harm (of any description)' to the plaintiff, but at using the plaintiff for the defendant's purposes, treating her as a means to an end rather than an end in herself. Whether we are looking at a sick practical joke, a fabric of threatening lies, a complex and wrongful charade or an extended pattern of abusive and demeaning conduct, the intention is invariably directed towards the ends of the defendant. Harming the plaintiff is an incidental consequence of the method adopted to further those ends, one to which the defendant apparently gave no consideration.

---

78   (1964) 111 CLR 384.
79   [1984] 1 WLR 1172.

In the dignitary torts the interests being protected are critical. Intention is read formally, as in trespass, to protect the plaintiff's interests, or marginalised, as in *Bunyan v Jordan*,[80] to deny protection. Tangles over intention are endemic. The nature of the interests protected encourages this ambiguity. Commonwealth courts (unlike those in the US[81]) remain ill at ease with an interests-based approach except where economic interests are involved. Economic interests seem precise, unambiguous and quantifiable in a way in which dignitary interests do not. Yet dignitary interests are ultimately far more important than economic interests and the lasting importance of actions such as trespass and *Wilkinson v Downton* may be found in their potential extension to affirm other dignitary interests. For this reason, I read *Midwest Radio* as a lost opportunity, and a lost opportunity in a critical area, that of workplace bullying.

Intention, at least in tort law, is a slippery signifier. Its meaning is not fixed, but contextual, not certain, but variable. If, in the economic torts, it comes when bidden, its meanings firmly grounded in ordinary language, in the dignitary torts it is a will-o-the-wisp, now formal, now apparently consequentialist, now immaterial. Intention is not singular, but plural. Different branches of the law of torts call forth different readings of intention. Readings of intention are, in turn, embedded in particular genres, and in the narratives and roles those genres suggest. Where the facts before the court fit securely within traditional narratives and the characters play out pre-ordained roles, whether in trespass or case, legal stories slide along familiar and comfortable channels. The script is played out in familiar ways. Where they do not, as in *Hegarty v Shine*,[82] *R v Brown*[83] and *Bunyan v Jordan*,[84] questions of intention, consent and dignity are up for grabs. In trespass, and its criminal alter ego, assault and battery, the action thriller with its clear and formal roles is replaced by the fatal ambiguities of *film noir* with its absence of any pre-ordained denouement. In case, melodrama with its twin motifs of dastardly villainy and wronged innocence makes

---

80   (1937) 57 CLR 1.
81   In this context it is worth recalling that in the US *Wilkinson v Downton* evolved seamlessly into the tort of insult and outrage and that privacy protection has long been available through the common law and through a variety of statutory torts. Neither is yet part of the law in any Commonwealth jurisdiction, although both Canada and New Zealand are taking tentative steps in that direction.
82   (1878) 14 Cox CC 145.
83   [1993] 2 All ER 75.
84   (1937) 57 CLR 1.

way for slapstick and, ultimately, farce. As the genre changes, the characters change as well. The villain disappears, only to be replaced by a Keystone Cop, while the wronged innocent metamorphoses into a dumb blonde. Within this genre, the bumbling defendant, epitomised by the drunken merchant in *Bunyan v Jordan*,[85] is hardly blameworthy. After all, he meant no harm! As for the dumb blonde, who knows what might have sparked her illness? The causal connection, clearly delineated within melodrama, is unstable within slapstick and irrelevant in farce. Legal stories, like other stories, move within predictable genres, their denouements as predictable as the precedents those denouements shape.

---

85   Ibid.

9 Intention: Meaning in Relation

MICHAEL J DETMOLD

Intention as Meaning

An action is an event with meaning. If a stone falls there is no meaning in the event itself. If, on the other hand, Smith delivers stones for Jones' rock garden there is a similar event but the event itself has meaning, ie it is an action. There is doubtless meaning in my description of the first event (the mere event). But I can just as well describe (with meaning) the second event (action). And here we see the point: in this second case there are two items of meaning, the action and the description, whereas in the first there is only the description.

The meaning of an action is what we call its intention. This meaning (intention) is not limited to the purpose of the action (what is desired). The perception of the circumstances in which the action occurs is part of its meaning. 'Why did you drop the stones in the driveway?', asks Jones, somewhat angrily. 'I was in a hurry', says Smith. 'It would have taken me longer to manoeuvre the truck into the backyard.' This perception of the spatial issues in the delivery is part of the meaning of the action, ie its intention. We get into terrible trouble if we try to explicate the complex issues that now arise between Jones and Smith by distinguishing between two mere purposes: acting to deliver stones or acting to deliver stones into the driveway.

Yet consider this: Smith is escaping from a bank robbery with the loot in the boot of his car when Jones, a police officer, attempts to arrest him by clinging to his car. Smith zigzags to throw her off, succeeds and Jones is killed.[1] The criminal law attempts to distinguish between an intention in Smith to harm Jones and an intention simply to escape. But such a

---

1   These are the facts of *DPP v Smith* [1961] AC 290, a case I discuss later in this essay.

distinction is meaningless. I agree with Grant Gillett's rejection of theories which support the idea that 'the beliefs and desires of the agent causally produce an intention which is expressed in, or causally produces, an action'.[2] Gillett argues that the moral life of the agent is much too complex for this sort of treatment, and I agree with this. My point, however, will be to show this not in relation to the moral life of the individual agent considered in itself, but in their life considered *exclusively* in relation to others. Meaning is always relational.

This calls up the question of the nature of minds and their way of relating by meaning. We will be looking at the way of relating by meaning in both perception (because that is part of the circumstances of an action) and desire.

Against the Private

Action and mind are in correspondence. It is the main argument of David Hodgson's *The Mind Matters*[3] to assert the existence of the mind in the world beyond the (determined) mechanisms of world (including body); and thus to find a special place for human action in the world. When all the physical, biological and neurological causes and effects are factored in, something is left for the mind itself which is of importance: the mind matters. But Hodgson argues for the individual mind (even to the point of the individual mind collapsing quantum states). Minds matter: what matters in my view is the mind in relation to other minds. Human action matters. But it is human action conceived as a relation to others that matters. I take Wittgenstein's view that private minds and private actions have no reality and no meaning.

John Searle founds an illuminating account of social reality on a conception of collective intentionality that is 'a primitive phenomenon' irreducible to individual intentionality.[4] An example of the difference between a collective intentionality and an individual one is the difference between my playing the cello in an orchestra and my playing it by chance in harmony with another player in the next room. The contrary argument, he says,

---

2   Grant Gillett, 'Intention and Agency', this volume, p 59.
3   David Hodgson, *The Mind Matters* (1991).
4   John Searle, *The Construction of Social Reality* (1995).

is that because all intentionality exists in the heads of individual human beings, the form of that intentionality can make reference only to the individuals in whose head it exists. So it has seemed that anybody who recognises collective intentionality as a primitive form of mental life must be committed to the idea that there exists some Hegelian world spirit, a collective consciousness, or something equally implausible. ... It is indeed the case that all my mental life is inside my brain, and all your mental life is inside your brain, and so on for everybody else. But it does not follow from that that all my mental life must be expressed in the form of a singular noun phrase referring to me ... The intentionality that exists in each individual head has the form 'we intend'.[5]

But how is this? How is a 'we intend' constituted? Searle's answer is that the sense of the other is biologically primitive:

We cannot explain society in terms of either conversation in particular or collective behaviour in general, since each of these presupposes a form of society before they can function at all. The biologically primitive sense of the other person as a candidate for shared intentionality is a necessary condition of all collective behaviour and hence of all conversation.[6]

But I would say there is a law here. The law which accounts for collective intentionality is the law of love. And when that is seen a much clearer account of Searle's problem can be offered: between individual minds there is the possibility of lawful union into collective intentionality.

The Law of Love

In Kant's kingdom of ends, humans respected each other as 'ends in self'. Kant sometimes called this the law of freedom and sometimes the law of love. I call it the law of love, and render it as: love the other as yourself. End in self is a phenomenal[7] category. It is both the way I appear to myself and the end point of all phenomenal experience. So Kant's law is the

---

5   Ibid 25.
6   Ibid 415.
7   By 'phenomenal' I mean how something in the mind (perception or desire) feels. I discuss this later in this essay.

fundamental law of the relation of phenomenal minds. In it there is a mutuality of place—you are your end (your phenomenal place of desire) and I am mine. This is the thing known to the law of contract as consideration: my active concession of a place for your desire, and yours of a place for mine, is both a fundamental element of the law of contract and the foundation of meaning. There is no meaning except by contract.

But in Kant the kingdom of ends was transcendental, and thus removed from the world to the private world of conscience. A removal to the private is an illusion, as Wittgenstein showed. The critical philosophical problem, then, is to recover Kant's law from the private. It then comes into its own as the foundation of what I call mind science, the science of the relation of minds. Kant's placement of the law of love in the individual private mind was actually an infringement of it.

The philosophical need is reciprocal: Wittgenstein needs Kant. The foundation of Wittgenstein's later philosophy was never fully explicated. But it could not actually be anything else than Kant's law. This is a proof by exclusion.[8] Anything else, any movement at all away from the lawful equality of the other, is a movement to the private, and the whole of Wittgenstein's argument is against the private. Many philosophers misunderstand Wittgenstein, thinking that he equated the phenomenal and the private and therefore denied the phenomenal. He did not. He denied that the phenomenal meant anything in itself. It only achieved meaning and reality in lawful public relation (ie in relation to another mind).

But how is it that the law of love is a law, and a law of the world? The world's laws are the way the world is. (If gravity is the way the world is then the law of gravity is one of its laws.) If Wittgenstein is, as I think, right about the way of meaning in the world, and if I am right about the place of the law of love in that way of meaning, then the law of love is the way the world is in the matter of meaning and is therefore one of its laws.

---

8   There is a more detailed argument towards this proof in Michael Detmold, 'Law as the Structure of Meaning' in Tom Campbell and Jeffrey Goldsworthy (eds), *Interpretation* (forthcoming).

Reality and Meaning

I define reality as that which is objectively[9] the case as opposed to that which simply appears to be the case to a *single* subjective (phenomenal) view or desire. It is the foundation of meaning and the focus of intention.

In Thomas Nagel's metaphor, reality (or meaning, which I will show is the same thing) is the view from nowhere.[10] From the proposition that reality is a function of a view, we infer that it is *a mind's* view—what the mind sees, to preserve the metaphor of view. Nagel writes that his book is about

> a single problem: how to combine the perspective of a particular person inside the world with an objective view of that same world, the person and his viewpoint included. It is a problem that faces every creature with the impulse and the capacity to transcend its particular point of view and to conceive of the world as a whole.[11]

Now, transcendence and its associated term, metaphysics, are permissible to mark the necessary presuppositions of our account of the world (the meaningful description that we give of the world). What I mean by this will become clear; but as an illustration we can think of the eye and the visual field and say that the eye, since it is precluded from being an object in the visual field, is transcendent to it (a necessary presupposition of it) and optics is at base a sort of visual metaphysics. This point was made by Wittgenstein, when in *Tractatus* 5.641 he drew the shape of the visual field and by the picture showed the sense in which the eye is not in its own field.

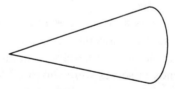

Figure 9.1

---

9   There are two sorts of objectivity. First, absolute reality, which I reject. And second, the objectivity of intersubjectivity, which my argument supports: see the cube analysis at the end of this section.

10   Thomas Nagel, *The View from Nowhere* (1986).

11   Ibid 3.

He added: 'the self of solipsism shrinks to a point without extension, and there remains the reality co-ordinated with it'.[12] That which is shaped to the eye is the world (the reality coordinated with it, Wittgenstein said). But as well as drawing the world, Wittgenstein has drawn a particular mind. He drew a particular eye, but we can extrapolate from the visual to the whole mind. So the drawing of the world shaped to the individual eye can be regarded as a mind's view of the world. Such an expansion of eye to mind (eye to I) is an expansion from vision to all our individual perceptions and desires. The expansion to the other perceptual senses is obvious enough: everything perceived by the senses is shaped in the Wittgensteinian way to a point of perception. But we can expand to desire as well. Just as vision itself is not an object of vision so desire itself is not an object of desire. We can draw the same conical shape for desire.

Kant's conception of an end in self confirms this idea of the extensionless point of vision. End in self is the extensionless point of desire. When a person is not treated as end in self, but as a means to another's end, they are an object (slave) within the other's field of desire. End in self is a precise equivalent of the Wittgensteinian point of vision. When I look at another as object, or treat them as object, they are object in my field of vision or desire. On the other hand, when I treat them as end in self I treat them as having their own field, and their own point of perception and desire.

The problem with my seeing in the shaped (and therefore personal) way that Wittgenstein pictured immediately becomes that of the temptations of solipsism. *Solus ipse*, myself alone, is a thought that carries the baleful question: is it perhaps the case that there is no real world but just my own view?

The issue of solipsism is a critical one in perception; but it is no less so in relation to desire: is it perhaps the case, asks a contracting party, that my own desire is the whole world (thereby contemplating the breaking of the contract)? Kant's ends in selves were supposed to keep their contracts. Wittgenstein's picture and analysis (including the language-game analyses of the later philosophy, to which we come shortly) shows that this is more an issue of sense (meaning) than moral duty.

---

12   Ludwig Wittgenstein, *Tractatus Logico-Philosophicus* (D F Pears and B F McGuiness (trans)) (1961) para 5.64.

Wittgenstein's shaped world of the mind is not solipsistic, but he is not perfectly clear here. He said that solipsism shrinks to a point without extension, and thus did not completely exclude solipsism, for a point without extension is not nothing. But there is a simple exclusion. The *shape* of vision itself implies the real world. This can be seen by comparing two shapes:

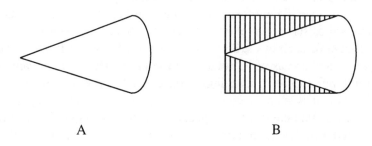

A   B

Figure 9.2

The shape of the visual field (A) implies that it is a view of a real world; otherwise the shape would be B. If there were no real world to be shaped there would be no shape of my view of it; there would just be B, where there is a shape constructed to include the blurred parts at the near edges of my vision but no shape of vision. There is no ground to construct that shape in B by giving priority to the clear part of B over the blurred parts: they are both just parts of the world, a clear part and a blurred part, and since there is no shape of vision, they are the parts of a solipsistic world.[13] B is the picture of solipsism. But it is A, not B, that gives the shape of vision, and therefore the real world. Though Wittgenstein is sometimes thought to have been a solipsist in the *Tractatus*, even by Nagel,[14] his picture of the mind's vision is the opposite of solipsistic.

The issue is critical to the existence of meaning. For a solipsist there can be no meaning. Suppose a solipsist sees a world and says 'this is mine alone'. For that to mean something there has got to be a further point of perception from which they judge it true or not true. And then there is a second cone with the first in its field of vision. This second cone then

---

13   Of course, I interpret the distinction between the clear and blurred parts as indicative
      of shape. But then I am interpreting B as A.
14   Nagel, above n 10, 62.

becomes the real world beyond the solipsist (distinguishing, as we have just done, A from B) and thus defeats the solipsism. If there is meaning, therefore, there can be no solipsism. The point without extension in Wittgenstein's picture is the mind and the place of meaning. But it is a non-solipsistic place. It implies other end points of perception and desire.

Let us now take an ordinary piece of matter with a shape we can easily talk about. Suppose I am a solipsist looking at a cube. It presents a certain shape to my eye. To another person standing near to me (as we know, but not the solipsist) it presents a different shape. This suggests a reality independent of each of us. So the cube is not what I see! It has at the same time another shape as well, in fact an infinity of shapes! No, it cannot be so queer a thing as to be many things at once! Such is my answer.

Further, it is many inconsistent things at once. Let us try to be very explicit here and take just two aspects of the cube's shape; and take them at a very reduced level, thinking of only one sense, the visual (the other senses present their own, but essentially similar, problems; any sense will only corroborate *after* we have attained reality under at least one of them):

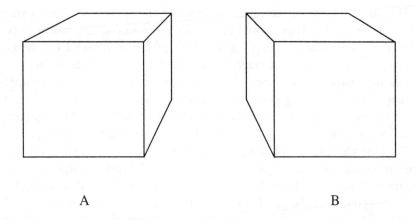

A   B

Figure 9.3

These figures correspond to the views of a cube of two human minds, from two positions in the world. Now, the reader must put aside their interpretation of the two views as views of a cube from different angles. We only get the cube after we get the relation of minds. When philosophy overlooks the relation of minds and limits itself to the relation of mind and matter it has no way of explaining the cube (or indeed any reality at all); it has no way of defeating solipsism; it has no way of seeing the mind as shaped.

The shape of vision is part of Wittgenstein's early philosophy (the *Tractatus*). He continued his campaign against solipsism in his later philosophy (*Philosophical Investigations*) of which the language game is the foundation. He wrote in *On Certainty*:

> It is queer: if I say, without any special occasion, 'I know'—for example, 'I know that I am now sitting in a chair', this statement seems to me unjustified and presumptuous. But if I make the same statement where there is some need for it, then, although I am not a jot more certain of its truth, it seems to me to be perfectly justified and everyday ... But as soon as I say this sentence outside its context, it appears in a false light.[15]

Wittgenstein is wondering about his knowledge of the chair and concludes that to say 'I know' beyond any language game is false (the falseness of false light):

> In its language-game it is not presumptuous. There, it ['I know'] has no higher position than, simply, the human language-game. For there it has its restricted application.[16]

The restricted application is the equivalent of our reflection on the cube. Run that reflection through in cubes rather than chairs. I look as hard as I can at the side of the cube, wanting to say 'I know'; but all I can do is play the language game of the cube with you and your mind's view.[17]

---

15   Ludwig Wittgenstein, *On Certainty* (Denis Paul and G E M Anscombe (trans)) (1969) paras 553–4.

16   Ibid para 554.

17   It is tempting to think that I might myself (without relation to another mind) construct the whole of reality by moving around the world to plot shapes from different points and then put the whole thing together (walking around the cube, say). This is a fallacy which I call the peripatetic fallacy. It is a false universality, this walk around the world; more modest than Hegel's walking of the universal through history, but essentially of the same order. First, taking vision alone (we shall introduce the corroboration of further senses shortly), there is no sense to tell me that I have moved except the changing shape of the objects of vision. So I have no reason to reject 'my solipsistic world changed in shape' in favour of 'I moved relative to an independent reality'. With more than one sense (ie the five) the point holds, but in a way that is a little more complex. Perhaps we think that our other senses corroborate the case for realism: the

The reality produced in the language game is meaning. When I look at the side of the cube, the meaning that I see is the cube. Of course, part of this meaning is the side of the cube; but the side of the cube only makes sense as part of the cube—the meaning of the cube makes the meaning of the side of the cube.

Sartre

Searle's account of collective intentionality was, as we saw above, underdeveloped in the matter of its law, and underdeveloped also in its real collectiveness. In fact his 'we-intentions' which exist *entirely inside my mind and your mind* do not improve upon the Sartrean I-thou which led Sartre to disaster.

Sartre's philosophy failed clearly to grasp the emergent reality and meaning implicit in the relation between self and other. Sartre stated Hegel's relational dialectic :

> According to Hegel the Other is an object, and I apprehend myself as an object in the Other. But the one of these affirmations destroys the other. In order for me to be able to appear to myself as an object in the Other, I would have to apprehend the Other as subject; that is, to apprehend him in his interiority. But in so far as the Other appears to me as object, my objectivity for him can not appear to me. Of course I apprehend that the Other-as-object *refers to me* by means of intentions and acts, but due to the very fact that he is an object, the Other-as-a-mirror is clouded and no longer reflects anything.[18]

(The reader will understand this by thinking of the two, self and other, as each having their own Wittgensteinian cones of vision; neither cone contains the other cone in its field.) But now Sartre quickly loses touch with the world. He considers a simple case where he is in a park looking at a lawn, and some benches and other objects, when a man passes by:

---

object emits a noise, let us say, which changes as I move, I feel my legs move and I touch the object and feel its shape change, and so on. But this does not help. There is now just a complex of changes: I still have no reason to reject the view that 'my solipsistic world underwent (the stated) complex of changes' in favour of the view that 'I moved relative to a (more complex) reality'.

18   Jean Paul Sartre, *Being and Nothingness* (H Barnes (trans)) (1958) 242.

If I were to think of him as being only a puppet [a Kantian object as opposed to end in self], I should apply to him the categories which I ordinarily use to group temporal-spatial 'things'. That is, I should apprehend him as being 'beside' the benches, two yards and twenty inches from the lawn, as exercising a certain pressure on the ground, etc. His relation with other objects would be of the purely additive type; this means that I could have him disappear without the relations of the other objects around him being perceptibly *changed*. In short, no new relation would appear *through* him between those things in my universe: grouped and synthesised *from my point of view* into instrumental complexes, they would *from his* disintegrate into multiplicities of indifferent relations. Perceiving him as a *man*, on the other hand [a Kantian end in self], is not to apprehend an additive relation between the chair and him; it is to register an organisation *without distance* of the things in my universe around that privileged object.[19]

The new relation without distance is Sartre's conception of the other's view from somewhere. Distance is a difficult notion here.

The view from somewhere (the single-shaped view) is without distance, because whilst I can measure between two objects within my vision (the other standing 'beside the benches'—a metre, say, between the other and the bench) I cannot measure to the point of my vision. The reason is that that point is not in the field of my vision, and therefore not within my visual measuring capacity;[20] Sartre here is saying the very thing implied by Wittgenstein's cone analysis.

But now things go alarmingly wrong:

This new relation of the object-man to the object-lawn has a particular character; it is simultaneously given to me as a whole, since it is there in the world as an object which I can know (it is, in fact, an objective relation which I express by saying: Pierre has glanced at this watch, Jean has looked out the window, etc), and at the same time it entirely escapes me. To the extent that the man-as-object is the fundamental term of this relation, to the extent that the relation *reaches toward him*, it escapes me. I cannot put myself at the center of it. The distance which unfolds between the lawn and the man across the synthetic upsurge of this primary relation is a negation of the distance which I establish—as a pure type of external negation—between these two objects.

---

19 Ibid 254.
20 I can measure to the tip of my nose, or the front of my eye, perhaps; but not to my point of vision, not to my eye; nor to my I, fully considered. (How could I measure I?)

> The distance appears as a pure *disintegration* of the relations which I apprehend between the objects of my universe.[21]

And now the objects flee from Sartre:

> There is a regrouping in which I take part but which escapes me, a regrouping of all the objects which people my universe. This regrouping does not stop there. The grass is something qualified; it is *this* green grass which exists for the Other; in this sense the very quality of the object, its deep, raw green is in direct relation to this man. This green turns toward the Other a face which escapes me. I apprehend the relation of the green to the Other as an objective relation, but I can not apprehend the green *as* it appears to the Other. Thus suddenly an object has appeared which has stolen the world from me.[22]

Sartre's mistake is to overlook *the relation between* the two minds in his story, the self and the other. The world was in fact falling into place by virtue of that relation of minds, which he very perceptively describes. Yet he thought it was disintegrating. What was disintegrating was the solipsistic wholeness of his original view. What we learn from this is that we have no access to the world except in the relation of minds. If Sartre were not so intent on self through other and other through self—as though self and other were individually the final source of value[23]—the reality of the world would be plain to him. His mistake was to seek to establish the reality of whole humans. But we are partial; we are defined only by love.[24]

Sartre was never able to think his way out of the disintegration of his reality. There could be no dialectical resolution of the disintegration but only a circle from which we can never escape:[25] 'nothing remains for the for-itself [the subject] except to re-enter the circle and allow itself to be indefinitely tossed from one to the other of the two fundamental attitudes'.[26] The two fundamental attitudes, examined by Sartre in great

---

21   Sartre, above n 18, 254–5.
22   Ibid 255.
23   As Roger Scruton put it in *Sexual Desire: A Philosophical Investigation* (1986) 111. Scruton's account is defective in a way quite like Sartre's.
24   Or: we are defined only by the science of the relations of minds. It will be apparent when the exposition of mind science is finished that it defines only love. The intuition that love is part of the world (encountered one way or another in the work of most of the great writers) gets its exposition in mind science.
25   Sartre, above n 18, 363.
26   Ibid 412.

depth, are masochism and sadism. First, I try to achieve being with the other by making myself object for the other (masochism); then by making the other object for me (sadism). It is obvious that Sartre has nowhere to go except into perpetual alternation; constantly looking at one side of the hellish sado-masochistic alternation or the other, never at their relation; never at the world (of matter and desire) constituted by the lawful relation of minds.

To return to Searle. His 'we-intentions' *entirely inside my mind and your mind* do not improve upon the Sartrean I-thou. 'We' simply equals the Sartrean 'I-thou' without saying so. A real 'we'-ness is in the world, as Wittgenstein held.

Intention and Action

Much of Wittgenstein's *Philosophical Investigations* is directed against our conception of the privacy of sensations such as pain. So I shall take as my example of intention and action something concerned with pain. At first pain seems like a relatively trivial philosophical issue. But it isn't, for if pain is a private thing within us then so, too, is our perception of the outer world. The whole world would become private—my private incorrigible knowledge of my pain would have its equivalent in my private incorrigible knowledge of the world. This is an insidious incorrigibility. Of course my knowledge of the world would continue to change; but it would not change because the world changes. It would itself just change as a pain sometimes diminishes or just goes away. Pain was simply a more difficult case for Wittgenstein's argument, hence his preoccupation.

My example is this. I have a pain, so I go to the doctor. What action have I performed? What is my intention? The relevant body events have their causes. The events are not actions and these causes are not reasons. When do they become this? I feel the body pain and make the noise 'Ooh!' (the natural selection advantages in my being helped are obvious). Or: I feel the body pain and say 'Doctor I have a pain.' Is there a difference? Only in the relation of minds—the second is an only slightly more complex effect than the first (with the same natural selection advantages). Or: I feel the body pain, notice that I am too close to the fire, and move. The pain ceases. With a different pain I move to the doctor's surgery. The pain ceases. Is there a difference? Only in the relation of minds.

It is just like the cube. The side of what we now know as the cube causes certain body effects in me which we call perception. And we have seen that this only has meaning in the relation of minds. It is the same with the pain. When there is a relation of minds then there is meaning and action with intention.

Let us compare the two cases:

A: *The Eye of Pain*
  1. I say 'I am in pain'.
  2. It is the case that there is a pain to feel.
  3. It is the case that *I* am in pain.
  4. I have a pain-feeling 'eye' (that by which I sense pain).

B: *The Eye of Vision*
  1. I see a side (of a cube).
  2. It is the case that there is a cube to see.
  3. It is the case that *I* see the cube.
  4. I have an eye (this is a statement in optics).

The progression from 1 to 4 in B is the progression to the full meaning of the cube (as we saw above). Now, it is easy to think that B2 follows from B1. That is what we think now, when we are already in practice with others in the cube language game. In fact, without a lawful relation to another viewer I cannot get past B1 (I cannot assert B2 as the meaning of B1). And I cannot assert B3 or B4, which are further removed than B2. With the lawful relation to another viewer, all falls into place. Once I 'get' the cube, its manner of getting becomes real as well and the objective world includes the cube *and* optics.

We should dwell a little on this last point about optics. Roger Scruton argues long, hard and persuasively in favour of the embodiment of selves; the situating of persons entirely in the world.[27] Nevertheless, says Scruton, we cannot escape the metaphysical illusion of our first person viewpoint; the illusion (Scruton's illusion; Wittgenstein's cone picture) persists no matter how hard we try to think of ourselves as in the world. But in the relation of minds the reality of the world is recognised as independent of vision. We still see in the same shaped way and the cone still makes sense;

---

27   Scruton, above n 23.

but the point is that the illusion is now a real one *and physics has embraced optics*. Optics embraces all eyes, including mine; thus we have B4 in the Eye of Vision, that is, I have an eye. The eye (first person viewpoint) is real, no longer an illusion.

The equivalent is true of the A sequence. All that can be said is A1. (I cannot get past it.) A3 cannot be said. (A3 is more removed than A2.) And since A3 cannot be said, A1 is just the equivalent of a groan (Wittgenstein's point all along in the private pain argument). The notion that we can say A3 is the notion of private knowledge; but privately (without lawful relation to another) 'it is the case that' adds nothing, so A3 collapses into A1. A3 and B3 can be said when there is a lawful relation to another: in the pain language game for A3 and in the visual language game for B3. With these lawful games, there is a painful and a visual reality and a meaning, marked in each case by 'it is the case that', which now makes a radical distinction between the 3s and the 1s. And the last step, once reality is established, is real self-reflection. There is a private eye and a private pain sense—but these things (each proposition 4) are said publicly, in the one case in optics, in the other in medicine or sympathy.

Perhaps in the comparison between A (pain) and B (vision) the viewer–viewer symmetry of B is tricking some readers. Though each view is inconsistent, it is still a symmetrical viewer–viewer in the relevant language game rather than, say, pain feeler–doctor. This is in the first place a function of the fact that we are comfortable with the reality of cubes (etc) but not yet with the reality of pain—we have not yet fully accepted Wittgenstein's argument. There are no viewers prior to the cube. In a perfectly constituted reality, the difference between pain feeler and doctor is equivalent to the difference between line-sloping-right-knower and line-sloping-left-knower (the lines of the cube: figure 8.3). Nevertheless there are some symmetries in the cube case which do not obtain in the pain case; for example, there is symmetry in right and left, as compared with the apparently asymmetrical pain feeler–doctor. But there is nothing in this asymmetry: it is simply a function of the fact that the doctor is a specialist. An equivalent specialist for the cube would be a geometrician, who would see it a little differently from us. And the issue of the reality of pain is the same if we think of pain-feeler and lay sympathiser; now we have a symmetry almost equal to the cube—sometimes I'm in pain (left) and you sympathise (right), sometimes you're in pain (left) and I sympathise (right). For pain-feeler/doctor a good perception comparison is with viewers of

Mount Everest (some at the bottom, some at the top). Some viewers of pain have taken the trouble to go to medical school; some viewers of Mount Everest have taken the trouble to get to the top.

To return to my action of going to the doctor for my pain. Without the relation of minds there is a series of causes and effects through which my body ends up at the doctor's surgery (just as my dog's body moves from a hot fire); and the doctor's body responds likewise. With the relation of minds, the causes and effects are reasons and actions. Beyond step 2, in The Eye of Pain there is meaning and intention.

Epiphenomenon (Love Makes the World go Round)

I have said quite a bit about the phenomenal without fully defining it. I adopt Chalmers' definition. For Chalmers the distinction between the phenomenal and psychological aspects of the mind is the distinction between how some mental thing feels subjectively and what it does.[28] In my view, the phenomenal thus conceived defines the mind. The mind is a person's subjectivity, their phenomenal life, what they care about. The whole set of a person's perceptions and desires make a phenomenal appearance at the point we call their mind. Now, there is a well-known objection to the idea that reasons and actions are just, as it were, the phenomenal inside of body causes and effects. If that were so, they would be mere epiphenomena: gratuitous extras with no function in the world. The body causes and effects would be doing it all. There would be no way to explain the epiphenomena's existence. This is a formidable objection to an individualistic conception of intention. But, as Searle shows, it is collective intentionality that gets the job done. What job?

Collective intentionality must be the product of selection. This is obvious. Humans survive only in community. But why could that not be all a matter of body causes and effects? Earlier we compared my saying 'Ooh!' to my saying 'Doctor I have a pain'; and the suggestion there was that the latter is as much a matter of body cause and effect as the former. The whole of human history might thus be explained. In one sense it must be. The whole of history is these causes and effects; to pursue the

---

28   David Chalmers, *The Conscious Mind: In Search of a Fundamental Theory* (1996) 11–31.

particular example, without the cause and effect nobody goes to a doctor. Given this, has the epiphenomenal objection re-established itself in large?

The phenomenal relation mediated by the law of love contributes a sense of self-worth and other worth indispensable to communal growth. Our interest in others is dependent upon them being as self, and our own sense of self-worth grows from this. Strawson's distinction between the reactive and the objective is relevant here.[29]

Wittgenstein said of a lion: 'If a lion could talk we could not understand him.'[30] Suppose I am attacked by the lion. This is an event against which I must (objectively) defend, but the idea of my resenting the lion's 'action' is entirely out of order. (Resentment is a typical reactive attitude.) If, on the other hand, I am attacked by a human, the same objective issue of defence is raised, but Strawson's distinction is shown by the fact that I shall also react with resentment. In the opposite direction, gratitude is also reactive. Suppose my dog retrieves a bird I have just shot. An objective response follows, but not the reactive attitude of gratitude; whereas if it is another person who makes me the present of a bird, gratitude is entirely in order. Wittgenstein and Strawson are in agreement here. It is only in reaction that there is any question of understanding and meaning.[31] Interpersonal relations and language games are the same thing. We would not *react* to the lion, and therefore would not understand him.

The distinction is not just the distinction between human and animal: it is interpersonal not inter-human. I may have a human slave to fetch the birds I shoot, rather than a dog, and I shall respond entirely objectively; this is simply because the slave is means (object) to my end, not end in self (person). It is very important to emphasise this point and see how wide it goes. The distinction is not one between response to humans and response to animals and other objects. The slave is human, but is treated non-reactively as animal or object. And many people treat other humans in this way without calling them slaves (as means to ends rather than ends in self). In the other direction, some people treat certain animals reactively. (The whole gamut of interpersonal reactions is often applied to pet dogs or cats; whole legal systems have done this when they have attributed criminality

---

29 Peter Strawson, *Freedom and Resentment and Other Essays* (1974). There is a more extensive discussion of Strawson in Detmold, above n 8.

30 Ludwig Wittgenstein, *Philosophical Investigations* (G E M Anscombe (trans)) (3rd ed, 1968) 223.

31 This is demonstrated in Detmold, above n 8.

204 Intention in Law and Philosophy

to animals; and large systems of philosophy now attribute rights to animals.) The distinguishing point is interpersonal not inter-human; that is, it is dependent upon the phenomenal relation of minds.

It is obvious that Kant's distinction between ends in self and means to ends corresponds to Strawson's distinction between reactive and objective attitudes. But Strawson shows an important quality of reactive relations. This quality makes a difference to our natural selection. When a person reacts to another (Strawson's sense) a new and different set of causes and effects is injected into the world—someone is punished or praised—and this makes a difference to the evolution of the species. Interpersonal (reactive) relations have causal power.

This solves the epiphenomenal problem. With individualistic intention there is a one-to-one correspondence between the causal (c) and the phenomenal (p), hence the problem of the epiphenomenal. We might say in this case the world goes: cp cp cp cp cp; and p would indeed begin to look like a mere epiphenomenon. With intention in the relation of minds, the correspondence is not one-to-one. The world goes: cp pp pc cp pp pc cp.

Intentional Fault

Lawyers are often muddled about the distinction between negligence and intention. The law of torts often puzzles over the relation between negligence and the seemingly peripheral cases of intention. And the criminal law does the same from the other side (thinking negligence peripheral).

Consider five cases: (1) Smith drives too fast and accidentally kills Jones. (2) Smith is escaping from a bank robbery with the loot in the boot of his car when Jones, who is a police officer, attempts to arrest him by clinging to his car. Smith zigzags to throw her off, succeeds and Jones is killed.[32] (3) Smith is confronted by Jones in the bank. He knows that Jones can identify him, so he kills her to avoid identification. (4) Jones insults Smith, so Smith kills her to avenge the insult. (5) Smith is a serial killer and Jones is one of the victims.

---

32   These were the facts of *DPP v Smith* [1961] AC 290.

Our law struggles with case 2. In *DPP v Smith* the House of Lords caused a scandal[33] when it said that Smith must be deemed to intend the natural consequences of his actions. The result of this is that Smith, by virtue of the dangerousness of his act, is said to have intended to kill or cause grievous bodily harm to Jones. *DPP v Smith* was quickly consigned to the scrap heap of legal history on the ground that the issue of intention was a subjective not objective one. But the distinction (from both sides) is nonsensical. If the jury were to decide Smith's subjective intention, they would do it by nothing but objective evidence. The subjective intention then would be objective (whatever that means). The House of Lords distinguished case 2 from case 1 by saying that the act in question in a case of type 2 must be 'aimed at someone'.[34] But the act was not aimed at Jones. It was aimed at *any* police officer who tried to arrest him. Jones happened to be the one. In case 1 the dangerous act is 'aimed at' whoever happens to be in the street at the time. Jones turns out to be the one and is killed. We are tempted to say here that (in case 1) the act was not aimed at anyone; it was just dangerous driving. But in the same sense, no act was aimed at Jones in case 2; it was just dangerous escaping. In neither case was Jones' death or serious harm desired by Smith. Perhaps the House of Lords had in mind an objective sense of 'aim': the act in case 2 was aimed at Jones in the sense that it was fixing exclusively upon Jones. But the same applies in case 1. Someone in a helicopter above the road might see Smith speeding around a corner into a street where Jones is stepping onto the road; they would see Smith's action fixing exclusively upon Jones. And if it is thought relevant that Jones, however fleetingly, is known by Smith, then let Jones in case 1 be a passenger in Smith's car. The particularisation of Jones is in fact a red herring.

One clear distinction between the cases is that in case 2 Smith has an opportunity to stop after the inevitability of harm to Jones becomes apparent; whereas in case 1 the opportunity to stop arises after the inevitability of harm to *someone* becomes apparent (though with Jones as a passenger the distinction is not quite so clear). This is a difference, but it doesn't make the difference between murder and innocence. (It is easy to think of examples where case 1 is more culpable: speeding in the vicinity of a crowd of children, for example.) It is desiring the harm that makes a

---

33 So much of a scandal that the Australian High Court decided they were no longer bound by House of Lords decisions.

34 [1961] AC 290, 327.

radical distinction in culpability such as might mark the crime of murder. In neither case 1 nor 2 was the harm desired.

I do not think it was desired in case 3 either. The act is aimed at anyone who can identify Smith. Jones happens to be the one. In this case the death is required (whereas in 1 and 2 it is not, though in both cases the harm implicit in the actions is required if the actions are to continue). But it was not desired.

Only cases 4 and 5 are cases where the act is subjectively aimed at the particular person killed. The first three cases are cases of negligence. The fourth is as well, for reasons that I will explain shortly. Only the fifth is a case of what I will define as intentional murder. This is as it should be, because only the fifth is a case of an evil mind (*mens rea*). The others are cases of unlawfulness (varying degrees of the breach of the law of love).

A great deal of the law's confusion about intention is attributable to a misconceived belief in the private mind. Intention is thought to be something that operates in the private mind (the guilty mind of Smith, for example). So when we do away with the private mind, what is intentional fault? I propose that it be seen as part of a continuum constituted by the degree of my foreknowledge of, and attention to, the other and the consequences of my actions for the other. The continuum ranges over intention, recklessness, negligence and accidental fault.

I suggest all fault can be graded like this:

- Accidental fault: My body did it.
- Negligence: I did not accord equality to your place in our relation; and could have by better attention to the circumstances of the relation and the likely consequences of its events.
- Recklessness: The same; plus the fact that my inattention to the circumstances and likely consequences was deliberate.
- Intention:[35] My not according equality to your place in our relation was deliberate.

Accidental fault I discuss in the next section.

Our first three Smith and Jones cases are cases of negligence or recklessness, depending on the degree of deliberation in the exclusion of

---

35 Here 'intention' has something like the specific meaning that it has in ordinary parlance. The main meaning of intention in this essay is to cover all the grades of meaning in action.

the other. Deliberation is quite apparent in case 3, where Smith deliberates about the one person who can identify him. It may be present in cases 2 and 3, though case 1 is more likely to be one of recklessness than case 2. This is because in fairly extreme versions (eg speeding past a school) it is more inherently dangerous than robbing a bank; hence the inattention to the other's interest is more likely to have been deliberate.

Case 4 is a case of response to a wrong—provocation, as it is usually called. It is a paradigm of negligence. If my response to the wrong is appropriate to the wrong, it preserves, not breaks, the relation in question. If it goes beyond the other's wrong, then it breaks the relation (but may be partially pardonable, as the defence of provocation recognises). I have argued this case elsewhere.[36]

Case 5 is intentional murder. The death is desired. But how do we know this? Do we not breach the Wittgensteinian condition of our discussion and look into the private mind of the killer to find the stated desire there?

No. In saying the death is desired we simply describe a biological fact. Suppose I am hungry and desire food. This is a biological fact about me, and there is no meaning in it. We are misled into thinking there is meaning in it because we can (with meaning) describe it. When, however, I go to the shop to buy food, my desire for food and the shopkeeper's desire for money come out of their biological state into the world of meaning and intention. This act of contracting and the act of describing are but small parts of the large communal act of creating and playing language games. That large act is itself contractual: the law of love is the condition of language games, and the law of love is the law of contract.[37]

The formulation of intention in the grading of fault given in this part is one that looks simply to the structure of the relation in issue. Case 5, we have said, is one of intentional murder. What is happening in case 5 is that the killer is deliberately excluding the other from the equality of the relation. He is deliberately breaking the relation,[38] deliberately reverting to

---

36   Michael Detmold, 'Provocation to Murder: Sovereignty and Multiculture' (1997) 19 *Sydney Law Review* 5.

37   Michael Detmold, 'Australian Constitutional Equality: The Common Law Foundation' (1996) 7 *Public Law Review* 33.

38   It is not the simple deliberate killing that counts (consider euthanasia); it is the deliberate killing without consent. This breaks the relation of (contractual) equality. Of course, sometimes with a loss of capacity there is a question of who may consent. For

the meaningless private. How do we know this (since there is no meaning in it[39])? I would say we know it *because* there is no meaning in it. It is an absence of meaning.[40] The structure of any relation gives it meaning. The breaking of the structure is the breaking of meaning, and the fault. In fact all four cases are progressive breakdowns in meaning.

Accidental Wrong

In tort law theory, there is a large debate about the fundamental relevance of blameworthiness to the commission of a tort. One of the main supporters of the case for relevance is David Owen, who expresses the issue succinctly:

> In *Brown v Kendall*, decided in 1850, a man accidentally struck another with a stick while trying to break up two fighting dogs. Holding that negligence was necessary to liability Chief Judge Shaw of Massachusetts officially proclaimed the central role of fault in accident law, opening a century of largely unchallenged dominance of fault in the law of torts ... And as the twentieth century opened its doors the explicitly fault-based standard of responsibility for accidents was solidly endorsed by the scholars of the period. Harvard Law School dean James Barr Ames, for example, noted with approval that '[t]he ethical standard of reasonable conduct has replaced the immoral standard of acting at one's peril'.[41]

Peter Birks is an opponent:

> The reality of the common law of negligence is that it imposes what is in effect strict liability for bad practice as for example, in the control of a motor vehicle on the roads. It sets an objective standard of competence to define bad practice

---

the serial killer the power implicit in the breaking of the relation of equality is the whole point; the killer is not up to the relation of equality, so must destroy it.

39　Though, of course, as we have just said, we may describe it. It is this description that makes it look as though there is meaning. The power that the serial killer thinks he is acquiring is an illusion: hate is always illusory.

40　We always see that when we try to explain the mind of a serial killer. We can see causes but not meaning.

41　David Owen, 'Philosophical Foundations of Fault in Tort Law' in David Owen (ed), *Philosophical Foundations of Tort Law* (1995) 201.

but does not ask whether the particular defendant was in fact worthy of reproach for the particular incident in which he fell below that standard.[42]

Birks adheres to the positivist conception of torts as the imposition of an objective standard of behaviour on citizens. This is actually the fallacy that the critics of *DPP v Smith* were aiming at. They attacked the idea that Smith must be deemed to intend the natural consequences of his actions by virtue simply of the dangerousness of his act. The act was indeed dangerous, so Smith must have intended to kill or cause grievous bodily harm. But the idea that it is not Smith who is being tried, but 'the man on the Clapham omnibus', is (as the critics thought) offensive and nonsensical. Who would be punished if there were a conviction?

And it makes no more sense in the law of torts. Take Doe and Roe on the road. The usual formulation of the law of negligence in its reference to the standard of care of the reasonable person is misleading here (and it has misled Birks). It looks as though there is in this standard of care an evaluation—what a reasonable person would do in the circumstances—that is required over and above Doe's and Roe's choices, which is then imposed upon them (in Birks's sense). This appearance is false.

The reasonable person is simply the lawful person, the one free from the selfish subjectivities in question. And that is not a third person; it is Doe and Roe themselves on condition that they are lawful between themselves.[43]

Birks's conception of negligence is a reflection of the common idea that contract and tort differ in that in contract the parties make the obligation whereas in tort the law imposes it. In fact, there is no fundamental difference between the law of contract and the law of tort. In the law of contract (say there is the sale of a book) the parties make the standards (Doe will give the book; Roe will pay the money) and the law that binds is the law of love (each has equal status). In the law of tort (say Doe is driving north and Roe south) the parties also make the standards— each decides for themselves what they want to do (as they do in contract)— and the law that binds them together is the law of love. Fundamentally, on one side Doe wants the money and the north and on the other Roe wants

---

42   Peter Birks, 'The Concept of a Civil Wrong' in ibid 45.

43   This rejection of the reasonable person as a standard imposed in negligence is argued in more depth in Detmold, above n 36, 11–17; and in Detmold, above n 37, 37–41.

the book and the south; the law that binds these enterprises into a collective intentionality is the same law.[44]

Even if Birks were right about negligence, fault is more complex than his position allows. On the *Brown v Kendall*[45] facts, was an apology in order when the plaintiff was accidentally struck? Make this case as strong as you can. Suppose it was a perfect accident, no-one at all thinking the defendant had acted in any sense carelessly. So was an apology in order? Of course it was. So there is fault. The relation is a reactive one where a failure to apologise would be a failure to understand the nature of the relation, and therefore its meaning (intention). Part of its meaning is that there is fault (albeit a low degree) in the event. Whether there is also a ground for holding the defendant liable to an action in the courts is a quite different question, depending on all sorts of issues of policy, and depending also on the degree of accidental fault.

Accidental fault is actually a very instructive case for the whole discussion of mind. Presumably those who adhere to the idea of the private mind as the place where guilt is found (the guilty mind) do not find accidental fault there. Then where is it?

Scandalous Conundrums

Individualised intention produces a scandalous array of insoluble conundrums. I will take a common one as the basis of my discussion and show how a relational conception of intention solves it easily.

The problem is this: A bandit has captured 15 people and tells me I can save 14 of them by the execution of one of them.[46] Otherwise the bandit will kill all of them. Now, let us say I judge that I should do this. I draw lots and shoot one of them (Jones). Did I intend to kill her? On one view yes, and I am guilty of murder (with extenuating circumstances). On another view no, because my intention was to save the 14. Each of these

---

44   See Detmold, above n 37, 37–41.
45   60 Mass (6 Cush) 292 (1850).
46   This is a version of Ivan Karamazov's question to his brother, Alyosha: if you could purchase perpetual happiness for humankind by the torture of one innocent child, would you do it? The question is confused by the pathological (Kant's meaning) abhorrence that we have of torture; a much more rigorous version is: would you purchase perpetual happiness for humankind by the commission of a small tort on a dying adult?

views is unsatisfactory. There is a strong sense in which I intended Jones' death; it was a central part of the meaning of my action. But am I at fault?

When it is alleged that one person has wronged another (Jones) the question of the intention in the action must focus on the place of Jones in its meaning. In this respect in the bandit case I am faultless, for this reason. A relation of minds is in place when all relevant persons are respected under the law of love. Was Jones respected? Clearly so. If given the opportunity I would have called the 15 together and offered them the gift implicit in the bandit's condition, that is 14 chances in 15 of their lives being saved. They get this for nothing, and they would accept it. More to the point perhaps, Smith would accept it. And were I not given the opportunity to discuss the matter with them, I would still know what they would decide; and I would act accordingly, respecting them all, including the unlucky one.

Conclusion: The Brute Phenomenal

There is no private mind, but there are still phenomenal perceptions and desires, and there are individuals who have their own phenomenal perceptions and desires—just as Wittgenstein never denied pain, so he never denied the phenomenal or the individual. But the question of intention is one of meaning, and meaning is always shared. That there are no private minds means only that meaning and intention are relational. Everyone accepts that meaning and intention are functions of mind; the issue is whether they are (as I hold) solely functions of the relations of minds.

I am in pain. Could I be mistaken about this? Hardly. Pain is a phenomenal thing, and there is no issue of mistake in the middle of a phenomenal experience. (To think otherwise is a category error: it would be like asking whether the twitch of a toe were a mistake.) Further, the pain is *my* phenomenal experience, and that statement of fact precludes mistake. The issue of mistake comes later than the brute phenomenal, when, for example, I seek to say something about the pain. Then, and only then, is there an issue of interpretation of events, meaning and possible mistake.

Now, I might groan or I might say 'I am in pain.' Is there a difference? This is the question of meaning. Of course, groans themselves can have meaning. So let us make this groan a brute one. Is there a difference between the brute groan and 'I am in pain'? (But 'I am in pain' could also be brute—the species could be selected for four distinct sounds rather than one long one—so we'll say it is not.) The difference between the two is that the latter has meaning. And the condition of this is that it is a shared thing under the law of love. If it is not shared, if, for example, I say to a doctor 'Only I know that I am in pain, you don't', I have caused my statement to revert to the brute; it is now the equivalent of the groan, and there is no meaning in it. There might be meaning. The doctor might take my statement to be the first sally in a philosophical discussion. But here the pain itself is not the topic.

Suppose, eschewing the philosophical in favour of the medical, the doctor says: 'I don't doubt that you are experiencing pain, but you are actually imagining it by virtue of a certain experience you had as a child.' I reply: 'No, Doctor, it's my pain. I know it's real.' But now the conversation has again reverted again to the brute (or the philosophical).

Take another example. Suppose I'm playing cricket, and I bowl out the opposing team's opening batsman with a ball that pitches outside off stump and comes back. 'A great wrong 'un', you say. 'Well, actually no', I reply. 'It was intended to be a leg break.' Am I an authority on my intention in this matter? When I bowled the ball there was a lot of phenomenal activity in place in my mind including my desire to bowl a leg break. Could I be mistaken here? Of course not. The bruteness of the phenomenal is a critical thing in the understanding of Wittgenstein. As with pain, no issue of mistake (or of knowledge, or meaning) arises in the middle of the brute phenomenal. But when I'm asked, moments later, about my intention as to the ball I bowled, the issue is radically changed to one of knowledge, meaning and possible mistake.

Moments later and you will probably have no reason to doubt my memory and interpretation (the meaning I'm now offering). But what if it is months later? And what if it is not a deliberate action like the bowling of a ball that is in issue, but a hectic, confused one, such as what I did in a run-out crisis? My memory is entitled to status here but it is hardly conclusive.

However, these issues attaching to my memory and my interpretation of events are not what Wittgenstein's opponents are getting at. I'm sure they will concede the fallibility of memory. What I think they want to say is that there is a special authority that I have over my own intention. But they confound the brute phenomenal, where I cannot be mistaken (because the idea makes no sense), with my memory and subsequent interpretation of events, where I am but one player in their meaning and intention.

I will conclude with a simpler example than Wittgenstein's of pain or mine of the art of leg-spin bowling. The issue of the relation between intention and phenomenal desire in the Smith and Jones cases is resolved in the same way we resolve the colour red.[47]

I have no access to your phenomenal experience of red, and it makes no sense for me to think I do. But we practise red together under the condition of the law of love—your phenomenal experience (whatever it is) is equal to mine. If our game works it works,[48] and we have the colour red. There is no other way to get the colour. If I say 'only I see it' we can have no practice of red and there is no meaning to red. ('The meaning of red is what *I* see' is a meaningless statement.) All meaning comes from language games, the condition of which is the law of love—love the other as self, which in the case of red is: your red is as my red.[49]

There can therefore be no meaning of red except in relation. And there can be no meaning to phenomenal desire (no intention) except in relation. In the various relations between Smith and Jones neither has access to the other's phenomenal desire. But their respective desires have meaning when they practise them under the law of love (the condition of all language games). Another way of saying this is that they have meaning when they practise them in contract: contract is the model of all lawful human relations,[50] and its law is the law of love, the same law as the law of language games.

When their practice starts to go wrong (and so an issue of fault arises) we do not generate meaning by pretending that we then have access to one

---

47   There is a fuller discussion of colour and meaning in Detmold, above n 8.

48   It is like natural selection in the biological world. What evolves evolves. But there is such an intricate and marvellous biological display that we think there must be meaning behind it. The power of the theory of natural selection lies in the fact that what evolves evolves: it simply needs a world with the possibility of mutation and therefore complexity. Language is the same. It also presents an intricate and marvellous display; and so we are tempted to think there must be prior meaning behind it. But what works in the relations of minds works.

49   Detmold, above n 8. There is, of course, colour blindness. You see red where I see green. This is merely a slight complication in the practice, to which the reflections in the text apply completely: you see red when I see green, but is the red that you see the same red as I see when I do see red, and so on? This question of sameness is the meaningless one.

50   Including tort and crime. See 'Accidental Fault', above; and Detmold, above n 37, 33.

or the other's phenomenal state of desire. When the practice goes wrong we are losing meaning, not gaining it. But we do have access to the condition of this loss of meaning—the breach of the law of love. The issue of intentional fault (in the varying degrees proposed in this essay) is always the structural one of the relation of the minds involved and its breach.

So the issue in the Smith and Jones cases is the issue of the loss of meaning between them. In contract, two brute phenomenal desires come out of their bruteness to meet each other in the meaning of the contract (language game[51]). To the extent that Jones is excluded from contract-like respect[52] in Smith's exploits the matter reverts to (or stays in) the realm of his brute phenomenal (where there is no issue of meaning or intention). The issue in the Smith and Jones cases is how much respect for Jones (and therefore meaning) there was in Smith's attitude throughout the events of the cases.

Contract and crime (stealing[53]) are opposites. In contract we are examining the building-up of meaning; in crime (and tort), its breakdown.[54] The philosophical substance of each is, however, the same.

Now think of Smith of *DPP v Smith* (case 2) cross-examined in his trial. The answers I shall invent are intended to be honest answers. This is a substantive as well as an expositional matter. There is, of course, a tendency for accused persons to give dishonest answers. But there is obviously no meaning in such talk. Lying at the trial would be the loss of meaning between Smith and the other participants in the trial (specifically, it would be a breach of the conversational contract between them). But this *further* issue of the loss of meaning in the court conversation we put aside. We are concerned with the initial (substantive) loss of meaning, that between Smith and Jones. Now the cross-examination.

---

51   All contracts are language games. Some are big (our form of governance), some are very big (the language itself) and some are little (buying a newspaper). There is much intersection, interdependence and overlapping.

52   This is Kantian respect. It distinguishes contracting from stealing. If other is as self, then self is required to negotiate with the other if they want something from them. If the self thinks they can get it without negotiating and contracting, then they are not allowing that other is as self. They are stealing. This applies to every aspect of human relations. In respect of everything I get from another the choice is: contract or steal.

53   Murder is the stealing of someone's life.

54   Breach of contract is, of course, breakdown, like crime. In fact it is like tort; tort and breach of contract are the same thing. In contract we build up meaning. In crime/tort/breach of contract we destroy it.

'What were you doing?', asks the lawyer. 'Intending to hurt the constable, intending to escape arrest? Both? One more than the other?' 'I don't know', says Smith. (At least with red he could point to something.) And nor do we.[55] Now, think of a different set of questions. 'You were trying to escape arrest, right?' 'Yes.' 'And the constable was trying to arrest you?' 'Yes.' 'Did you accept that the constable's project was entitled to the same respect as your own?' 'Well, I couldn't, could I? They were inconsistent.' 'When you planned the robbery did you think there might be someone in the vicinity whose job it was to stop you?' 'Yes, of course.' 'Did you plan as carefully about their safety as you planned about your own?' 'No.' 'So when you shook the constable off you were thinking more about your own enterprise than her safety?' 'Yes.' 'Did it occur to you then that she might be seriously injured, even killed?' 'Well, I don't know that I thought about it, but it's obvious, isn't it?'[56]

The first line of questioning of Smith makes no more sense than if Smith were asked to explain what his phenomenal view of red was really like. The second line exposes Smith's fault exactly. And it is the opposite of the first. In the first (traditional) way of thinking, Smith's intention is supposed in some way to have focused on the constable. But his fault lies in the fact that it didn't.

---

55 It is a confused, hectic event like the run out discussed earlier in this section.

56 This may constitute recklessness under the definition set out above. There would have to be a deliberate rejection of concern for the consequences to Jones. In the heat of the moment this is perhaps unlikely. If the danger to Jones is just in the background of Smith's thought at the time then it is no different from a serious case of negligent driving. It is the particularisation of Jones that appears to make a difference; but this is a red herring, as discussed above.

10 Intention to Contract: Public Act or Private Sentiment?

MARGARET THORNTON

An act of the united choice of two persons by which anything at all that belongs to one passes to the other is a *contract*.[1]

Introduction

By and large, the role of intention within liberal legalism is functional; it is employed as a device to give retrospective meaning to a situation or text in order to assign responsibility for an act. Judges are formally charged with performing the interpretive role in a way that accords with legal and social norms. Because the purposive role of intention is paramount, law is not overly concerned with speculating about what might have transpired within the secret recesses of the mind of an accused, litigant or legislature, months, or even years, before. Pragmatism, not philosophical inquiry, is the dominant *modus operandi*.

Within the criminal law, intention operates as a device for affixing culpability, usually in individualistic terms, in order to assuage societal angst. In civil law, intent is invoked to steer a course between private wishes, objective legal phrases and just ends.[2] In the case of legislative intent, an individualised concept has to be transmuted into one that is corporatised and publicly sanctioned but, as Waluchow asks, 'How does one meaningfully ascribe intentions to a disparate body like a legislature?'[3]

---

1   Immanuel Kant, *The Metaphysics of Morals* (Mary Gregor (trans)) (1996) 91.
2   Eg Jane Baron, 'Intention, Interpretation, and Stories' (1992) 42 *Duke Law Journal* 630.
3   W J Waluchow, *Inclusive Legal Positivism* (1994) 255. Statutory interpretation is one of the sites identified by Julius Stone where judges are able to exercise creative choices, or what he termed 'leeways of choice':

217

In determining what can reasonably be attributed to the legislative brain at the time the relevant statute was enacted, fictional meanings may be constructed to serve particular ends.[4] However, as Balkin points out, 'All decision making makes use of ideological constructions of social reality. What we call "non-ideological" decisions are ideological decisions whose ideology is simply not noticed.'[5] It is in this way that intention is filtered through prevailing legal discourse so that suitable accounts of dispute resolution are effected for public consumption. I am interested in looking at the fictions and the ideology of contractualism, particularly in the way that intention is construed according to the legal hermeneutic tradition in which it is embedded.

Within classical liberalism, both the marketplace and the domestic sphere are deemed to be private and beyond state intervention. It will be shown, however, that law adopts quite a different stance towards market-based 'contracts' compared with intimate 'agreements', when viewed through the lens of intention. Privacy is deemed to shield domestic agreements from scrutiny; they operate in an extra-legal space where 'domesticated command' has traditionally prevailed. In contrast, the law is predisposed to uphold 'private' contracts emanating from the market because they underpin free enterprise.

To illustrate the thesis, I will first consider the nature of the transition that has occurred from will theory to objectivism, with particular regard to commercial contracts. Secondly, I will have regard to the marriage contract, which is a very curious type of contract because of its status, or non-negotiable, elements. Thirdly, I will interrogate the resistance towards

---

> Where the ordinary meaning of the words yields a single acceptable result, reference beyond the words seems unnecessary. But where the words do not yield such a single acceptable result reference to the supposed intention is, as Gény pointed out, a fiction covering over the inescapable judicial activity of creative choices.

Julius Stone, *Legal System and Lawyers' Reasonings* (1968) 350.

4   The so-called 'persons cases', a spate of which occurred in the common law world in the late-nineteenth and early-twentieth centuries, are a good illustration. In these cases, in which women sought to be admitted to the professions and to stand for election to public office, statutes using the gender-neutral word 'person' were interpreted to exclude women on the basis that the relevant legislation did not 'intend' women to be lawyers, doctors, etc: Albie Sachs and Joan Hoff Wilson, *Sexism and the Law: A Study of Male Beliefs and Judicial Bias in Britain and the United States* (1978); Mary Jane Mossman, 'Feminism and Legal Method: The Difference it Makes' (1986) 3 *Australian Journal of Law and Society* 30; Margaret Thornton, *Dissonance and Distrust: Women in the Legal Profession* (1996) esp 56–63.

5   J M Balkin, 'Ideology as Constraint' (1991) 43 *Stanford Law Review* 1133, 1153.

domestic contractualism. Although a shift is occurring from 'contract as commerce to contract as relationality',[6] the focus is still on property and financial agreements in accordance with market contractualism. The effect is to leave unchallenged the fact that women assume overwhelming responsibility for housework and child care, functions deemed to be carried out for 'love and affection'. The absence of an intention to enter into legal relations continues to be invoked to cordon off affectivity from scrutiny.

From Will Theory to Objectivism

Kant is a useful starting point for thinking about the philosophy of intention, for he is the progenitor of will theory, which dominated contract theory until the end of the nineteenth century.[7] A consideration of the Kantian approach enables us to appreciate the ideological changes that have occurred. Kant believed that the will emerged from the reason of the subject and encompassed the capacity for desire.[8] Hence, the will is able to incorporate both *choice* and *wish*. While the will is primarily a product of reason, freedom of choice means that the will can be affected by impulses other than pure reason. The exclusive cerebral focus means that all the contractee acquires is the promise of the other, not the thing promised.[9] In the meeting of two minds, a unity of the two wills occurs which must be respected in the fulfilment of mutual obligations.[10] The reciprocal promise constitutes the foundation of the moral right against the other person to carry out their promise. The contract as a promise enshrines the liberal notion of the right which embodies the self's capacity to determine its own conception of the good. Will theory emphasises the importance of the rights of the individual, rather than collective interests, because the will of the collective is much harder to ascertain. Religious significance attached to the promise through the belief that God was a witness to it, or that the promisor actually communicated with God, as well as the mundane person and the law.[11] There was thought to be something unconscionable about changing one's mind. Accordingly, promises could be pleaded and

---

6   Elizabeth Kingdom, 'Cohabitation Contracts and the Democratization of Personal Relations' (2000) 8 *Feminist Legal Studies* 5, 6.
7   Charles Fried, *Contract as Promise* (1981) 60.
8   Kant, above n 1, 42.
9   Ibid 93.
10   Ibid.
11   Peter Goodrich, 'Gender and Contracts' in Anne Bottomley (ed), *Feminist Perspectives on the Foundational Subjects of Law* (1996) 21.

enforced in spiritual courts. Will theory displays scant concern for the content of the contract, including proof of inequality, which does not suffice to vitiate a contract at common law.[12]

The contemporary legal approach to contract is significantly more pragmatic and purposive than that suggested by will theory. By the end of the nineteenth century, the will theory of contract, with its subjective meeting of the minds, had been 'objectivised' by jurists, such as Holmes, in the United States.[13] Although the discourse of contract continues to be infused with high-sounding moral concepts, including promise, obligation, mutuality, autonomy and trust, a contracting party in modern commercial relations may not be held to its bargain if it has changed its mind, provided that it is deemed reasonable in the circumstances. It would seem that a transition has occurred from 'the Age of Principle into the Age of Pragmatism'.[14] De Moor suggests that the move to an objective approach has been bolstered by the need for certainty in commercial relationships,[15] although she argues strongly that intention should not be forsaken, for it remains the backbone of contract.

Indeed, in the commercial sphere courts rarely look for the subjective intention of the parties at all.[16] Lord Steyne succinctly encapsulates the contemporary position:

> It is true the objective of the construction of a contract is to give effect to the intention of the parties. But our law of construction is based on an objective theory. The methodology is not to probe the real intentions of the parties but to ascertain the contextual meaning of the relevant contractual language. Intention is determined by reference to expressed rather than actual intention. The question therefore resolves itself in a search for the meaning of language in its contractual setting. That does not mean that the purpose of a contractual provision is not important ... But the court must not try to divine the purpose of the contract by speculating about the real intention of the parties. It may only be inferred from the language used by the parties, judged against the

---

12 Though in some cases equity may provide some relief: see, for example, *Commercial Bank of Australia Ltd v Amadio* (1983) 151 CLR 447. Some jurisdictions have introduced legislation permitting release from unconscionable contracts, such as *Contracts Review Act 1980* (NSW).

13 Clare Dalton, 'An Essay in the Deconstruction of Contract Doctrine' (1985) 94 *Yale Law Journal* 997, 1040 et passim.

14 P S Atiyah, *The Rise and Fall of Freedom of Contract* (1979) 649 ff.

15 Anne de Moor, 'Intention in the Law of Contract: Elusive or Illusory?' (1990) 106 *Law Quarterly Review* 632, 655.

16 Geoffrey Samuel and Jac Rinkes, *Law of Obligations and Legal Remedies* (1996) 210.

objective contextual background. It is therefore wrong to speculate about the actual intention of the parties.[17]

A formalistic approach to contract does not accord with the ambiguity, flexibility, mediation, negotiation and variation that is more likely to typify contemporary business practice.[18] As with other sites of legal revisionism, it is not the *subjective* intent that matters, but the *appearance* of intent that is important.[19] The contract must nevertheless be grounded in the subjectivity of the promise for the court to construe an intention to be bound from external indicia:

> What has to be shown is that there is objective evidence of an apparently subjective *consensus ad idem*. If the offeree objectively appears to have knowledge of, and be accepting, the offeror's promise then the promise will be binding: 'what is necessary is that the intention of each as it has been communicated to and understood by the other (even though that which has been communicated does not represent the actual state of mind of the communicator) should coincide'.[20]

It therefore cannot be said that contract has moved away altogether from the subjectivity of the will to an objective manifestation, for an 'elusive correspondence between subjective intent and manifested form'[21] remains. This subjectivity tends to be invoked selectively by courts in order to legitimise particular incarnations of the 'objective'. However, no court is likely to find a contract in existence in the absence of any evidence of an intention to enter into a contract. Conversely, it is not going to find the existence of a contract in the absence of any objective evidence of a relationship that will ground liability. Contract law necessitates a reconstruction of events for the purpose of determining liability:

> In singling out these two parties and bringing them together in this way, private law looks neither to the litigants individually nor to the interests of the community as a whole, but to a bipolar relationship of liability.[22]

---

17   *Genossenschaftsbank v Burnhope* [1995] 1 WLR 1580, 1587.

18   Goodrich, above n 11, 33.

19   P S Atiyah, 'Contracts, Promises and the Law of Obligations' (1978) 94 *Law Quarterly Review* 193, 203.

20   Samuel and Rinkes, above n 16, 222, elaborating upon the words of Lord Diplock in *The Hannah Blumenthal* [1983] 1 AC 854, 915–16.

21   Dalton, above n 13, 1100.

22   Ernest Weinrub, *The Idea of Private Law* (1995) 2.

Contract is considered to represent the paradigmatic act of liberal legalism whereby strangers voluntarily agree to come together and effect binding pacts free from intervention by the state. It is the function of the law to give effect to private autonomy.[23] Despite the rhetoric of individualism, the state creates the conditions of freedom for the parties. In any case, the notion of untrammelled freedom is qualified by judicial revisioning of intent on breach of a term by one of the parties.

Under the guise of facilitating private wills, law privileges the free market and the workings of capitalism. Contract is the central plank of the market economy.[24] Contract is always shaped by public policy which, in turn, informs the notion of what is a contract in the first place.[25] Thus, an intention to create legal relations will be deemed to inhere within a bipolar relationship by virtue of its market setting: 'No one supposes that two merchants who make a deal must entertain some additional intention to create legal relations in order for that deal to be binding in law.'[26] Indeed, some substantive evidence, normally of an express kind, is required to rebut the presumption that there was no intention to create legal relations in the marketplace.

This presumption is the direct opposite of the situation in a domestic setting. Lord Salmon describes the presumption against legal relations in the domestic sphere as a presumption of fact, not law, which derives from life and human nature, relying on family ties of mutual trust and affection.[27] Although some family contracts involving donative transactions may advance community interests, such as a gift from a parent to a child, the values of harmony and community associated with idealised family life are thought to be corroded by contractualism: 'A family arrangement of this type cannot be measured just in terms of dollars and cents.'[28] 'Arm's-length' contractualism is deemed appropriate for a legalised space, which is underpinned by the assumption that the parties are on an equal footing, but not for the family where dependency and inequality are normative. While

---

23 Atiyah, above n 19, 193.

24 Thomas Wilhelmsson, 'Questions for a Critical Contract Law—and a Contradictory Answer: Contract as Social Cooperation' in Thomas Wilhelmsson (ed), *Perspectives of Critical Contract Law* (1993) 16–17.

25 Beverley Brown, 'Contracting Out/Contracting In: Some Feminist Considerations' in Bottomley, above n 11, 11.

26 Fried, above n 7, n 38.

27 *Jones v Padavatton* [1969] 2 All ER 616, 621.

28 *Aras v Schmutz* (Unreported, New South Wales Court of Appeal, 9 December 1997) [26] per Brownie AJA.

the family is not in fact unregulated,[29] resistance to regulation has had the effect of creating what Frances Olsen refers to as a 'limited "state of nature", in which the state refused to protect one family member from the harmful acts of any other family member'.[30] By invoking the language of love and affection, the domestic sphere has been judicially constituted as non-rational and outside the domain of law.

The existence of intent is therefore primarily determined by the geographical site of the relationship within the liberal landscape. The courts have recourse to familiar aids and interpretive techniques to assist in the construction of an intention to justify different outcomes for different sites. Wightman argues that commercial contracts can draw on the context of a contracting community as a source of norms to fill in the gaps, a context which is lacking in the case of intimate relationships.[31] However, I would suggest that courts draw on the norms of a *non*-contracting community in the case of intimate relations, a context long shaped by the marriage contract. In the domestic sphere generally, there is unlikely to be a written contract drawn up by lawyers, but a casual remark embedded in an overture of affection on which the plaintiff relies:

> The parties did not use and are unlikely even to have known formal language which would unmistakably express the intention to create enforceable equitable interests.[32]

In a commercial setting, the parties are assumed to be at arm's length, for suspicion and distrust underpin the normative contractual relationship which may crystallise into adversarial legal relations; contract is corrosive of trust among intimates. The idea that one's competitor is one's contracting partner whose will merges with one's own at one moment, but who may turn on one the next, highlights the parlous and tenuous nature of trust in the market. There is a masculinist character to 'arm's-length' contractualism which transcends the identity of the parties, the range of life

---

29 Katherine O'Donovan, *Sexual Divisions in Law* (1985); Margaret Thornton, 'The Cartography of Public and Private' in Margaret Thornton (ed), *Public and Private: Feminist Legal Debates* (1995) 2.

30 Frances Olsen, 'The Family and the Market: A Study of Ideology and Legal Reform' (1983) 96 *Harvard Law Review* 1497, 1521.

31 John Wightman, 'Intimate Relationships, Relational Contract Theory and the Reach of Contract' (2000) 8 *Feminist Legal Studies* 93, 106–7.

32 *Aras v Schmutz* (unreported, New South Wales Court of Appeal, 9 December 1997) [6] per Priestley JA.

experiences, stock gender roles and sex specific language.[33] The rules of contract, underpinned by competitiveness, aggression, self-interest and mistrust, are deemed to be unsuited to non-commercial settings:

> These rules express a reluctance to allow contract law to intrude at all upon the world of family and friendship, lest by doing so it destroy their peculiar communal quality.[34]

At one level, the rhetoric of love and affection that envelopes the domestic sphere is attractive, but feminist critiques have exposed how this seductive language conceals patriarchal ordering that is conceptualised as a space beyond law: the home must be maintained as a 'haven in a heartless world'[35] for men who have to deal with the dehumanised world of the market.[36] The dichotomy between public and private must therefore be maintained because it is functional.

Judges themselves are also discomfited by affectivity and would prefer the 'arm's-length' approach, which comports with the universality, abstraction, neutrality and objectivity of law. Dealing with company A versus company B is much easier than the case of a child suing a parent[37] or a parent suing a child.[38] In a commercial law dispute, it does not really matter who 'wins'; the outcome has no more significance than a sporting contest because the tables may soon turn. Thus, the softer, feminised language conflating society and connectedness with relational contracts is deceptive.[39] All contracts are 'relational', in that they necessarily involve a relationship between two parties, even if they are adversaries. In the case of a family dispute, the outcome may be devastating, rending asunder family ties forever. For this reason, intimates with 'undoubted legal rights' may 'forbear from mercy' to enforce them.[40]

---

33 Mary Joe Frug, *Postmodern Legal Feminism* (1992) 60–124.
34 Roberto Mangabeira Unger, *The Critical Legal Studies Movement* (1983) 62. Cf Hugh Collins, *The Law of Contract* (3rd ed, 1997) 64–6.
35 Christopher Lasch, *Haven in a Heartless World: The Family Besieged* (1977).
36 Olsen, above n 30, 1524.
37 *Aras v Schmutz* (unreported, New South Wales Court of Appeal, 9 December 1997).
38 *Jones v Padavatton* [1969] 2 All ER 616.
39 Alice Belcher, 'A Feminist Perspective on Contract Theories from Law and Economics' (2000) 8 *Feminist Legal Studies* 29, 44. Belcher acknowledges the significance of the work of Macneil on relational theory, although it is primarily concerned with market contracts. See Ian Macneil, *The New Social Contract: An Inquiry into Modern Contractual Relations* (1980).
40 *Jones v Padavatton* [1969] 2 All ER 616, 622.

Unger acknowledges the traditional power exercised by a husband over a wife within the family as a reason for treating the family as a private community beyond the realm of contract.[41] A nascent contract theory that 'preaches equality in distrust'[42] threatens the hierarchical norms of the traditional heterosexual family type in which the husband is the head of the household: 'The redemptive union of authority and affection provides the alternative to legal or at least to contractual ordering.'[43]

The Marriage Contract

Few contract textbooks today mention the marriage contract, in contradistinction to the nineteenth century when entry into marriage was viewed as the quintessential site of contract formation:

> The relation of marriage is founded upon the will of God, and the nature of man; and it is the foundation of all moral improvement, and all true happiness. No legal topic surpasses it in importance; and some of the questions which it suggests are of great difficulty.[44]

As contract became the preserve of the market, marriage and other particular forms of contract, such as the social contract and the employment contract, disappeared from texts and treatises on contract law and were dealt with in specialist works.[45] It may be that the marriage contract is not viewed as a true contract by lawyers because the parties are not free to set their own terms,[46] a criticism that feminists have also been making for almost two hundred years.[47] The retention of a status element in the marriage contract contributes to its unique character as a contract.

The conjunction of the Christian idea of marriage as a sacrament and the ascendancy of the will theory of contract contributed to the view that marriage was the most perfect form of contract.[48] In contrast to the ephemeral union of parties to a commercial contract, the two wills merged

---

41   Unger, above n 34, 65.
42   Ibid.
43   Ibid 66.
44   Theophilus Parsons, *Law of Contracts* (first published 1853, 1980 ed) 556–7.
45   Unger, above n 34, 58.
46   Cf Brown, above n 25, 7; Marcia Neave, 'Private Ordering in Family Law: Will Women Benefit?' in Thornton, above n 29, 146–7.
47   Carole Pateman, *The Sexual Contract* (1988) 154.
48   Goodrich, above n 11, 7.

and remained permanently indivisible. Nevertheless, according to Blackstone, the will of the wife was subsumed into that of the husband,[49] which would seem to suggest something less than perfect unity. But, as already intimated, will theory had little regard for reality. Carole Pateman's radical thesis is that the marriage contract was effected between men in order to secure access to women's bodies.[50] Thus, rather than contracting partners, women were merely the objects of exchange, and the real parties were fathers, brothers, guardians and prospective husbands. The exclusion of married women from contract, other than at the moment of crystallisation of the formal marriage contract, has meant that contractualism has historically been a deeply gendered phenomenon.[51]

Despite the patriarchal heritage, the formation of the marriage contract at common law mirrored the basic elements of the contract in a commercial setting. Provided that the elements of offer and acceptance, intent, capacity and consideration were present, even if in fictional form, the contractual requirements were satisfied. The civil action for breach of promise to marry, now generally repealed,[52] in which damages were payable in the breach, clearly illustrates the point. The action, which originated in the ecclesiastical courts, epitomises the will theory of contract in that it was predicated on the promise alone. Hence, a breach of the promise was regarded as more serious than embarking on a bad marriage for life.[53] As with commercial contracts, intention was established by the presence of objective evidence, such as the purchase of an engagement ring. The action, instituted almost entirely by women, revealed the social pressure on men to uphold monogamy and heterosexuality.

Once the parties move beyond the threshold, a different incarnation of the marriage contract emerges, one that hovers between status and contractualism. Maine's famous aphorism 'from status to contract'[54]

---

49 Blackstone has expressed this idea most famously: 'By marriage, the husband and wife are one person in law: that is, the very being or legal existence of the woman is suspended during the marriage, or at least is incorporated and consolidated into that of the husband; under whose wing, protection, and *cover*, she performs everything.' William Blackstone, *Commentaries on the Laws of England* (first published 1765–69, 1979 ed) 442.
50 Pateman, above n 47.
51 Cf Goodrich, above n 11, 23.
52 *Law Reform (Miscellaneous Provisions) Act 1970* (UK); *Family Law (Amendment) Act 1976* (Cth).
53 Margaret Thornton, 'Historicising Citizenship: Remembering Broken Promises' (1996) 20 *Melbourne University Law Review* 1072.
54 Sir Henry Sumner Maine, *Ancient Law: Its Connections with the Early History of Society and its Relation to Modern Ideas* (first published 1861, 1917 ed).

encapsulates the idea of the transition that has been effected from feudalism to modernity. Freedom of contract could be said to be the *leitmotif* of modernity, as society sloughed off the rigidity of feudal status in favour of individual liberty and the free market. The marriage *contract,* however, is something of a misnomer because it retains pre-modern, status elements in which there are still legally binding terms that are non-negotiable. The parties cannot be said to inhabit that domain of freedom that is supposedly characteristic of liberalism, apart from choosing to enter marriage or depart from it. It has been suggested that the static nature of the rights and duties makes marriage the paradigmatic status relationship.[55] The result is that an intention which is contrary to the status provisions of marriage cannot be accorded legally binding effect.

In respect of the formation stage, it may appear to be self-evident that a marriage can take place only between a man and a woman, but this traditional status requirement imposes a profound limitation on freedom of contract.[56] The universal prohibition of same-sex marriage in favour of heterosexual unions[57] may also exclude transsexual partners[58] and other non-normative unions.[59] The intention of the parties in such cases is legally irrelevant. Whereas contractual capacity in the marketplace is restricted by the requirements of sound mind and attainment of the age of majority, the sex and number of parties to a marriage contract constitute crucial limitations. The *sexual* nature of the contract is another.

As Kant pointed out, 'A marriage contract is *consummated* only *by conjugal sexual intercourse (copula carnalis).*'[60] What Pateman refers to as

---

55   Cf Stephen Cretney, 'From Status to Contract?' in F D Rose (ed), *Consensus Ad Idem: Essays in the Law of Contract in Honour of Guenter Treitel* (1996) 269.

56   That a marriage must be heterosexual is the common law position, adapted from ecclesiastical law, and now incorporated into statute. See, eg, *Matrimonial Causes Act 1973* (UK) ss 11, 12; *Family Law Act 1975* (Cth) s 43(a).

57   In 2000, the Dutch Cabinet enacted legislation which made Holland the first country in the world with full marriage rights for gays and lesbians. See 'Dutch Same-Sex Couples Get Break' *The Age*, 14 September 2000, 13. Denmark has had a system of registering same-sex relationships (not marriages) since 1989. See also John Culhane, 'Uprooting the Arguments against Same Sex Marriage' (1999) 20 *Cardozo Law Review* 1119; Heather Lauren Hughes, 'Same-Sex Marriage and Simulacra: Exploring Conceptions of Equality' (1998) 33 *Harvard Civil Rights-Civil Liberties Law Review* 237.

58   *Corbett v Corbett* [1971] P 83; Mary Coombs, 'Transgenderism and Sexual Orientation: More than a Marriage of Convenience' (1997) *National Journal of Sexual Orientation Law* 3 <http://metalab.unc.edu/gaylaw/issue5/issue5.html> 1.

59   O'Donovan, *Family Law Matters* (1993) 45.

60   Kant, above n 1, 98.

the 'sex act', which is intercourse constituted in terms of male sexuality,[61] is a fixed term of the contract. The agreement of the parties to live a celibate life, for example, cannot alter the status requirement. Similarly, an agreement to separate that is made during marriage or before the parties are married is invalid.[62] This would include an agreement to separate after a fixed period or when the children have grown up. Although married people effect informal arrangements of this kind all the time, pre-nuptial contracts are not legally enforceable at common law.[63] There is no problem as to the validity of such an arrangement once the parties are formally separated, when a disaggregation of wills occurs and the parties are free to enter into new agreements. It is at the threshold of marriage, when the minds of the parties are supposedly *ad idem,* that their intent may be frustrated by status elements.

Marriage represents a contemporary site of contestation, and increasing numbers of men and women are not marrying at all. Marriage nevertheless remains the template for legal recognition of intimate relationships. To qualify as a de facto relationship, the essential requirement of a de jure marriage has to be satisfied, that is, the relationship must consist of a man and a woman; a same-sex relationship does not qualify. Legislative moves to recognise same-sex relationships have challenged directly the notion of enforceable status terms that can only be heterosexual.[64] While the freedom and autonomy associated with contractualism are ostensibly liberatory, there is nevertheless a certain disquiet associated with transposing the values of the marketplace into family settings. The provocative question that has been posed is: 'should the family become more like the market (or vice versa)'?[65]

---

61   Pateman, above n 47, 164. See also O'Donovan, above n 59, 45 ff; Richard Collier, *Masculinity, Law and the Family* (1995) 147 ff.

62   G H Treitel, *The Law of Contract* (9th ed, 1995) 400.

63   The Australian Government has tabled legislation which will enable couples to make binding financial agreements before, during and after marriage. See Family Law Amendment Bill 1999 pt VIIIA: 'Financial Agreements'. The agreements would have to be in writing and legal advice would be mandatory. The Family Court would be the arbiter of disputes. For a critique of the proposal, see Belinda Fehlberg and Bruce Smyth, 'Pre-Nuptial Agreements for Australia: Why Not?' (2000) 14 *Australian Journal of Family Law* 80.

64   For example, *Property (Relationships) Legislation Amendment Act 1999* (NSW); Hon Justice Michael Kirby, 'Same Sex Relationships: Some Australian Legal Developments' (1999) 19 *Australian Bar Review* 14; Jenni Millbank, 'If Australian Law Opened its Eyes to Lesbian and Gay Families, What Would it See?' (1998) 12 *Australian Family Law Journal* 99.

65   Olsen, above n 30, 1529.

Contracting in the Haven

In view of the vagaries surrounding entry into marriage, the extent to which contractualism *within* marriage is permitted has remained uncertain, although greater autonomy is accorded the parties on breakdown of marriage.[66] Hobbes said that if a man and woman contract in the state of nature, the children are the mother's but, in a civil government, if there be a contract of marriage, any children belong to the father because 'the domesticated command' belongs to the man under the civil law of matrimony.[67] This theory of 'domesticated command' has shaped the ideology of contractualism in the context of marital relations. Coverture denied a married woman all civil rights, including the right to contract. As a *feme covert*, her legal personality merged with that of her husband at common law, and any contracts into which she entered were void.[68] Once under the cover, or wing, of her husband, the wife's will was vitiated; marriage meant a state of civil death for her.

Despite the passage of married women's property Acts, enfranchisement and other progressive initiatives designed to remove sex-based disabilities affecting women during the nineteenth and twentieth centuries, a residual assumption of indivisibility of the legal personalities of husband and wife has lingered on,[69] a factor that has impeded their ability to enter into pre-nuptial and nuptial contracts.[70] Equality, freedom and autonomy, the qualities presumed to characterise contractees in the marketplace, have largely eluded married women.

The predilection in favour of contractualism in the marketplace has permitted the interpolation of an intention to create legal relations. In the domestic sphere, there has been an unwillingness to interpolate this intention. Judicial revisioning has thereby effectively upheld the separation between public and private spheres in accordance with the dominant liberal

---

66 Cretney, above n 55, 251; Olsen, above n 30, 1535. Community of property regimes that recognise an equal division of marital property on divorce represent an attempt to move beyond former models of dominance and dependence.

67 Thomas Hobbes, *De Cive or The Citizen* (Sterling Lamprecht (ed))(first published 1642, 1949 ed) IX 6.

68 David Berkowitz and Samuel Thorne (selectors), *Baron and Feme: A Treatise of the Common Law concerning Husbands and Wives* (first published 1700) in *Classics of English Legal History in the Modern Era* (1979) 214 ff.

69 Mary Lyndon Shanley, *Feminism, Marriage, and the Law in Victorian England, 1850–1895* (1989) 46; Margaret Thornton, 'The Judicial Gendering of Citizenship: A Look at Property Interests During Marriage' (1997) 24 *Journal of Law and Society* 486.

70 Eg *F v F* [1995] 2 FLR 45; *Zamet v Hyman* [1969] 3 All ER 933.

paradigm. In this way, the Hobbesian concept of 'domesticated command' has been instantiated as an ancillary status element to the marriage contract.

The leading case on domestic contractualism is *Balfour v Balfour*,[71] in which the husband agreed to pay maintenance to the wife on their informal separation; she was to remain in England while he returned to (what was then) Ceylon. When the husband reneged and the wife instituted suit, the King's Bench held that 'the King's writ does not seek to run' in the private sphere *qua* family because the family has been constituted as a realm beyond law. From the facts, it is apparent that there was an intention that the husband would pay maintenance to the wife on the understanding that she would not pledge his credit or make further financial claims on him. This common intention, which satisfied the Kantian prescript, did not suffice in the Court of the King's Bench, for the parties also needed to evince an *intention* to enter into legal relations. Here, we see the functional invocation of intention to contain wives' new-found independence and to affirm the conventional cartography of public and private spheres. The element of consideration was also found to be defective for, rather than accepting the agreement on the part of the wife to reside in England and not to pledge the husband's credit, consideration was deemed to be no more than the ubiquitous 'love and affection', the familiar trope signifying 'domesticated command'. This would seem to be an example of consideration as 'fig leaf to cover a decision driven by other concerns'.[72] The facts suggest that 'love and affection' were in short supply,[73] but the courts declined to take judicial notice of the actual state of affairs; they construed their role as including a mandate to uphold marriage, however imperfect.

Balfour v Balfour remains significant, even after more than eighty years, particularly so far as spousal agreements are concerned but also so far as social and domestic agreements generally are concerned.[74] *Balfour* underscores the way that intent, like consideration, operates in contract

---

71   [1919] 2 KB 571.
72   Wightman, above n 31, 97.
73   The headnote in *Balfour v Balfour* tells us that the plaintiff had obtained a decree nisi for restitution of conjugal rights, and an order for alimony following the breach of their 'alleged verbal agreement'.
74   It has been suggested that *Balfour* would be decided differently today because of the development of the equitable remedy of estoppel. See Ray Mulholland, 'Nay, This Be Estoppel' [1998] *New Zealand Law Journal* 179, 181. Equity allows advertence to conscionability. The focus is then on the promise and the expectation, rather than the mutuality of intention. Nevertheless, equity, like the common law, has tended to uphold market, rather than domestic, relations.

discourse as a 'fig leaf' to reify the separation between the market and the family, as well as to privilege the former over the latter. *Balfour* attests eloquently to the judicial resistance to 'contracting in the haven'.[75] Freeman appraises the arguments commonly raised against domestic contractualism—public policy, privacy and intention—and shows that they are unpersuasive and riddled with contradictions.[76] Despite the liberal myth that a clear line of demarcation between public and private life is 'natural', it is apparent that regulation of these spheres is judicially authorised in accordance with ideological sub-texts. The malleability of the concept of intention, particularly when it is likely to be implied rather than express, provides ample scope for a judicial hermeneusis that appears rational and persuasive.

The assumption that responsibility for housework or child care fall within women's domain is yet another dimension of status correlative to the marriage contract which wives might . wish to alter. Cohabitation contracts are presently not a viable option in this regard because they lack legal force. Kirsty Clarke pithily refers to domestic agreements as '"near" contract experiences', for judges find that the constituent elements invariably fall just short of a legally binding contract in order to sanction the status quo in gender relations.[77] By definition, status is resistant to change, particularly when nurturing and housework have conventionally been perceived as a 'natural part of cohabitation'.[78] The conceptualisation of what women do in the home is deemed to be of no value in economic terms.[79] The privileging of property as the basis of contract ensures that domestic responsibilities remain unexamined in the privacy of the home. These responsibilities also continue to be feminised, while contracting in the marketplace continues to be marked as a masculinist activity.

---

75 Michael Freeman, 'Contracting in the Haven: *Balfour v Balfour* Revisited' in Roger Halson (ed), *Exploring the Boundaries of Contract* (1996) 68.

76 Ibid 73–5.

77 Kirsty Clarke, 'A "Near" Contract Experience' (1994) 1 *E Law* <*http://www.murdoch.edu.au/elaw/*>.

78 Soile Pohjonen, 'Partnership in Love and Business' (2000) 8 *Feminist Legal Studies* 47, 49.

79 Marilyn Waring, *Counting for Nothing: What Men Value and What Women are Worth* (1988); Marty Grace, 'The Work of Caring for Young Children: Priceless or Worthless?' (1998) 21 *Women's Studies International Forum* 401. The undervaluation of the homemaker and caring contributions of wives continues to be marked on divorce. See Neave, above n 46, 160 ff.

Although courts are loathe to enforce contracts for personal services,[80] property has always occupied a privileged status in the eyes of the law. Not only is it the basis of market transactions, it also forms the backbone of civil society. While the right of married women to contract and to hold their own property was specifically recognised a century ago, vestigial disquiet remained as to their wills.[81] Indeed, contractualism was opposed in the domestic sphere not simply because of the familiar floodgates argument, but because of the invidious situation of married women, who generally did not own property. Ownership of property engendered a sense of free will and enabled effect to be given to intention. Property was the basis of enfranchisement and full citizenship, as well as of civil society itself.[82] Setting up as an independent householder qualified one as an autonomous individual. Sons were able to assert their will independent of their fathers;[83] daughters were unable to do so. Without being grounded in property, the individual did not mature into a fully fledged contractee; property was necessary to animate the will. Hence, the conceptualisation of housework and caring as a dimension of love and affection, rather than as property or as a means of generating property, has perpetuated the view that women, particularly wives, are still not fully autonomous.

Agreements between family members, other than spouses, are also caught by the rubric of 'love and affection', but legal intervention in such cases has a pragmatic social utility in the absence of the hierarchisation of authority denoted by 'domesticated command'. As Lord Denning has pointed out, the contention that an agreement between family members is not intended to have legal consequences belies the facts, as such arrangements *do* have legal consequences when it is the courts that are called upon to effect a resolution of a dispute. The uncertainty with regard to intent appertains to the substantive arrangements effected:

---

80 Marcia Neave, 'The Hands that Sign the Paper: Women and Domestic Contracts' in Glyn Davis, Barbara Sullivan and Anna Yeatman (eds), *The New Contractualism?* (1997) 84.

81 The point is underscored by the recent abolition of the immunity of a husband charged with rape. The immunity was predicated on the common law assumption that the wife's will was vitiated on marriage. When she consented to the marriage, she surrendered the right to say 'no'. See *R v L* (1991) 174 CLR 379; *R v R* (1991) 3 WLR 767.

82 Jean Jacques Rousseau, *The Social Contract and Discourses* (G D H Cole (trans)) (1973) 151; Kant, above n 1, 126.

83 Anna Yeatman, 'Contract, Status and Personhood' in Davis, Sullivan and Yeatman, above n 80, 44.

[T]hese family arrangements do have legal consequences; and, time and time again, the courts are called on to determine what is the true legal relationship resulting from them. This is especially the case where one of the family occupies a house or uses furniture which is afterwards claimed by another member of the family, or when one pays money to another and afterwards says it was a loan and the other says it was a gift, and so forth. In most of these cases the question cannot be solved by looking to the intention of the parties, because the situation which arises is one which they never envisaged and for which they made no provision. So many things are undecided, undiscussed and unprovided for that the task of the courts is to fill in the blanks.[84]

Reiterating the view that there is no intention to enter into legal relations allows the court to avert its gaze from possible injustice, leaving the dispute to be resolved in the interests of the defendant and the status quo. The boundary between the market/civil society and the domestic sphere is thereby affirmed. These lines of demarcation are by no means rigid, however, and the 'elusive correspondence between subjective intent and manifested form'[85] provides a fluid backdrop against which the leeways of choice operate in a way that appears to be rational. The test as to whether a binding contract exists in the domestic sphere is dependent on the judicial interpretation of the seemingly 'objective' factors surrounding the agreement. Despite increasing fluidity in spousal contractualism as a result of legislative changes, judges remain the arbiters of what constitutes a legally binding contract.[86]

Sex exercises an ambivalent role in contractualism, which, once again, can be traced to the marriage contract, where sex is an implied term. In any other setting, sex is corrosive of the rationality of law. Contracts for sexual services between parties, such as paying the rent for a 'mistress',[87] were customarily held to be void as contrary to public policy, regardless of the actual intent of the parties. A changed social climate has subsequently led to legal recognition of de facto relations and the somewhat more grudging recognition of same-sex relations. As a result, the interpolation of an intention to create legal relations has been used to change the parameters of contractualism. In the trailblazing United States case of *Marvin v Marvin*, the court found that an agreement to live together was enforceable unless it

---

84   *Hardwick v Johnson* [1978] 2 All ER 935, 938.
85   Dalton, above n 13, 1100.
86   Eg *Family Law Act 1975* (Cth) s 86. See also above n 63.
87   *Upfell v Wright* [1911] 1 KB 506.

234 Intention in Law and Philosophy

explicitly rested 'upon the immoral and illicit consideration of meretricious sexual services'.[88]

In *Seidler v Schallhofer*,[89] an agreement to cohabit on a trial basis was upheld, and the court found that such an agreement no longer involved a sexually immoral consideration for a sexually immoral purpose. The sexual dimension in *Seidler*, however, was incidental to the main focus of the agreement which was directed to financial arrangements regarding purchase of a property and the nature of the refund if the parties decided not to marry. Nevertheless, the more interesting question in *Seidler* is the sexual hypothetical posed by Hutley JA which, perhaps unsurprisingly, does not appear to have been addressed to date:

> I would have thought that if at the end of the first month one party expressed an intention to entirely withhold sexual favours from the other, that party could treat this behaviour as a fundamental breach and seek remedies for breach of contract.[90]

In the past, actions for restitution of conjugal rights and loss of consortium formally recognised sexuality in the context of marital relations, but an action in contract for damages or specific performance of sexual relations in respect of de facto or same-sex parties, regardless of the actual intent of the parties, would seem to be a long way off. The emergence of more liberal attitudes towards alternative forms of cohabitation does not constitute evidence of a radical leap in favour of sexual contractualism. Sexuality, after all, lies at the heart of the private sphere of liberal legalism.

Cohabitation agreements governing the financial affairs of de facto couples have come to be widely accepted, particularly in the United States, since *Marvin*.[91] Such agreements are likely to be upheld if they are in writing with an express intention to be legally bound.[92] In non-marital

---

88   *Marvin v Marvin* 18 Cal 3d 660, 668 (1976).
89   (1982) 8 Fam LR 598.
90   Ibid 612.
91   Eg *Wilcox v Trautz* 427 Mass 326 (1998); Jennifer Robbennolt and Monica Kirkpatrick Johnson, 'Legal Planning for Unmarried Committed Partners: Empirical Lessons for a Preventive and Therapeutic Approach' (1999) 41 *Arizona Law Review* 417.
92   In the absence of written contracts, equity may assist the parties, thereby bypassing the fiction of intent altogether. See, eg, *W v G* (1996) 20 Fam LR 49 in which a New South Wales court found that promissory estoppel (a promise to parent) on the part of the lesbian partner of the plaintiff birth mother grounded liability. For analysis, see

unions, both parties retain their independent legal personalities. With a certain sleight of hand, courts are more likely to conceptualise same-sex relationships as 'commercial', than as relationships based on 'natural love and affection'.[93] The discomfiting sexual element is then bypassed. However, if the 'meretricious' intent of *Marvin* is raised at all, it is in relation to same-sex cohabitation.[94] While a more liberal approach towards de facto and same-sex couples in respect of contracts pertaining to their financial affairs is apparent,[95] agreements as to who is going to be responsible for housework or child care will be unenforceable, as is the case for married couples. As courts wrestle with new affective relationships, we see the instantiation of the Kantian idea of a linkage between free will, independent personhood and property.

Conclusion

The dominant discourse of contract has tended to focus on the market and commercial relations. Contractualism has been resisted in the domestic sphere, supported by the marriage contract, with its public carapace and paradigmatically private underside. Hence, neither will theory nor objectivism proffer adequate explanations of domestic contractualism; such explanations have to be supplemented by an ideology of private life and 'domesticated command'. However, the family, understood as increasingly diverse and heterogeneous, is becoming more like the market in the way that it is tentatively reaching out towards acceptance of contractualism. Conversely, the market appears to be heading towards the acceptance of more status-like terms. The movement away from subjective intent to objectivism in commercial contracts is exemplary. Indeed, Anna Yeatman rejects the mutual exclusivity of status and contract, attacking the accepted wisdom of Maine as specious. Contractualism, she argues, has its own distinctive legal order, as has a kinship-based social order: 'Contract ... does not free "the individual" from "society" but reshapes the status of the

---

Jenni Millbank, 'An Implied Promise to Parent: Lesbian Families, Litigation and *W v G* (1996) 10 Fam LR 49' (1996) 10 *Australian Journal of Family Law* 112.

93   Millbank, ibid 8.
94   *Fitzpatrick v Sterling Housing Assn Ltd* (1999) 3 WLR 1113. See also Mark Pawlowski, 'Cohabitation Contracts: Are They Legal?' (1996) 146 *New Law Journal* 1125. For a survey of the position of cohabitants in a range of European countries, see Anne Barlow and Rebecca Probert, 'Cohabitants: A Survey of European Reforms' (1999) 149 *New Law Journal* 1738.
95   See above n 64.

person in society so as to become an individualised one'.[96] The way that citizens are presently being transmuted into consumers, students into customers, and recipients of welfare into clients—relationships with little freedom—provide evidence of this new order.[97] What might be termed postmodern manifestations of status are not synonymous with the frozen forms of pre-modernity, as exemplified in residual form in the marriage contract.

I do not wish to suggest that contracting 'in the haven' will necessarily bring equitable solutions, for 'contracts among lovers and friends may reflect and perpetuate the inequalities in their relationships'.[98] Similarly, I do not wish to suggest that the courts are the best forum for resolving disputes between intimates,[99] nor that adjudication is an inevitable corollary of contractualism. Despite the caveat raised by Yeatman that all contractualism possesses a 'status' element, I have sought to show that the transition from 'status to contract', in Maine's words, has been retarded so far as marriage is concerned.

The status of marriage continues to occupy a privileged position as a heterosexual institution. An intention to marry on the part of same-sex partners has no legal effect; their wills are vitiated in light of the powerful counter-ideology. Although the prohibition against contractualism is changing in the case of married couples, the assumption of indivisibility of their wills has not disappeared altogether. Paradoxically, an intention on the part of either heterosexual or homosexual partners to cohabit without marriage places them in a superior position as autonomous legal persons, for they tend to be treated as though they were strangers in the marketplace.

The role of intention in cohabitation agreements is equivocal. Elizabeth Kingdom is cautiously optimistic about the role of cohabitation contracts for women, provided that they are drafted in an open and transparent manner,[100] although the limited evidence regarding pre-nuptial agreements, from the perspective of divorcing couples, is less favourable.[101] Ideologies of status, gender and the family, which have traditionally operated to delimit free will, are likely to continue to do so within new

---

96   Yeatman, above n 83, 43.
97   Eg Davis, Sullivan and Yeatman, above n 80.
98   Olsen, above n 30, 1537–8. Cf Neave, above n 46; above n 80, 79; Fehlberg and Smyth, above n 63, esp 91–2.
99   *Hardwick v Johnson* [1978] 2 All ER 935, 940 per Roskill LJ.
100 Kingdom, above n 6, 23.
101 Fehlberg and Smyth, above n 63, 93. It is apparent that the sense of obligation identified at the beginning of an intimate relationship is likely to alter with the evolution of the relationship. See Wightman, above n 31, 102.

forms of contractualism. The challenge of modernisation is to give legal expression to individual wills in a range of intimate relations without the corrosive effects associated with the aggressive individualism of contractualism in the market.

I have suggested that intention in contract law plays a key ideological role in the way that it both reflects and constitutes public and private spheres. On the one hand, intent acts as a facilitative technology which enables law to 'oil the wheels of capitalism'. On the other hand, it endeavours to immunise the affective realm from the principle of equality of bargaining power, not from the formal rules and juridification attaching to contractualism in the market. While 'arm's-length' contractualism, with its aggressive underside ('equality in distrust'), has been deemed to be repugnant to family life, this can no longer be rationally maintained in a contract society. Cloaking housework and care with the language of love and affection ensures that these activities remain cordoned off from contractual norms. In this way, 'domesticated command' continues to be upheld, albeit in a somewhat shadowy sense, so as to impede the acceptance of women, particularly married women, as fully autonomous social actors. The hermeneusis of intent allows particular gender and sexual relationships to be juridically instantiated under the guise of freedom of contract.

PART III:
INTENTION AND THE COLLECTIVE

11 Collective Intentions

PHILIP PETTIT

We all know, or think we know, what it is for a singular agent to have an intention and how to go about telling what their intention in a given case is. But things are not at all so clear when it comes to plural or collective agents. Or so at any rate I mean to argue.

The argument should be of some interest, as the divination of collective intention is often a pressing problem in legal and political life. It arises with respect to bodies like a legislature, for example, when interpreters seek to identify the intent of this or that constitutional provision, this or that law, or this or that administrative decree. And of course it regularly arises in contexts, legal or moral, where there is an issue of whether a collective agency exhibits *mens rea* and can be held responsible in the associated sense.

My argument is this. First premise: there is no intention without a minimum of rationality on the part of the relevant agent. Second premise: collectives can display that minimum of rationality only so far as they collectivise reason, as I shall put it. Conclusion: only groups that collectivise reason can properly have intentions. The first and second sections deal respectively with the two premises, while the third section sets out the conclusion and looks at some of its implications.

First Premise: No Intention Without Rationality

The conditions required for the existence of intentions can be summed up in a single word: 'rationality'. Intentions, for the purpose of this discussion, are plans that shape an agent's actions at a time and across different times.[1] If we are to see certain subjects as centres of intention in

---

1   Michael Bratman, *Faces of Intention: Selected Essays on Intention and Agency* (1999).

this sense, then we must be able to represent them as forming beliefs and desires in a more or less rational manner and then as rationally forming intentions—and performing actions—on the basis of those beliefs and desires.[2]

Here, intuitively, is why. The intention-forming subject has to be able to represent its environment in a more or less reliable fashion and then to pursue its desired goals in a manner that makes sense according to that representation. And that is just to say that the subject must form beliefs about its environment in a more or less rational way and that it must act in such a manner that, if the environment is as represented, then the action is a rational means to advancing its desired goals. The subject must be rational in evidence-related and action-related ways; it must be well-behaved on both these fronts.

Or at least that must be the case within intuitively feasible limits and under intuitively favourable circumstances. We are ready to think that a machine counts as a mathematical calculator, even though it doesn't work with numbers above a certain size or complexity, or under conditions of electromagnetic interference. And so we will be ready to think that a certain subject counts as a belief-desire system—and as a system, therefore, that can form intentions—even if it doesn't always operate to expectations. It may not work well when it comes to achieving consistency among very complex beliefs, for example; and it may not work well under the influence of alcohol.

I am going to take it as an assumption that an intention-forming system has to satisfy such minimal constraints of rationality. The assumption should not be difficult to accept. It is not clear how we could ever get to think of a mute system—say, a non-human animal—as forming intentions if we did not find it responsive to evidence, and poised for action, in the manner envisaged. And neither is it clear why we should take the words of a talking, intention-avowing system seriously if we did not find that its words could be taken as expressions of more or less rationally formed and effective states: if we did not find, as we say, that its words could be taken at face value.

Is this all that there is to say about the conditions required for the existence of an intention in any agent, whether that agent be singular or plural? Not quite, for we can readily specify the requirements of rationality

---

2 Daniel Dennett, *The Intentional Stance* (1987); Philip Pettit, *The Common Mind: An Essay on Psychology, Society and Politics* (1993, paperback edition 1996); and David Braddon-Mitchell and Frank Jackson, *The Philosophy of Mind and Cognition* (1996).

that bear in particular on intention. I shall mention three plausible candidates: consistency, closure and completeness, each of which has a theoretical and a practical aspect.

An agent will satisfy the relevant form of consistency, theoretical and practical, so far as it holds only by such beliefs, and sticks only to such intentions and actions, as are rationally co-tenable with the things it is rightly said to intend. We would have real difficulty in taking an agent seriously as a centre of intention if the intentions it avowed, or the intentions we were supposed on any other basis to ascribe to it, did not satisfy such a consistency constraint; or at least if it did not satisfy such a constraint under intuitively favourable conditions and within intuitively feasible limits.

An agent will satisfy the relevant form of closure, theoretical and practical, so far as it forms all those beliefs and intentions, and performs those actions, that are rationally required by the things it is rightly said to intend. The idea here is that if such an agent intends to perform a certain action, for example, and if performing that action rationally requires its forming a certain belief—say, the belief that it is able to act—or doing something else as well—say, adopting a certain means—then it will comply. Or at least it will comply under the usual qualifications to do with favourable conditions and feasible limits.

An agent will satisfy the relevant form of completeness, theoretical and practical, so far as it forms or is disposed to form beliefs and intentions on all of those issues that are rationally relevant to the things it is rightly said to intend, and so far as it acts or is disposed to act on those beliefs and intentions. Suppose that it intends to bring about some goal G and that whether it does so by this means or that—this salient means or that salient means—depends on the belief it comes to form as to which is easier. Well then, we will generally expect it to form a belief on the required matter. Or, as always, we will expect this under favourable conditions and within feasible limits.

Second Premise: No Collective Rationality Without Collectivising Reason

The first premise of my argument sums up the drift of two decades of discussion in the philosophy of mind. But the second premise of the argument takes me into relatively new territory. It is a proposition that becomes salient and compelling only in light of the doctrinal paradox, as it is sometimes called, that has recently received attention in jurisprudential circles.[3] I have discussed various aspects of the paradox elsewhere and my presentation here draws heavily on those discussions.[4]

The doctrinal paradox arises when a multi-member court has to make a decision on the basis of received doctrine as to the considerations that ought to determine the resolution of a case: that is, on the basis of a conceptual sequencing of the matters to be decided.[5] It consists in the fact that the standard practice whereby judges make their individual decisions in a case, and then aggregate them, can lead to a different result from that which would have ensued had they decided instead on whether the relevant considerations obtained, and let those decisions dictate how the case should be resolved.

A good example of the doctrinal paradox is provided by a simple case in which a three-judge court has to decide whether a defendant is liable for breach of contract.[6] According to legal doctrine, the court should find against the defendant if and only if it finds, first, that a valid contract was in place, and second that the defendant's behaviour was such that it would have breached a contract of that kind, had a contract been in place; the judge's decision on the second issue will be by way of an *obiter dictum*, of course, if he or she does not think that a contract was in place. Now imagine that the three judges, 1, 2 and 3, decide as follows on those issues

---

3   Lewis Kornhauser and Lawrence Sager, 'Unpacking the Court' (1986) 96 *Yale Law Journal* 82; Lewis Kornhauser, 'Modelling Collegial Courts: I Path-Dependence' (1992) 12 *International Review of Law and Economics* 169; Lewis Kornhauser, 'Modelling Collegial Courts: II Legal Doctrine' (1992) 8 *Journal of Law, Economics and Organization* 441; Lewis Kornhauser and Lawrence Sager, 'The One and the Many: Adjudication in Collegial Courts' (1993) 81 *California Law Review* 1. See too B Chapman, 'Law, Incommensurability, and Conceptually Sequenced Argument' (1998) 146 *University of Pennsylvania Law Review* 1487; B Chapman, 'More Easily Done than Said: Rules, Reason and Rational Social Choice' (1998) 18 *Oxford Journal of Legal Studies* 293; and G Brennan, *Collective Irrationality and Belief* (1999).

4   Christian List and Philip Pettit, 'The Aggregation of Reason: An Impossibility Result' (paper presented at the Isaac Levi Conference, Columbia University, New York, November 2000); Philip Pettit, 'Deliberative Democracy and Discursive Dilemma' (2001) 11 *Philosophical Issues* (forthcoming); Philip Pettit, 'Groups with Minds of their Own' (paper presented at Yale University Political Theory Workshop, September 2000).

5   B Chapman, 'Law, Incommensurability, and Conceptually Sequenced Argument', above n 3.

6   Kornhauser and Sager, 'The One and the Many: Adjudication in Collegial Courts', above n 3.

and on the derivable matter of whether the defendant is indeed liable. The 'yes' or 'no' on any row represents the disposition of the relevant judge to accept or reject the corresponding premise or conclusion.

Matrix 11.1

	Valid contract?	Breach?	Liable?
1	yes	no	no
2	no	yes	no
3	yes	yes	yes

There are two ways in which the court might in principle make its decision in a case like this. It might have the judges do their individual reasoning and then aggregate their decisions on the conclusion—the liability issue—on, say, a majority basis. Since the conclusion does not command majority support, the defendant would go free. Or the court might have the judges aggregate their decisions on the individual premises—the contract and breach issues—and let the resulting, collective judgments on those premises determine what it rules on the conclusion. Since each premise commands majority support, the result in this case is that the defendant would be found liable. The doctrinal paradox, as presented in the jurisprudential literature, consists in the fact that the two procedures described yield different outcomes.

This sort of paradox will arise, not just when legal doctrine dictates that certain considerations are conceptually or epistemically prior to a certain issue—an issue on which a conclusion has to be reached—and that judgments on those considerations ought to dictate the judgment on the conclusion. It arises more generally whenever a group of people discourse together with a view to forming an opinion on a certain matter that rationally connects, by the lights of all concerned, with other issues. It constitutes a discursive, not just a doctrinal, dilemma.

For an example that is close to the case just discussed, consider an issue that might arise for politicians rather than for judges. The issue is whether to build a new public prison or not. Let us suppose, for simplicity, that everyone involved in the decision-making committee—this might be the cabinet, a party committee, or whatever—agrees that three considerations should determine the issue. The committee members involved are to make the decision on the basis of considering: first, whether a new prison is desirable overall; second, whether a public prison would serve the community better than a private prison; and third, whether a decision in favour of a public prison would be electorally feasible: that is, would not significantly reduce the government's chance of re-election. If a member of the committee thinks that a prison is needed, that a public prison would be better than a private, and that building a public prison would be electorally feasible, then he or she will vote for the prison; otherwise they will vote against. And so each will have to consider the three issues and then look to what should be concluded about the prison.

Imagine now that after appropriate dialogue and deliberation the members are disposed to vote on the relevant premises and conclusion in the pattern illustrated by the following matrix for three members.

Matrix 11.2

	Prison needed?	Public better?	Electorally feasible?	To build or not?
1	yes	no	yes	no
2	no	yes	yes	no
3	yes	yes	no	no

If this is the pattern in which the members are inclined to vote, then a different decision will be made, depending on whether the group judgment is driven by how members judge on the premises or by how they judge on the conclusion. Looking at the matrix, we can see that though everyone individually rejects the prison, a majority supports each of the premises. If we think that the views of the members on the conclusion should determine the group decision, then we will say that the group conclusion should be to reject the prison: there are only 'no's' in the final column. But if we think that the views of the members on the premises should determine the group decision, then we will say that the group conclusion should be to build the prison: there is a majority of 'yes's' in each of the premise columns.

The doctrinal or discursive paradox generalises in many different ways. It may arise with disjunctive as well as conjunctive reasoning, since a disjunctive set of premises, P or Q, will support a conclusion R just in case the negation of the conjunctive set of premises, ¬P and ¬Q, supports that conclusion. It may arise whenever there are three or more propositions involved. It may arise whenever there are three or more persons involved. And it may arise even if we allow the rejection of the premises to leave some individuals with an open mind—they fail to say 'yes' or 'no'—on the conclusion.

What does the paradox show? Negatively, that even if the members of a group each have a perfectly consistent set of judgments on a range of issues, still majority voting on each of the issues can lead the group to an inconsistent set of collective judgments. And positively, that if the members of the group are to ensure the consistency of their collective judgments on such a range of issues, then they will have to restrict majority voting and, more generally, restrict responsiveness to the views of their individual members. They will have to ensure that the discipline of reason is applied at the collective level to the views they endorse. They will have to collectivise reason rather than just being content to find that members are individually rational.

In the examples given, the members restrict responsiveness to individual views, and ensure collective rationality, by letting the collective judgment on the conclusion be determined by the collective judgments on the premises. But they might equally have taken other steps to collectivise reason. They might have explored where majority voting on each issue would lead and then, in the event of a collectively non-rational output, decided on which vote to amend; this could involve a reversal of the conclusion vote, or a reversal of one or more premise votes. Or they might have authorised some agency or individual to decide on the amendment required in the event of a collectively non-rational profile of views; the decision might have been left to a chairperson, for example.

The particular cases given show that under majority voting it is necessary for a group to impose the discipline of reason on itself at the collective level—in particular, it is necessary to restrict majority voting—if it is to achieve consistency. Might the members avoid such inconsistency by other means? Well, they could insist on unanimity, so that a collective judgment would be available on any issue only so far as all go along with a certain view. Or they could deny that the group has to endorse a conclusion just because it endorses premises that entail it. But such moves would compromise the rationality of the group in other ways. While either move might serve to guard the group against inconsistency, the second would involve the rejection of closure and the first would involve the rejection, in effect, of completeness: no group could hope to be able to form a collective view on any significant range of issues if unanimity were required for the formation of such a view.[7]

Conclusion: No Collective Intention Without Collectivising Reason

The claims of the first two sections combine to support the conclusion that there is no possibility of collective intention unless a group actively works to ensure that it satisfies the discipline of reason at the collective level: unless it works, in particular, to ensure that it satisfies relevant forms of consistency, closure and completeness. We saw in the first section that any agent that is going to be a centre of intention formation will generally have to satisfy such constraints. And we have now just seen that a plural or collective agent can hope to do so only by collectivising reason. It follows, then, that only a group that collectivises reason can constitute a centre of intention formation.

The General Implications

This conclusion has quite significant implications. Since any group that is going to collectivise reason must have a minimal degree of organisation, it means in the first place that only such organised collectivities can have intentions. The intention-forming group cannot involve just a random selection or a random juxtaposition of individuals: a mere aggregate, as distinct from something properly incorporated into a whole.[8] Thus it must amount to more than the set of pedestrians on a given street, or a crowd at a football match, or even a mob of looters. And it must amount to more than the set of people with red hair, or the set of people who live in areas

---

7   I say no more here on the general possibilities that arise in the area, as what we have seen is sufficient for the conclusion I wish to draw. Christian List and I have argued elsewhere for an associated impossibility theorem that bears on such matters. Let a satisfactory set of views be required to display strict forms of consistency, closure and completeness. Our impossibility theorem shows that no voting procedure that allows for any profile of individually satisfactory views on a rationally connected set of issues can ensure that a collectively satisfactory set of views will emerge, if it treats both the issues and the members even-handedly: that is, if it does not let the group's views on some issues determine the group's views on others, and if it does not appoint an authority to make required amendments. List and Pettit, above n 4.

8   Peter French, *Collective and Corporate Responsibility* (1984).

with even postcodes, or the set of people who are firstborn to their mothers.

Since any organised group that is going to collectivise reason must be organised so as to authorise certain attitudes and actions, the conclusion means in the second place that not just any organised groups will be capable of forming intentions. They cannot be groups and groupings whose members relate to one another in a distinctive way but who need not jointly authorise anything. Such groups might include families, hobby groups, internet chat groups, and other enduring or episodic networks of individuals.

Groups and groupings whose members do authorise things jointly—and the members will usually relate to one another in the course of doing this—come in a number of varieties.[9] They include organisations which have a specific function to discharge. For example, museums, libraries, trusts and states, as well as more episodic entities like appointments committees, juries or commissions of inquiry. And they also include groups and groupings which do not have any one specific function but which are associated with a characteristic goal, involving the outside world or the group's own members or perhaps a mix of both. Examples in this category might include political parties, trade unions and business corporations, as well as pairs of colleagues involved in collaborative research and sets of friends arranging joint holidays.

There is a general argument why any group or grouping that has a purpose to advance, specific or otherwise, is likely to collectivise reason at some level and is likely therefore to constitute an intention-forming subject. This applies even to groups and groupings which are happy to be able to find only incompletely theorised agreements on many issues:[10] that is, agreements that different people support for different reasons.[11] The lesson it teaches is of the first importance.

The argument I have in mind can be spelled out in these considerations:

- So far as the pursuit of an assumed purpose requires reasoning and judgment—so far as it is not like the goal of a tug-of-war team—any group or grouping is going to generate a history of judgments which it

---

9   S J Stoljar, *Groups and Entities: An Inquiry Into Corporate Theory* (1973).
10   Cass Sunstein, *One Case at a Time: Judicial Minimalism on the Supreme Court* (1999).
11   Pettit, 'Groups with Minds of their Own', above n 4.

is on record as making; these will be judgments that shape how it acts in pursuit of the purpose.

- Those past judgments will inevitably constrain the judgment that the group or grouping ought to make in various new cases; only one particular judgment in this or that case will be consistent or coherent with the past judgments.
- The group or grouping will not be able to constitute or present itself as a credible promoter of its assumed purpose if it tolerates inconsistency in its judgments across time; not all the actions shaped by those discordant judgments can be simultaneously represented as advancing the same purpose.
- Thus the group or grouping which assumes a purpose of any kind, whether in relation to the outside world or its own members, must routinely ensure, by whatever means, that the judgments it endorses across time satisfy constraints of consistency.

To sum up the point to which we have been led, then, a collectivity will constitute a centre for the formation of intention only so far as it is an organised, authorising group or grouping. And that is to say that it will constitute a centre for the formation of intention only if it imposes the discipline of reason on itself at the collective level. Many collectivities will do this, for any group or grouping that claims to advance a purpose is bound at some level to collectivise reason.

Two Fallacies

It may be useful to spell out some more concrete implications of the position defended here. I do so by identifying two fallacies, as they must appear in the light of the analysis presented.

Commentators on US politics often say that the American people do not like to have the same party holding executive and legislative power at the same time. And so they routinely comment that, in dividing their support between a Democratic President and a Republican Congress, the American people reveal this intention to divide power. Under the analysis of this paper—perhaps under any serious examination—this comment is downright silly. A group as amorphous as the American people cannot be held to form intentions of any kind, let alone such a sophisticated intention as that which is here attributed to them. The only sense in which we might speak of the intention of such a group is the metaphorical or summative sense in which we say that a group has any intention that is supported by a majority of its members.[12] The commentators envisaged here are guilty of a fallacy in speaking as they do. The fallacy is one of composition, as it is often described, since it involves illicitly moving from an attribute of individuals—assuming the individuals do intend that power be divided—to an attribute of the group they compose.

This fallacy of composition pairs off with a fallacy of decomposition that becomes equally salient under the analysis sketched here. Consider a case where a group agency, say a committee of some kind, advances a particular line and is clearly worthy of being credited with an intention to do so. Consider in particular a case where on this basis the group is held responsible for what it does, and responsible in a manner involving *mens rea*. The fallacy I have in mind would consist in assuming that, because the group as a whole is responsible in this intention-involving sense, the members of the group must be responsible in the same sense: the intention, and the responsibility, must apply to the individuals into which the group can be decomposed. That this is a fallacy appears in the fact that the committee in our prison example can clearly he held responsible for recommending the building of a public prison if they follow a procedure under which the premise votes dictate the conclusion; yet under that scenario the individual members cannot be held responsible in the same way: after all, each of them voted individually against building a public prison.

I hasten to add that the fact that a group can have such a non-decomposing form of intention and responsibility does not mean that the individuals escape all relevant forms of responsibility. Consistently with the group and only the group having responsibility for recommending the construction of a public prison, each of the individuals involved can be responsible for playing his or her part, say in going along with the decision-making procedure adopted or in voting as he or she does. There are complex issues here but, happily, we need not engage with them in the current context.

A Lesson for the Analysis of Collective Intention

I conclude with a comment on the implications of our discussion for a tendency in recent analyses of collective or joint intention. The usual, if

---

12   A Quinton, 'Social Objects' (1975) 75 *Proceedings of the Aristotelian Society* 17.

not the only, approach in such analyses is to take a grouping of two or perhaps three agents and, focussing on this example, to try to identify the conditions under which we would ascribe a collective intention to them.[13] And that approach has led to an emphasis on the need for rich structures of common belief that may be misleading rather than helpful.

The analyses generally agree that, in order for joint intention to appear, there must be common belief present as to what each believes about others, as to how each is ready to act in the event of others acting in a complementary way, and so on. The relevant notion of common belief in play here is reasonably familiar. It will be a matter of common belief among a number of people that p so far as each believes that p; each believes that each believes that p; each believes that each believes that each believes that p; and so on. And so on, most plausibly, in this mode: while not everyone may believe the required condition at each higher level, at least no one disbelieves it at any such level.[14]

There are interesting issues that have been raised in the literature on joint intention, many of them connected with themes we have discussed. For the record, some of the more prominent issues have been:

- the effect-of-intention question: whether it is necessary for collective intention that those who comply are licensed—perhaps licensed on the basis of an implicit agreement—in rebuking those who fail to do their part in advancing or securing the intention;
- the intended-content question: whether it is necessary that each of us in the group intend not just that I, this individual, behave in a certain way—presumably this is necessary—but also that we, the group, do so; and
- the intending-subject question: whether in addition we, the group, must form an intention to do something—at whatever locus this is to be formed—such that this may not reflect anything that I or you intend that we do.

But interesting though those issues are, the analysis of this paper must raise a question about the focus on small groupings and the consequent

---

13   Margaret Gilbert, *On Social Facts* (1989); A Meijers, *Speech Acts, Communication and Collective Intentionality: Beyond Searle's Individualism* (1994); John Searle, *The Construction of Social Reality* (1995); R Tuomela, *The Importance of Us* (1995); and Bratman, above n 1.

14   David Lewis, *Convention: A Philosophical Study* (1969).

insistence on the need for rich structures of common belief. The reason is that if we impose such requirements generally on collectivities that are to be held capable of forming intentions, then we may unduly restrict the range of collective intention.

Any collectivity that is to be capable of forming intentions, by the account defended here, must be able to discipline itself by reason at the collective level and it must therefore have the flexible ability to recognise collective irrationality—lack of consistency, closure or completeness—and to respond appropriately. A small grouping might display this flexibility, and yet manifest the rich structure of common belief that is generally posited in the literature. But it is doubtful if any large-scale group could instantiate such a structure of common belief without seizing up.

The costs of maintaining and adjusting the sort of common belief envisaged would obviously increase dramatically with increasing size and complexity on the part of a group. How could a large-scale group be expected to register and respond to a collective irrationality, if such registering and such responding had to involve transformations in structures of common belief? Getting the group to shift in the required respects would be like trying to turn around an ocean-going liner. It would take so much effort and time as not to be feasible.

But happily there is no need for a rich structure of common belief among the members of large-scale, intention-forming groups. There is no reason why each and every member of such a group has to share in anything other than a very abstract common belief to the effect that such and such procedures will generally be followed. Indeed, some members of the group may be involved in the things it does only to the extent that they have a power of protest in the event of not approving of the actions of officials. In order to adapt to circumstances, then—in order to respond, for example, to a perceived inconsistency—officials will not have to consult individual members or establish any form of belief in common with them; they will only have to be sure that the line they take will not cause members to instigate an effective revolt.

We saw earlier that a group or grouping cannot be a centre of intention formation without being organised in quite specific ways. The lesson of these last observations is that neither can it be a centre of intention formation if it is so intensely organised—in particular, so bound to incorporating each and every member into a community of belief—that it loses flexibility and adaptability. The loose-limbed multitude cannot constitute an intending agent. But neither can the muscle-bound pachyderm.

12 Bad Faith and Bad Intentions in Corporate Law

SUZANNE CORCORAN

A truth that's told with bad intent
Beats all the lies you can invent.[1]

This essay considers the problem of intention in the sphere of corporate law. It considers the problem at three levels: the level of the corporate entity, the level of the corporate organ (for example, the board of directors) and the level of the individual actor. It concerns itself with the integrity of the corporate entity and the propriety of corporate actions and not with the consequences occasioned by them. Propriety in corporate law refers to what is permitted of a particular corporation as a corporation (its integrity), in relation to decisions and actions which are, or will be considered to be, the decisions and actions of that particular corporation.

My argument will be that intention is fundamental to corporate law. I will argue that it is a derivative, complex and artificial notion of intention in which free will, to the extent it exists, derives from what is known as the substratum of the corporation (the membership together with the purpose of the corporation), while responsibility is assigned to the corporate entity itself. This gives the corporation *agency* in a moral sense and anchors it to a certain historical philosophical position in the way that original intent theory provides a starting point for constitutional interpretation. But, as with constitutional theory, the substratum (and thus the free wills that constitute the corporate entity) continues to evolve and extend the intention of the entity in ways which may depart from that original intention. Nevertheless, the constitutional arrangements of a corporation continue to

---

1   William Blake, *Auguries of Innocence.*

remain relevant. As Robert Frost has observed so famously, the point of departure will often make all the difference.[2]

The word 'intention' comes from the Latin verb *intendere* meaning to stretch out or extend, for example *intendere animum* 'to turn one's mind to' or what we call in corporate law 'purpose' or 'active discretion', that is, mental application. This essay focuses on bad faith and bad intentions. The reason for focusing on bad faith and bad intentions in corporate law, rather than the more positive aspects of intention, is twofold: perspective and philosophy.

Perspective involves the evaluation of something from a particular vantage point. Looking at intention from the vantage point of bad faith, or bad intention, is interesting because in corporate law the issue of good faith most often arises when it is thought to be lacking. Also, this essay is concerned with questions concerning bad faith from the perspective of civil liability. It will not venture into the debate about criminal intent and the *mens rea* requirements of criminal law. Criminal law and civil law often treat intention quite differently.[3] This essay is about civil responsibility.

The philosophical reason for focusing on bad faith is that it permits me as a lawyer to retreat to pragmatism. Pragmatism appeals to the professional corporate lawyer who must achieve closure in a defined time frame. Political pragmatism also underlies much of the corporate regulatory framework that continues to redefine our concepts of the modern corporation.

Bad faith is not the stuff of high drama, either in life or law. But it will sustain civil liability of serious proportions. It should also be noted that breaches of the law do not operate in isolation from the standards or rules of evidence, the presumptions attached to evidence, the burdens of proof required to establish breaches of the law and the remedies available once breach has been established.

The burdens of proof that must be met to establish particular breaches of a good faith requirement operate as indicators of the human value attached to the specific underlying legal obligation. Also, available civil

---

2   Robert Frost, *The Road Not Taken*.
3   While intention is relevant to both civil and criminal liability, it is usually an element in the definition of a crime (a stipulated level of intention). Also, the burden of proof necessary for proof of intention is different, depending on whether the attendant liability is civil or criminal.

law remedies can mitigate the imprecision which low burdens of proof will produce. This holistic view of civil liability has an impact on the rigour with which 'bad faith' is defined in a given set of circumstances. For example, if the only remedy available for an exercise of bad faith is monetary damages, the intellectual and philosophical purity of the legal requirement of good intent becomes less urgent than the simple need to have such a requirement in the first instance.

Complexity and Intention

Corporate law is littered with references to intent and to other concepts which are indicative of intent, such as proper purpose and good faith. But, as I hope to show, intent in corporate law is contrived and consequential. It is not the same as human intent where the actor and the action are unified.[4] In corporate law, it is possible to have a very good intention and still act in bad faith or for an improper purpose, if the legal or practical consequences of that act are legally proscribed. It is also possible that an otherwise morally neutral act in corporate law will, if performed with bad intentions, become a breach of trust.

Corporations are complex organisations. They are complex in three ways: structurally, theoretically and legally. These complexities require some description because they affect the location of intention within the corporation.

Structurally one must view the corporation not just as a collectivity, but as a series of collectivities many of which are imbedded within each other. One may talk about the corporate group, the parent or subsidiary corporation, the board of directors, corporate or executive officers, senior management, employees and members or shareholders of the corporation. Some of these collectivities have recognised status and operate as organs of the corporation or group, for example the board of directors or the body of members. The intention of the board of directors may not be the same as the intention of an individual director. Within a corporate group, it is the

---

4   Definitions of intent focus on the individual. For example, intent has been defined as 'the design, resolve, or determination with which a person acts': *Witters v United States* 106 F2d 837, 840 (1939). It has also been described as 'A mental attitude which can seldom be proved by direct evidence, but must ordinarily be proved by circumstances from which it can be inferred': *State v Gantt* 217 SE2d 3, 5 (1975).

individual corporation which not only has corporate status but is recognised, by law, as a separate legal person. This last fact means that the decision-making structure of the corporate group may be at odds with legal responsibility since legal responsibility can only attach to legal personality.

Theoretical complexity in corporate law flows from the structural complexity of the corporate entity. It can be seen in the fact that many individuals within the corporation act in more than one capacity. An individual may be a director and a shareholder as well as an individual employee. When that person intends something, the first question that will be asked is: in what capacity is that individual acting? The difficult area of conflicts of interest is replete with questions concerning intent and capacity—for example, are we dealing with the 'director acting in the capacity of director' or the 'director acting in the capacity of member'? This problem arises when it is unclear whether a person is acting upon knowledge that he or she has obtained as a director of a corporation or whether that person is acting upon knowledge received as a member of the corporation. Similarly, one person may act as principal in one situation but as an agent in another. Complicated questions of attribution of knowledge or information follow from the problem of dual capacity. Does a director of a corporation know something as a director or as an individual?[5]

The legal complexity of corporations is due to the fact that corporate law is equally dependent on all three major streams of modern law: common law, equity and statute. It relies heavily on the common law of contract, especially implied contract. Many people believe that the corporation is simply a nexus of contracts. But corporate life is not that simple and essentially tort law concepts of proximity and reliance have entered corporate law in a big way. Alongside the common law doctrines of corporate law sit equitable principles. Corporations have their historical roots in continental law (indeed Roman law). In the development of the English legal system, this has led to the use of trust law and general equitable principles as the basis for much corporate law. Equity, of course, sets a high premium on good conscience and fiduciary principles. Thus, in many cases intentions must not only be good, but exemplary. Within a corporation, when an individual moves into a corporate office or assumes substantial power (de jure or de facto) equitable principles will apply. Finally, one must recognise that the modern corporation is as much a

---

5   See *Queensland Mines Ltd v Hudson* (1978) 18 ALR 1 (PC).

creature of statute as of the general law and that statutory directives often alter, while not necessarily destroying, the established rules of corporate action, intention and attribution.

Locating Intention Within the Corporate Entity

When we consider the complexity of the corporation, intention has to be seen as operating on several levels. If we compare the corporation to a mosaic (something made of many pieces but which is different in its impact from a mere collection of pieces of stone or tile) and then ask what the intention of the mosaic is, that intention cannot be found in the individual pieces which make up the whole. It must be located somewhere in the whole, that is in the collective impact of the organisation.

In corporate law I would suggest that this intention of the corporate entity, which is the primary level of intent, is to be found in what one might call the empathetic collectivity of the organisation. That is, it is to be found in the organisational objective or purpose which explains the membership of the substratum of the association. That objective is whatever it is that attracts these individuals to the particular corporation: the desire to build railroad cars, to make a better computer, to establish a hospital or simply to invest money at an expected rate of return. It is that empathy which provides a foundation for the trust relationships between the individual parts which is necessary for the functioning of the whole. Those trust relationships are the mortar between the pieces of the mosaic which hold it together and create the distinctive legal personality.

When we consider the organisational objective or objectives, the 'corporate purpose', as the site of intention of the corporation as a whole, then we will immediately see that free will, in the conventional sense, does not operate. Furthermore, individual free will within the corporation is limited by agency or trust relationships which are contractual and fiduciary and which relate to the corporate objectives or purpose. At the same time, the free will of the entity as a whole is limited by its dependency on individual actions and individual ambits of discretion.

In addition to the primary intention of the corporation, that of the corporate entity, there are of course two other levels of intention. A secondary institutional level of intent is the intent of corporate organs, which is manifested through formal actions such as resolutions of the board. And, finally, there is a tertiary level of intent: that of individuals acting on behalf of the corporation.

The Corporate Constitution as Corporate Intention

Corporations are recognised as legal persons when their charters or constitutions are registered or otherwise approved by the relevant sovereign power. While corporate constitutions have been around since the earliest periods of Roman law, it is the modern corporate constitution which has a defining role to play in the operation of intention within contemporary corporations. It is the corporate constitution which defines the purposes of the corporate association, places limits on the power of the corporate entity and defines the legal relationships (what is called the statutory contract) between the corporate entity and the members. The modern corporate constitution developed with the rise of the business corporation in the nineteenth and twentieth centuries. It was at that time that the corporate form adapted to include the internal rules of the large partnership, the joint stock company. Those internal rules defined two critical aspects of the corporate entity which have a bearing on the question of intention: the limited purpose (and therefore power) of the association; and the relationship between the individual members of the substratum (the statutory contract). The primary intention of the corporate entity is limited by its purpose because that purpose limits its powers. The secondary intention of corporate organs is also limited by power and purpose. Corporate organs must act within power and must act to further the purpose of the corporate entity. The good faith of corporate organs will be measured within that framework. The tertiary intention of individuals acting on behalf of the corporate entity is subject to legal duties which relate back to the corporate purpose and the special relationship (contractual or fiduciary) which the law recognises between the individual members of the corporation, the corporate organs and the corporate entity itself.

The Duty to Act Bona Fide in the Best Interests of the Corporation

To illustrate the operation of all three levels of intention (that of the corporate entity, corporate organs and individuals) within a particular area of corporate law, one can consider the requirement of good faith found in the duty to act in the best interests of the corporation. This equitable duty ties the individuals and corporate organs acting on behalf of the corporation to the corporate purpose while providing a large ambit of discretion regarding the particular action to be taken. That discretion to act one way or another is only limited by the good faith qualification. The test for good faith is whether the act was done in good faith and in the best interests of the corporation, rather than for personal or other advantage.[6]

This duty is sometimes referred to as the duty of loyalty (particularly in the United States) since it requires loyalty to the organisation and prohibits potential conflicts which would undermine that loyalty. In Australia, the duty is codified in a number of general incorporation statutes including the *Corporations Law* s 181(1). While the statutory language does not always use the exact wording of the classic duty, courts tend to hold that the statutory formulations mean the same thing. Whatever linguistic arguments one might consider, the important point for this discussion is that one must *intend* to act for the benefit of the corporation whether or not one's actions are in fact beneficial. One may take risks— even big risks—but they must be taken with the intention of benefiting the corporation. Any act taken to benefit oneself or some other person or group without full disclosure to, and approval of, the corporation's members will be a breach of duty.[7]

The Positive Content of the Duty to Act in Good Faith

For the corporate lawyer this immediately raises the problem of how one establishes *intent* in the context of actual transactions. How does one define the positive content of good faith? Good faith was once defined as personal honesty according to a Christian morality of clear conscience.

---

6   *Peter's American Delicacy Co Ltd v Heath* (1939) 61 CLR 457, 509; *Harlowe's Nominees Pty Ltd v Woodside (Lake Entrance) Oil Co NL* (1968) 121 CLR 483; see also *Hogg v Cramphorn Ltd* [1967] 1 Ch 254, 256.
7   See *Re Tivoli Freeholds Ltd* [1972] VR 445.

Over time, and in the face of moral plurality, it transformed into a more positive and objective professionalism. For example, in the early cases good faith often served as an excuse for stupidity or laziness. It could excuse both gross incompetence and gross negligence. In more modern cases, more diligence is expected and objective considerations of reasonableness and fairness will be part of the equation. There is also a trend in the very recent cases to move to negligence, where feasible, thereby avoiding the need to establish lack of good faith. In other words, we may observe a shift from the use of equitable principles, based upon relationships and conscience, to common law principles based on proximity and due care. Although the move to negligence is tempting where possible, it will not always be an option for the corporate lawyer. While the concept of negligence is expanding in corporate law, the concept of intentional bad faith is still alive and well.

Intention and, in particular, the concept of proper purpose, still operate as determinants of liability in many areas of corporate law. This is particularly true when substantial parts of the mosaic which is the corporate entity no longer trust each other. A standard example would be the cases involving takeovers. If groups of members within a corporation have intentions that are at odds with each other, the intentions behind their action will be scrutinised carefully for indications of bad faith. Thus, while the core obligation is one of good faith, the objective examples one sees in the litigated cases are, more often than not, examples of bad faith or bad intentions.

Bad Faith and Corporate Intentions

For that reason I will move to the subject of bad intentions and consider some of the kinds of behaviour which have been found to involve bad faith, bad intentions or improper purposes in a positive sense. These examples of bad faith occur across all three levels of corporate intention, although they occur most often at the individual or corporate organ level, as opposed to the corporate entity level. There can be a point, however, at which bad faith can so permeate the mosaic that the bad faith of the corporate organs and individuals becomes the bad faith of the corporate entity.

Below, I have identified seven kinds of activity that may be equated with positive bad intent (as opposed to negligent bad intent) on the part of a corporation. The determination of whether positive bad faith is involved, rather than negligent bad faith, will usually depend on the knowledge and will of the corporate organ or corporate agent. These acts may occur at the general corporate level, at the corporate organ level (eg board of directors) or at the individual agent level. The most critical level of intention is that of the corporate organ. It is at this level that the link is made between the intention of the entity and the intention of the individual natural persons. This is the level at which the informal act becomes the formal act of the corporation. It is also the level at which intention is connected to actuality, thereby providing evidence and a basis for legal remedies. The categories of bad intent or bad faith listed below may result in legal liability, but not necessarily so. Whether the intent of the corporate organ or agent can result in legal liability for the corporate entity will depend on whether that intent can be attributed to the corporation. This in turn depends upon a series of legal rules concerning the nature and authority of the agent.

Deceit and Audit Failure

These situations involve wrongful or blameworthy actions by individuals within the corporation which are fraudulently concealed from the appropriate corporate organs such as the board. For example, in *Friedrich's* case, the managing director of the National Safety Council altered the company accounts without the knowledge of other senior executives or the board of directors.[8] Another example is the *AWA* case.[9] In that case a foreign exchange dealer sustained loses and concealed them from senior management and the board of directors. In both cases, the corporation and the board of directors were found to be liable for damages despite the fact that they did not condone or participate in the individual deceit. Liability was imposed because they did not adhere to normal industry standards and their own internal audit procedures, which would have brought the fraud to their attention.

---

8 *Commonwealth Bank of Australia v Friedrich* (1991) 5 ACSR 115.
9 *Daniels v Anderson (AWA Case)* (1995) 37 NSWLR 438.

Misleading Statements

These instances of bad faith involve formal corporate statements that are not true, or only marginally true, or misleading, either because of the context in which the statements are made or because of the failure to provide necessary context.[10] In situations in which the agents involved know that the statements could mislead, bad faith is involved. An example is the statement in a prospectus that shares would be free without also stating that important membership rights would be sacrificed to take up the shares.[11] It is also well settled that one may mislead by silence,[12] but that is generally treated as a separate category, as discussed below.

Non-Disclosure of Material Facts

This category of bad faith includes numerous situations in which important information is withheld, in particular information relating to conflicts of interest. An example of this category of bad faith is the non-disclosure by the managing director of the State Bank of South Australia (Tim Marcus Clark) of his relationship with Equiticorp Ltd.[13]

The Systematic Absence of Diligence

The systematic absence of diligence or a systematic pattern of unreasonable actions is another category of bad faith. Here there is a failure to do the task entrusted to the relevant corporate organ or officer.[14] An example is the case of the company director, Mrs Moreley, who delegated all of her authority as a director to her incompetent son.[15] Other examples include the case of the major shareholder and director who always voted the same way as the person he mistakenly thought was the controlling shareholder.

---

10   *NRMA Limited v Ian Francis Yates* (1999) 18 ACLC 45.
11   *Fraser v NRMA Holdings Limited* (1995) 127 ALR 543, 544.
12   *Henjo Investments Pty Ltd v Collins Marrickville Pty Ltd* (1988) 79 ALR 83, 95; *Rhone-Poulenc Agrochimie SA v UIM Chemical Services Pty Ltd* (1986) 68 ALR 77.
13   *South Australia v Marcus Clark* (1996) 66 SASR 199, 234. See also *R v Byrnes & Hopwood* (1995) 130 ALR 529; *Shears v Chisholm* [1994] 2 VR 535, 627–8.
14   See *Re Equitable Fire Insurance Co Ltd* [1924] All ER 485 (Romer J).
15   *Statewide Taxation Services Ltd v Morley* (1990) 2 ACSR 405.

Abuse of Power

Situations involving an abuse of power, including taking unfair advantage of an individual or group and the misuse of position or office, are also examples of bad faith. This kind of bad faith or bad intention is often found in contests for control of a corporation, such as company takeovers and proxy contests for positions on a board of directors. In such situations, boards or majority shareholders often use their powers in a way that can be said to be an abuse of the underlying trust inherent in the original grant of power. Simply put, power is used in a way that it was not meant to be used. Many of these cases concern the constitutional arrangements of the relevant corporation. This occurs when the abuse of power consists in the exercise by one corporate organ of power in a way that interferes with power which properly belongs to another corporate organ. For example, the board of directors may exercise a power that properly belongs to the shareholders or vice-versa.[16]

Improper Purpose

There are a number of cases which also involve improper purpose but which are not really an improper use of power. They are only improper in the sense of not playing by the rules. The distinction between these cases and those involving abuse of power is often that the person exercising power for an improper purpose is seeking to use a constitutional or statutory right for an ulterior and improper motive. Again, many examples can be found in the cases involving contests for corporate control. There is also a large group of cases dealing with the inspection of corporate documents and registers which fall into this category. They are cases in which inspection or access to corporate information is sought for the wrong reason.[17]

---

16   See *Howard Smith Ltd v Ampol Petroleum Ltd* [1974] AC 821 (PC); *Darvall v North Sydney Brick and Tile Co Ltd* (1989) 16 NSWLR 260.

17   See eg *Re Augold NL* [1987] 2 Qd R 297; *Knightswood Nominees Pty Ltd v Sherwin Pastoral Co Ltd* (1989) 15 ACLR 151; *Garina Pty Ltd v Action Holdings Ltd* (1989) 7 ACLC 962.

Misuse of Information

Bad faith also arises in situations where individuals or groups have legitimate access to information but use it for the wrong purpose. The most typical situations are those involving the use of corporate information for personal gain (at the extreme end, insider trading) and situations involving the use of corporate information for the benefit of a competitor.

In all of these situations individual acts of bad faith may have an impact on the constructed intention of the corporate organ or the corporation as an entity. All of the above factual situations may in isolation be legally and morally neutral, but in a given set of circumstances depend on intent for their moral and legal validity.

Some Conclusions on the Nature of Corporate Intention

I believe that some conclusions can be drawn on the legal nature of corporate intention from the above examples. These conclusions attempt to bring together the general corporate intent with the intent of the individualised actors within the organisation. The following is a tentative list of the characteristics of corporate intention in the civil law sphere.

1. Corporate intention does not equate with free will, but it does assume residual freedom at the level of the substratum (the pieces of the mosaic). If that were not the case, the existence of bad faith or improper purpose would not be an issue.
2. Corporate intention is not individual. It always assumes another person or, at the very least, another capacity. It is of its very essence relational, that is dependent upon relationships. Individual acts of bad faith by corporate agents will not necessarily destroy the good faith of the corporation.
3. Corporate intention is neither subjective, nor objective. It is legally contrived and consequential. It is consequential in the sense that corporate intention is constructed from, and follows as a result of, the corporate act. It must be established through evidentiary rules.
4. Corporate intention includes oblique intention (the unintended, and sometimes unforeseen, result of an action). This is clear from the legal remedies available for breach of duty.

5. Corporate intention is not necessarily rational. For example, there are situations where corporate agents cannot act to protect the interests of the majority.[18] Nevertheless, corporate intention is legally rational in the sense that it is constructed from legal rules. Also, good faith will sometimes be measured by reference to the extrinsic reasonableness of an action or transaction. Thus, rationality and the concept of the reasonable person may affect a determination of whether intent is good or bad.

6. Corporate intention is not morally determined. For example, the good intention of the individual actor will not be enough to establish proper purpose. Also, the operation of rules regarding burdens of proof means that a finding of bad faith only means that it is more probable than not that bad faith or improper purpose infected the transaction.

The Impact of Legal Developments on Concepts of Corporate Intention

A number of legal developments have affected both the interpretation and the importance of intention in corporate law. Of greatest significance is the growth of statutory provisions which supplant or avoid the use of intention as a legal requirement for civil liability. In this essay, the role of corporate law statutes is that of 'the dog that didn't bark'. Statutes have three important roles to play with regard to intention. The first is that a statute will often remove the need to prove intent as a prerequisite for liability. The second is that a statute can define the type of intent required for liability. For example, a statutory provision requiring proof of 'the intent to deceive' is more restrictive than the requirement that one show intent to do the relevant act. Finally, and most importantly, statutes have to be interpreted as to their own intent and meaning.

Another legal development one must consider is the increasing use of negligence as a basis for liability rather than intentional breach of duty. The increasing use of negligence is related to other phenomena such as the institutionalisation of management and the growth of corporate groups, neither of which have formal legal recognition or rules which facilitate the attribution of intention. Insurance as a routine method of prudential

---

18   See *Howard Smith Ltd v Ampol Petroleum Ltd* [1974] AC 821.

management has also limited the need to attribute intent. Finally, flexible non-public dispute resolution also removes the need for intent in the settlement of claims.

The Impact of Other Disciplines on Concepts of Corporate Intention

In addition to legal developments, changes in other areas and disciplines cannot help but influence the way lawyers and courts view intention and define concepts such as bad faith. It is clear, for example, that cultural and moral plurality has had an impact on industry expectations and definitions of commercial morality. Disagreements as to moral standards have led to the growth of statutory prescriptions. Similarly, the growth of psychology and the deprecation of the concept of free will have affected legal ideas about responsibility and liability. Social, political and organisational theories also influence the view of the modern corporation and its autonomy and responsibility to the community.

Final Observations

I want to end this essay by asking what all of this tells us about corporate law generally and, more specifically, what it tells us about the importance of classic concepts of intention for principles of corporate governance and corporate decision making. It seems clear that the traditional rules for attributing criminal intent to the corporation—the 'directing mind' or 'control group' tests—are not more than part of the civil law mosaic. These tests focus on individual agency and attribute that individual agency to the institutional entity. This is done using definitions of intent that rely upon philosophical principles and jurisprudential standards relevant to personal responsibility and criminal liability. Such definitions of intent do not begin to address the nature and definition of collective intent.

With bad faith and bad intentions in corporate law, the definition of intent must encompass the entire mosaic. Despite the influence of developments elsewhere which limit or minimise the centrality of intention, as a general proposition I would say that the importance of intention in corporate law is not diminishing. What also seems clear is that where intention is important in corporate law it is often the critical issue.

When this is the case, higher standards of good faith will be demanded as the corporate entity or organ becomes more complex and more artificial. These more exacting standards or norms will depend upon corporate law expectations that have their legal foundations in the collective empathy of the corporate substratum, in current corporate practice and the current regulatory framework.

This essay has considered the definition of corporate intention, and the various ways in which intention has an important role to play in the assignment of legal responsibility and legal liability at all levels of corporate activity: the corporate entity level, the level of corporate organs and the level of individual actors and agents. The collective nature of the enterprise must be a reference point for defining intention at each level. What is particularly distinctive in corporate law theory is that bad intentions at the corporate entity level can cause the corporate entity to more or less self-destruct.

While individual and unorganised collective action may not affect the general corporate intention, corporate strategies involving a pervasive organisational and institutional campaign to deceive or mislead will. Strategies which depend on bad faith at all levels of the corporation, and which have an impact on the empathetic collectivity of the organisation, will provide further proof of intention and consequently may trigger civil liability. This is true because here the very integrity of the corporation, as a corporation, is called into question. When that happens, the protective veil, which is the corporate form, dissolves. In that event, it is not just legal liability that may result from bad intentions. The corporation itself may lose its legal personality.

Pollock and Maitland called the corporate form a 'blank form of legal thought'.[19] If the intention which is brought to enliven that 'blank form' is corrupt, the corporate form itself has been misused. In an historical and philosophical sense, the corporation has failed to achieve its identifying truth. At law, it presents an injustice for which the law must seek a remedy. The tobacco companies may provide a contemporary example of bad faith at all levels of corporate intent. To the extent that these large corporations seek to hive off their cigarette producing subsidiaries—sending dividends

---

19   Frederick Pollock and Frederic Maitland, *The History of English Law Before the Time of Edward I, Vol I* (2nd ed, 1899) Book II, ch II, sec 12, p 486.

to the parent corporation while isolating legal liability in a subsidiary corporation—one can expect that smoke will permeate the corporate veil.

13 Postulated Authors and Hypothetical Intentions

NATALIE STOLJAR[1]

Introduction

Theories of legal interpretation commonly, though controversially, characterise the meaning of legal texts such as statutes and constitutions using the notion of legislators' intention. This approach is an example of the interpretive theory of intentionalism, in which the author's intended meaning is said to determine interpretation. According to intentionalism, only those interpretations corresponding to the author's intended meaning are correct. Thus, like most theories of interpretation, intentionalism is not a 'mere' decision procedure, or aid to discovering interpretive meaning. Rather, it is a *legitimating* or *justifying* theory; it provides an answer to the question of which of a number of possible interpretations of a text is the correct or justified interpretation.

This essay examines a particular version of intentionalism which I call the *postulated author thesis*. Most versions of intentionalism characterise interpretation using the intentions of actual authors. The postulated author thesis uses the hypothetical intentions of postulated—or fictitious—authors. The aim of the essay is to argue that appealing to the postulated author thesis undermines the plausibility of intentionalism. The first section explains the place of the postulated author thesis in the context of intentionalism. It sketches different varieties of intentionalism and outlines the postulated author thesis in contrast to these. The next three sections each describe a way of arguing for intentionalism and hence for the postulated author thesis. The first treats legal interpretation as a species of conversational interpretation in which participants in the conversation

1   I am grateful to Ian Gold and John Williams for comments on an earlier draft of this essay. I have benefited also from comments from participants in an ARC Workshop at Monash University Law School, June 2000, especially those from Heidi Hurd, Michael Moore and Walter Sinnott-Armstrong.

make inferences about what others intend to communicate. On this approach, the postulated author thesis is offered as a supplement to, and extension of, intentionalism. The second approach conceives of legal interpretation as constructive, not conversational, and therefore as *not* determined by actual intentions of actual authors. Nevertheless interpretation is *intentional* in the sense that it relies on a 'structural' intention implicit in the practice or text; in other words, it relies on a postulated intention. The final approach argues that texts have meaning only if they are conceived as the products of intentional agents. Hence, even if there is no agent we know about, or no actual agent, there is a postulated author whose intentions determine interpretation. I argue that all three approaches fail. I also argue that the postulated author thesis should not be considered a legitimating theory, but at most a convenient heuristic device.

Intentionalism and the Postulated Author Thesis

Intentionalists claim that the meaning of legal texts is the speaker's or author's meaning. Although it is acknowledged that, in addition, sentences and texts bear conventional or dictionary meaning, which may diverge on particular occasions from the speaker's meaning, it is argued that legal texts are the legislators' 'attempt to communicate what they have determined ought to be done, and *that* text's meaning is the [speaker's meaning] not [the dictionary meaning]'.[2] Such arguments often rely on H P Grice's analysis of speaker's meaning. The analysis requires that for a speech-act to be an act of communication, and hence for a speaker to *mean* something by an utterance, there must be a complex hierarchy of communicative intentions accompanying the utterance. In short, a speaker must have an intention to produce a belief or other response in the hearer, as well as higher-order intentions that the hearer recognise that first intention, and that the hearer's belief come about through the recognition of the first intention.[3] If something like Grice's intentional analysis is true, it is plausible that successful interpretation requires interpreters to make inferences about the author's intentions.

---

2   Larry Alexander, 'All or Nothing at All? The Intentions of Authorities and the Authority of Intentions' in Andrei Marmor (ed), *Law and Interpretation* (1995) 365.
3   Grice, H P, 'Meaning' (1957) 66 *Philosophical Review* 377, 383. See Scruton's exposition for an example of an analysis of Grice using these three intentions: Roger Scruton, *Modern Philosophy: A Survey* (1994) 254.

Legal authors have different kinds of intentions and intentions at different levels of abstraction. Which intentions determine meaning? Broadly speaking, proponents of intentionalism have suggested four alternatives. The first two understand 'intention' to refer to a psychological state of an author or authors. Consider a regulation that prohibits the use of toxins without a licence, and suppose that the legislative body passing the regulation has some specific examples of toxins in mind that it wishes to prohibit. The approach of 'strict' intentionalism argues that the interpretation of the regulation is determined by the specific beliefs of the legislators about the application of the word 'toxin'—that is to say, by their *application* intentions. Thus, for example, if the legislators believe that insecticides are toxins, but caffeine is not, the regulation prohibits the use of insecticides without a licence but does not prohibit the use of caffeine without a licence. The approach of 'moderate' intentionalism, however, argues that the author's *enactment* intentions—the intentions regarding the *sense* of the clause—determine interpretation. Therefore, the regulation applies to everything to which the term 'toxin' applies, even if the legislators do not have specific beliefs about all those things.[4] Enactment intentions can be *abstract*, such as an intention to enact an abstract moral principle.[5] For instance, the framers of the Equal Protection clause of the United States Constitution intended to enshrine an abstract moral principle of equality in addition to the specific applications of that principle that they had in mind. Moderate intentionalists argue that the fact that the framers thought that racial segregation was permissible is not relevant for the interpretation of the Equal Protection clause. Their abstract intention was to enshrine equality, and hence segregation is unconstitutional. Application, enactment and abstract intentions are all actual psychological states of the author.

A third approach is to allow *counterfactual* intentions (in addition to actual intentions) of the author to determine interpretation. Suppose the authors of the regulation prohibiting toxins did not consider the case of caffeine. *Had* they considered it, however, they *would not have intended* to require a licence for its use. The legislators therefore had a counterfactual

---

4   See Goldsworthy's discussion of the difference between enactment and application intentions: Jeffrey Goldsworthy, 'Originalism in Constitutional Interpretation' (1997) 25 *Federal Law Review* 1, 30.

5   See Dworkin, 'The Forum of Principle' in Ronald Dworkin, *A Matter of Principle* (1985) and D O Brink, 'Legal Theory, Legal Interpretation and Judicial Review' (1988) 17 *Philosophy and Public Affairs* 105 for discussions of the distinction between abstract and specific, or concrete, intentions.

intention not to prohibit the use of caffeine under the regulation. Intentionalists often employ counterfactuals to enlarge the scope of their theory: for example, laws often attempt to regulate the use of some category of things—insecticides, weapons, toxins, firearms, etc—in which there are new discoveries or inventions after the law is passed. It is sensible to think that any laws regulating these categories also apply to new instances that the legislators could not have foreseen, and hence it is prima facie plausible to employ a counterfactual intention.[6]

The fourth approach is that of the postulated author thesis. This departs even further from the use of actual intentions, because 'intention' refers to a hypothetical intention of a postulated author. Ronald Dworkin writes that

> interpretation is by nature the report of a purpose; it proposes a way of seeing what is interpreted—a social practice or tradition as much as a text or painting—as if this were the product of a decision to pursue one of a set of themes or visions or purposes, one 'point' rather than another. This structure is required of an interpretation even when there is no historical author whose historical mind can be plumbed.[7]

Dworkin adopts this thesis to explain the character of social practices, such as that of law, for which there are no single authors, yet for which, he claims, interpretation is 'intentional'. Alexander Nehamas endorses a similar position for literary interpretation: 'To interpret a text is to consider it as its author's production ... But just as the author is not identical with a text's fictional narrator, so he is also distinct from its historical writer.'[8] In principle, therefore, Freudian psychoanalytic theory could provide a correct interpretation of *Oedipus Rex*, even though the historical writer Sophocles did not intend to convey Freud's principles. The interpretation of *Oedipus Rex* is governed by the intentions of a postulated author not those of the historical writer.

---

6   For discussions of counterfactuals and intentionalism see Natalie Stoljar, 'Counterfactuals in Interpretation: The Case Against Intentionalism' (1998) 20 *Adelaide Law Review* 29 and Natalie Stoljar, 'Vagueness, Counterfactual Intentions and Legal Interpretation' *Legal Theory* (forthcoming).

7   Ronald Dworkin, *Law's Empire* (1986) 58–9. Dworkin's commitment to intentionalism is a matter of some controversy. Some would argue that Dworkin at times supports an actual intention theory rather than a postulated author theory, eg Jeffrey Goldsworthy, 'Dworkin As An Originalist' (2000) 17 *Constitutional Commentary* 49.

8   Alexander Nehamas, 'The Postulated Author: Critical Monism as a Regulative Ideal' (1981) 8 *Critical Inquiry* 133, 144.

The postulated author is a theoretical construct of the interpreter. However, the sense in which the postulated author thesis is constructive should be distinguished from two senses in which standard conceptions of intentionalism relying on actual intentions may be constructive. First, standard conceptions may be constructive in that they require interpreters to theorise on the basis of available evidence—diaries, notebooks, constitutional debates, etc—about what the author intended. For these conceptions, the *process* of making the interpretive judgment—the decision procedure—is constructive in the same way that all empirical theorising is constructive and its conclusions fallible. However the outcome of the process in this case is a judgment about an *actual* author's *actual* intention.

Second, the postulated author thesis must be distinguished from theories in which *actual* intentions are posited as theoretical constructs. Consider again Grice's theory of speaker's meaning. It requires that, for speakers to mean something by their utterances, the utterances be accompanied—consciously or unconsciously—by the complex hierarchy of intentions identified by the analysis. In passing legislation, legislators may intend to command, regulate, control, admonish, set an example, punish, express a moral view, state the law, persuade, and so forth. Do they, in addition to these intentions, have the higher-order intentions required by Grice's analysis for their speech-acts to be meaningful acts of communication? Suppose that there is no evidence that these complex higher-order intentions are actually held by the legislators when they pass laws. Then there is no reason to posit that the required intentions accompany their utterances and no reason to conclude that their utterances are acts of communication. On the other hand, the legislators' utterances are *obviously* acts of communication, and hence the complex set of intentions required by the analysis (assuming it is correct) *must* be present. A way out of the dilemma is to treat the communicative intentions required by Grice's analysis as theoretical constructs. In the same way that unobservable particles are posited as theoretical constructs by scientific theories, 'unobservable' intentions are posited by Grice's theory of meaning and communication. That is, a hierarchy of intentions is deemed to be present and to accompany speech-acts such as the passing of laws.

The postulated author thesis therefore should be distinguished from intentionalism conceived as constructive in the sense that it requires a process or decision procedure of a certain kind—one in which the interpreter theorises about the author's intention on the basis of evidence; and it should be distinguished from theories in which intentions are posited as theoretical constructs. Here, the intentions in play are actual psychological states of actual authors, whereas, on the postulated author thesis, the intentions and authors do not actually obtain.

On standard conceptions of intentionalism, interpretations that correspond to the appropriate actual intention are correct. Is the postulated author thesis a mere decision procedure, or heuristic device, or does it also provide a criterion of correctness of interpretation? One way of articulating the postulated author thesis as a justifying theory (and not merely a decision procedure) is to draw on models from moral and political theory, in which correct moral judgments have been held to correspond to the judgments of ideal moral observers or reasoners. In the same way, correct interpretations of legal texts could correspond to what postulated authors operating under ideal conditions would intend.

Consider for example the way in which John Rawls uses the notion of an ideal reasoner to develop the principles of justice that are fundamental to his political theory.[9] The ideal reasoner, on Rawls' account, is said to be reasoning in the 'original position'. The original position is a hypothetical situation in which free and rational agents aiming to further their own interests choose the principles of justice behind a 'veil of ignorance'. The notion of the veil of ignorance is designed to remove the biases inherent in the situation of particular rational choosers; hence Rawls claims that the principles of justice are *fairly* chosen.[10] Other theorists build different features into the notion of the ideal reasoner. For example, some suggest conditions in which a reasoner is free from a list of negative qualities such as distortion, malfunction, error, irrationality, or inattentiveness,[11] or alternatively conditions in which the reasoner has special abilities such as a capacity for vivid imaginative awareness, an ability to keep all relevant facts before one's mind, and infinite patience.[12] Some of these qualities are suitable as the conditions for an ideal balancer or an ideal valuer.[13] In order to *balance* values properly, one would need to perceive all the relevant

---

9   I am grateful to Heidi Hurd for pointing out the possibility of a parallel between postulated author theses and Rawls' notion of a reasoner in the original position.

10   John Rawls, *A Theory of Justice* (1971) 118 ff.

11   For example, Harman characterises the ideal reasoner this way: Gilbert Harman, *The Nature of Morality* (1977) 129–30.

12   John Rawls, 'Outline for a Decision Procedure for Ethics' (1951) 60 *Philosophical Review* 177; R Firth, 'Ethical Absolutism and the Ideal Observer' (1952) 12 *Philosophy and Phenomenological Research* 213 and David Lewis, 'Dispositional Theories of Value' (1989) Supp 63 *Proceedings of the Aristotelian Society* 133 are examples of philosophers who suggest that 'ideal conditions' are conditions in which an observer or reasoner has certain *positive* qualities.

13   Lewis, ibid.

facts, know about all the costs and benefits of applying a particular value, as well as know how other values are affected. In order to establish that something *is* a value, it may be sufficient to engage in 'hard thought' or vivid imaginative awareness. On all these accounts, the notion of the ideal reasoner is not just a heuristic device. The outcome of the reasoning process is *justified* because the reasoning agents have certain ideal features: on Rawls' account, for instance, they are rational and unbiased and hence the outcomes of their reasoning processes are justified. Therefore, the outcome of the decision procedure *itself* provides the criterion of correctness of judgments about the principles of justice. An important question for the postulated author thesis is whether the postulated author can fulfil a parallel role in answering questions of legal interpretation. I argue below that the answer is 'no'.

I have sketched four possible approaches to characterising authors' intentions. The key feature of the postulated author thesis, which distinguishes it from the other approaches, is that it potentially offers a justifying theory of legal interpretation using non-actual intentions of fictitious authors. I now turn to an examination of three strategies for arguing for the postulated author thesis. The next section explores the claim that the postulated author thesis is an extension of standard conceptions of intentionalism in which interpretation is determined by actual intentions; the following section looks at the argument for the postulated author thesis derived from the notion of 'constructive' interpretation; and the final section focuses on the proposal that a postulated author thesis can be inferred from an analysis of the notion of a meaningful text.

Conversational Interpretation and the Postulated Author

Grice's account of speaker's meaning is proposed as an analysis of utterances of single speakers in conversational contexts. Intentionalists sympathetic to Grice treat legal interpretation as a species of conversational interpretation in which the speech-acts to be interpreted (statutes or constitutions) are conceived as acts of communication by their authors. It is claimed that the meaning and therefore the interpretation of such acts is determined by the author's intentions. One strategy for arguing for the postulated author thesis is to adopt this model of legal interpretation in conjunction with a negative claim, namely that the intentions needed for interpretation cannot be restricted to those of the actual author. Marmor argues as follows. Interpretation is a matter of grasping what is being communicated by a speaker or author. But successful communication cannot be achieved using rules and conventions alone. It depends on speakers *intending* that their utterances be understood relative to certain contexts. For example, when a speaker utters 'The cat is on the mat', this is intended to be understood as referring to a cat sitting on a horizontally placed mat, not to a cat hanging on the edge of a vertically placed mat.[14] Marmor claims that, because the specification of context cannot be reduced to rules and conventions, meaning and interpretation require an intentional analysis. An interpretive statement is a 'statement on the communication intentions of an author'.[15] Marmor notes, however, that we make interpretive judgments even in the absence of plausible actual intentions corresponding to the judgment. The judgment 'The Sophocles play *Oedipus Rex* has a psychoanalytic moral' is an interpretive judgment about the play despite the fact that Sophocles presumably had no intentions about psychoanalysis. It follows, according to Marmor, that the appropriate communication intentions in this case are the hypothetical intentions of a fictitious speaker.[16] On this approach, the postulated author thesis supplements the standard conception of intentionalism in which interpretation is determined by actual authors' actual intentions: when there is no plausible actual intention corresponding to an interpretive claim, an intention of a fictitious author fills the gap.

Conceiving of legal interpretation on the conversational model, and hence relying on authors' actual intentions, has several well-known advantages over other theories of interpretation.[17] Since in this context the postulated author thesis is offered as a supplement to intentionalism, one would expect these advantages to be maintained even when a postulated author's intentions are introduced. My aim in this section is to point out that, on the contrary, once the move is made from actual intentions to hypothetical intentions of postulated authors, some of these advantages are

---

14   Andrei Marmor, *Interpretation and Legal Theory* (1992) 26–7.
15   Ibid 31.
16   Ibid.
17   I divide theories of interpretation into the following categories: intentionalist, textualist, value-maximising, historical, pragmatist, and critical. Each category offers distinctive notions of constraint on interpretation. In intentionalism, they are author-centred, based on the author's intention; in textualism, they are text-based; in value-maximising theories, correspondence with appropriate moral values is important; in historical approaches, interpretations are constrained by history; and in pragmatist approaches constraints are generated by the intersubjective features of our practices. The critical approaches in the last category often attempt to undermine the notion of constraint and hence perhaps are not strictly speaking 'theories' at all.

lost. Intentionalist theories that adopt the postulated author thesis therefore do not have the same advantages as standard conceptions of intentionalism over other theories. Moreover, there is a tension within intentionalist theories that endorse both the conversational model and the postulated intention thesis. The reasons for holding the former (for example, that it offers a neat criterion of correctness of interpretation) may be reasons for *rejecting* the latter. In order to resolve the tension, intentionalism must reject the postulated author thesis. I discuss two prominent advantages of intentionalism here, those of *validity* and *stability*.

Michael Moore poses the question of validity as follows: 'in what sense are interpreters discovering meaning (as opposed to creating it) and in what sense can their interpretations be true or valid?'[18] As Moore notes, intentionalism provides an easy answer to this question. Interpreters are discovering meaning because they are describing the intentions of authors, and interpretations are correct only when they correspond to these intentions. Moreover, it has been suggested that a reason for upholding intentionalism is precisely that it solves the problem of validity. E D Hirsch says that, since intentionalism is the only genuine alternative to wholly subjective 'reader-response' theories, it is the 'only compelling normative principle' providing a solution to the problem of validity.[19]

Can the postulated author thesis maintain the advantage? Are the intentions of a postulated author discovered or created? Is there a single stable intention of a postulated author that can determine correct interpretation? Characterising the intentions of a postulated author in the legal context depends on characterising the conditions that an ideal legal author would have to meet. For example, should the postulated author be subject to historical constraints that would constrain the actual author? Nehamas suggests in the literary context that if the historical writer *could not* have had a particular intention, this intention should not be attributed to the postulated author.[20] If this is right, a Freudian interpretation of *Oedipus Rex* would be ruled out if it is judged that Sophocles would have had to know about Freud to intend to comment on the principles of Freudian theory. Alternatively, should the postulated legal author be characterised as ideally rational on the model of ideal reasoner theories in ethics and politics? Or should an ideal legal author be characterised as someone who has special insights that are specific to the area of law being

---

18   Michael Moore, *Educating Oneself in Public: Critical Essays in Jurisprudence* (2000) 440; see also 225, 227.
19   E D Hirsch Jr, *Validity in Interpretation* (1967) 5.
20   Nehamas, above n 8, 145–6.

interpreted? For example, an ideal legal author might be required to have before his mind all the possible cases to which a regulation or clause could apply, or the ability to vividly imagine the morality of future generations, or even special insight into the morally correct application of legal texts. The conditions that a postulated author would have to meet will be an artefact of the interpretive theory that is developed, and there will be many equally reasonable accounts of ideal conditions available. It is implausible therefore to think of the intentions of postulated authors as discovered, or as offering stable criteria of correctness of legal interpretation.

Suppose however that there is a single set of conditions appropriate for the ideal legal author. It is often thought that ideal conditions imply that there is in principle a single correct answer available at the limit of inquiry, even if it is inaccessible to us. For instance, Nehamas advocates 'critical monism' because our practices of literary interpretation converge on an ideal in which all the features of the literary text are explained. He argues against 'pluralism' in literary interpretation by distinguishing methodological pluralism from pluralism of content. There can be many different interpretations of literary texts in the sense that interpreters can offer different perspectives on the text and different approaches to interpreting them. Yet, unless the contents of these different interpretations are both equally compelling and incompatible, methodological pluralism does not entail content pluralism. Nehamas develops monism using the notion of an ideal interpretation. He writes:

> The critical monism which I advocate is a regulative ideal and identifies the meaning of the text with whatever is specified by that text's ideal interpretation. Such an interpretation would account for all of the text's features, though we can never reach it since it is unlikely that we can even understand what it is to speak of 'all the features' of anything. What we do have (and that is what we need) is the notion of one interpretation answering more questions about a text than another and thus being closer to that hypothetical ideal which would answer all questions. The direction in which this ideal lies may change as new interpretations reveal features of a text previously unnoticed.[21]

Nehamas' idea is that as interpretations of a literary work are revised, and hence improve, they explain more and more features of the text. Therefore, interpretations are approaching a hypothetical ideal in which *all* features of the text are explained, and *all* questions that we might have about a text are answered. The meaning of the text is identified with the

---

21   Ibid 144.

ideal interpretation. Similarly, Dworkin's device of the ideal judge, Hercules, who has 'superhuman skill, learning, patience and acumen',[22] is meant to avoid the epistemological difficulties of real judges, and hence to reduce or eliminate the risk of pluralism in interpretation.

It is not the case, however, that ideal conditions ensure single correct interpretive answers. Consider a parallel with Rawls' reasoner in the original position. Even if it is agreed that one of the features of the reasoner is ideal rationality, the ideally rational agent may still face dilemmas. Rawls' derivation of the principles of justice in the original position depends on the claim that behind the veil of ignorance ideal reasoners will identify with the least well-off members in the society to which the principles of justice will apply. However this assumes that choosers are extremely risk-averse and they identify with the least well-off members of the society. In fact, it is highly probable that once in the society they will not be one of the least well-off. Why not take this small risk when considering what principles of justice to formulate for the society? In other words, the conditions of ideal rationality may not distinguish between agents who are extremely risk-averse and agents who are willing to take very small risks, but the differences between such agents may generate a difference in the principles of justice endorsed. Thus, accounts of a concept that depend on reasoners operating in ideal conditions are compatible with pluralistic characterisations of the concept. The notion of the ideal legal author therefore does not solve the problem of validity because, *pace* Nehamas, pluralism is probable even on theories invoking ideal conditions. There will be considerable, yet reasonable, disagreement over how to specify ideal conditions, and different answers to interpretive questions are likely to emerge, even if a single set of conditions is specified.

A second advantage of intentionalism as a theory of legal interpretation is that it maintains *stability*. Intentionalism is a version of originalism, namely of the thesis that the meaning of a legal text corresponds (and should correspond) to its original meaning—its meaning at the time that it was written. Intentionalism therefore is taken to have the justifications offered for originalism. It is argued that interpretation is a matter of discovery not creation, and hence that it maintains important 'rule of law' values such as stability. However, relying on postulated rather than real authors undermines the originalist element in intentionalism. The shift to the notion of a postulated author is in effect a shift from an author-

---

22   Ronald Dworkin, *Taking Rights Seriously* (1977) 105.

centred to an interpreter-centred approach to interpretation. And, as we have seen, specifying the characteristics of an ideal author is a significantly value-laden enterprise, and hence is creative not descriptive. These shifts undermine the originalist impetus for intentionalism. Correct interpretations no longer correspond to the actual intentions of a historical author.

The advantages of intentionalism conceived according to the conversational model of interpretation do not hold for the postulated intention thesis. Moreover, not only does the postulated author thesis not have these advantages, it is likely to be significantly more pluralistic than some alternative theories of interpretation, and hence to be worse off with respect to validity and stability than these other theories.[23] Holding both the standard conception of intentionalism and the postulated author thesis is therefore likely to result in an internally inconsistent position. Intentionalists should jettison the postulated author thesis and acknowledge that intentionalist interpretation is incomplete and 'gappy'. When questions arise for which there is no actual intention determining an answer, interpreters have *discretion*. Thus, judgments about texts and practices that do not correspond to an actual author's intention are not judgments about intention in any substantive sense. Rather, they are judgments that rely on subjective criteria introduced by the interpreter. And, if there are a great many instances in which intentionalism must admit of interpretive gaps, even standard versions of intentionalism may end up being worse off on the measure of validity than at first thought.

Interpretation is Intentional

An alternative approach is to argue for the postulated author thesis directly by claiming that interpretation is intentional, but not conversational. Hence it does not rely on actual intentions of actual authors but on some other notion of intention. For example, Nehamas writes: 'To interpret a text is to place it in a context, and this is to construe it as someone's production, directed at certain purposes ... But just as the author is not identical with a text's fictional narrator, so he is also distinct from its historical writer.'[24] Dworkin says 'interpretation is by nature the report of a purpose ... even

---

23   For example, textualist theories and some versions of value-maximising theories may offer better solutions to the problem of validity.

24   Nehamas, above n 8, 144.

when there is no historical author whose historical mind can be plumbed'.[25] Both claim therefore that interpretation is essentially intentional; the intention is a 'structural' intention implicit in the text or practice, or, in Nehamas' terms, an intention of a postulated author. I argue in this section that, on these accounts, the postulated author's intention does not do the work of justification. Hence, it is a heuristic device only, and does not add anything to intentionalism conceived as a justifying theory.

Nehamas says that the meaning of the text is identified 'with whatever is specified by that text's ideal interpretation ... Such an interpretation would account for all of the text's features though we can never reach it'.[26] Moreover, 'the author is postulated as the agent whose actions account for the text's features. He is a character, a hypothesis, which is accepted provisionally, guides interpretation and is in turn modified in its light'.[27] Thus, it is easy to distinguish the justifying criterion from the decision procedure in Nehamas' account. The work of justification is done by the text's 'ideal interpretation', whereas the way in which we are guided to that interpretation is through adopting the device of the postulated author.

Dworkin's argument turns on his elaboration of the notion of 'constructive' interpretation, the type of interpretation appropriate for social practices and texts, and therefore for law. Constructive interpretation is analogous to, but not the same as, conversational interpretation. According to Dworkin, when engaging in the process of interpretation, the participants in a practice adopt an 'interpretive attitude' in which they conceive of the practice as having 'value or purpose'.[28] These participant interpreters seek to 'see [the practice] in its best light' and to 'restructure' it on that basis.[29] Suppose that one of the rules of the social practice of courtesy is that men should stand whenever a woman enters the room; suppose also that participants in the practice consider that the point of the practice is to promote interpersonal respect. Dworkin's claim is that if it becomes the case that standing when a woman enters the room is no longer always required to express respect, participants will reinterpret or modify the rule accordingly.

---

25 Dworkin, above n 7, 58–9.
26 Nehamas, above n 8, 144.
27 Ibid.
28 Dworkin, above n 7, 52. There are too many expositions of, responses to, and arguments against Dworkin's approach to list here. One comprehensive exposition is Stephen Guest, *Ronald Dworkin* (1991).
29 Dworkin, ibid 47.

Dworkin seems to advocate a postulated author thesis because he claims that to ascertain the point of a text or practice, interpreters must treat a text or practice *as if* it constituted a single work written by a single author, and *as if* the single author had a single purpose in mind. He identifies the author of social practices and laws as the community personified. Thus the interpreter theorises about the purpose of the community personified—the postulated author of the social practice in question. Let us accept for the sake of argument that this is a plausible description of the phenomenology of interpretation. Nevertheless, the description does not establish that interpretation is intentional. An alternative account (advocated by Dworkin in other places) is that interpreters are theorising about the *values* embedded in the practice and modifying the rules of the practice in the light of those values. Moore points out that the notion of purpose is ambiguous: 'purpose' understood as function or value must be distinguished from 'purpose' understood as an author's intention.[30] Dworkin's model of legal interpretation may offer a helpful heuristic device for interpreters to theorise the value of a social practice. It may be helpful to consider large and unwieldy historical practices such as that of American constitutional law *as if* they were written by a single author with a single vision or purpose in mind. But what is doing the work of justification on Dworkin's account is not an intention but rather a value or set of values that is conceived by interpreters as implicit in the practice.

The postulated authors described by Nehamas and Dworkin are at most heuristic devices. It is questionable however whether they are truly useful ones. On Nehamas's account, giving a good interpretation of a literary text is giving one that explains as much of the features of the text as possible. It is an open question whether theorising about a postulated author will be helpful to achieve that goal. Similarly, constructive interpretation may be equally well, or better, achieved by interpreters who theorise directly about the values appropriate to a practice or text.

The Nature of a Text

A third way of arguing for the postulated author focuses on the nature of a meaningful text. It is claimed that a necessary condition of marks being meaningful texts is that they are the creations of 'intentional agents'. Marks that are washed up in the sand that resemble poetry, or cloud

---

30 Moore, above n 18, 438–9.

formations that resemble language, therefore cannot carry meaning and cannot be objects of interpretation because they are natural processes rather than the products of agents. Interpretation therefore is determined by the intentions of the agent producing the object of interpretation. And, since the intention is not, or is not always, an actual intention of an actual author, in some or all cases it must be the intention of a fictional or postulated author. I argue in this section that even if interpreters are required to postulate an author when interpreting texts, it does not follow from this that the interpretation of these texts is determined by the author's intentions. The argument that texts are products of intentional agents does not entail intentionalism.

Steven Knapp and Walter Benn Michaels, and Stanley Fish, develop a theory of interpretation along these lines. Fish writes:

> *Words are intelligible only within the assumption of some context of intentional production, some already-in-place pre-decision as to what kind of person, with what kind of purposes, in relation to what specific goals in a particular situation is speaking or writing* ... All interpretation is intentional—assuming as the ground of its possibility a purposeful agent who has produced its object.[31]

Knapp and Michaels ask us to consider marks washed up on the sand that resemble the stanzas of a poem. According to Knapp and Michaels, on coming across the first stanza in the sand, we automatically assume that they are meaningful and are the work of an intentional agent. However, as we watch, a second stanza is washed up. As there is no obvious intentional agent at work here, Knapp and Michaels claim that we must question whether these marks are meaningful at all:

> As long as you thought the marks were poetry, you were assuming their intentional character ... you had without realising it, already posited an author. It was only with the mysterious arrival of the second stanza that your tacit assumption (e.g. someone writing with a stick) was challenged ...
>
> The example of the second stanza made clear that what had seemed to be an example of intentionless language was either not intentionless or not language. The question was whether the marks counted as language; what

---

31 Stanley Fish, *Doing What Comes Naturally: Change, Rhetoric and the Practice of Theory in Literary and Legal Studies* (1989) 295–6 (emphasis in original).

determined the answer was a decision as to whether or not they were the product of an intentional agent.[32]

According to these writers, therefore, interpreters must assume that the object of interpretation has been produced by an intentional agent. One way to justify this conclusion is through Grice's distinction between natural and non-natural meaning.[33] Many natural effects 'mean', or are natural signs of, something else. For example, dark clouds 'mean' rain and red spots 'mean' measles. However the notion of natural meaning should be distinguished from the notion of meaning that is appropriate to languages and other symbolic systems, in Grice's terms, non-natural meaning. Since 'mere' marks on the sand are natural effects only, they bear at most natural meaning. Hence they are not proper objects of interpretation. Only objects that are conceived as the products of intentional agents have non-natural meaning and are texts.

Two writers on legal interpretation challenge this conclusion. Frederick Schauer proposes a conception of 'semantic autonomy', and Michael Moore argues that even natural effects, such as cloud formations, may have non-natural meaning. Both approaches rely on adopting the perspective of the interpreter or audience as the arbiter of non-natural meaning. Schauer's argument for semantic autonomy claims that marks looking like C-A-T have an 'acontextual' meaning for speakers of English that is independent of what an author on a particular occasion intended the marks to mean. This is the case even if these marks are the product of arbitrary forces such as waves on the sand at a beach. The acontextual meaning derives from the conventions and rules of English which competent speakers of English employ when they interpret such marks.[34] Moore argues that if interpreters find some value in treating natural effects such as cloud formations as a text, so that treating the clouds as a text

---

32 Steven Knapp and Walter Benn Michaels, 'Against Theory' (1982) 8 *Critical Inquiry* 4, 16. Note that Knapp and Michaels can be characterised as advocating an actual intention thesis, not a postulated intention thesis. See Steven Knapp and Walter Benn Michaels, 'Intention, Identity and the Constitution: A Response to David Hoy' in Gregory Leyh (ed), *Legal Hermeneutics: History, Theory and Practice* (1992) in which they seem to adopt the former rather than the latter. I am assuming for the purposes of the discussion here that their position is committed to the postulated author thesis at least for some cases of interpretation—namely those in which there is no obvious actual author whose intentions determine meaning.

33 Grice, above n 3, 377.

34 Frederick Schauer, 'Formalism' (1988) 97 *Yale Law Journal* 509. Endicott 1996 argues persuasively that there is no such thing as acontextual meaning: T Endicott, 'Linguistic Indeterminacy' (1996) 16 *Oxford Journal of Legal Studies* 667.

potentially gives either reasons for belief or reasons for action, then the clouds *are* a text.[35] If either Schauer or Moore is right, even natural effects can be conceived as texts and hence as bearers of non-natural meaning. There is no need to postulate an agent, and hence no need to treat interpretation as determined by the intentions of that agent.

My argument here does not depend on characterising natural effects as having non-natural meaning. Rather, I concede for the sake of argument that marks must bear non-natural meaning to be texts, and that the hallmark of non-natural meaning is its production by an intentional agent or agents. I deny however that this claim implies an intentionalist approach to interpretation. It does not imply, as Moore puts it, 'that the meaning of the text must be sought in the propositional attitudes of their authors'.[36] Knapp and Michaels' intuition is that once we establish that the object of interpretation is the product of an intentional act, there is some intention accompanying or 'behind' the act that corresponds to the meaning of the object of interpretation. They conclude:

> The point ... is not that there *need* be no gulf between intention and the meaning of its expression, but that there *can* be no gulf. Not only in serious literal speech but in *all* speech what is intended and what is meant are identical ... [W]hat a text means and what its author intends it to mean are identical.[37]

This conclusion is flawed, however, because there are cases of intentional acts for which there is no actual intention 'behind' the act that corresponds to the meaning of the act.

One example is that of social practices such as courtesy. Moore suggests that such social practices 'grow up gradually and unwittingly' and hence have no individual creator.[38] Yet it is generally agreed that social practices are in some sense products of intentional agency as well as being interpretive practices with non-natural meaning. Since there is no individual creator, their meaning cannot be tied to an individual author's intention. Thus, in this case, the meaning of an intentional act cannot be governed by an actual intention 'behind' the act. A second example is that of legislation. Jeremy Waldron points out that most legal interpretation is interpretation of statutes and constitutions, namely of acts which are 'the

---

35   Moore, above n 18, 431; see also the discussion at 437–9.
36   Ibid 438.
37   Knapp and Michaels, 'Against Theory', above n 32, 18–19.
38   Moore, above n 18, 436.

product of a multi-member assembly, comprising a number of persons of quite radically different aims, interests and backgrounds'.[39] Suppose in a parliament there are three factions, divided over the questions of whether the rule 'No vehicles in the park' has exceptions for ambulances or bicycles and of whether the rule includes state as well as municipal parks. Faction 1 thinks the rule excepts ambulances and bicycles and does not include state parks. Faction 2 thinks it excepts only ambulances and applies to parks. Faction 3 thinks it excepts only bicycles and applies to parks. On the basis of counting the relevant intentions in each case, the resulting piece of legislation is that the rule excepts both ambulances and bicycles and includes state parks. But there was no faction which intended such a combination. Thus, while the legislation is plausibly described as an intentional act because it is the product of a group of intentional agents, there is *no* actual intention that is the intention behind the act.

The point applies to cases of single agents and hence to interpretation quite generally. Knapp and Michaels' analysis involves a slide from the claim that objects of interpretation are products of intentional agents to the claim that the interpretation of these objects must be intentionalist. But this slide depends on what Michael Bratman calls 'the simple view' of the relation between an intentional act and having an intention, namely that for the act to be intentional, it must be done *with* an appropriate intention. As Bratman points out, the simple view is false. Consider his example of playing a video game and hitting a target intentionally but without an intention to do so. According to Bratman, when I hit the target in a video game I hit it intentionally because I want to hit it, and am trying to hit it, and hitting it depends on my skills in playing video games. However, suppose I am playing two games simultaneously and it is known to me that they are linked up in such a way as to be impossible to hit both targets. On the simple view, if I am playing and using my skill to try to hit the targets, I am engaging in the intentional acts of trying to hit each target and hence I have intentions to hit both targets when I know this to be impossible. Bratman argues that since I am not irrational, I cannot have both intentions, and hence the simple view is false.[40]

Bratman's critique of the simple view assumes that there are certain rationality constraints on intentional action. It has been suggested however that these constraints do not obtain in all cases and at all levels of generality, and if this is so, Bratman's argument against the simple view is

---

39 Jeremy Waldron, 'Legislators' Intentions and Unintentional Legislation' in Marmor, above n 2, 336.

40 Michael Bratman, *Intention, Plans and Practical Reason* (1987) 114.

questionable.[41] Is there support for Bratman's conclusion that does not presuppose that his rationality constraints always hold? I claim that Bratman's insight can be defended as *explanatory* of the way in which many literary works, and artworks in general, are sometimes produced. The creative process of writers and artists is an intentional process but one which often does not seem to involve particular intentions to execute particular plans. The production of expressionist artworks is a case in point. Although Jackson Pollock intentionally produced the colours and patterns on the canvas we call 'Blue Poles', arguably there was no particular plan or intention attributable to him during the creative process of producing that complex of colour and pattern. Although the production of works of literature may not be expressionistic in the same way, certain portions of writing are sometimes described as being produced in the absence of particular plans or intentions that they turn out that way. For example, characters in novels have been described by writers as having a life of their own, so that character development is felt by the writer to be in some sense unintended. In the context of the production of artworks, therefore, the simple view does not hold.[42]

The examples that I have outlined are designed for cases of actual authors and actual intentions. For instance, Waldron's point about legislation is significant because it is an example of an object of interpretation for which there is no *actual* psychological state of a single agent corresponding to its meaning. However, the moral to be drawn from the examples applies just as well to postulated as to real authors. Suppose when the stanza of poetry mysteriously appears on the sand it is necessary for interpreters to postulate an author to characterise the marks as meaningful. The act of postulating an author does not itself imply that the interpretation of a text must be guided by the author's intention; it does not imply that interpretation is intentionalist.

---

41 See Moore's discussion of Bratman's rationality constraints in Michael Moore, *Placing Blame: A General Theory of the Criminal Law* (1997) 313–15.

42 Moore notes that the simple view is denied implicitly by the following claim of criminal law: all actions done knowingly are done intentionally. Ibid 314. The simple view is denied because doing something knowingly does not imply that it is done with an intention.

Conclusion

This essay has explored arguments in the literature on legal interpretation, and interpretation generally, that adopt the postulated author thesis in one form or another. My response has been threefold. First, proponents of the conversational model who also adopt the postulated author thesis should jettison the thesis because it undermines the advantages that they implicitly attribute to their theory. Second, when the postulated author thesis is offered as a component of 'constructive' approaches to interpretation, it is no longer a legitimating theory; it is a mere decision procedure or heuristic device, and probably not a very useful one. Third, intentionalists who endorse the postulated author thesis on the basis of an analysis of the nature of meaningful text mistakenly assume that *intentionalist* interpretation is required when one is interpreting an intentional object. This is not the case, so even if interpreters are required to postulate an author, they are not required to analyse interpretation as corresponding to that author's intentions.

14 Legislative Intent and Democratic Decision Making

TOM CAMPBELL

The concept of intention is crucial in the interpretation of law by judges and by citizens. It is also fundamental with respect to the theory of legislation in a democracy and to the understanding of the authority and functions of law in general. Bringing these aspects together, I argue in this essay that legislative intent should be analysed first in relation to the idea of a democratic political system and only secondarily, and derivatively, in relation to issues concerning statutory and constitutional construction. The substantive thesis I defend refines an institutional conception of legislative intent to propose that it is the duty of a democratic legislature to enact statutes which make formally good law, that is law which is clear, unambiguous, readily applicable and unproblematic in that it can be understood and followed without difficulty. This means that citizens have a right to expect that statutes mean what they say, that legislatures have a duty to enact laws which can be understood, followed and applied on the basis of the contextually evident meaning of the words, and that courts have as their prime, if defeasible, duty the responsibility of applying the text, so understood.[1] In other words, in a democratic context, legislatures ought to be taken to intend the contextually evident meaning of their enactments. This is part of what I call 'democratic positivism'.[2]

This thesis takes legislative intent to be a normative concept which relates to the responsibility of legislatures, the members of which can be held politically accountable for, amongst other things, their formal enactments. It does not require interpreters and subjects to discover the

---

1   This position is partially articulated in Tom Campbell, *The Legal Theory of Ethical Positivism* (1996) ch 6.
2   See Tom Campbell, 'Democratic Aspects of Ethical Positivism' in Tom Campbell and Jeffrey Goldsworthy (eds), *Judicial Power, Democracy and Legal Positivism* (2000) 3.

actual or subjective intent or purpose shared by a majority of individuals within a legislative assembly. Yet it retains the link between the legitimacy of law and the originating political will, in this case the will of the people, which is crucial to democratic forms of legal positivism and, indeed, to any form of democracy which incorporates the rule of positive law, that is law which can be understood, followed and applied without recourse to speculation, controversial evaluation and political calculation.[3]

The proposed conception of legislative intent in a democracy is that the legislating assembly must be taken to intend that its enacted words be law and that those words be understood in terms of their public meaning as captured by the conventions of language and legislation in that society at the time they are made, unless the legislators make it clear, through the text itself, that this is not the case. This may be achieved through the provision of stipulative definitions or some other way of making known what it is that the legislators intend to enact, provided this is consistent with the making of good positivist law. And so, while the intention of the legislature is the source, and the basis for the authority, of law, it is not the actual intent of the members of the legislature that directly determines the meaning of the words used in the enactment. The justification for this normative theory of legislative intent derives from the right of legislatures to make law: law being a set of publicly available rules for the control and facilitation of interpersonal conduct. Because the public nature of law is necessary to its operations it is the legislature's right to choose the words and sentences of the law but not to dictate what they mean. This ultimately empirical justification is, as we shall see, reinforced by other considerations relating to moral form and political accountability.

The view that democratic legislatures should be taken to intend the contextual plain meaning of their enactments is not what is called in the literature an 'intentionalist' theory. Intentionalists regard the text as merely evidence of a subjective intent that is the real source of, and authority for, an enactment.[4] I argue that legislators are responsible for the public, not the private, meaning of their enactments. My view may be called 'textualist', although, as we will see, it is a contextual form of textualism and one which is governed by appropriate conventions for reading legislative texts.

---

3   See Tom Campbell, 'Legal Positivism and Deliberative Democracy' in Michael Freeman (ed), *Current Legal Problems* (1999) 65.

4   Larry Alexander, 'All or Nothing at All? The Intentions of Authorities and the Authority of Intentions' in Andrei Marmor (ed), *Law and Interpretation* (1995) 357, 361.

Further, it is a textualism which traces its authority to legislative intent as a political construct necessary for the institutional operation of what I call democratic positivism. It might, therefore, be labelled 'textual intentionalism'. My position is 'originalist' in so far as it takes the text in its public meaning at the time of enactment. However, it would be confusing to give it this label since 'originalism' is tied in the literature to original intention in a sense which goes beyond that which is to be found through the text and contemporary understanding of it and draws on the denotations originally present to the minds of legislators.[5] This diverges from the traditional idea of orthodox originalism, that is that the meaning of legislation is the specific intention of the legislators as it is revealed in the text plus our knowledge of their beliefs and assumptions. Orthodox originalism suggests that the relevant intention is a meaning the legislature tries, but may fail, adequately to express in words, thus licensing us to use evidence of what the legislators actually meant, and in so doing to put aside the contextually plain meaning of the text. I am not, therefore, even a 'moderate intentionalist', to use Jeffrey Goldsworthy's useful label for a theory which accepts that the meaning of a statute is its 'original intended meaning'[6] but restricts evidence as to what legislators' intentions actually were to that which 'was readily available to their intended audience'.[7] Goldsworthy confines evidence of legislators' intent to what their audience can 'reasonably be expected to know' about those intentions, whereas I hold that citizens have a right and a duty to read the text in terms of the contextually evident meaning at the time of enactment, irrespective of evidence that legislators failed to get their actual meaning across through the text.[8]

The thesis is that the political will is expressed through the conscious and overt choice of language in a particular context, a choice made under the above assumptions. We can thereby relate the authority of legislation to the political authority of the representatives of the adult voting population which elects them to make law and governments to rule via positive law.

---

5   Paul Brest, 'The Misconceived Quest for Original Understanding' (1980) 60 *Boston University Law Review* 204.

6   Jeffrey Goldsworthy, 'Originalism in Constitutional Interpretation' (1997) 25 *Federal Law Review* 1, 12.

7   Ibid 20.

8   For the terminology of intentionalism, textualism and originalism see Marmor, above n 4; Gregory Bassham, *Original Intent and the Constitution: A Philosophical Study* (1992); and Sandford Levinson and Steven Mailloux (eds), *Interpreting Law and Literature: A Hermeneutic Reader* (1988).

This does not require us to undertake a, usually fruitless, search for the subjective intentions of selected individual, or groups of, legislators. Legislative intent does not relate to private meanings or to any purposes, public or private, that are not stated or evidently implied in the text, but to the intentions which citizens and courts of the jurisdiction, conversant with the relevant linguistic conventions and implications of the process of making and transmitting laws, are entitled to find in the enacted text. This thesis does not derive from an abstract analysis of 'intention' or from an apolitical theory of interpretation but from a combination of the ideal of governance through law and the democratic thesis that the right to determine the content of that law derives from the decisions of the populace as a whole. In brief, democratic governments are elected to govern through laws and are accountable in terms of the laws they make. Given the functions of law, on the positivist analysis I adopt, this is not a feasible system unless they are accountable for the contextually evident plain meaning of the legislation enacted.

In summary, this notion of legislative intent brings together commitments to:

(1) the democratic sources of legislation;
(2) the ideal of governance through positive law;
     and, as is implicit in the combination of (1) and (2) above,
(3) priority for the adjudicative, rather than discretionary or law-making, role for courts.

The purposes of this thesis are to promote the utility and justice of law in societies marked by individual and group disagreement, to bolster the legitimacy of democratic process in dealing with disagreement by arriving at a working compromise as to legal rights and duties, and providing a framework within which courts can aspire to carry out functions which are part of, and yet routinely subordinate to, this political process. The political assumption here is that law is the creation of authoritative determinations of mandatory conduct through the selection and specification of moral and instrumental rules from the range of alternatives available in society.[9]

Some theorists will doubt the wisdom of running together three apparently distinct concerns: a theory of politics (the sources of legitimacy), a theory of law (particularly a theory of legal authority) and a

---

9   In this I follow Joseph Raz, 'Authority, Law and Morality' (1985) 62 *The Monist* 295; and Alexander, above n 4, 359–60.

theory of adjudication. I take the contrary view. These three areas of theorising are inextricably intertwined and must be dealt with coherently and comprehensively. We cannot know what judges ought to do until we have a view on the role of law in a justifiable political system. The compartmentalisation of discourses in legal philosophy is implicated in the current ideological shift to legitimating free-ranging judicial control of legal content. The concept of legislative intent is a crucial meeting place of theoretical concerns. A clear and coherent notion of legislative intent is required to give expression to the distinct concepts of democratic sovereignty, the rule of (positive) law and the methodology of legal adjudication. We have to make sense of the idea of the sovereign will of the people in connection with the making of rules which can be accurately and consistently applied by independent judicial officers without recourse to controversial moral and political judgments. In enabling us to make these connections the concept of legislative intent has the potential to unite the central strands of legally oriented political philosophy.

The Thesis

I have argued that a theory of legal interpretation which offers any guidance for practice requires a normative theory of legislative intent, that is a prescriptive conception of what counts as legislative intent which lays down the sort of legislative intent that should be adopted as the source of law, indicates what citizens have a right and a duty to assume about legislative intent, and establishes what sort of legislative intent judges have a duty to respect.

A normative theory cannot be derived from conceptual analysis alone. It follows that there is no prospect of deducing any useful conception of legislative intent from the concept of intention as such. Indeed, 'intention' covers a multiplicity of complex notions relating to action. The discourse of 'intention' may be used to identify, for example, (1) the objectives of conduct, (2) ulterior purposes, (3) commitments to future action, (4) decisions between alternative conduct, (5) motives for these commitments and decisions, (6) attempts to do something and (7) agents' knowledge of the consequences of their actions.[10] There is nothing in the concept of

---

10 For useful explorations of these alternatives, see Gerald MacCallum, 'Legislative Intent' in Robert Summers (ed), *Essays in Jurisprudence* (1970) 237; and Bassham, above n 8.

intention that requires us to adopt one of these multifarious conceptions, let alone give it a specific content, when we seek to identify what is to count as 'legislative intent'. The clarification of legislative intent requires that we make an articulate and overt choice between the range of meanings available, limited only by the contexts we are dealing with and the evaluative stance we decide to adopt.

Because we are dealing with a normative theory of legislative intent, what legislators and legislatures actually intend does not in itself qualify as legislative intent. Normative legislative intent may be regarded as a fiction, a counterfactual assumption. It is not about what individual legislators would have intended if they had thought about the matter, but about what citizens and judges have a right to assume legislators intended, the meanings for which they can be held responsible, even if they had no such actual intentions.[11] Nevertheless, a prescriptive conception of legislative intent must be capable of instantiation, otherwise it would not be reasonable to hold someone or body of persons accountable in its terms. Moreover, it need not be a fiction. Indeed, the theory is that it ought not to be. With respect to my particular normative thesis, contextually evident plain meaning is what legislators both can and ought to intend. Contextually evident plain meaning is what citizens and courts have a duty to accept and a right to assume, just as, in making their wedding vows, a bride and groom have a reciprocal duty to mean what they say and a correlative right to assume that their about-to-be spouse means it when they say 'I do'.

The thesis is that legislators should be taken to intend the contextual plain meaning of words and sentences they enact as rules. However, legislators may make it clear (in plain language) in the text of the legislation in question that they are departing from, or seeking to give more clarity and definition to, what the words and sentences in the legislation mean in terms of the linguistic rules and conventions currently used to understand the communicative discourse of the people concerned. Further, contextual plain meaning takes into account the conventions assumed to hold with respect to legislative communication in general, as well as the shared assumptions of those who operate in the area of social life to which the legislation is addressed. This involves a defeasible commitment to plain meaning, any departure from which must be brought about through the use of further plain meanings.

---

11 For a discussion of counterfactual intentions see Natalie Stoljar, 'Counterfactuals in Interpretation: The Case Against Intentionalism' (1998) 20 *Adelaide Law Review* 29.

The contextually evident plain meaning thesis has three types of advantage: (1) democratic, (2) rule of law and (3) adjudicative.

(1) A core democratic advantage of legislative intention as contextual plain meaning is that plain meaning can serve as the shared intention of all members of the legislature. This applies equally to those who support and those who oppose the legislation in question, in that they accept it or reject it in these same terms. Agreement on meaning precedes acceptance and rejection. Those who accept or reject a piece of legislation can be held accountable for their action with respect to an agreed public meaning of the enactment in question. Contextually evident meaning provides the common ground on which choice and responsibility may be grounded.

One advantage of this approach is that we do not have the problem of aggregating individual wills by settling on the coincidence of subjective intentions, be they linguistic intentions about how the individual legislators understand the words in question, purposive intentions about what the individual legislators hope to achieve by the legislation, or motive intentions about why the individual legislators support (or oppose) the legislation in question. No assumption is required that the individuals comprising the majority supporting the enactment have the same motives or the same reasons or the same further intentions, only that they share the intention to adopt (or in the case of the minority who oppose it, reject) the text in question on the assumption that it 'means what it says'.[12]

It may be argued that this notion of legislative intent undermines the democratic authority of legislation if that is thought to depend on legislation being the embodiment of the political purposes of the people's representatives, or a majority thereof.[13] But that is not so in a democracy that incorporates the rule of law. In such a system what matters is that the people, or their representatives, get to choose what the *law* is to be and that cannot be done except through a choice of text which can be understood and utilised without recourse to the very controversies which give rise to the need for a process for the resolution of political disagreement. Democratic process may, of course, either decrease or increase policy disagreements. Legislative enactment does not remove such disagreement as remains, but it does provide a decision in the form of an authoritative

---

12 Jeremy Waldron makes a similar and perhaps stronger point in Jeremy Waldron, *Law and Disagreement* (1999) 142–6.

13 See David Lyons 'Constitutional Interpretation and Original Meaning' (1986) 4 *Social Philosophy and Policy* 75, 81–2.

text by a majority, the members of which may continue to disagree with respect to objectives and motives.

In short, legislative intent as contextually evident meaning gives intelligible and realisable meaning to the concept of the will of 'the people' or their representatives, and provides a basis for assuming the democratic legitimacy of legislation adopted where the controlling assumption in the logic of the process is that the words mean not what the legislators think they mean or would like them to mean, but what they do mean in terms of the social and political community concerned. This meaning forms the content of the citizen's duty of conformity to law and the basis on which they may hold their representatives accountable.

(2) A core legal theory advantage of seeing legislative intention as contextual plain meaning with respect to, for instance, the idea of legal authority, is that contextual plain meaning has to be assumed in the formulation of many of the reasons which can be given for having mandatory rules applying to a given population. For instance: as a means to establishing a framework for cooperation; reaching agreement on what constitutes unacceptable conduct; setting up procedures for dispute; and administering a system for ordering the distribution of benefits and burdens in a society. All these functions require, I have argued elsewhere,[14] a shared understanding of authoritative rules in common. In crude early positivist terms, legislative intent as contextual plain meaning can make sense of the idea of law as the command of the sovereign in a way which gives us a basis for understanding why we might wish to have a sovereign: namely, to achieve the decisive ordering of social relationships for the improvement of the lives of all subjects.

All this does not entail that only the text and the conventions of the language in question are relevant to our reading of it. The context in which the legislation occurs is an indispensable part of our understanding of it. Even linguistic conventions are often context-relative. However, law making is an endeavour to arrive at relatively decontextualised general norms. More generally, the semantics and syntax of a language must be used in a context and take into account the social setting of the type of discourse involved, the general circumstances of the type of utterances in question (sometimes referred to as the pragmatics of discourse), and something of the particular circumstances of the enactment in question. In the case of legislation these contexts include not only the pragmatics of the

---

14   Campbell, above n 1, ch 3.

conventional understanding of what it is to legislate, but also the political and social situations from which the particular legislative proposals emerge and to which the legislation in question is addressed. Such contextual understandings of legislation exclude the personal or subjective intentions of legislators in the sense of their beliefs about the meaning of the words enacted as well as their motives and ulterior objectives, but it is inclusive of a shared understanding of the area of social life which is being regulated and the perceived problems and prospects which give rise to the legislative innovation.

Contextual understanding is constrained by the normative structures of institutional intention I have outlined, which require that when we look at context we do so selectively. We are not, for instance, interested in the motives of the legislators, which may be no more than keeping their jobs. Nor are we interested in grand statements of legislators' objectives which may bear little relationship to the enacted text. In seeking to understand context, we do so in order to determine what the text means as law, not to override the text in order to serve some other assumed or identified goal, such as the alleged or assumed objectives of legislators.

With formally good legislation, there can be 'contextually evident meanings' that are prior to any interpretation. By interpretation I mean here the processes to which we have recourse when we fail to find such plain meanings in an actual text and have to find some way of resolving ambiguities and vaguenesses. Interpretation in this sense is far removed from the creative so-called 'interpretation' that takes place when interpretation goes beyond the choice between alternative contestants for the category of plain meaning and becomes a more or less unbounded re-authorship of the text in the light of the values and beliefs of the so-called interpreters. It is this contextually evident meaning that the legislators may be assumed to intend and that may therefore be said to be law. It suffices to give content to the ideal of legislative intent in a way which makes sense of the sovereignty of an assembly, that is its right to make law. It provides a basis for developing ways of understanding the substance of law that makes it useable by citizens and sets the judiciary a manageable and appropriate task within a democratic polity.

The contextual plain meaning approach fits in with the rule of law thesis that sovereign authority must be exercised under and through the medium of rules, on the grounds that this provides advantages of predictability in the use of centralised power which enhances negative liberty, makes possible formal equality of opportunity, enables efficient administration and presents itself in a form which makes it amenable to moral and technical criticism. In other words legislative intention as contextual plain meaning makes it possible for us to conceive of legislation as law in a sense which connects with standard and acceptable normative theories of the purpose and functions of law in a pluralist society.

(3) Finally, there is a core adjudicative advantage in the contextual plain meaning approach in that legislative intention as contextual plain meaning enables us to conceive of a feasible judicial duty to apply the laws the legislators intended to enact. We can use it to frame a description of the judicial role which is compatible with an initial presumption as to the propriety of excluding judges from law making. It can also form the basis for developing a theory of how courts ought to tackle problems of interpretation, that is problems which arise when it is not clear if there is a contextual plain meaning to be applied.

The thesis assumes that interpretation is required not to understand clear legislation, but to deal with the uncertainties which arise from the elusiveness of plain meaning. When interpretation does feature in judicial process it is not a matter of delving into the subjective intentions—be they linguistic, political or personal—of individual legislators or selected legislators or drafters. The initial orientation of courts must be, however, an earnest endeavour to give significance to the choice of terms in the light of the alternatives that were available at the time of enactment and an appreciation of the assumptions at work in the area of life to which the legislation pertains. This makes clear that problems of adjudication are inseparable from ideals of legislation. More specifically, if legislators do not enact legislation which has contextually plain meaning then judges cannot carry out their allotted function.

To make this theory of legislative intent persuasive and acceptable we have to show that there is a clear idea of contextual plain meaning which:

(1) accords with a philosophically defensible theory of meaning; and
(2) fits with the rationales of democratic legitimacy that cohere with an acceptable prescriptive theory of the rule of law; and
(3) can be the basis for an acceptable judicial method and ethic.

I deal with each in turn.

Contextual Plain Meaning

Stipulating that legislative intent should be understood as the intention to enact laws in accordance with the public meaning of the terms used in the adopted text is initially simply that: a stipulation. The technical terminology of the philosophy of language can facilitate the clear articulation of the thesis, but it cannot itself justify the theory.

Thus, in general, the contextual plain meaning approach emphasises sentence meaning rather than speaker's meaning. Sentence meaning depends on semantics and syntax and is often spoken of as semantic or dictionary meaning, although this does not exclude shared assumptions in the contexts in which the discourse normally takes place, which are more readily understood as social or contextual. Even dictionary definitions standardly point to contexts. The contextual plain meaning approach is to say that words and sentences have meanings in terms of the linguistic rules and conventions of the community within which they have a communicative role.[15] This means, that, in theory, words or other signs can have meanings even if they originate from an inanimate source, such as a random natural (ie non-human) process. At any rate, we can understand a text without knowing anything about the psychological states or social situation of those uttering those sentences.

But is this enough to take us to an understanding of meanings in a specific enough manifestation to be of use in legal contexts? Goldsworthy points out that semantic meaning is a relatively thin conception of meaning which leaves out a great deal of what we need to understand a sentence in practical contexts. In ordinary conversation we rely on what is called utterance meaning, which takes into account those pragmatics of discourse that cannot be expressed in semantic rules. Goldsworthy's example is 'the cat is on the mat'. We cannot know, for instance, which cat and which mat is meant until we know the context of the utterance on a specific occasion. However, in asking what the sentence means, we need not take into account any private meanings the speaker may be utilising. Goldsworthy's utterance meaning, as part of his theory of moderate intentionalism,[16] involves only conventions and facts known to the audience by means of which they are able to understand such matters as the specific reference of a sentence.

---

15   Thus, Marmor, above n 4, esp 16–19.
16   Goldsworthy, above n 6, 19–21.

This would suggest that the meaning of a law depends in part on the pragmatics connected with legal utterances in specific contexts. However, legislative utterances do not aim to identify particular cats and particular mats, but require conformity to general rules, such as 'cats shall not sit on mats'. In other words, the functions of legislation routinely require excluding a lot of what Goldsworthy takes in under the heading of everyday utterance meaning.[17] On the other hand, there is room for a theory of legislative utterance that provides the institutional context in which are embedded many assumptions, such as the conventions of statutory interpretation, as to what it is to enact and apply legislation. A narrow view of semantic meaning is clearly insufficient for legislative as well as everyday communication. Indeed the understanding of what legislation involves, and what a particular piece of legislation is about—which may be termed 'legislative utterance'—is important to, and part of, what I mean by contextual plain meaning, for it brings in that part of the context which marks the communication not only as an enactment, with all the social, political and legal understandings that go with this, but also as an enactment addressed to relatively specific types of situation.

What can be resisted in this context is the reduction of legislative meaning to 'speaker's meaning', a concept which takes us back from semantics and syntax to the intentions involved in particular speech acts. Speaker's meaning puts the emphasis on what the speaker intended to say or do in the saying rather than on what she did say, and allows for the fact that a speaker may have an idiosyncratic understanding of the meaning of certain words and phrases or an incapacity to frame sentences with which she is satisfied as expressing her views and may have all sorts of further purposes in expressing the words in question. This is not the case with legislative meaning, which is, at the very least, closer to semantic meaning than to speaker's meaning.

It is worth noting that the classic theory of speaker's meaning developed by H P Grice is a rather more objective matter than such subjective intentionality.[18] Grice's theory is that meaning is, or involves, speaker's intention: 'a speaker S means that p by a declarative utterance of x to an audience A if and only if (a) S intends that A should come to

---

17 See Jeffrey Goldsworthy's 'utterance meaning' which combines semantics, syntax and the pragmatics of the contexts in which language is used: 'Implications in Language, Law and the Constitution' in Geoffrey Lindell (ed), *Future Directions in Australian Constitutional Law: Essays in Honour of Professor Leslie Zines* (1994) 150, 151.

18 H P Grice, 'Meaning' (1957) 66 *Philosophical Review* 377.

believe that *p*; (b) S intends that A should recognise that S uttered *x* with intention (a); and (c) S intends that this recognition (b) should be among A's reasons for coming to believe that *p*.' (In more accessible formulation: S means something if she uses words intending that the audience believe that something and intending that the audience recognise this intention and intending that her use of these words in this way will be taken by the audience as a reason for believing that something.)

If this is what is meant by 'speaker's intention' then there is no difficulty in incorporating it into the conception of contextual plain meaning, as long as the speaker is taken as a legislator or legislators. For our purposes, we might want to have a version of Grice's speaker's meaning which relates to imperatives rather than propositions. The equivalent analysis might be: 'a commander C means do *s* by a declarative utterance of *x* to an audience of subjects A if and only if (a) C intends that A should come to do *s*; (b) C intends that A should recognise that C uttered *x* with intention (a); and (c) C intends that this recognition (b) should be amongst A's reasons for doing *s*'. (In simpler language: a commander means do something when she uses words intending that the audience do that thing and that the audience realise that she so intends, and that her uttering the words will be taken by the audience as a reason for so doing.)

This is helpful in so far as legislation is viewed as an act of communication.[19] All communication involves some such intentions, as Grice outlines, as well as an understanding of the conventions that make successful communication feasible. But it tells us nothing about how audiences are to begin to know what it is that is meant by the utterances in question. All that we have is that communication requires audiences to be aware that utterances are made for purposes: for instance, in order to alter their beliefs or actions. Audiences must recognise that speakers are making utterances in order that they (audiences) come to believe what they (speakers) say, but this does not help us understand how audiences know what it is that is being said. In other words, Grice's account of speaker's meaning presumes semantic or sentence meaning. This takes us back to

---

19   Serious doubts can be raised about viewing legislation as communication. Although legislation must be communicated, it may be misleading to think of it simply in terms of legislators communicating with citizens, sometimes via judges, for legislation sets up rules to be followed by all (legislators included) rather than conveying a message about what some people want other people to do or be permitted to do. See Heidi Hurd, 'Sovereignty in Silence' (1990) 99 *Yale Law Journal* 945; and Jeremy Waldron, 'Legislators' Intentions and Unintentional Legislation' in Marmor, above n 4, ch 9.

accounts of mutual understanding via conventions of language and communication that are shared by those concerned. And this involves understanding a text by deploying the shared conventions of the communicators, an understanding that can readily be conjoined to the thesis that an act is an act of legislation if and only if the legislators intend that their utterances be taken as rules to be followed and that this is understood by those to whom they are addressed. That is the intent of legislation and that intent may even be regarded as a constitutive element of legislation.

Grice's scheme of ideas is thus helpful in expressing my thesis of legislative intent more precisely, but this does not, of course, make the thesis correct. It may be argued, for instance, that legislators are doing all sorts of different things when they legislate. Thus, symbolic legislation may be enacted to affirm values rather than effect conduct, and a great deal of legislation may have more to do with gaining voter approval than altering citizen behaviour. This is an objection which can be made to Grice's analysis of speaker's meaning. Speakers may have all sorts of intentions other than changing other people's beliefs. For instance, speakers may intend to deceive or dissemble. Why then should we adopt Grice's assumptions? His analysis may be correct if we are out to answer the question 'did she really mean that?' But it will not help with the question: 'what is she up to this time?' One answer is that it is possible to argue for some sort of fundamental commitments on which other intentions are parasitic. Perhaps we cannot have the intention to deceive unless we routinely have the intention to convey propositions accurately, thus making the intention to convey propositions more basic than the intention to deceive. This approach is reminiscent of the natural law argument for the priority of truth telling over deceit.[20] It may also be read into the Habermasian assumption of sincerity in dialogue.[21] And similarly, we may argue, symbolic legislation presumes or is parasitic upon the norm of ordinary legislation and ordinary legislation is command intentional.

Here it is helpful to introduce the terminology of speech act theory: the locution, the illocution, and the perlocution.[22] Locutions, according to J L Austin's scheme, are utterances with a certain sense and reference. Illocutions are what a person is doing in making an utterance (like giving

---

20   Thus, Thomas Aquinas, *Summa Theologica* (T C O'Brien (trans)) (1972) vol 41, q 110, art 1.

21   Jurgen Habermas, *The Theory of Communicative Action* (1984–87).

22   See J L Austin, *How to do Things with Words* (1962).

an order or issuing a warning), including utterances whose performance are doing things (like getting married or enacting a law), which are sometimes called speech acts. Perlocutions are utterances whose performance have certain effects, such as changing people's beliefs or conduct, or are utterances seen from the point of view of their effects. Legislation, we may say, is a paradigmatic performative speech act, the act of making words into laws. And legislation may, and usually does, have all sorts of effects, many of them intended, such as to change behaviour, to bring about social justice, and so on. There may be a whole range of perlocutions which are not part of the locution, the sense and reference of the words whose illocutionary enactment makes them into legislation and has certain effects on action.

In this scheme we may hold that locutions are primary. They are the basic datum whose utterance may also become an illocution or a perlocution. Therefore the assumptions which belong to locutions, or utterances per se, are basic. And, it may be argued when we consider locutions, then we can see that they are fundamental to all discourse. If this is correct, then we may say that speaker's meaning must presuppose locutions, which thus have philosophical priority. Only because locutions have meaning per se can we use locutions to tell lies, by turning them into perlocution.

However, we do not require recourse to such quasi-sophistries, which are suspect because of the way in which they draw on an essentialist conception of discourse. Instead we can simply accept that the idea of speaker's meaning is normative. It is a prescriptive model about what we have a right to expect that speakers are intending to do in what they say. It sets up acceptable terms of conversation, which aid successful communication. Not only is it speaker's meaning rather than poet's meaning or mad person's meaning, it is a certain type of speaker's meaning. A communicator speaker's meaning perhaps, or maybe a 'good speaker's meaning', an idea which might put us on the scent of a conception of 'good legislative intent', a norm or standard which sets out what it is that ought to be intended in enactment. Good legislative intent involves such matters as choosing texts which, when read in terms of standard linguistic conventions, have the formal characteristics of clarity, consistency, precision and generality. These derive from a theory of the nature of the function of law as an instrument of, and limitation on, legitimate political power.

There are advantages, therefore, to a Gricean variation in terms of legislative meaning being tied to the intention to make law (which we can understand through Austin's conception of illocutionary acts) and to the idea of utterance meaning as a broader view than pure semantic or dictionary meaning, but not, I think, so broad as Goldsworthy's notion of discourse pragmatics in general. This enables us to have a conception of contextual plain meaning that does not go down the subjectivist path of postulating a meaning which legislators have in their minds which they then put into words when trying to express their meaning and thereby communicate it to their audience. On that view we read the words in order to get at subjective speaker's meaning, that is, what is in the speaker's mind, if anything. In other words, texts are taken to be attempts to communicate the prior meanings or determinations of their authors.

This I take to be Alexander's analysis when he writes: 'It [a text] is whatever that author intended to communicate through the marks or sounds'. Legislators make determinations which they then seek to communicate through texts, so 'we must look at their texts with an eye to discovering authorial intentions'.[23] However, while this is a possible view it is not one that we 'must' accept as following from the very idea of what it is to have a text. It may be that we want to leave room for legislatures to indicate that they are using something different from dictionary meaning, provided they do this with stipulations which can be understood in terms of plain meanings. And I can accept that it is contingently feasible that legislators have a sense of knowing what they mean but fail in the attempt to communicate their beliefs. But, if it is a requirement of understanding of legislation that we grasp the subjective intentions, even just the individual semantic intentions of the legislators who vote for the enactment in question, then I suggest that most legislation does not have a meaning. This prospect seems to be admitted by Alexander in his category of 'failed legislation', which refers to legislation, for instance, that has been passed by a majority whose members have in mind very different instantiations of the terms adopted in the legislation.

The issue here comes to a head when appeal is made to the beliefs of legislators regarding the legal changes made by an enactment, particularly with regard to whether the legislation would, for instance, make this or that specific and concrete example of conduct illegal. Are we to read a general term like 'cat' in the light of the images that the legislators have of cats

---

23   Alexander, above n 4, 363.

(which may include tigers) or the plain meaning (which, we may hazard, excludes tigers, unless the context makes it clear that the legislation is dealing with zoos). In other words, should we seek to discover and follow the specific or concrete intentions of legislators with respect to what they would (perhaps counterfactually) accept as instantiations of a classificatory term?

Alexander argues that the assumptions of legislative authority require us to take evidence of such specific intentions seriously. I argue that we should not. My approach has the pragmatic advantage that it saves us from hopeless inquiries into subjective intent, and from even more hopeless inquiries into counterfactual specific intent. Would the legislators have considered leopards as cats if they had thought of the matter? On the other hand, it does not exclude the right of legislators to make it plain that they do indeed include or exclude tigers and leopards.

Does that make me a 'moderate intentionalist' in Bassham's sense,[24] in that I accept the legislators' semantic intentions relating to the definitions of the classificatory terms but not their exemplars, or list of instantiations of the classification? I think not, for, unless the legislators give a stipulative definition of the term, it is to be understood as the audience understands it in terms of the public meaning of the language. This does not make me an immoderate intentionalist but rather not an intentionalist at all. In particular, I deny the right of legislators either to give authority to private meanings of general terms or to give authority to anything which the audience may care to make of the general terms chosen.

In trying to make clearer what I mean by contextually plain meaning I may be thought to have drifted from identifying legislative intention into placing normative constraints on what is to count as legislative intention. I plead not guilty to drifting, as normative constraints are in the driving seat all the way, right into the core of identifying a particular notion of legislative intent. My conception of legislative intent is a notion of responsibility intention. What the legislators can be held accountable for is the public meaning of the words they enact, and, to tie up with what I have just said, they are responsible for the foreseeable meaning which will be given to their legislation.

However, this seems to make the content of the legislators' responsibility relative to the expectations and practices of their audience, and perhaps the audience do not accept that legislators ought to be

---

24   Bassham, above n 8, 28–34.

responsible only for contextual plain meaning. Perhaps audiences take the view that they can read the text in any way they like and that is what legislators ought to have foreseen they would do. This is not so. Audiences also have duties, and the duties of both legislators and audiences have to be read against a theory of law and a theory of democracy.

Democratic Legitimacy

My account of contextual plain meaning may seem quite removed from reality in a number of ways.[25] Thus it may be argued that a prescriptive conception of legislative intent is unhelpful because a norm can offer no way of settling interpretive disputes in law, whereas there is at least the prospect of an inquiry into the actual intentions of legislators producing an objective grounds for settling interpretive disputes. However, this objection neglects to note that the norm in question seeks to establish the authority of what is ultimately a matter of fact, namely contextually evident meaning understood in terms of actual social conventions and practices. Moreover, it may be argued that evidence as to meaning in this sense is more readily available than knowledge of speakers' intentions since each competent speaker of a language has competence in determining plain meaning.

In support of this thesis, it can be argued that the whole logic of the legislative exercise is directed towards the adoption of certain words as the text of a statute. Why do legislators argue over the words? Why do they bother over how these words will be understood? Why do they worry over what they believe the results of conformity to or use of those texts will be? All this only makes sense if we see a certain logic in the legislative process, a logic which assumes that the choice of words matters, that the intelligibility of those words is significant and that the consequences of their adoption as rules of action will have certain consequences.

This logic may not match the reality of what goes through the mind of the individual legislator. The text is drafted by bureaucrats on the instructions of members of the executive. Many members of a legislative assembly either do not read most legislation or do not understand what the text says. But they know that they have the right to suggest changes to the text of a bill. They know that the choice of words in the enactment matter.

---

25   See Neil MacCormick 'Ethical Positivism and the Practical Force of Rules' in Campbell and Goldsworthy, above n 2, 51–3.

They know that they will be held accountable by electorates for what happens as a result of the application of the text of the enactment unless it can be shown that the rules were not enforced as enacted. There is, therefore, a powerful democratic argument in favour of plain meaning.

It is important to note that there is no sense of empirical impossibility or even unlikelihood of such a legislative intent being a reality within an operative democracy. The traditional idea of sovereign intent, it may reasonably be claimed, is a ridiculous fiction. It never has had much application to any particular system of law. Certainly it has no bearing at all on modern legal systems in which the sources of law are various, and the legislative process—the paradigmatic locus of the sovereignty fiction—is the outcome of many factors. Some of these factors are intentional acts of a large number of human beings, but these rarely add up to *a* will or *an* intention in the sense of an agreed objective. And the idea of a sovereign will has no significant place in any remotely postmodern view of law as a diffuse network of social relationships mediated by multiple shifting discourses, none of which have any foundational basis in a shared objective reality. But the same difficulties do not apply to the notion of an agreement that enacted texts be read in terms of contextual plain meaning. It can be concluded that this theory may help us to make sense of the actual politico-legal process and is central to any democratically acceptable legal philosophy.

It could, however, be argued that electorates hold governments responsible for the results of their legislation whether or not these results are the outcome of conformity to their plain meaning. It could also be argued that courts have a duty to promote the outcomes intended by an elected government rather than apply the legislation in its contextually evident meaning. Yet, in a system of government subject to the rule of law it is necessary for governments to pursue their objectives in a law-like manner. Obtaining desired objectives in a manner which bypasses governance by rules is not legitimate within a democratic system that incorporates an ideal of the rule of law. It is certain, therefore, that courts do not have a duty to directly foster government objectives rather than apply democratically authorised rules. Indeed, it is also arguable that citizens have a duty to reject governments that pursue their policies by non-legal means.

This position presupposes a theory along the lines of what I call democratic positivism.[26] Positive law, in the hard prescriptive sense in which I use the term, is law which is identifiable and intelligible without reference to contentious moral and political values. Democratic positivism is an ideal which advocates a system of government in which institutions are designed to give effect to the idea of equality of political power, that power being confined as much as possible to the choice of positive laws, that is mandatory rules which can be identified and understood, followed and applied without recourse to contentious moral and political values. It is a system in which all adult persons as citizens share equally in the making of law and in the liabilities and capacities which arise from the law that they have made. It is a system which depends on the sustenance of institutions that give effect to equality in law making, and to law application and utilisation that are an accurate reflection of the laws which have been made. Democracy is thus a matter of democratic will formation in the form of clear mandatory rules which are to be accurately and consistently operationalised.

It follows from these starting points that legislative intent is central to the understanding of law in a democracy, for legitimate law making must be seen as an expression of democratic, that is the people's, will. Conversely, determinative political intentions in a democracy must be primarily concerned with law making, that is the will is expressed in the form of law in the positivist sense of general standing commands which have force until such time as the sovereign withdraws or amends them.

It is this thread of will-in-the-formation-of-law which gives force to the role of intention in such a politico-legal system. Personifying this, we say that the people's will rules through the medium of positive law. Positive law must, therefore, in some sense embody that popular will, or else the rationale for the system collapses. If laws do not embody the popular will then they lack legitimacy. Legislative intent is central to democratic positivism because valid law must be an expression of the will of the people. Law making must not only be an intentional or purposive activity, it must embody the intentionality of the people. If this is unsustainable then democracy is unsustainable.

Collaterally, it may be thought, the idea of legislative intent may serve to provide a source of authoritative guidance in the case of laws whose meaning is in doubt in the process of application. After all, if, in a

---

26   See Campbell, above n 3, 75.

democracy, law is the expression of the will of the people, what better place to seek guidance as to the interpretation of muddy law than the intention of the parliament which is constituted by the people's representatives. Hence the growing practice of looking to extra-legal sources, such as *Hansard*, or white papers, or political manifestos, as bases for clarifying and extending the text of enacted legislation.[27]

This is a mistake, or, at least, largely a mistake. Indeed, the primacy of the decision making of the people as the proper source of law argues in precisely the opposite direction. Only if we distinguish what is enacted from why it is enacted, that is what legislators intend when they make law and what motivates them to make law, can we make sense of the idea of the will of the people in a way that coheres with an intelligible conception of legal legitimacy. Democratic will formation of law proscribes going behind those laws to subjective intentions of legislators to alter that law. Indeed, even if we make the strange assumption that parliamentary debates are themselves part of the text of the legislation, these debates must then be read in accordance with their contextual plain meaning and not as evidence of the subjective intentions of the proponents of the legislation.[28]

In support of such formalism there are at least two rationales that relate to democratic positivism, that is, the idea that 'the people' are entitled to rule, but only via law making.

In the first place, the legislative process is a matter of making a decisive choice of authoritative words whose positivistic purpose is to reach a decision that binds until that decision is legitimately changed, thus attracting all the familiar positivist benefits of certainty, predictability and authoritativeness that enable communities to enjoy the benefits of coordination, conflict resolution and conduct control. These benefits are not associated with hunting subjective intentions.

Second, what legislators ultimately agree upon through the process of voting is not reasons, or objectives, or motives, but words: agreed formulations in the language of the community to which the law is addressed. The decisions of the people which are binding are their choice of rules or laws, not decisions or views about particularities, which may well feature as the motives for their law-making activities. This is essential to the rule of law which requires publicly identifiable rules with publicly identifiable meanings. The notion of intention here is unashamedly

---

27   *Pepper v Hart* [1992] 3 WLR 1032. See Enid Campbell, Lee Poh-York and Joycey Tooher, *Legal Research* (4th ed, 1996) ch 15.
28   See Waldron, above n 12, 146.

312 Intention in Law and Philosophy

normative: it expresses what legislative intention ought to be in a democratic polity that embraces the rule of positive law. At the same time, it attempts to encapsulate a realistic psychology and represents an almost necessary logic of legislative process.

However, we may reasonably ask: 'Why do we require democracies to be subject to the rule of law?' That is a gigantic question and here I provide only one, illustrative, answer. The rule of law makes democratic decision making more democratic by minimising the standing shame of democracies, namely their tendency to neglect the interests of minorities.[29] By making democratic assemblies enact general rules we make it more difficult for government coercion to be selectively applied to minority groups, and there is pressure to debate and to choose in terms of general principles which conform to the necessary logic of moral acceptability, the test of universalisability. Majorities may want to feather their own nests at the expense of minorities but they have to do so by means of general rules which at the very least help to make their self-preference explicit and, given the pressure of democratic debate, may modify their predations. In brief, if members of the majority wish to promote their self-interest in disproportionate and morally unacceptable way, the requirement that they can choose only general laws and not particulars makes this more difficult to achieve. If so, this means that, in the interpretation of law, should we fall back on the intentions of the assembled legislators, we are undoing the moral disciplining effects of this aspect of the rule of law.

Thus Senator X presses her fellow senators to support the bean growers of her state because she wants to save the jobs of her friends, relatives and constituents, but has to do so by proposing a law which provides benefits for all bean growers, thus ensuring that her buddies and supporters are not the only ones to benefit, and raising the issue of why it is bean growers rather than pea cultivators or vegetable gardeners generally that should benefit. If that legislation is passed, and becomes a matter of interpretative debate in court proceedings, we would not want to go back to Senator X's desire to benefit her own people as the basis for settling ambiguities or gaps in the enacted law. Rather it is the words for which Senator X received majority support that have the authority. If they are unclear or incomplete we should not go back to the partial interests which promoted the legislation in the first place for authoritative guidance.

---

29   Much of this analysis flows from Jean Jacques Rousseau, *The Social Contract* (first published 1762, 1963 ed). See also Cass Sunstein, *The Partial Constitution* (1993) and John Rawls, *Political Liberalism* (1993).

It is often argued that when we seek clarification of legislation through consulting the legislative debate we are not seeking to draw on the no doubt often unworthy motives of the individual legislators but the reasons which were given and accepted in the debate. It is not the fact that Senator Y voted one way on an amendment so as to get home early, but the explanation of that amendment professed by its proposers that gives us guidance as to the meaning of the clause in question. Yet legislation is not even in part constituted by the reasons given in favour of it by members of a legislative assembly or their promoters or those who vote for the legislation. I may accept an amendment for my own reasons while rejecting the reasons given by its proposer. There may be as many reasons prompting support for a piece of legislation as there are members of the majority that vote for it, indeed many more, given that individuals may have more than one reason for their support.

Those evident facts of legislative psychology are often taken as a *reductio ad absurdum* of the view that legislative intent is relevant to anything: there is no one legislative intent to which appeal can be made for any purpose. Indeed, this is clearly the case if by legislative intent we mean the reasons the legislators have for supporting the enacted text. The whole point of legislation is to respond to the diversity of views as to what should be done and why it should be done, by establishing procedures through which we can make determinative decisions about what is to be done, but not why it is to be done.

Similar conclusions follow even if we adopt more restrictive understandings of legislative intent which exclude motives but include reasons or at least reasons of an acceptable type, such as the public purpose which the legislation is intended to serve, the problems it is intended to solve, or the goals that it is intended to promote. These may, of course, feature in the ulterior purposes legislators have for supporting the legislation, but they are a type of reason, and a type which may be thought more acceptable, particularly if the objectives in question can be described as some conception of the common good or public interest. Indeed, this is precisely the sort of thing that is meant by intention in statutory interpretation of the purposive sort, which has led to purposive preambles and the acceptability of purposive legal arguments in not only understanding but stretching a text so that the law better serves the desired objective.

This 'public reason' approach may appear to have democratic credentials if the purposes involved are those shared by the majority supporting the legislation,[30] and this can certainly be validated by having purposive preambles, or even by incorporating ministerial statements into the law by modifying the rule of recognition to include such currently extra-legal material. But this is not compatible with democratic *positivism*, for such an approach undermines the point of law, which is intended to prevent the sovereign issuing commands of the form: 'do whatever promotes goal X or objective Y', and which requires that the sovereign commands be expressed in terms of specific general rules.

A mildly purposive approach may be considered acceptable if it is not used to create or develop or put aside legal rules but rather to gain a better understanding of them. There is a role for subjective intention as part of the context which helps us to establish the meaning of rules as distinct from their purpose. The investigation of legislative intention here is undertaken in relation to what meaning is intended by the use of the words embodied in the text. The idea is not to vary the rule in the light of legislative purpose, but to consult legislative purpose to get a better hold on the meaning of the rule. This may be done without extrapolating from exemplars or even the classificatory criteria which were in the minds of legislators but with the objective of comprehending the social situation to which the legislation is addressed and the role which legislation might have in that context.

Judicial Method

The perceived Achilles heel of legal positivism and the textual theory of legislative intent is the problem of interpretation. What does the theory of contextual plain meaning have to say to us when there is no clear contextual plain meaning? Are we in the whirlpool of judicial discretion, which draws in all vague and ambiguous rules and thus, ultimately, all law deep into the sea of arbitrary will?

The problems of interpretation arise when conventional meanings seem elusive and ambiguous. The assumption that legislators intend plain meaning as it will be perceived by the audience to which the legislation is addressed does not settle what that meaning is, in many cases. Hence the democratic impulse is to look to the legislators to determine an authoritative meaning. We have said that this path is not open to us

---

30 See Rawls, ibid 225–7.

because of the difficulty of identifying any such authoritative intention behind the words. Indeed, vague and ambiguous words are often chosen to obtain a majority for a text where no political agreement exists. An assembly is a group of individuals and does not normally have an intention as distinct from a number of intentions equal to the number of the members involved. It follows that appeal to legislative intent as the state of mind of those supporting or opposing the legislation will not settle matters of interpretation even if we could know what these legislators intended independently of what they said. They may say one thing but intend another.

Indeed if legislators know that what they say in the assembly can be used to interpret the legislation they may say things in the assembly in order to influence that interpretation. And these things may be contrary to what others in the assembly intend citizens and courts to accept as their intentions. Moreover, going into legislative history brings to light all sorts of reasons why members of the assembly support or oppose the legislation in question, what their further intentions or ulterior motives were in so supporting or opposing. These often relate to the results they think will follow from the law and why they believe these to be beneficial or detrimental. This may be to confuse what the legislation says with the reasons why it has been enacted, muddling the what with the why and undermining the social and moral functions of law by returning us to the morass of disparate opinions.

Where does this leave legal positivists in their search for the implementation of democratic positivism? We should note that this issue is not simply a matter of adjudication. The initial injunctions for formally good law are addressed to legislatures rather than courts. Second, we should note that, under the positivist regime, courts do have an adjudicative prescription to read the text in its plain and stipulated meaning, and it has to be assumed that this injunction does have considerable bite, given good legislative intent and drafting expertise. Third, we may note that the approach is suspicious of perlocutionary meanings, however worthy, for varying the plain and stipulated meanings. Moreover, we have seen that it can allow use of extra-enactment data, such as *Hansard*, either to help with understanding rather than changing the rules, or, more realistically, to give meaning where there is no clear conventional meaning, or to choose between meanings where there is ambiguity and indeterminacy by exhibiting the context, but not by privileging the subjective intentions of individual legislators.

Here we have to look again at the conventions of discourse. These arise out of, and make most sense in, relatively restricted dialogic communities in standard situations.

All communication needs to be seen in context. I have referred to contextually plain meaning to bring this out. However, legislation is not a standard situation. It aims at both generality and precision. It has wide communicative ambition. It is supported by the system of separate adjudicative courts which can utilise conventions to help us grapple with meaning out of its primary contexts. This is part of the general objective of institutionalising government through rules. In this respect legislation is not well conceived as a matter of communication at all. It is more a matter of setting up an authoritative text.

The practical implication of this thesis is that citizens and courts ought to be aware of the social situations to which the legislation applies and the sources of concern that led to the legislation in question. That does not mean identifying the precise reference that legislators would give to their general terms if asked, as an original intentionalist would require. The originalist approach assumes that the meaning of a general term is an extrapolation from paradigm exemplars, that sense is a generalisation of reference, so that we can extrapolate, but we cannot detach, the general terms from the specific examples which legislators had in mind. There is some attraction in this since it turns interpretation into a factual inquiry. But legislators are making laws and laws are general and identify the features which any paradigm examples may be believed to possess. In this laws identify the criteria of relevance that the assembly is prepared to see enforced. Legislators are not entitled to legislate on particulars. It would not be legislation if they did. It is possible for them to be mistaken as to whether the paradigm examples did have the characteristics attributed to them. And they certainly cannot require that we consider only *their* exemplars or standard examples. What we are bound by is the text: the general terms and not the examples that give that generalisation meaning. So there is logical space here for accepting the generalisation but rejecting the examples, and so taking the sense without the reference.

This still leaves us with the problem of how to deal with positivistically poor legislation. What of the interpretive problems that remain after plain meaning has run out? What is to be done with the imprecision, the gaps, the penumbral cases that remain? Legal positivists are castigated for having recourse to judicial discretion here, but they are right to speak of discretion because it draws attention to the fact that there are in these cases alternatives open to judges that are not determined by the content of the law. Further, legal positivists are as free as anyone to suggest interpretative rules and need not argue that it is a matter for individual judges to decide which rules to adopt. One such rule may be individual judicial discretion. Another is to dismiss any charge or suit where the law is not clear. No clear law can be taken to mean no remedy, or no conviction. Another, not very practical, rule for routine use is to refer the matter to the legislature. A further approach is to draw on positive morality, if there is any consensus on the matter. Others include arguing from the nearest perceived analogies with settled law, drawing on basic legal principles, or considering what enhances the internal consistency of the legal system. All of these are regrettable, in that it would be better to do without them altogether, and some are worse than others because of the scope they allow for the operation of unlegitimated values, but in second best situations they may be acceptable stopgaps pending further legislative clarification.

A general problem with such default conventions is that they may be misused to overturn plain meanings. However, any interpretive method may be misused. The legal philosopher's task is to make clear that there is a distinction between use and misuse. Indeed, we can hope that an efficient system will have a legislative intent here, that is, an intent about what to do when the legislators make formally poor legislation. These then become part of the contextual legislative assumptions. They, too, may be misused, this time by legislatures, as excuses for fudging the difficult political choices.

In summary, the implications for interpretation of textual intentionalism are:

- we have no need to assume that the theory requires a counterfactual claim about a legislative assembly having a psychological unitary state of mind;
- we should not be intimidated by theories of language to say that indeterminacy is a necessary feature of a text-based system of law;
- such indeterminacy as there is, and there is a great deal, presents a problem for which we can reasonably seek solutions more or less compatible with democratic principles and the preferred functions of law;
- these solutions are partly in the conventions of interpretation we commend for mutual adoption by legislatures, courts and citizens;

- the problems of interpretation can be minimised by adoption and adherence to shared and recognised standards as to what counts as good legislative intent;
- minimising the need for interpretation is first a job for legislatures and only secondarily a job for courts;
- courts and citizens should not be expected to find the meaning of legislation in the subjective understandings of members of the legislature, whose legislative intention should be to express their subjective intentions in the public discourse which enables the words of the enactment to become law.

Conclusion

Anxieties about, and denunciations of, legal positivism take a number of forms, one of which is that legal positivism serves as a theory to cloak the exercise of power by vested interests to the exclusion of the oppressed, outsider groups within a hierarchical society.[31] We may note, in conclusion, that the thesis of contextual plain meaning provides one avenue of response to what is undoubtedly a danger which arises in the application of all legal philosophies and judicial methods.

First, the capacity for democratic change through political process requires that officials are limited by laws enacted by representative assemblies. Given that in a hierarchical society there is a tension between democratic will and elite power, the democratic output must be formed in such a way as to minimise the capacity of the power elites to ignore and evade the democratic will. I suggest that this is helped rather than hindered by precise, clear laws free of contestable terms.

Second, if we assume that administrative and judicial officials share the prejudices or rationality of the powerful then it is appropriate to limit their discretion and to enact rules which explicitly exclude what are perceived as legal contributions towards oppression and discrimination. The alternative strategy of replacing existing officials with more enlightened ones and giving them power unrestricted by anything but vague purpose-oriented guidelines is unrealistic. The best that we can hope for from enlightened adjudicators, I suspect, is the capacity to see the potential for abuse through the neglect of plain meaning, through the

---

31 See Margaret Davies, 'Legal Separation and the Concept of the Person' in Campbell and Goldsworthy, above n 2, 115.

pretence that it exists when it does not and general human incapacity to envisage factual situations with which they are unfamiliar.

Third, attention must be paid to the discrimination-defying potential of rules which exclude official action on the basis of offending categories such as race, religion and social class and the significance of requiring political decisions to be made in accordance with a general form that makes the nature of the political moral choices that are at stake more transparent.

That said, we may be worried by the apparent conservatism of the use of conceptual plain meaning, a conservatism which will be unwelcome to those who see many existing social relationships as unacceptable. I would suggest that conceptual plain meaning, when conjoined with the specificity and concreteness embraced by ethical positivism, is anything but conservative. The requirement that we formulate laws in the conventions of existing language gives us the capacity to formulate, for instance, rules forbidding common but unacceptable conduct. Plain meaning does not restrict; it enhances the range of alternatives. Only where plain meaning is associated with vague terminology about 'reasonableness', 'honesty', 'fairness' etc does plain meaning produce conservative results. Hence the goal of precision of language, minimisation of official discretion and effectiveness of legislative review of judicial discretion.

There are undoubted limits to the utility of plain meaning in addressing profound social change. For many reasons law must generally follow social and educational processes in which the discourse of a society is developed to express new insights and address new problems. In this respect, law can rarely be in the vanguard of social progress. But it can be a vital part of institutionalising and sustaining such progress as is built on other and deeper foundations.

15 Constitutional Intention: The Limits of Originalism

JOHN WILLIAMS*

Introduction

At 3 am on 11 February 1948 the debate as to the original intent of the framers of the Australian Constitution was born. At that moment the 92-year-old Isaac Alfred Isaacs died in his home in Melbourne.[1] He was, by four months, the last surviving of the delegates to the 1890s Constitutional Conventions. With him died, in one sense, the chance to recapture an authentic original intent.

The question of original intention within the Australian constitutional context can be traced back nearly sixty years before Isaacs' death, to Sydney in 1891. In that year John Murtagh Macrossan, the Queensland delegate to the Australasian Federal Convention chided his fellow delegates for their disregard for the facts of political life. 'Do not let us forget the action of party. We have been arguing all through as if party government were to cease immediately we adopt the new constitution.'[2] A fortnight after uttering these prophetic words, Macrossan was dead. After that day, and with the demise of each of the framers, a fragment of Australia's constitutional intention, its authorial authority, was lost.

The above example, of course, is not the original intent that those who subscribe to this theory of interpretation would seek to find.[3] Questions of the subjective, private intentions of individual drafters or framers are usually excluded from any originalist theory. Likewise they are not the focus of this essay. However, the above history provides an example of the

---

* I wish to thank my colleague Rosemary Owens for her comments and suggestions on the draft of this essay. The responsibility for any errors, of course, remains mine.
1 Max Gordon, *Sir Isaac Isaacs* (1963) 214.
2 *Official Record of the Debates of the Australasian Federal Convention* (1891) 434.
3 Jeffrey Goldsworthy, 'Originalism in Constitutional Interpretation' (1997) 25 *Federal Law Review* 1, 20.

temporal and fleeting intentions that can be identified when discussing this method of constitutional adjudication.

This essay will investigate the role of the framers and their constitutional imprint on the lives of those who succeed them. It does so primarily from an Australian perspective, though analogous situations from other countries will often be considered. It will argue that originalism, even in its moderate guise, misunderstands the role of the framers and rests the dead hand of the past too heavily on the lives of the current generation. However, it is not an argument for unfettered 'living force' or non-originalist interpretation of the document. Rather, it argues that the current holders of the Constitution need to embrace the hand of the past in order to give meaning to the operation of the Constitution. Critical in this argument is the role of the courts in the 'discovery' of intention. In a larger sense this essay deals with the distinction between legal process and historical process in the determination of intention.

Arthur Boyd, Manning Clark's Kitchen and the Problem of the Author

Manning Clark's presence remains in the house in Canberra where he and Dymphna raised their children and Manning penned his six volume *History of Australia*.[4] Watching over the kitchen table in the house is a portrait of Clark which Arthur Boyd painted in 1972. In 1998 I stood beside Boyd as he reviewed his artwork. As he surveyed the brush work and moved around it I could see he was becoming agitated by his creation. I asked him about his thoughts. He replied that he had 'not done Manning justice'. Boyd gave an account of what he was attempting to capture and the meaning he tried to leave on the canvas.

The visual arts appear to be a good starting point to consider authorial intent.[5] In understanding or interpreting an artwork there are a number of perspectives to be considered. First, that of the artist. Is the value or understanding to be supplemented by the views of the artist? Is it necessary to know the artist? Their age or gender? Does the viewer's opinion of the painting change because it is an early Boyd or one from the later period? A known painter or a house painter? What of the context? Does it matter if the painting was painted during a particular period? During war or

---

4   Manning Clark, *A History of Australia* (1962–1987) vols I–VI.
5   Joseph Raz, 'Interpretation Without Retrieval' in Andrei Marmor (ed), *Law and Interpretation* (1995).

prosperity? Does the place where the painting is viewed matter? In Manning Clark's house or in the National Gallery? What of the topic itself? A floral still life as against a tin of Campbell's soup? Or are all of the above superfluous? Is it that the artist, having moved their pen or the brush across the page or canvass, disappears from the landscape. Are all artists, for the purpose of interpretation, dead? Is meaning, like beauty, solely in the eye of the beholder?

This discussion raises many familiar issues to those who confront the interpretation of legal statutes and constitutions. There remains, of course, an important difference between art and law. Art, unlike a legislative enactment or a constitution, is not normative. Thus, while we can look to the world of visual art for analogies in the understanding of intention, there is a need to be cautious about its immediate application to the area of law. But having said that it is also worth noting that the question of intentionalism is not solely a legal problem and artists, philosophers and historians have much to offer the constitutional lawyer.

Originalism and the Constitutional Question

The debate as to the virtues or otherwise of approaching a constitution by recapturing its original meaning has filled the shelves of university libraries. There would be few modern constitutional or quasi-constitutional disputes that cannot be discussed in terms of the intentions of the framers of the document.

Recourse to a text, and the original meaning that it presumably contains, could be made for any number of reasons. It could be to glean an account of the 'evil' that was being resolved at the time of drafting. For example, endless disruptive custom duties prompted the framers to include section 92 in the Australian Constitution so that trade would be 'absolutely free'. In doing so, they attempted to end barriers that marked intercolonial relations in the 1890s.[6]

Second, an account of the drafting of the Constitution might highlight the various alternatives that were being proposed and the means by which they were considered. In contrast to the first approach, which highlights the outcome of the deliberation, this second approach focuses on the *quality* of the debate and the means by which it was conducted. Thus an account of

---

6   *Cole v Whitfield* (1988) 165 CLR 360.

the Australian or American constitutional histories might highlight, for instance, the role of the press or the nature and extent of the public debate.

Third, a search of the historical record could reveal the intentions of individual framers of the Constitution and their contribution to the debate. Unlike the first approach, which may project a collective outcome, this last approach focuses on individuals. Thus it would be possible to highlight the consistency or otherwise of individuals and their role in subsequent considerations of the Constitution. For instance, Isaac Isaacs' discussion at the Melbourne Convention of 1898 as to the limits of section 80 of the Australian Constitution dealing with trial by jury was replicated in his determination of the issue as a justice of the High Court.[7]

All of the above enquiries are legitimate ways to consider the historical context of a constitution. The question however remains whether or not that historical context, or an understanding of that context, must dictate the interpretation of the document. Clearly, it is possible to have an historical understanding of an event or agreement without projecting that understanding onto the text in an exhaustive and conclusive manner. Thus, for example, I may arguably know the events of the 1890s, but that does not necessarily mean that I must employ that knowledge in the interpretation of the document. The search for this general historical context means that, to some degree, we are all originalists now.[8]

The problem of ascertaining original intention and its application to particular constitutional controversies has given rise to a large body of constitutional literature. Antonin Scalia has described 'the Great Divide' in the literature.[9] This is a division between those who plump for *original* meaning and those who find persuasive the *current* meaning of the words of the constitution. The latter school adheres to the idea of a 'living constitution', a document that grows to address the concerns of each successive age, while the former sees the authority in the words or intentions of the drafters.

The original intent debate has primarily occurred within the United States context. Cases such as *Brown v Board of Education*[10] have generated

---

7　*Official Record of the Debates of the Australasian Federal Convention* (1898) 352 and *R v Bernasconi* (1919) 20 CLR 629, 637.

8　As Paul Brest argues, in terms of non-originalist adjudication the 'text and history' has 'presumptive weight' but is not treated as being 'authoritative or binding': Paul Brest, 'The Misconceived Quest for the Original Understanding' (1980) 60 *Boston University Law Review* 204, 205.

9　Antonin Scalia, *A Matter of Interpretation: Federal Courts and the Law: An Essay* (1998) 38.

10　347 US 483 (1954).

protracted arguments as to the aspirations of the framers of the American Constitution and their continuing presence in the constitutional landscape.

The next section will briefly outline the approaches that have been propounded on the question of originalism. Within the broad school of originalism there are various sub-categories and approaches. Often these approaches highlight the type of material that is to be considered when ascertaining the original meaning of a document. Further, originalists have been divided into those who espouse what is sometimes called 'hard' or 'extreme' originalism, 'moderate' originalism and 'soft' originalism.

What is meant by originalism, and how it differs from intentionalism, remains problematic. Often the two terms are used interchangeably and drawing a clear distinction between them is difficult. While originalism is generally said to concentrate on the text, and intentionalism on the authors who drafted the text, this itself creates an artificial division as the authors' intent is, to some degree, implicated in the choice of words.

'Originalism', for writers such as Robert Bork, concentrates on the meaning of the text at the time of its drafting. As he states:

> All that counts is how the words in the Constitution would have been understood at the time [of its drafting]. The original understanding is thus manifested in the words used and in secondary materials, such as debates at the conventions, public discussion, newspaper articles, dictionaries in use at the time, and the like.[11]

Bork is clear that the search for original intent does not include an enquiry into the subjective mental states of the authors of the text. Other writers in the area have not been as assiduous in eliminating the subjective element. For instance, Frederick Schauer suggests that '[p]rescriptive language is to be understood by reference to evidence of the actual, contemporaneous mental states of the inscribers of the language at issue'.[12]

'Hard' or 'extreme' originalism requires the establishment of the framers' intention with respect to particular words or phrases and a rigid application of that intention. Thus the meaning of a set of words or a phrase is dependent on what the framers intended them to mean. The framers meant what they said and said what they meant. This approach is arguably workable when there is some textual support for their intention. Thus the framers' publicly expressed understanding of 'excise' in section 90 or

---

11   Robert Bork, *The Tempting of America* (1990) 144.
12   Frederick Schauer, 'Defining Originalism' (1995) 19 *Harvard Journal of Law & Public Policy* 343.

326 Intention in Law and Philosophy

'chosen by the people' in sections 7 and 24 of the Australian Constitution can be ascertained and applied by the courts to establish the intended meaning.

However, what if when there is no textual support for an intention? Take, for example, section 51(vi) of the Australian Constitution, which grants to the Federal Parliament power to legislate with respect to 'naval and military defence'. Historically, we know that the framers did not intent 'air defence' given that it did not exist. Taking a strict approach to their intention (as expressed in the words of the Constitution), we would conclude that the Federal Parliament does not have a capacity to legislate with respect to this type of defence. Within the 'hard' or 'extreme' form of originalism it is not permissible, according to writers such as Bork, to look to purpose, as the original meaning is 'manifest' in the words. Thus originalism in its extreme form will often be of limited assistance given the fading relevance of the framers' intentions to contemporary events. It is for these reasons that there has been no support for the 'hard' or 'extreme' form of originalism in Australia.

The second form of originalism, known as 'moderate' originalism, attempts to deal with the twin issues of historical sources and the intentions of the framers. Jeffrey Goldsworthy has argued that 'moderate' originalism is superior to originalism for three important reasons.[13] First, it is only interested in the public utterances and not the private thoughts of the framers. Secondly, it is interested only in the 'enactment intentions' of the framers, not their 'application intention'. In other words, the search is for the meaning of the provision they enacted, not their thoughts as to its application to particular circumstances. Finally, 'moderate' originalism concedes that the founder's intention will not answer all questions and thus recourse must be made to other interpretive methods.

It is this final aspect of 'moderate' originalism that in essence differentiates it from its more extreme versions. Taking again the example of 'air defence', it is clear that the framers of the Australian Constitution could not have a public opinion (an enactment intention) on this form of defence given that it did not exist.

Goldsworthy deals with this issue within the American context by applying an interpretation that is consistent with his view of 'moderate' originalism. Article I section 8 of the American Constitution empowers the Congress to raise and regulate 'land and naval Forces'. Using this article and the issue of 'air defence', Goldsworthy argues that recourse can be

---

13   Goldsworthy, above n 3, 20.

made to what he calls 'non-literal, purposive interpretation'.[14] The inclusion of air defence is appropriate because, in Goldsworthy's view, the 'underlying purpose' is clear ('to give Congress power to raise and regulate all military forces of the United States'). But how does this relate to the intentions of the framers?

There are a number of options. The first would appear to be some form of counterfactual enquiry of the framers.[15] Such an enquiry must be in the form of: 'If the framers knew of this new form of defence would they have included it in the section?' For Goldsworthy the answer would appear to be in the affirmative. But, stepping back from this process, it must surely be fictitious. What we are doing is removing the framers from their context, transporting them to our own, and then putting a question to them after they fully appreciate the new context. It would be the equivalent of asking Shakespeare of his opinion of the film adaptation of *King Lear*. This is not to doubt that purpose is important. Rather it is to question the value of projecting the reconstructed (or fabricated) intention of framers onto a contemporary constitutional question. To be fair to Goldsworthy, he rejects what appears to be a subjective enquiry of the framers. However, establishing the 'clear underlying purpose' of any constitutional provision must involve, at some point, a reconstruction of the intention of the framers if we are to be consistent with the overall originalism that he prefers.

Alternatively Goldsworthy removes (to some degree) the framers from the interpretative inquiry. This is due to the fact that the historical record may be inadequate or contradictory. As Goldsworthy concedes:

[R]esort to the founders' intentions cannot answer all, or probably even most, interpretative disputes of the kind which appellate courts are required to resolve. It [moderate originalism] holds that interpretation begins with an examination of all relevant evidence of the law-makers' intentions, but not that, in difficult cases, it very often ends there. If relevant evidence of those intentions does not resolve a dispute, then judges may be forced to act creatively, and after considering matters such as consistency with general legal doctrines and principles, public policy, and justice, stipulate what the disputed provision should thenceforth be taken to mean. They must settle the dispute: they cannot wash their hands of it and leave the parties to fight it out in the street. Furthermore, when judges act creatively in this way, they are free to take into account contemporary concepts and values.[16]

---

14   Ibid 33.
15   Natalie Stoljar, 'Counterfactuals in Interpretation: The Case Against Intentionalism' (1998) 20 *Adelaide Law Review* 29.
16   Goldsworthy, above n 3, 20–1.

This obvious concession leads to two interpretative conclusions. If, for argument's sake, it is accepted that after an 'examination of all relevant evidence' an intention can be found on a particular constitutional issue (say the meaning of what the framers thought a lighthouse was) then, consistent with the 'moderate' approach, this meaning would be given prominence in the interpretation of the relevant section. However, say that there was no publicly expressed intention (or at best an inconclusive one) for the meaning of 'marriage' or 'coinage'; following the Goldsworthy approach the courts would be free to 'act creatively' using other non-originalist methods. This must surely be an unsatisfactory outcome as it would lead to a patchwork Constitution. Some sections of the Constitution would be constrained by the chance event that there is an intact historical record, while others could be freely interpreted according to non-originalist precepts.

Further, what if the framers' publicly expressed intention were proved to be incorrect by future events? What if, as was the case with persons of 'the aboriginal race', the framers' belief was that they were a dying race and thus their enacted intention was that there was no need to make constitutional provisions for them?[17] How would that intent assist a court in its interpretation of the race power, s 51(xxvi)?[18]

Originalism, in its 'moderate' guise, suffers from further difficulties. While 'moderate' originalists like Goldsworthy attempt to resolve the issue of indeterminacy by limiting intention to the publicly known evidence of the collective intention of the framers, this does not fully solve a number of problems. First, publicly expressed intention may bear little relation to actual intention for an event. In Australia Latham alluded to this in relation to the *Engineers* case[19] when he stated:

> [T]he real ground [for the *Engineers* decision] was the view held by the majority that the Constitution had been intended to create a nation, and that it had succeeded; that in the Great War the nation had in fact advanced in status while the States stood still, and (as was a patent fact) that the peace had not

---

17 John Williams and John Bradsen, 'The Perils of Inclusion: The Constitution and the Race Power' (1997) 19 *Adelaide Law Review* 95.

18 The history of the section is problematic in that there are a number of aspects to it including the events of 1967. The point being made here is that the framers' incorrect historical judgment was that Aboriginal peoples were a dying race.

19 *Amalgamated Society of Engineers v Adelaide Steamship Co Ltd* (1920) 28 CLR 129.

brought a relapse into the *status quo ante bellum*; that a merely contractual view of the Constitution was therefore out of date.[20]

While this observation may point merely to the difference between the *legal* explanation for an event and the *historical*, it highlights the fact that the public and private expressions of an event may diverge. Presumably the 'moderate' originalist would reply by suggesting that private impulse may differ from public intention and that it is the latter that is critical.

Even if we determine intention by counting 'votes' in the case of a legislature or a constitutional convention (so that the collective may be said to have spoken), what we construct as intention may not be representative of the whole.[21] Moreover, what of the minority which has voted against a proposal? Is the intention of the individuals who comprise the minority meaningless? Take, for example, the 1999 referendum on the republic in Australia. What intention was evident when both republicans and monarchists voted 'no'? Presumably the enacted intention was against the proposal, yet this would appear to be a distortion of the different views of the various individuals who voted against it.

Shifting to the last of the approaches to originalism, what Cass Sunstein has described as 'soft' originalism, we find a less constraining historical framework. 'For soft originalists it matters very much what history shows; but the soft originalist will take the framers' understanding at a certain level of abstraction or generality.'[22] This thesis sees originalism in terms of an abstract agreement and has been developed further in Sunstein's later work. I will return to his application in the last part of the essay. For the moment I merely wish to note this third form of originalism for completeness.

So far the essay has outlined three broad approaches to historical enquiry and their proposed use in constitutional interpretation. It has been argued that both 'hard' and 'moderate' originalism equip us poorly for the task of establishing the meaning of a constitution. Before investigating further the role of the framers in constitutional interpretation, it is worth pausing and considering a fundamental question. What is it that constitutional courts and historians are doing when they investigate the

---

20   R T E Latham, 'The Law and the Commonwealth' in W K Hancock (ed), *Survey of British Commonwealth Affairs Vol 1* (1937) 564.

21   David Lyons, 'Original Intent and Legal Interpretation' (1999) 24 *Australian Journal of Legal Philosophy* 1, 17–18.

22   Cass Sunstein, 'Five Theses on Originalism' (1996) 19 *Harvard Journal of Law & Public Policy* 311, 313.

past? If the search is for a publicly expressed intention by the framers then there would appear to be some overlap between the methods that historians and lawyers use to establish that intention.

What do Historians and the High Court do with History?

The first High Court bench in 1904 dealt swiftly with the problem of history. When B R Wise, appearing for the State of New South Wales, attempted to quote the views of various framers from the Constitutional Convention Debates of the 1890s, the members of the court intervened to halt the submission. To Griffith CJ the Convention Debates had authority

> no higher than parliamentary debates, and [were] not to be referred to except for the purpose of seeing what was the subject-matter of discussion, what was the evil to be remedied and so forth.[23]

It would appear that the first judges were not interested in the original intent of the framers as contained in the debates or, at least, did not need reminding of it. This is not to suggest that the High Court has not assumed a critical role in the development of Australian history.

In *The Use and Abuse of Australian History*, Graeme Davison has argued that the past has become a troubling thing for the present.[24] Using Friedrich Nietzsche's[25] critique of historical knowledge, Davison expounds the monumental, the antiquarian, and the critical uses to which history has been deployed in contemporary Australia. The 1970s in Australia, so it is argued, saw a sharp break with the monumental tradition of history and the adoption of a critical approach. Of the critical tradition, Nietzsche wrote:

> Man must have the strength to break up the past, to apply it, in order to live. He must bring the past to the bar of judgement, interrogate it remorselessly and finally condemn it ... Every past is worthy of condemnation.[26]

Davison cites the *Mabo*[27] decision as 'the most striking victory of critical history' in Australia. In that case

---

23   *Municipal Council of Sydney v Commonwealth* (1904) 1 CLR 208, 214 per Griffith CJ *arguendo*. Barton and O'Connor JJ made similar remarks.
24   Graeme Davison, *The Use and Abuse of Australian History* (2000).
25   Friedrich Nietzsche, *The Use and Abuse of History* (1957).
26   Nietzsche, cited in Davison, above n 24, 14.
27   *Mabo v Queensland (No 2)* (1992) 175 CLR 1.

six of the seven judges on the High Court of Australia overturned the doctrine of *terra nullius*—the belief held since the earliest days of the colonies that, since Aborigines were a nomadic people who did not lead a settled existence, they enjoyed none of the rights customarily associated with land ownership. In doing so, the Court had relied heavily upon the arguments first developed by Henry Reynolds in his book, *The Law of the Land* (1987). By upholding the principle of native title, documented by Reynolds in the legal debates surrounding early colonisation, the judges had created the basis for the most fundamental re-examination of land rights since European colonisation.[28]

If Davison is correct then clearly a certain view of history has influenced the judicial process in Australia. Since 1998, with the High Court's decision in *Cole v Whitfield*,[29] historical interpretation has taken on added importance. The use of history, and the High Court's method, has caused some concern amongst legal commentators.[30] But what do historians and lawyers do when they embark on historical enquires? F W Maitland in his famous essay, 'Why the History of English Law is Not Written', pointed to a critical distinction between historians and lawyers. As he stated, the

> process by which old principles and old phrases are charged with a new content is from the lawyer's point of view an evolution of the true intent and meaning of the old law; from the historian's point of view it is almost of necessity a process of perversion and misunderstanding. Thus we are tempted to mix up two different logics, the logic of authority, and the logic of evidence. What the lawyer wants is authority and the newer the better; what the historian wants is evidence and the older the better.[31]

However, it would be wrong to suggest that historians form a homogeneous group. What historians do, and the histories that they write, can be seen in a number of different genres or tropes.[32] For instance, some

---

28   Davison, above n 24, 15.
29   (1988) 165 CLR 360.
30   Greg Craven, 'Original Intent and the Australian Constitution: Coming Soon to a Court Near You?' (1990) 1 *Public Law Review* 166; Sir Daryl Dawson, Intention and the Constitution: Who's Intent?' (1990) 6 *Australian Bar Review* 93 and Paul Schoff, 'The High Court and History: It Still Hasn't Found(ed) What It's Looking For' (1994) 5 *Public Law Review* 253.
31   H A L Fisher (ed), *The Collected Works of F W Maitland* (1911) 491.
32   Mark Tushnet, 'Symposium on the Trends in Legal Citations and Scholarship: Interdisciplinary Legal Scholarship: The Case of History-in-Law' (1996) 71 *Chicago-Kent Law Review* 909, 914–17.

histories are stories of progress and development. Often labelled as 'Whig' history, the institutions and ideas of today are explained in terms of a starting point or genesis in the past. This is a story of continuity in which subsequent generations share, modify and expand historical notions.

A variation on this theme is the story of decline and fall.[33] Within this genre the historian tells the story of degeneration of institutions or ideals, with the author sometimes celebrating or regretting the events. This theme often carries with it some moral story or narrative that reflects upon past events with an eye to the present. Perhaps the most obvious example here is Edward Gibbon's classic, *The History of the Decline and Fall of the Roman Empire*.

A further approach to history is to highlight and make sense of the complex and contradictory nature of other periods. As Tushnet explains:

> Here the historian demonstrates that the past is a foreign country where people managed to think that things we find inconsistent were entirely compatible, indeed sometimes entailed by each other. The historian shows how complicated yesterday's ideas and institutions were. The simple fact that people in the past used words we use today does not mean that those words meant to them what they mean to us.[34]

Another dimension of the historical enterprise is ideological. Histories can, for instance, be written from a Marxist or neo-Marxist, liberal or Whig, feminist, indigenous, queer or conservative standpoint. Further, histories can build from archives oral or cultural accounts of the institutions or regions that are being investigated. They may seek to address shortcomings in previous accounts, challenge a traditional wisdom or support a particular interpretation.

Take for instance the history of the federation period when the Australian Constitution was being debated and drafted. The account of this period has changed over time, emphasising different places, events or individuals. As Stuart Macintyre has outlined, the accounts have variously described federation as a 'personal and patriotic' event, inspired by imperial wishes or achieved in spite of imperial meddling, as a New South Wales or Victorian project, as explicable by economic, defence, race or nationalist factors, as an anti-labour conspiracy, as a people's movement,

---

33   Ibid 915.
34   Ibid 915–16.

and as an institutional or cultural event.[35] Federation has also been described from women's perspectives. This single event of federation has therefore inspired numerous accounts and debates. Yet the historiography of federation demonstrates that context remains a critical feature of any history. Take for example, J A La Nauze's, *The Making of the Australian Constitution*, which remains a classic history of the drafting of the Australian Constitution. Writing in 1972, La Nauze described the framers' concern about the power of the Senate as a 'storm in a teacup' and provided only nine entries on the 'Senate and money-bills'.[36] However, if La Nauze had been writing after the dismissal of the Whitlam government in 1975 it may have been a very different account.

What the above discussion of the various themes and methods of historians indicates is that history is a contested terrain. Interpretation, as well as the method of interpretation, is an ongoing debate in which historical 'truths' are constantly revisited and revised.

The High Court is no stranger to historical method. As an institution the High Court, like all superior courts of appeal, is immersed in the historical as well as the legal project of the nation. The court makes or creates history, as well as authorising it.

The making of history by an institution like the High Court is the natural by-product of its constitutional function. For instance, the court helped shape the political and economic agenda of Australia by declaring that the legislation banning the Communist Party of Australia and the legislation which brought about nationalisation of the banks were both unconstitutional.[37] So too the United States Supreme Court's decisions in *Roe v Wade*[38] and *Lochner v New York*[39] informed and directed the political, economic and legal history of that nation. And yet there remains a debate as to whether or not the court actually 'makes' the history (in terms of changing social and political directions) or merely ratifies the already changed social reality.[40]

---

35   Stuart Macintyre, 'The Fortunes of Federation' in David Headon and John Williams (eds), *Makers of Miracles: The Cast of the Federation Story* (2000) ch 1.

36   J A La Nauze, *The Making of the Australian Constitution* (1972). See B Galligan and J Warden, 'The Design of the Senate' in Gregory Craven (ed), *The Convention Debates: 1891–1898 Commentaries, Indices and Guide* (1986) 89.

37   *Australia Communist Party v Commonwealth* (1951) 83 CLR 1 and *Bank of New South Wales v Commonwealth* (1948) 76 CLR 1.

38   410 US 113 (1973).

39   198 US 45 (1909).

40   As Gerald Rosenberg has argued, in the context of the United States, 'U.S. courts can *almost never* be effective producers of significant social reform. At best, they can

334 Intention in Law and Philosophy

Courts are more than the mere chroniclers of historical events; they also provide authorised accounts of history. History is transformed when it becomes part of judicial deliberation. Courts pass judgment on history and in doing so radically change that history.

History and its interpretation is a dialogue. It is a conversation through time between the past and the present, as well as a conversation within a particular period. The historian is the means by which the past speaks to the present and the present to the past. Likewise, as discussed above, historians debate between themselves the meaning of the past. So too the courts have a dialogue with the past and with the present, though it is usually through a much more limited set of material, the precedents. In applying precedent, courts deal in historical anachronisms. That is, historical material such as a case (with its precedential value) is stripped of its social, political or economic context. A legal precedent from another age may stand as solid as the day it was delivered.[41] Yet the world that informed the context has ceased to be. It is the ability to work with historical anachronisms that distinguishes the legal enterprise from the historical.

What then occurs when judges use history? Critical to the answer to this question is the means by which the judicial process turns the historical dialogue into the judicial monologue. History, like other evidence, becomes a fact and, within the legal context, a fact that is rigid. Take again, for example, the *Mabo* decision.[42] Davison suggests that the High Court 'relied heavily upon the arguments first developed by Henry Reynolds'.[43] Looking at the case, there are five references to Reynolds' *The Law of the Land* in the judgments of Deane and Gaudron JJ,[44] Dawson J[45] and Toohey J.[46] What is significant is the use by the High Court of the work of a historian like Reynolds to support conclusions of fact. For example, as Deane and Gaudron JJ (citing Reynolds) note, when dealing with the argument that colonial officials did not appreciate native title and thus ignored it:

---

second the social reform acts of the other branches of government.' Gerald Rosenberg, *The Hollow Hope* (1991) 338.

41 This is not to suggest that precedents are not challenged or distinguished within the legal paradigm. The point being made is that there is a distinction to be drawn between the legal and the historic framework.

42 *Mabo v Queensland (No 2)* (1992) 175 CLR 1.

43 Davison, above n 24.

44 (1992) 175 CLR 1, 107.

45 Ibid 142.

46 Ibid 181.

That explanation is not, however, a plausible one in respect of later events. Increasingly, the *fact* that particular tribes or clans enjoyed traditional entitlements to the occupation and use of particular lands for ritual, economic and social purposes was understood. Increasingly, that *fact* was even acknowledged by government authorities and in formal dispatches.[47]

Reynolds' 'facts' are now under attack. As the Editor of *Quadrant* thunders:

> The prevailing fashion in Aboriginal history is crumbling, under challenge by courts and dissident historians. The 'legacy of unutterable shame' to which a couple of High Court judges, Gaudron and Deane, referred hyperbolically in the Mabo judgment of 1992 is being questioned. How much of the legacy is the product of invention and exaggeration?[48]

Similarly Reynolds' other historical conclusions with respect to contact between indigenous and non-indigenous Australians have been challenged on empirical grounds.[49] Let us assume, for the sake of argument, that the attack on Reynolds is justified and that Reynolds was wrong. That is, his work is disproved by other historians on empirical or methodological grounds. What would be the impact on the High Court's decision in *Mabo*? Would the decision cease to have legal authority? I would argue that the case must continue to have legal authority. This is because the historical facts presented by Reynolds have been transformed into judicial facts. They are, in the judicial sense, no longer contestable within the historical paradigm. (They may be contested within the legal.) Unfortunately, the *Quadrant* attack fails to draw this distinction as it launches into Reynolds as a means of undermining the *Mabo* decision.[50]

Should the High Court, or other superior courts, then abandon the use of history in the search for intention? Some have counselled this course for a number of reasons. One argument is that lawyers using history (or indeed philosophy) can tend towards what Brian Leiter has described as a form of 'intellectual voyeurism'. This is a

---

47 Ibid 107 (emphasis added).
48 (2000) 371 *Quadrant* 2.
49 Keith Windschuttle, 'The Myths of Frontier Massacres in Australian History' Pt I (2000) 370 *Quadrant* 8; Pt II (2000) 371 *Quadrant* 17.
50 Obviously, if the law is a dialogue then such attacks will enter into the conversation. However, the correction of these judicial facts remains with the court and not the historians.

superficial and ill-informed treatment of serious ideas, apparently done for intellectual 'titillation' or to advertise, in a pretentious way, the 'sophistication' of the writer. In these cases, the promising scholarly endeavour of interdisciplinary research becomes a forum for posturing and misuse of knowledge.[51]

Others have suggested that the search for inspiration from the intention of the framers is a form of 'ancestor worship', and that it is neither possible nor desirable to 'look over one's shoulder and to refer to understandings of the text that were common in 1900 when the society which the *Constitution* addresses was so different'.[52]

While both objections may be true, they specifically relate to the use of history as being *conclusive* of an argument. The historical 'voyeurist' uses history in a clumsy way that a professional historian would not. Similarly the 'hard' or 'moderate' originalist uses history to guide and conclude a constitutional controversy, forsaking (where possible) the contemporary meaning of text. What then is to be the use of history and intention in the constitutional context if, as has been argued, historians and lawyers have dramatically different approaches to the same material? In the last section of this essay I wish to explore the alternatives.

Purposive Intention and Constitutional Meaning

Original intention as an interpretative method is ahistorical. There is no evidence that the framers of the Australian Constitution intended their views to be conclusive of any constitutional controversy. To the contrary, we know that those framers who discussed the issue noted the absurdity of imposing their will and intentions onto future generations. Inglis Clark proclaimed that

the Constitution was not made to serve a temporary and restricted purpose, but was framed and adopted as a permanent and comprehensive code of law, by which the exercise of the governmental powers conferred by it should be regulated as long as the institutions which it created to exercise the powers should exist. But the social conditions and the political exigencies of the succeeding generation of every civilized and progressive community will

---

51 Brian Leiter, 'Intellectual Voyeurism in Legal Scholarship' (1992) 4 *Yale Journal of Law and the Humanities* 79, 80.
52 The Hon Justice Michael Kirby, 'Constitutional Interpretation and Original Intent: A Form of Ancestor Worship' (2000) 24 *Melbourne University Law Review* 1, 14.

inevitably produce new governmental problems to which the language of the Constitution must be applied, and hence it must be read and construed, not as containing a declaration of the will and intentions of men long since dead, and who cannot have anticipated the problems that would arise for solution by future generations, but as declaring the will and intentions of the present inheritors and possessors of sovereign power, who maintain the Constitution and have the power to alter it, and who are in the immediate presence of the problems to be solved. It is they who enforce the provisions of the Constitution and make a living force of that which would otherwise be a silent and lifeless document.[53]

Thus it is difficult to understand why 'hard' and 'moderate' originalists would impose a function upon the framers that they themselves denied.

Further there is an unstated assumption being made by those who suggest that the framers' intent is to be preferred to contemporary views of the Constitution and its interpretation. The framers have become the unwitting repository of constitutional perfection. That is, the framers are regarded as holding a wisdom that the current generation does not possess and it is assumed that recourse to this wisdom will resolve constitutional controversies. This could only be so if their views and constitutional understanding have a degree of infallibility which trumps future generations. Again it is difficult to believe that the framers held such views.

So what do we make of the framers and their handiwork? Moreover does this mean the end of history and intention in the constitutional setting? The answer to both questions is no. What is needed is a more subtle appreciation of the framers and their place in determining constitutional meaning.

The starting principle in a purposive account of the framers' intention is that their actions must bind the current generation. This is a basic premise of all constitutions. Those who drafted the Constitution, and those who agree to or disagree with constitutional amendment, know that their decisions have a hold upon the future. To suggest otherwise is to undermine the very reason for a written constitution. Constitutionalism, amongst other things, is about creating the conditions whereby arbitrary and unaccountable power is checked. As Philip Pettit has argued, constitutionalism recognises the establishment of the 'empire-of-law condition', the 'dispersion-of-power condition' and the 'counter-

---

53   Andrew Inglis Clark, *Studies in Australian Constitutional Law* (1901) 21–2.

majoritarian condition'.[54] These terms suggest constitutions are about holding power within limits.

So what did the framers agree to when they drafted the Australian Constitution? It is difficult to maintain that they agreed to a particular interpretive process, outcome or meaning. What they did agree upon was a set of constitutional arrangements such as a federal system, the separation of judicial power from the other sources of power, the rule of law and representative government. These are all fairly abstract concepts relating to the institutions for the governance of the new nation. This type of agreement is, in Sunstein's words, an 'incompletely theorized convergence on an abstraction'.[55] It is incomplete in that a constitution does not spell out in detail the scope of any of the provisions that make up the document.

Often it was the very fact that the agreement reached between the framers had no fixed content that made the agreement possible. Take for instance the oft-appearing phrase in the Australian Constitution 'until the Parliament otherwise provides'. This phrase is connected with appeals to the Privy Council, many of the financial standards of the new Commonwealth and the electoral system.[56] The result of this shrewd 'putting off for another day' allowed both 'free traders' and 'protectionists' to agree on the economic union. It also allowed those who wished to see an end to appeals to the Privy Council and those who wished to maintain that link to agree on the relevant section.[57] Similarly the framers agreed on a federal system without knowing the ultimate shape of that federation, and on the separation of powers without fully appreciating the degree of that separation. Thus, their agreement was predicated upon the constructive use of silence. The unexpressed premise does not detract from the agreement. Rather it was a precondition for that agreement.[58]

This type of agreement on general constitutional text and structure is consistent with the 'soft' originalism that was described previously. The framers *do* have a presence, though not a strong one, in the interpretation of the Constitution. Their intention matters to the extent that they have established the 'incompletely theorised' agreement. It is at this point that a

---

54 Philip Pettit, *Republicanism: A Theory of Freedom and Government* (1997) 172–82.

55 Cass Sunstein, *Legal Reasoning and Political Conflict* (1996) 171.

56 For example Australian Constitution ss 29, 30, 31, 34, 65 and 67. Section 74 allows parliament to make laws limiting appeals and s 90 left open the question of what would be the quantum of the customs duty.

57 The agreement in these situations may be seen as one in relation to process, that is parliament would ultimately decide the issue. That does not detract from the argument that the framers avoided the need to agree on an outcome.

58 Sunstein, above n 55, 38–9.

purposive model is critical in providing theoretical substance to that agreement.

Before further consideration of 'soft' originalism as a method of constitutional interpretation, it is important to confront the most pressing criticism of it: that is, it lacks any guiding principle or standards. As Scalia argues, in relation to the United States Constitution,

> there is no agreement, and no chance of agreement, upon what is to be the guiding principle of the evolution. *Panta rei* is not a sufficiently informative principle of constitutional interpretation. What is it that the judge must consult to determine when, and in what direction, evolution has occurred? Is it the will of the majority, discerned from newspapers, radio talk shows, public opinion polls, and chats at the country club? Is it the philosophy of Hume, or of John Rawls, or of John Stuart Mill, or of Aristotle? As soon as the discussion goes beyond the issue of whether the Constitution is static, the evolutionists divide into as many camps as there are individual views of the good, the true, and the beautiful. I think that is inevitably so, which means that evolutionism is simply not a practicable constitutional philosophy.[59]

Scalia acknowledges that the charges he levels at evolutionists (or non-originalists) can equally be made against originalists who differ on the relative strength of the historical material and its discernible intention. Putting this to one side and dealing with the major criticism, it would appear that for Scalia non-originalist judges have no constraints, either professional or methodological, placed upon them. Scalia appears to deny the constraining nature of precedent, argument by analogy or judicial deference based on democratic legitimacy. What Scalia presents is a free-wheeling non-originalist judge who uses whim or fancy as an interpretative method. What Scalia and other 'hard' originalists attempt to deny is the essence of the judicial process: choice. It is an inescapable fact that judges make choices, yet what 'hard' originalists attempt to do is limit (if not deny) those choices by replacing them with rules that relate to the search for historical intention.

What then is to fill the constitutional silence and how does 'soft' originalism assist in that process? It is a truism, as Justice McHugh noted in *McGinty*, that:

---

59   Scalia, above n 9, 45.

The Constitution contains no injunction as to how it is to be interpreted. Any theory of constitutional interpretation must be a matter of conviction based on some theory external to the Constitution itself.[60]

For McHugh J the 'external' nature of any interpretative method or theory was itself a reason to reject it as a means to interpret the document.[61] Yet McHugh J's general point must be correct. The Constitution does not contain an instruction as to its interpretation, thus *all* interpretive methodology, be it originalism, non-originalist or textualism, must be 'external' to the Constitution. Therefore any contest between alternative meanings is a contest between the various theories of interpretation. Such a contest or justification 'must be independent of any texts that are being interpreted. Any understanding of the "meaning" of texts depends on judgments and commitments that are independent of the text themselves'.[62] As Sunstein notes, 'any approach to interpretation must be defended on the ground that it will produce the best system of law, all things considered'.[63]

This creates another level of contestation in interpretation, a further level of choice.[64] The constitutional silence is to be filled by a theoretical debate as to the meaning of the 'incompletely theorised' agreement of the framers. Their bequest to the present is the structure or the boundaries of that agreement contained in the words of the Constitution. The search for their intention is a search for the limits of that agreement, not the substance of that agreement. For instance, an interpretation of the Constitution that denied the continued existence of the federal system, or of the role of the jury or representative government, would transgress the limits of the framers' agreement. However, a theory of government would be within the limits of the agreement.

What all this suggests is the need for judges to have an expressed theory of representative government or federalism, be it literalist, originalist or non-originalist. Whether or not a particular approach is to be favoured is a matter for judicial discretion and the circumstances of the section being

---

60 *McGinty v Western Australia* (1996) 186 CLR 140, 230.
61 McHugh J drew upon the work of Posner to reject such 'top-down reasoning'. See Richard Posner, 'Legal Reasoning From the Top Down and From the Bottom Up: The Question of Unenumerated Constitutional Rights' (1992) 59 *University of Chicago Law Review* 433. Similar points are made by George Winterton, 'Extra-Constitutional Notions in Australian Constitutional Law' (1986) 16 *Federal Law Review* 223.
62 Sunstein, above n 55, 170.
63 Ibid.
64 See Kirby, above n 52, 13.

interpreted. To suggest otherwise is to impute an essentialism that a 'soft' originalism denies.

Jeremy Kirk has questioned whether an interpretative method that rests on theoretical assumptions and debate (such as 'soft' originalism) would satisfy the 'complex, multi-dimensional task of interpreting what is in the Constitution'.[65] However, I would argue that it is both consistent with the intention of the framers (that is to create incompletely theorised agreement) and an open legal pluralism that must be the nature of constitutional deliberation.

Conclusion

This essay has argued that the search for a rigid constitutional intention is both ahistorical and unlikely to provide the certainty or satisfaction that its proponents suggest. What becomes apparent, however, in the search for original intention is the distinction between the use of historical material by the discipline of history and the manner in which the judiciary treats the same material. This distinction, founded upon fundamentally different methodologies and relationships to disciplinary norms, provides a cautionary note in the use of history by lawyers.

Ultimately, it is argued, while 'hard' or 'moderate' originalism are unacceptable methods of establishing constitutional meaning, there is room for a weak or 'soft' originalism. Such an originalism is consistent with the historical intention of the framers and with broader constitutional premises. Such an originalism provides an opportunity to enter into an open constitutional debate as to the meaning of the incompletely theorised constitutional agreement of the framers.

---

65   Jeremy Kirk, 'Constitutional Interpretation and a Theory of Evolutionary Originalism' (1999) 27 *Federal Law Review* 323, 360.

PART IV:
BEYOND INTENTION?

PART IV

BEYOND INTUITION?

16 Intention Versus Reactive Fault

JOHN BRAITHWAITE

Building on ideas initially developed by Brent Fisse,[1] this essay argues that the conception of fault in criminal law should in most cases abandon intention in favour of what Fisse calls reactive fault.[2] Here reactive fault is conceived as restorative fault and articulated to a wider jurisprudence of restorative justice that is relevant to civil as well as criminal law. For that matter, the analysis is that the criminal law should in most cases abandon other mental states such as recklessness or wilful blindness that are believed to have caused the crime to occur. In other words, we are considering a shift from fault which is causally prior to the crime, of which intention is the most important variant, to fault based on how restoratively the offender acts after the crime.

The core intuition of restorative justice is that because crime hurts, justice should heal. Reciprocating hurt with hurt, in contrast, adds to the amount of hurt in the world. Indeed, punishing wrongdoing often creates vicious spirals of hurt begetting hurt.[3] Because the poor are disproportionately both victims of crime and convicted offenders,[4] these vicious spirals of punitive justice add to social injustice. The result is that more of the poor become victims of crime and more of them rot in prison or suffer death in custody.

---

1   Brent Fisse, 'Reconstructing Corporate Criminal Law: Deterrence, Retribution, Fault and Sanctions' (1983) 56 *Southern California Law Review* 1141.
2   Ibid 1201.
3   I am indebted to a talk I once heard Howard Zehr deliver for the idea of hurt begetting hurt.
4   Michael Hindelang, Michael Gottfredson and James Garofalo, *Victims of Personal Crime: An Empirical Foundation for a Theory of Personal Victimization* (1978). John Braithwaite and David Biles, 'Victims and Offenders: The Australian Experience' in Richard Block (ed), *Victimization and Fear of Crime: World Perspectives* (1984).

Making intention central to how we allocate responsibility is a mistake from the perspective of the philosophy of restorative justice. In the next section I argue that, while it might be philosophically coherent in some possible world, it is not in any existing world. It is self-defeating to make intention central in the way we sort out responsibility in any sociologically existing world. In part this is an extension of the argument that Philip Pettit and I have made about desert:[5] in all actually existing worlds just deserts is imposed successfully on the vulnerable, unsuccessfully on the most powerful.

Scapegoats of Intention

In the work Brent Fisse and I did together and separately on corporate crime over a period of many years,[6] the key problem with the application of *mens rea* to the real world of corporate crime was scapegoats. A criminal law based on intent was shown usually to result in no one being held responsible and when someone was it was usually a scapegoat. Large corporations, we found, have enormous capacities for creating smokescreens of diffused accountability, so everyone is freed of criminal intent by a capacity to blame someone else. The alternative is the designated scapegoat. In *Corporate Crime in the Pharmaceutical Industry*,[7] I discovered a species of American business executive called the Vice-President Responsible for Going to Jail. Lines of responsibility were drawn so that this Vice-President would be the patsy for the President in a difficult situation. I interviewed three of these Vice-Presidents and was told about others. After a period of faithful service in this role, the Vice President Responsible for Going to Jail would be promoted sideways to a safe Vice-Presidency. If our current conception of *mens rea* fosters this and various other forms of denial of corporate and individual responsibility, does a restorative conception of criminal fault offer an alternative? Before returning to that question I want to make the same point in more banal contexts than the high politics of crimes of the powerful.

---

5   John Braithwaite and Philip Pettit, *Not Just Deserts: A Republican Theory of Criminal Justice* (1990) 182–201.

6   Much of this work is integrated in Brent Fisse and John Braithwaite, *Corporations, Crime and Accountability* (1993).

7   John Braithwaite, *Corporate Crime in the Pharmaceutical Industry* (1984).

Recall this kind of family scene. Brother pushes sister. She falls, hurts her knee, and cries. You are the parent. You arrive at the scene of the crime. 'He pushed me and hurt my knee and he meant to. It wasn't an accident'.

Question: Do you conduct an enquiry, cross-examining the witnesses to reach a view on whether there was intent in the actions of the son?

Most wise parents I suspect will say that the best thing to do is get behind the pushing incident to settle its underlying cause. 'What are you two fighting over?' It turns out to be the TV program. The parent proceeds to resolve the underlying conflict because this is more important than the alleged assault: 'Wasn't there a better way for you to sort out your disagreement?' The parent's objective is (a) to heal the damaged relationship between brother and sister so there will be peace; and (b) if assault has occurred, to create a moral space where the brother might *take* responsibility for it, even apologise or do something nice for his sister to make up for his wrong.

Mutual recriminations about responsibility and intention are not the best path for getting to (b). The theory of restorative justice says that (a) is the best path for getting to (b).

This is not just a point about minor acts of violence between children. It is also true of the most major acts of violence between adults. For example, while there is an important place for prosecution of war crimes, there is less hope for preventing future violence in the former Yugoslavia through prosecuting alleged war criminals like Mr Milosovic than there is through restorative justice processes rather more like those that Nelson Mandela empowered Desmond Tutu to implement through the Truth and Reconciliation Commission in South Africa.[8] Of course, with murder restorative justice can not bring back the victim any more than a quick execution can balance a slow death at the hands of a torturer under a retributive philosophy. We have learnt over the past decade that living homicide offenders can, however, help considerably with healing for the families of victims, with both war crimes and common murders. In Manitoba we have even seen the John Howard Society organising a play in which murderers and the families of murder victims perform together in a play about the evils of violence and the potential of restorative justice to heal its victims.

---

8   Desmond Tutu, *No Future Without Forgiveness* (1999).

348 Intention in Law and Philosophy

I won't seek to argue in this essay that restorative justice is the best path for encouraging offenders to take responsibility for the above major and minor kinds of crime.[9] But let us assume you accept this. You might still say yes, you are right for children or crimes of the powerful, but in between, for run-of-the-mill serious individual adult criminals, enquiry into intent and then punishment proportionate to the offence is the way to go. That view I contend is wrong. It goes against the empirical experience of criminology that accused criminals respond with a variety of techniques of neutralization. The standard empirically established techniques are still those first identified by Sykes and Matza: denial of responsibility (eg I was drunk); denial of injury (eg they can afford it); denial of victim (eg we weren't hurting anyone); condemnation of condemners (eg she was asking for it); appeal to higher loyalties (eg I had to stick by my mates).[10]

Most important is blaming the victim and blaming the system (especially the police and the courts). My hypothesis is that attempts at enquiries oriented toward coerced imputation of intent mostly lead to mutual recrimination between accuser and accused, between victim and offender, between police and criminals, and between judges and criminals. And it leads to strategic moves to make scapegoats of others. Further, the hypothesis is that these are general effects. Shadd Maruna's important new study *Making Good: How Ex-Convicts Reform and Rebuild their Lives* found that serious repeat criminals who went straight rewrote their lives according to 'generative' scripts.[11] They were ex-offenders who acquired a desire to take active responsibility for making some important contribution to their communities, especially to individuals like themselves who found themselves in trouble with the law. Helping others, be they victims or other offenders, is one of the best ways of helping yourself out of the cycle of crime. The persisters, in contrast to the desisters, adopted 'condemnation' scripts, like blaming the victim and other standard Sykes and Matza neutralizations. Hence the argument for restorative justice is not just the negative of avoiding scapegoating, it is also the positive of creating spaces

---

9   I do so in my forthcoming book, John Braithwaite, *Restorative Justice and Responsive Regulation* ch 6.

10 Gresham Sykes and David Matza, 'Techniques of Neutralization: A Theory of Delinquency' (1957) 22 *American Sociological Review* 664.

11 Shadd Maruna, *Making Good: How Ex-Convicts Reform and Rebuild their Lives* (2001).

where taking responsibility is nurtured, where generative scripts help the offender find a pathway out of crime.[12]

The only reason we routinely play the punishment proportionate to intent game with burglars and street dealers of drugs is that they have no power to resist that counterproductive model. They have no benevolent parents to protect them from outsiders who might punish them if they found out about the violence transacted in the privacy of the family. They have no corporate or political power to protect them. The judge, the philosopher or the legal academic has experience of the world of violence between children and the world of cheating on expense accounts, plagiarism or sexual harassment at work. That experience teaches them that criminal process would be a crude and ineffective way of dealing with such problems. The world of the burglar or drug dealer, in contrast, is a strange and threatening world to them. They do not understand it. It is the world of the other, and a powerless other much vilified by those who do not understand. So they convince themselves that what they recognise as an utterly stupid intentionality-based way of regulating the family crimes of their children, as a counterproductive way of regulating the workplace infractions of their colleagues or others from workplaces like theirs, is a sensible way of regulating the crimes of men in black hats, men astride motor bikes in black leather jackets or women with black skins.

Reactive Fault

We turn to Brent Fisse's theory of reactive fault[13] (further developed in *Corporations, Crime and Accountability*[14]) for the alternative. All criminal justice systems incorporate notions of causal and intentionality-based fault and reactive or restorative fault. Causal fault is about being causally responsible, while reactive fault is about how responsibly one reacts after the harm is done. The balance between the two varies enormously from system to system. Western criminal justice systems (like the US) are at the causal end of the continuum, though Fisse showed that there were elements of reactive fault in US corporate criminal law.[15] Asian systems (such as

---

12   For the increasingly encouraging evidence that restorative justice can reduce crime compared to courtroom processing of offenders, see Braithwaite, above n 9, ch 3.
13   Fisse, above n 1.
14   Fisse and Braithwaite, above n 6.
15   Fisse, above n 1, 1195.

Japan) tend to the reactive end. Yet, even in the West, reactive fault sometimes dominates causal fault, as in our intuition that with hit-run driving, the running is the greater evil than the hitting.

In *Crime, Shame and Reintegration*, I told two stories to illustrate the extremes in the cultural balancing of causal and reactive fault.[16]

> The first is of two American servicemen accused of raping a Japanese woman. On Japanese legal advice, private reconciliation with the victim was secured; a letter from the victim was tabled in the court stating that she had been fully compensated and that she absolved the Americans completely. After hearing the evidence, the judge leaned forward and asked the soldiers if they had anything to say. 'We are not guilty, your honor', they replied. Their Japanese lawyer cringed; it had not even occurred to him that they might not adopt the repentant role. They were sentenced to the maximum term of imprisonment, not suspended.
>
> The second story is of a Japanese woman arriving in the US with a large amount of American currency which she had not accurately declared on the entry form. It was not the sort of case that would normally be prosecuted. The law is intended to catch the importation of cash which is the proceeds of illicit activities, and there was no suggestion of this. Second, there was doubt that the woman had understood the form which required the currency declaration. After the woman left the airport, she wrote to the Customs Service acknowledging her violation of the law, raising none of the excuses or explanations available to her, apologizing profusely, and seeking forgiveness. In a case that would not normally merit prosecution, the prosecution went forward *because* she had confessed and apologized; the US Justice Department felt it was obliged to proceed in the face of a bald admission of guilt.[17]

These are stories about how the US justice system creates disincentives for reactive fault, while the Japanese justice system requires it. In its most radical version, reactive fault would mean that, in a case of assault, the alleged assailant would go into a restorative justice conference not on the basis of an admission of criminal guilt, but on the basis of admitting responsibility for the *actus reus* of an assault ('I was the one who

---

16   The first story is from John Haley, 'Sheathing the Sword of Justice in Japan: An Essay on Law Without Sanctions' (1982) 8 *Journal of Japanese Studies* 262. The second story is from H Wagatsuma and A Rossett, 'The Implications of Apology: Law and Culture in Japan and the United States' (1986) 20 *Law and Society Review* 486.

17   John Braithwaite, *Crime, Shame and Reintegration* (1989) 165.

punched her').[18] Whether the mental element required for crime was present would be decided reactively, on the basis of the constructiveness and restorativeness of his reaction to the problem caused by his act. If the reaction were restorative, the risk of criminal liability would be removed; only civil liability might remain. However, if reactive criminal fault were found by a court to be present, that would be insufficient for a conviction; the mental element for the crime would also have to be demonstrated before or during its commission.[19] But it would be the reactive fault that would be the more important determinant of any penalty than the causal or *mens rea* fault. If the offender responded in as restorative a way as was possible or reasonable, if conscientious steps were taken to right the wrong, there is no reactive fault and there should be no escalation beyond restorative justice to a further punitive response. If reparation is spurned, apology scoffed at, steps to prevent recurrence not taken, escalation to a punishment that might achieve social control through deterrence or incapacitation might be justified. So might giving the offender a second chance to acquit his or her reactive fault.

This gives us an answer to the retributivist who says: 'Where is the justice with two offenders who commit exactly the same offence: one apologises and heals a victim who grants him mercy; the other refuses to participate in a restorative justice conference and is punished severely by a court?' The answer is that, while the two offenders are equal in causal fault, they are quite unequal in reactive fault. It is not the whole answer, however. The other part of it is that the just deserts theorist may be morally wrong to consider equal justice for offenders a higher value than equal justice for victims.[20]

From Denial to Active Responsibility

If the argument is that conducting an enquiry into who intended to commit a crime triggers defensiveness, denial and pointing the finger at others,

---

18   Functionally, New Zealand law already accomplishes this result in the *Children, Young Persons and Their Families Act 1989* by putting cases into family group conferences not on the basis of an admission of criminal guilt, but on the basis of formally 'declining to deny' criminal allegations.

19   Brent Fisse has been known to advance the more radical view that if criminal liability is about punishing conduct known to be harmful and if failure to respond responsibly is harmful, then such reactive fault can be sufficient to establish criminal liability.

20   The second part of this argument will be developed further in Braithwaite, above n 9.

how does restorative justice do things differently? Restorative justice privileges active over passive responsibility.[21] Passive responsibility means holding someone responsible for something they have done in the past. Active responsibility means the virtue of taking responsibility for putting things right for the future. It is taking active responsibility that acquits reactive fault.

Good training manuals in restorative justice processes urge participants not to point the finger of responsibility at others. Rather the idea is that through the simple process of discussing the consequences, what the victim and the offender's family have had to endure as a result of the crime, the offender will accept responsibility. In part we rely here on Carol Heimer and Lisa Staffen's insight that 'it is the humanity of other people that inspires responsibility'.[22] In the toughest cases of everyone wanting to deny responsibility, in advance of the conference, Ted Wachtel and Paul McCold suggest asking participants to consider if there is even a small part of the responsibility that they would be willing to own at the conference.[23] The idea is that taking responsibility is contagious, is reciprocated. Instead of a vicious circle of unacknowledged shame and anger, we get a virtuous circle of acknowledged shame and mutual acceptance of responsibility.[24] In the famous Hollow Water program, there was the extraordinary accomplishment of persuading 52 adults in a community of 600 First Nations people to admit that they had sexually abused children.[25] Much of this was accomplished by making admission easier for offenders by putting them in the circle with other sexual abuse offenders who had already confessed, who were reaping the benefits of acknowledging their shame. These ex-offenders could also 'get under the

---

21   This distinction, is developed in John Braithwaite and Declan Roche, 'Responsibility and Restorative Justice' in Mara Schiff and Gordon Bazemore (eds), *Restorative Community Justice: Repairing Harm and Transforming Communities* (forthcoming). It in turn builds on distinctions in Mark Bovens, *The Quest for Responsibility* (1998).

22   Carol Heimer and Lisa Staffen, *For the Sake of the Children: The Social Organization of Responsibility in the Hospital and the Home* (1998) 369.

23   Ted Wachtel and Paul McCold, 'Restorative Justice in Everyday Life' in Heather Strang and John Braithwaite (eds), *Restorative Justice and Civil Society* (forthcoming).

24   This idea is being developed further in a forthcoming book by Eliza Ahmed, Nathan Harris, John Braithwaite and Valerie Braithwaite, *Shame Management Through Reintegration*.

25   See Berma Bushie, 'Community Holistic Circle Healing: A Community Approach' in T Wachtel (ed), *Proceedings of Building Strong Partnerships for Restorative Practices* (1999); Rupert Ross, *Returning to the Teachings: Exploring Aboriginal Justice* (1996).

skin' of the offenders, see through their tactics of denial, explaining that they had used the same tactics in their own denial.

In more standard juvenile justice conferences we often observe victims own some responsibility ('I should not have left the keys in the car') and see that this can immediately trigger the reaction: 'It's not your fault. I am the one who is responsible.' These are virtuous circles of acknowledgment rather than vicious circles of denial. Or we see parents accept responsibility. Again it is easier to see dramatic manifestations of this in Japanese culture than in our own:

> The boy was a troublemaker in school who intimidated his classmates and extorted money from them. His father, who was a former school principal, went to see the son's homeroom teacher in response to the latter's request. When he was told of his son's robbery, he apologised with a deep bow, saying 'I am very sorry.'
>
> Watching his father thus apologizing on his behalf, the offender was moved to tears. This was a turning point for him that changed his way of life completely.[26]

In many of the world's cultures, it is common to see attributions of intent for wrongdoing eschewed in favour of giving the offender gifts.[27] For example, in the highlands of New Guinea when one tribe is owed substantial compensation by another who has wronged them, the process that leads to the paying of that compensation starts with the wronged tribe offering a gift to the wrongdoer. In New Guinea even when the offender acts first by offering compensation to a victim, the preserving of relationships will often also involve the expectation of a smaller but significant reciprocal gift back to the offender by the victim. Such a way of thinking is not unknown in the West. We see it in Les Misérables, part of the Western literary canon, and in Pope John Paul bringing a gift to the man who shot him. The message of Les Misérables, and the biblical one, is that the grace of the gift, refraining from casting the stone, nurtures the voluntary acceptance of responsibility and the need to transform a life to a caring path.

---

26 T Lebra and a letter to the editor of the *Asahi Shinhum*, quoted in John Haley, 'Apology and Pardon: Learning from Japan' in Amitai Etzioni (ed), *Civic Repentance* (1999) 105.

27 For a number of examples, see ch 3, box 3.3 of Braithwaite, above n 9.

354 Intention in Law and Philosophy

Moving Up the Pyramid

Restorative justice is a way of doing justice designed to focus on the *actus reus* of the offence, on its consequences and how to repair them, normally to the exclusion of a discussion of *mens rea*. If the wrongdoer takes responsibility for repairing the harm that has been done, apologises and remorsefully commits to reform, we will say that his reaction means that we should no longer hold him at fault for the crime. More than that, according to the theory of reintegrative shaming we must commit to rituals to decertify the deviance of the wrongdoer.[28] This theory says that reintegrative shaming can prevent crime, but that shaming will increase crime if ceremonies that certify deviance (like laying of charges by the police) are not terminated by ceremonies to decertify deviance. These can be very minor rituals, as in the police officer after a recent restorative justice conference in Canberra who said to a shaken young man walking out of the conference 'When you walk out of that door this is all over.' It can take the emotional form of a hug. It can take standard ritual forms of sharing a beverage or meal or a speech of reconciliation by an indigenous elder about making a fresh start.

The reaction of the offender (and the reaction of the community to that reaction) signifies that there is no longer any criminal fault to be found in the case. If in contrast the reaction of the offender was to scoff at the suffering of the victim, to refuse compensation or community work, to refuse to change, the reactive fault has not been acquitted. Nor have the features of restorative justice that theorists like myself believe assist in the prevention of crime been delivered. These are remorse,[29] the acknowledgement of shame,[30] and the experience of loving acceptance and commitment to preventive measures freely chosen and embedded in social support.[31] What then?

Then restorative justice has failed morally and preventatively. One option is to try again, perhaps with some different supporters who can offer special kinds of support to the victim and the offender that might draw out active responsibility. On my consequentialist view, if restorative justice fails repeatedly, it will be best to seek to prevent further crime with a strategy that operates with a very different psychology from restorative

---

28   Braithwaite, above n 17.
29   See Gabrielle Maxwell and Alison Morris, *Reducing Reoffending* (1999).
30   See Ahmed *et al*, above n 22, pt III.
31   See above, notes 17, 24, 27.

justice. This strategy is deterrence and it involves a shift to the psychology of self-interested calculation, a shift from the psychology of the gift of the ethic of care with restorative justice. Then, when deterrence fails, it will be best to shift to a strategy that assumes no psychology at all. This is incapacitation, which by forbidding the fraudulent director from holding the office of director, stripping the incompetent nursing home owner of their licence, locking up the armed robber, renders the offender incapable of committing this kind of offence again. This is the crime prevention story of the pyramid (see figure 15.1).[32] What of the story on fault as we move up the pyramid?

ASSUMPTION

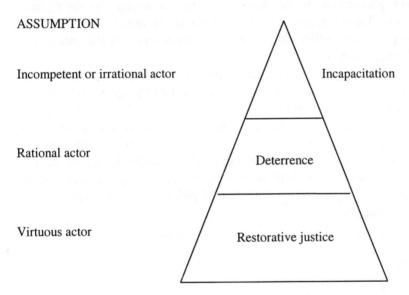

Incompetent or irrational actor — Incapacitation

Rational actor — Deterrence

Virtuous actor — Restorative justice

Figure 15.1: Towards an integration of restorative, deterrent and incapacitative justice

The beauty of restorative justice at the base of the pyramid is that it gets us out of the sometimes messy adjudication of *mens rea*. Was there intention? Yes but were there any of a raft of defences in play: coercion, duress, mistake, self-defence, provocation, insanity, necessity, and so on? When there were multiple actors involved, as there usually are, how do we sort out the various intended and unintended contributions to the

---

32   See Ian Ayres and John Braithwaite, *Responsive Regulation* (1992); Braithwaite, above n 9, ch 2.

wrongdoing of the different actors? But if there is still reactive fault, if there is a need to escalate to deterrence, we have seen that we need to revert to *mens rea*. Deterrence will not work unless there is a freely chosen action (or omission to act) to deter. An accidental death that was intended by no one and was not caused even by the negligent action of another cannot be deterred. In consequentialist terms, it is therefore necessary to establish some sort of *mens rea*, the most important variant of which is intent. Of course desert theorists and other deontologists reach the same conclusion about punishment via a different route. They say it is morally wrong to punish unless the punishment is deserved and the most standard reason for punishment to be deserved is that a wrong has been done intentionally. However one gets there, it seems uncontroversial that it is wrong to purposely inflict hard treatment without fault on the part of the agent who is punished.[33]

Hence in a regime of restorative justice and responsive regulation, reactive fault supplants intention at the base of the regulatory pyramid, but intention or some other form of *mens rea* is needed before moving up the pyramid to deterrence as a strategy. Since restorative justice is how most law breaking is dealt with in such a regime, reactive fault replaces intention in most cases as the dominant fault paradigm. However, in that minority of cases where there is a need to escalate up the pyramid to deterrence or incapacitation, intention replaces reactive fault as the dominant paradigm.

Summary

1. Attempts to impose intentionality-based fault lead to vicious circles of mutual recrimination, condemnation of the condemners in what shame scholars call shame-rage spirals. It tends to worsen the evil we seek to prevent.
2. Intentionality-based fault results in punishment focused on society's scapegoats. Justice has little to do with it in practice. It is a coherent theory for some possible world, but not for any existing world of serious imbalances of power.

---

33 Of course a standard charge of retributivists against utilitarians and other consequentialists is that they have an inferior theory of why it is wrong to punish the innocent. Beyond noting it, this tedious debate need not delay us here.

3. Reactive fault does less injustice at lower cost and fosters virtuous spirals of active responsibility rather than vicious circles of passive responsibility such as shame-rage spirals. Reactive fault helps healing to beget healing while passive responsibility helps hurt to beget hurt.

4. It follows that restorative justice is much more than just a new technology of disputing. In involves a radically transformed jurisprudence where intention and *mens rea* are pushed off a centre stage that is occupied by the cultivation of restorative virtues.

5. At the same time, restorative justice needs a theory of when it should be abandoned because it fails to do the work claimed of it in this essay. Responsive regulation is such a theory. One of its implications is that, as we move away from the restorative base of a regulatory pyramid, intention is reinstated as the paradigmatic form of *mens rea*.

Bibliography

Ahmed, Eliza, Nathan Harris, John Braithwaite and Valerie Braithwaite, *Shame Management Through Reintegration* (Cambridge University Press, Melbourne, forthcoming).

Alexander, Larry, 'All or Nothing at All? The Intentions of Authorities and the Authority of Intentions' in Andrei Marmor (ed), *Law and Interpretation* (Oxford University Press, Oxford, 1995) 361.

Ames, J B, 'How Far an Act May be a Tort Because of the Wrongful Motive of the Actor' (1905) 18 *Harvard Law Review* 411.

Anscombe, Gertrude E M, *Intention* (Blackwell, Oxford, 1957).

Anscombe, Gertrude E M, *Intention* (2nd ed, Blackwell, Oxford, 1963).

Aquinas, Thomas, *Summa Theologica* (T C O'Brien (trans)) (Eyre and Spottiswoode, London, 1972).

Ashworth, Andrew, 'Criminal Liability in a Medical Context: The Treatment of Good Intentions' in A P Simester and A T H Smith (eds), *Harm and Culpability* (Clarendon, Oxford, 1996) 179.

Ashworth, Andrew, *Principles of Criminal Law* (3rd ed, Oxford University Press, Oxford, 1999).

Ashworth, Andrew and Meredith Blake, 'The Presumption of Innocence in English Criminal Law' [1996] *Criminal Law Review* 306.

Atiyah, P S, 'Contracts, Promises and the Law of Obligations' (1978) 94 *Law Quarterly Review* 193.

Atiyah, P S, *The Rise and Fall of Freedom of Contract* (Oxford University Press, Oxford, 1979).

Audi, Robert, 'Intending' (1973) 70 *Journal of Philosophy* 387.

Aune, Bruce, *Reason and Action* (D Reidel, Dordrecht, 1977).

Austin, J L, *How to do Things with Words* (Clarendon Press, Oxford, 1962).

Australia, Criminal Law Officers Committee of the Standing Committee of Attorneys-Generals, *Model Criminal Code—Chapter 2: General Principles of Criminal Responsibility, Discussion Draft* (1992).

Australia, Criminal Law Officers Committee of the Standing Committee of Attorneys-Generals, *Model Criminal Code—Chapter 2: General Principles of Criminal Responsibility, Final Report* (1993).

Australia, Model Criminal Code Officers Committee of the Standing Committee of Attorneys-General, *Report* (1998).

Australia, Model Criminal Code Officers Committee, *Model Criminal Code—Chapter 5: Non Fatal Offences Against the Person, Report* (1998).

Australia, Model Criminal Code Officers Committee, *Model Criminal Code—Chapter 5: Sexual Offences Against the Person, Report* (1999).

Ayres, Ian and John Braithwaite, *Responsive Regulation* (Oxford University Press, New York, 1992).

Bagshaw, Roderick, 'Can the Economic Torts be Unified?' (1998) 18 *Oxford Journal of Legal Studies* 729.

Bagshaw, Roderick, 'Inducing Breach of Contract' in Jeremy Horder (ed), *Oxford Essays in Jurisprudence, Fourth Series* (Oxford University Press, Oxford, 2000).

Balkin, J M, 'Ideology as Constraint' (1991) 43 *Stanford Law Review* 1133.

Barlow, Anne and Rebecca Probert, 'Cohabitants: A Survey of European Reforms' (1999) 149 *New Law Journal* 1738.

Baron, Jane, 'Intention, Interpretation, and Stories' (1992) 42 *Duke Law Journal* 630.

Barthes, Roland, *Image, Music, Text* (Stephen Heath (trans)) (Fontana, London, 1977).

Bassham, Gregory, *Original Intent and the Constitution: A Philosophical Study* (Rowman and Littlefield, Lanham MD, 1992).

Belcher, Alice, 'A Feminist Perspective on Contract Theories from Law and Economics' (2000) 8 *Feminist Legal Studies* 29.

Bennett, Jonathan, 'Morality and Consequences' in Sterling McMurrin (ed), *The Tanner Lectures on Human Values, Vol II* (University of Utah Press, Salt Lake City, 1981) 45.

Bentham, Jeremy, *An Introduction to the Principles of Morals and Legislation* (Clarendon, Oxford, 1996 (reprint of 1781 ed)).

Berkowitz, David and Samuel Thorne (selectors), *Baron and Feme: A Treatise of the Common Law concerning Husbands and Wives* (first published 1700) in *Classics of English Legal History in the Modern Era* (Garland, New York, 1979).

Berns, Sandra, 'The Hobart City Council Case: A Tort of Sexual Harassment for Tasmania?' (1994) 13 *University of Tasmania Law Review* 112.

Berns, Sandra, *To Speak as a Judge: Difference, Voice and Power* (Ashgate, Aldershot, 1999).

Birk, Peter, 'The Concept of a Civil Wrong' in David Owens (ed), *Philosophical Foundations of Tort Law* (Oxford University Press, Oxford, 1995) 31.

Blackstone, William, *Commentaries on the Laws of England* (University of Chicago Press, Chicago, 1979).

Bovens, Mark, *The Quest for Responsibility* (Cambridge University Press, New York, 1998).

Braddon-Mitchell, David and Frank Jackson, *Philosophy of Mind and Cognition* (Blackwell, Oxford, 1996).

Braithwaite, John, *Corporate Crime in the Pharmaceutical Industry* (Routledge & Kegan Paul, London, 1984).

Braithwaite, John, *Crime, Shame and Reintegration* (Cambridge University Press, Cambridge, 1989).

Braithwaite, John, *Restorative Justice and Responsive Regulation* (Oxford University Press, Oxford, forthcoming).

Braithwaite, John and David Biles, 'Victims and Offenders: The Australian Experience' in Richard Block (ed), *Victimization and Fear of Crime: World Perspectives* (US Dept. of Justice, Washington, DC, 1984).

Braithwaite, John and Declan Roche, 'Responsibility and Restorative Justice' in Mara Schiff and Gordon Bazemore (eds), *Restorative Community Justice: Repairing Harm and Transforming Communities* (Anderson Publishing: Cincinnati, forthcoming).

Braithwaite, John and Philip Pettit, *Not Just Deserts: A Republican Theory of Criminal Justice* (Clarendon Press, Oxford, 1990).

Bratman, Michael, *Faces of Intention: Selected Essays on Intention and Agency* (Cambridge University Press, Cambridge, 1999).

Bratman, Michael, *Intention, Plans and Practical Reason* (Harvard University Press, Harvard, 1987).

Brennan, G, *Collective Irrationality and Belief* (Research School of Social Sciences, Australian National University, Canberra, 1999).

Brest, Paul, 'The Misconceived Quest for Original Understanding' (1980) 60 *Boston University Law Review* 204.

Brink, D O, 'Legal Theory, Legal Interpretation and Judicial Review' (1988) 17 *Philosophy and Public Affairs* 105.

Brink, D O, 'Semantics and Legal Interpretation (Further Thoughts)' (1989) 2 *Canadian Journal of Law and Jurisprudence* 181.

Brown, Beverley, 'Contracting Out/Contracting In: Some Feminist Considerations' in Anne Bottomley (ed), *Feminist Perspectives on the Foundational Subjects of Law* (Cavendish, London, 1996) 5.

Burchell, E M and P M A Hunt, *South African Criminal Law and Procedure, Vol I* (Juta & Co, Cape Town, 1970).

Bushie, Berma, 'Community Holistic Circle Healing: A Community Approach' in T Wachtel (ed), *Proceedings of Building Strong Partnerships for Restorative Practices* (Vermont Department of Corrections and Real Justice, Burlington, Vermont, 1999).

Campbell, Enid, Lee Poh-York and Joycey Tooher, *Legal Research* (4th edn, LBC, Sydney, 1996).

Campbell, Tom, 'Democratic Aspects of Ethical Positivism' in Tom Campbell and Jeffrey Goldsworthy (eds), *Judicial Power, Democracy and Legal Positivism* (Dartmouth, Aldershot, 2000) 3.

Campbell, Tom, 'Legal Positivism and Deliberative Democracy' in Michael Freeman (ed), *Current Legal Problems* (Clarendon Press, Oxford, 1999) 65.

Campbell, Tom, *The Legal Theory of Ethical Positivism* (Dartmouth, Aldershot, 1996).

Cane, Peter, 'Fleeting Mental States' (2000) 59 *Cambridge Law Journal* 273.

Cane, Peter, *The Anatomy of Tort Law* (Hart Publishing, Oxford, 1997).

Cane, Peter, *Tort Law and Economic Interests* (2nd ed, Clarendon Press, Oxford, 1996).

Carty, Hazel, 'Joint Tortfeasance and Assistance Liability' (1999) 19 *Legal Studies* 489.

Chalmers, David, *The Conscious Mind: In Search of a Fundamental Theory* (Oxford University Press, New York, 1996).

Chapman, B, 'Law, Incommensurability, and Conceptually Sequenced Argument' (1998) 146 *University of Pennsylvania Law Review* 1487.

Chapman, B, 'More Easily Done than Said: Rules, Reason and Rational Social Choice' (1998) 18 *Oxford Journal of Legal Studies* 293.

Chisholm, Roderick, 'The Structure of Intention' (1970) *Journal of Philosophy* 633.

Clark, Andrew Inglis, *Studies in Australian Constitutional Law* (Charles F Maxwell, Melbourne, 1901).

Clark, Manning, *A History of Australia* (Melbourne University Press, Melbourne, 1962–1987) vols I–VI.

Clarke, Kirsty, 'A "Near" Contract Experience' (1994) 1 *E Law* <http://www.murdoch.edu.au/elaw/>

Collier, Richard, *Masculinity, Law and the Family* (Routledge, London, 1995).

Collins, Hugh, *The Law of Contract* (Butterworths, Lonodn, 3rd ed, 1997).

Cooke of Thorndon, Lord, 'The Right of Spring' in Peter Cane and Jane Stapleton (eds), *The Law of Obligations: Essays in Celebration of John Fleming* (Clarendon Press, Oxford, 1998) 37.

Coombs, Mary, 'Transgenderism and Sexual Orientation: More than a Marriage of Convenience' (1997) *National Journal of Sexual Orientation Law* 3 <http://metalab.unc.edu/gaylaw/issue5/issue5.html>.

Cretney, Stephen, 'From Status to Contract?' in F D Rose (ed), *Consensus Ad Idem: Essays in the Law of Contract in Honour of Guenter Treitel* (Sweet and Maxwell, London, 1996) 269.

Cross, R, 'The Mental Element in Crime' (1967) 83 *Law Quarterly Review* 215.

Cross, R, 'The Mental Element in the Crime of Murder' (1988) 104 *Law Quarterly Review* 30.

Culhane, John, 'Uprooting the Arguments against Same-Sex Marriage' (1999) 20 *Cardozo Law Review* 1119.

Curley, E, 'Excusing Rape' (1976) 5 *Philosophy and Public Affairs* 325.

D'Arcy, E, *Human Acts: An Essay in Their Moral Evaluation* (Clarendon, Oxford, 1963).

Dalton, Clare, 'An Essay in the Deconstruction of Contract Doctrine' (1985) 94 *Yale Law Journal* 997.

Davidson, Donald, *Essays on Actions and Events* (Clarendon Press, Oxford, 1980).

Davies, Margaret, 'Legal Separation and the Concept of the Person' in Tom Campbell and Jeffrey Goldsworthy, *Judicial Power, Democracy and Legal Positivism* (Aldershot, Dartmouth, 2000) 115.

Davison, Graeme, *The Use and Abuse of Australian History* (Allen & Unwin, Sydney, 2000).

Dawson, Sir Daryl, 'Intention and the Constitution: Who's Intent?' (1990) 6 *Australian Bar Review* 93.

de Moor, Anne, 'Intention in the Law of Contract: Elusive or Illusory?' (1990) 106 *Law Quarterly Review* 632.

Dennett, Daniel, *Brainstorms: Philosophical Essays on Mind and Psychology* (Harvester, Hassocks, 1979).

Dennett, Daniel, *Consciousness Explained* (Alan Lane, Penguin, London, 1991).

Dennett, Daniel, *The Intentional Stance* (MIT Press, Cambridge, Mass, 1987).

Dennis, I H, 'The Critical Condition of Criminal Law' (1997) 50 *Current Legal Problems* 213.

Dennis, I H, 'The Mental Element for Accessories' in Peter Smith (ed), *Criminal Law: Essays in Honour of J C Smith* (Butterworths, London, 1987) 40.

Detmold, Michael, 'Australian Constitutional Equality: The Common Law Foundation' (1996) 7 *Public Law Review* 33.

Detmold, Michael, 'Law as the Structure of Meaning' in Tom Campbell and Jeffrey Goldsworthy (eds), *Interpretation* (forthcoming).

Detmold, Michael, 'Provocation to Murder: Sovereignty and Multiculture' (1997) 19 *Sydney Law Review* 5.

Duff, Antony, 'Codifying Criminal Law: Conceptual Problems and Presuppositions' in I H Dennis, *Criminal Law and Justice: Essays from the W G Hart Workshop, 1986* (Sweet & Maxwell, London, 1987) 95.

Duff, Antony, *Intention, Agency and Criminal Liability: Philosophy of Action and the Criminal Law* (Blackwell, Oxford, 1990).

Duff, Antony, 'Intentions Legal and Philosophical' (1989) *Oxford Journal of Legal Studies* 76.

Duff, Antony, 'Law, Language and Community' (1998) 18 *Oxford Journal of Legal Studies* 189.

Dworkin, Ronald, *A Matter of Principle* (Harvard University Press, Cambridge, Mass 1985).

Dworkin, Ronald, *Law's Empire* (Belknap Press, Cambridge, Mass, 1986).

Dworkin, Ronald, *Taking Rights Seriously* (Harvard University Press, Cambridge, Mass, 1977).

Eells, Ellery, *Rational Decision and Causality* (Cambridge University Press, Cambridge, 1982).

Endicott, T, 'Linguistic Indeterminacy' (1996) 16 *Oxford Journal of Legal Studies* 667.

Fehlberg, Belinda and Bruce Smyth, 'Pre-Nuptial Agreements for Australia: Why Not?' (2000) 14 *Australian Journal of Family Law* 80.

Fingarette, Herbert, *The Meaning of Criminal Insanity* (University of California Press, Berkeley, 1972).

Finnis, John, 'Intention and Side-Effects' in R G Frey and Christopher Morris (eds), *Liability and Responsibility: Essays in Law and Morals* (Cambridge University Press, Cambridge, 1991) 32.

Finnis, John, 'Intention in Tort Law' in David Owen (ed), *Philosophical Foundations of Tort Law* (Clarendon Press, Oxford, 1995) 229.

Firth, R, 'Ethical Absolutism and the Ideal Observer' (1952) 12 *Philosophy and Phenomenological Research* 213.

Fish, Stanley, *Doing What Comes Naturally: Change, Rhetoric and the Practice of Theory in Literary and Legal Studies* (Duke University Press, Durham, 1989).

Fisher, H A L (ed), *The Collected Works of F W Maitland* (Cambridge University Press, Cambridge, 1911).

Fisse, Brent, *Howard's Criminal Law* (5th ed, Law Book Company, Sydney, 1990).

Fisse, Brent, 'Reconstructing Corporate Criminal Law: Deterrence, Retribution, Fault and Sanctions' (1983) 56 *Southern California Law Review* 1141.

Fisse, Brent and John Braithwaite, *Corporations, Crime and Accountability* (Cambridge University Press, Cambridge, 1993).

Flannery, Kevin, 'Natural Law Mens Rea Versus the Benthamite Tradition' (1995) 40 *American Journal of Jurisprudence* 377.

Fleming, John, *The Law of Torts* (9th ed, Law Book Company, Sydney, 1998).

Freeman, Michael, 'Contracting in the Haven: *Balfour v Balfour* Revisited' in Roger Halson (ed), *Exploring the Boundaries of Contract* (Dartmouth, Aldershot, 1996) 68.

French, Peter, *Collective and Corporate Responsibility* (Columbia University Press, New York, 1984).

Fried, Charles, *Contract as Promise: A Theory of Contractual Obligation* (Harvard University Press, Cambridge, Mass, 1981).

Frug, Mary Joe, *Postmodern Legal Feminism* (Routledge, New York, 1992).

Galligan, B and J Warden, 'The Design of the Senate' in Greg Craven (ed), *The Convention Debates: 1891–1898 Commentaries, Indices and Guide* (Legal Books, Sydney, 1986) 89.

Gardner, David and Frances McGlone, *Outline of Torts* (2nd ed, Butterworths, Sydney, 1998).

Gibbon, Edward, *The History of the Decline and Fall of the Roman Empire* (John Murray, London, 1962).

Gilbert, Margaret, On Social Facts (Princeton University Press, Princeton, NJ, 1989).

Gillett, Grant, 'Consciousness and Lesser States: The Evolutionary Foothills of the Mind' (1999) 74 *Philosophy* 331.

Gillett, Grant, 'Free Will and Mental Content' (1993) 6(2) *Ratio* 89.

Gillett, Grant, 'Husserl, Wittgenstein and the Snark' (1997) 57 *Philosophy and Phenomenological Research* 331.

Gillett, Grant, *Representation, Meaning and Thought* (Clarendon, Oxford, 1992).

Gillett, Grant, *The Mind and its Discontents: An Essay in Discursive Psychiatry* (Oxford University Press, Oxford, 1999).

Goff of Chieveley, Lord, 'The Mental Element in Murder' (1988) 104 *Law Quarterly Review* 30.

Goldsworthy, Jeffrey, 'Dworkin As An Originalist' (2000) 17 *Constitutional Commentary* 49.

Goldsworthy, Jeffrey, 'Implications in Language, Law and the Constitution' in Geoffrey Lindell (ed), *Future Directions in Australian Constitutional Law: Essays in Honour of Professor Leslie Zines* (Federation Press, Sydney, 1994) 150.

Goldsworthy, Jeffrey, 'Originalism in Constitutional Interpretation' (1997) 25 *Federal Law Review* 1.

Goode, Matthew and Ian Leader-Elliott, 'Criminal Law' in *An Annual Survey of Australian Law* (Law Book Company, Sydney, 1992) 199.

Goodrich Peter, 'Gender and Contracts' in Anne Bottomley (ed), *Feminist Perspectives on the Foundational Subjects of Law* (Cavendish, London, 1996) 17.

Gordon, Max, *Sir Isaac Isaacs* (Heinemann, London, 1963).

Grace, Marty, 'The Work of Caring for Young Children: Priceless or Worthless?' (1998) 21 *Women's Studies International Forum* 401.

Grice, H P, 'Meaning' (1957) 66 *Philosophical Review* 377.

Grice, H P, *Studies in the Way of Words* (Harvard University Press, Cambridge, Mass, 1989).

Guest, Stephen, *Ronald Dworkin* (Stanford University Press, Stanford, 1991).

Habermas, Jurgen, *The Theory of Communicative Action* (Beacon Press, Boston, 1984–87).

Haley, John, 'Apology and Pardon: Learning from Japan' in Amitai Etzioni (ed), *Civic Repentance* (Rowman & Littlefield Publishers, Lanham, 1999) 105.

Haley, John, 'Sheathing the Sword of Justice in Japan: An Essay on Law Without Sanctions' (1982) 8 *Journal of Japanese Studies* 262.

Harman, Gilbert, *The Nature of Morality* (Oxford University Press, New York, 1977).

Harre, Rom and Grant Gillett, *The Discursive Mind* (Sage, Thousand Oaks, 1994).

Hart, H L A, *Punishment and Responsibility* (Oxford University Press, Oxford, 1968).

Heimer, Carol and Lisa Staffen, *For the Sake of the Children: The Social Organization of Responsibility in the Hospital and the Home* (University of Chicago Press, Chicago, 1998).

Heuston, R F V and R A Buckley (eds), *Salmond and Heuston on the Law of Torts* (21st ed, Sweet & Maxwell, London, 1996).

Heydon, J D, *Economic* Torts (2nd ed, Sweet & Maxwell, London, 1978).

Heydon, J D, 'The Defence of Justification in Cases of Intentionally Caused Economic Loss' (1970) 20 *University of Toronto Law Journal* 131.

Hindelang, Michael, Michael Gottfredson and James Garofalo, *Victims of Personal Crime: An Empirical Foundation for a Theory of Personal Victimization* (Ballinger Publishing, Cambridge, Mass, 1978).

Hirsch, E D, Jr, *Validity in Interpretation* (Yale University Press, New Haven, 1967).

Hobbes, Thomas, *De Cive or The Citizen* (Sterling Lamprecht (ed))(Appleton, New York, 1949).

Hodgson, David, *The Mind Matters* (Clarendon, Oxford, 1991).

Horder, Jeremy, 'Intention in the Criminal Law: A Rejoinder' (1995) 58 *Modern Law Review* 678.

Horder, Jeremy, *Provocation and Responsibility* (Oxford University Press, Oxford, 1992).

Horwich, Paul, *Probability and Evidence* (Cambridge University Press, Cambridge, 1982).

Howard, Colin, *Australian Criminal Law* (Law Book Company, Melbourne, 1965).

Hughes, Heather Lauren, 'Same-Sex Marriage and Simulacra: Exploring Conceptions of Equality' (1998) 33 *Harvard Civil Rights-Civil Liberties Law Review* 237.

Hume, David, *A Treatise of Human Nature* (Oxford University Press, Oxford, 1888).

Hurd, Heidi, 'Sovereignty in Silence' (1990) 99 *Yale Law Journal* 945.

Jackson, Frank, 'A Probabilistic Approach to Moral Responsibility' in Ruth Barcan Marcus *et al* (eds), *Proceedings of the Seventh International Congress of Logic, Methodology, and Philosophy of Science* (North-Holland, Amsterdam, 1986) 351.

Jeffrey, Richard, *The Logic of Decision* (McGraw-Hill, New York, 1965).

Kant, Immanuel, *The Metaphysics of Morals* (Mary Gregor (trans)) (Cambridge University Press, New York, 1996).

Kenny, A J P, *Freewill and Responsibility* (Routledge, London, 1978).

Kenny, A J P, 'Intention and Purpose in Law' in Robert Summers (ed), *Essays in Legal Philosophy* (Blackwell, Oxford, 1968) 146.

Kingdom, Elizabeth, 'Cohabitation Contracts and the Democratization of Personal Relations' (2000) 8 *Feminist Legal Studies* 5.

Kirby, Hon Justice Michael, 'Constitutional Interpretation and Original Intent: A Form of Ancestor Worship' (2000) 24 *Melbourne University Law Review* 1.

Kirby, Hon Justice Michael, 'Same-Sex Relationships: Some Australian Legal Developments' (1999) 19 *Australian Bar Review* 14.

Kirk, Jeremy, 'Constitutional Interpretation and a Theory of Evolutionary Originalism' (1999) 27 *Federal Law Review* 323.

Kornhauser, Lewis, 'Modelling Collegial Courts: I Path Dependence' (1992) 12 *International Review of Law and Economics* 169.

Kornhauser, Lewis, 'Modelling Collegial Courts: II Legal Doctrine' (1992) 8 *Journal of Law, Economics and Organization* 441.

Kornhauser, Lewis and Lawrence Sager, 'The One and the Many: Adjudication in Collegial Courts' (1993) 81 *California Law Review* 1.

Kornhauser, Lewis and Lawrence Sager, 'Unpacking the Court' (1986) 96 Yale Law Journal 82.

Knapp, Steven and Walter Benn Michaels, 'Against Theory' (1982) 8 *Critical Inquiry* 4.

Knapp, Steven and Walter Benn Michaels, 'Intention, Identity and the Constitution: A Response to David Hoy' in Gregory Leyh (ed), *Legal Hermeneutics: History, Theory and Practice* (University of California Press, Berkeley, 1992).

La Nauze, J A, *The Making of the Australian Constitution* (Melbourne University Press, Melbourne, 1972).

Lacey, Nicola, 'A Clear Concept of Intention: Elusive or Illusory' (1993) 56 *Modern Law Review* 621.

Landes, William and Richard Posner, *The Economic Structure of Tort Law* (Harvard University Press, Cambridge, Mass, 1987).

Lasch, Christopher, *Haven in a Heartless World: The Family Besieged* (Basic Books, New York, 1977).

Latham, R T E, 'The Law and the Commonwealth' in W K Hancock (ed), *Survey of British Commonwealth Affairs Vol 1* (Oxford University Press, London, 1937) 510.

Leader-Elliott, Ian, 'Criminal Cases in the High Court of Australia: *Hawkins'* (1994) 18 *Criminal Law Journal* 347.

Leiter, Brian, 'Intellectual Voyeurism in Legal Scholarship' (1992) 4 *Yale Journal of Law and the Humanities* 79.

Levinson, Sandford and Steven Mailloux (eds), *Interpreting Law and Literature: A Hermeneutic Reader* (Northwestern University Press, Evanston IL, 1988).

Lewis, David, *Convention: A Philosophical Study* (Harvard University Press, Cambridge, Mass, 1969).

Lewis, David, 'Dispositional Theories of Value' (1989) Supp 63 *Proceedings of the Aristotelian Society* 113.

List, Christian and Philip Petitt, 'The Aggregation of Reason: An Impossibility Result' (Paper presented at the Isaac Levi Conference, Columbia University, New York, November 2000).

Lyons, David, 'Constitutional Interpretation and Original Meaning' (1986) 4 *Social Philosophy and Policy* 75.

Lyons, David, 'Original Intent and Legal Interpretation' (1999) 24 *Australian Journal of Legal Philosophy* 1.

MacCallum, Gerald, 'Legislative Intent' in Robert Summers (ed), *Essays in Jurisprudence* (Blackwell, Oxford, 1970) 237.

MacCormick, Neil, 'Ethical Positivism and the Practical Force of Rules' in Tom Campbell and Jeffrey Goldsworthy, *Judicial Power, Democracy and Legal Positivism* (Aldershot, Dartmouth, 2000) 37.

Macintyre, Stuart, 'The Fortunes of Federation' in David Headon and John Williams (eds), *Makers of Miracles: The Cast of the Federation Story* (Melbourne University Press, Melbourne, 2000) 3.

Mackie, John, *Ethics: Inventing Right and Wrong* (Harmondsworth, New York, 1977).

Macneil, Ian, *The New Social Contract: An Inquiry into Modern Contractual Relations* (Yale University Press, New Haven, 1980).

Maine, Henry Sumner, *Ancient Law: Its Connections with the Early History of Society and its Relation to Modern Ideas* (Dent, London, 1917).

Marmor, Andrei, *Interpretation and Legal Theory* (Oxford University Press, Oxford, 1992).

Marmor, Andrei (ed), *Law and Interpretation* (Oxford University Press, Oxford, 1995).

Maruna, Shadd, *Making Good: How Ex-Convicts Reform and Rebuild Their Lives* (Washington, DC, American Psychological Association, 2001).

Maxwell, Gabrielle and Alison Morris, *Reducing Reoffending* (Institute of Criminology, Victoria University of Wellington, Wellington, 1999).

McDowell, John, *Mind and World* (Harvard University Press, Cambridge, Mass, 1994).

McIntyre, Alasdair, *The Unconscious: A Conceptual Analysis* (Routledge, London, 1958).

Meijers, A, *Speech Acts, Communication and Collective Intentionality: Beyond Searle's Individualism* (de Jonge, Utrecht, 1994).

Mercier, Charles, *Crime and Insanity* (Williams & Norgate, London, 1911).

Michaels, Alan, 'Acceptance: The Missing Mental State' (1998) 71 *Southern California Law Review* 953.

Mill, John Stuart, *System of Logic, Ratiocinative and Inductive* (Harper, New York, 1874).

Millbank, Jenni, 'An Implied Promise to Parent: Lesbian Families, Litigation and *W v G* (1996) 10 Fam LR 49' (1996) 10 *Australian Journal of Family Law* 112.

Millbank, Jenni, 'If Australian Law Opened its Eyes to Lesbian and Gay Families, What Would it See?' (1998) 12 *Australian Family Law Journal* 99.

Millikan, Ruth, *White Queen Psychology and Other Essays for Alice* (MIT, Cambridge, Mass, 1993).

Moore, Michael, *Educating Oneself in Public: Critical Essays in Jurisprudence* (Oxford University Press, Oxford, 2000).

Moore, Michael, *Placing Blame: A General Theory of the Criminal Law* (Clarendon Press, Oxford, 1997).

Mossman, Mary Jane, 'Feminism and Legal Method: The Difference it Makes' (1986) 3 *Australian Journal of Law and Society* 30.

Mulholland, Ray, 'Nay, This Be Estoppel' [1998] *New Zealand Law Journal* 179.

Nagel, Thomas, *The View from Nowhere* (Oxford University Press, New York, 1986).

Neave, Marcia, 'Private Ordering in Family Law: Will Women Benefit?' in Margaret Thornton (ed), *Public and Private: Feminist Legal Debates* (Oxford University Press, Melbourne, 1995) 144.

Neave, Marcia, 'The Hands that Sign the Paper: Women and Domestic Contracts' in Glyn Davis, Barbara Sullivan and Anna Yeatman (eds), *The New Contractualism?* (Macmillan Education Australia, South Melbourne, 1997) 71.

Nehamas, Alexander, 'The Postulated Author: Critical Monism as a Regulative Ideal' (1981) 8 *Critical Inquiry* 133.

Nietzsche, Friedrich, *The Use and Abuse of History* (Bobbs-Merril, Indianapolis, 1957).

O'Donovan, Katherine, *Family Law Matters* (Pluto Press, London, 1993).

O'Donovan, Katherine, *Sexual Divisions in Law* (Weidenfeld and Nicholson, London, 1985).

Odgers, Stephen, 'Contemporary Provocation Law: Is Substantially Impaired Self-Control Enough?' in Stanley Yeo (ed), *Partial Excuses to Murder* (Federation Press, Sydney, 1990) 101.

Official Record of the Debates of the Australasian Federal Convention, Sydney, 1891 (Government Printer, Sydney, 1891).

Olsen, Frances, 'The Family and the Market: A Study of Ideology and Legal Reform' (1983) 96 *Harvard Law Review* 1497.

Owen, David, 'Philosophical Foundations of Fault in Tort Law' in David Owens (ed), *Philosophical Foundations of Tort Law* (Clarendon Press, Oxford, 1995) 201.

Parfit, Derek, *Reasons and Persons* (Clarendon Press, Oxford, 1986).

Parsons, Theophilus, *Law of Contracts* (W S Hein, Buffalo, 1980).

Pateman, Carole, *The Sexual Contract* (Polity, Cambridge, 1988).

Paulsen, Monrad and Sanford Kadish, *Criminal Law and its Processes: Cases and Materials* (Little, Brown, Boston, 1962).

Pawlowski, Mark, 'Cohabitation Contracts: Are They Legal?' (1996) 146 *New Law Journal* 1125.

Peacocke, Christopher, *Holistic Explanation* (Clarendon Press, Oxford, 1979).

Pettit, Philip, 'Deliberative Democracy and Discursive Dilemma' (2001) 11 *Philosophical Issues* (forthcoming).

Pettit, Philip, 'Groups with Minds of Their Own' (paper presented at Yale University Political Theory Workshop, September 2000).

Pettit, Philip, *Republicanism: A Theory of Freedom and Government* (Oxford University Press, Oxford, 1997).

Pettit, Philip, *The Common Mind: An Essay on Psychology, Society and Politics* (Oxford University Press, New York, 1993).

Pohjonen, Soile, 'Partnership in Love and Business' (2000) 8 *Feminist Legal Studies* 47.

Pollock, Frederick and Frederic Maitland, *The History of English Law before the Time of Edward I, Vol I* (2nd ed, Boston University Press, Boston, 1899).

Posner, Richard, *Economic Analysis of Law* (4th ed, Little, Brown, Boston, 1992).

Posner Richard, 'Legal Reasoning From the Top Down and From the Bottom Up: The Question of Unenumerated Constitutional Rights' (1992) 59 *University of Chicago Law Review* 433.

Posner, Richard, *The Problems of Jurisprudence* (Harvard University Press, Cambridge, Mass, 1990).

Quinton, A, 'Social Objects' (1975) 75 *Proceedings of the Aristotelian Society* 17.

Rawls, John, *A Theory of Justice* (Clarendon Press, Oxford, 1971).

Rawls, John, 'Outline for a Decision Procedure for Ethics' (1951) 60 *Philosophical Review* 177.

Rawls, John, *Political Liberalism* (Columbia University Press, New York, 1993).

Raz, Joseph, 'Authority, Law and Morality' (1985) 62 *The Monist* 295.

Raz, Joseph, 'Intention in Interpretation' in Robert George (ed), *The Autonomy of Law: Essays on Legal Positivism* (Oxford University Press, Oxford, 1996) 249.

Raz, Joseph, 'Interpretation Without Retrieval' in Andrei Marmor (ed), *Law and Interpretation* (Clarendon Press, Oxford, 1995) 155.

Robbennolt, Jennifer and Monica Kirkpatrick Johnson, 'Legal Planning for Unmarried Committed Partners: Empirical Lessons for a Preventive and Therapeutic Approach' (1999) 41 *Arizona Law Review* 417.

Rogers, W V H, *The Law of Tort* (2nd ed, Sweet & Maxwell, London, 1994).

Rogers, W V H (ed), *Winfield and Jolowicz on Tort* (14th ed, Sweet & Maxwell, London, 1994).

Rosenberg, David, *The Hidden Holmes* (Harvard University Press, Cambridge, Mass, 1995).

Rosenberg, Gerald, *The Hollow Hope* (University of Chicago Press, Chicago, 1991).

Ross, Rupert, *Returning to the Teachings: Exploring Aboriginal Justice* (Penguin, London, 1996).

Rousseau, Jean Jacques, *The Social Contract and Discourses* (G D H Cole (trans)) (Dent, London, 1973).

Sachs, Albie and Joan Hoff Wilson, *Sexism and the Law: A Study of Male Beliefs and Judicial Bias in Britain and the United States* (M Robertson, Oxford, 1978).

Sales, Philip and Daniel Stilitz, 'Intentional Infliction of Harm by Unlawful Means' (1999) 115 *Law Quarterly Review* 411.

Samuel, Geoffrey and Jac Rinkes, *Law of Obligations and Legal Remedies* (Cavendish, London, 1996).

Sartre, Jean Paul, *Being and Nothingness* (H Barnes (trans)) (Methuen, London, 1958).

Scalia, Antonin, *A Matter of Interpretation: Federal Courts and the Law: An Essay* (Princeton University Press, Princeton, 1998).

Schauer, Frederick, 'Defining Originalism' (1995) 19 *Harvard Journal of Law & Public Policy* 343.

Schauer, Frederick, 'Formalism' (1988) 97 *Yale Law Journal* 509.

Schauer, Frederick, *Playing By the Rules: A Philosophical Examination of Rule-Based Decision Making in Law and in Life* (Clarendon Press, Oxford, 1991).

Schoff, Paul, 'The High Court and History: It Still Hasn't Found(ed) What It's Looking For' (1994) 5 *Public Law Review* 253.

Scruton, Roger, *Modern Philosophy: A Survey* (Sinclair Stevenson, London, 1994).

Scruton, Roger, *Sexual Desire: A Philosophical Investigation* (Weidenfeld & Nicolson, London, 1986).

Searle, John, *The Construction of Social Reality* (Allen Lane, London, 1995).

Sereny, Gitta, *Cries Unheard: The Story of Mary Bell* (Macmillan, London, 1998).

Shanley, Mary Lyndon, *Feminism, Marriage and the Law in Victorian England, 1850–1895* (Tauris, London, 1989).

Shavell, Steven, *Economic Analysis of Accident Law* (Harvard University Press, Cambridge, Mass, 1987).

Shiner, Roger, 'Intoxication and Responsibility' (1990) 13 *International Journal of Law and Psychiatry* 9.

Sidgwick, H, *The Methods of Ethics* (6th ed, Macmillan, London, 1901).

Simester, A P, 'Moral Certainty and the Boundaries of Intention' (1996) 16 *Oxford Journal of Legal Studies* 445.

Simester, A P, 'Murder, Mens Rea and the House of Lords—Again' (1999) 115 *Law Quarterly Review* 17.

Smith, A T H, *Property Offences: The Protection of Property Through the Criminal Law* (Sweet & Maxwell, London, 1994).

Smith, Michael, 'A Theory of Freedom and Responsibility' in Garrett Cullity and Berys Gaut (eds), *Ethics and Practical Reason* (Oxford University Press, Oxford, 1997) 293.

Smith, Michael, 'The Coherence Argument: A Reply to Shafer-Landau' *Analysis* (forthcoming).

Smith, Michael, *The Moral Problem* (Blackwell, Oxford, 1994).

Stapleton, Jane, 'Duty of Care: Peripheral Parties and Alternative Opportunities for Deterrence' (1995) 111 *Law Quarterly Review* 301.

Stephen, James, *A Digest of the Criminal Law* (Herbert Stephen and Harry L Stephen (eds)) (5th ed, Macmillan, London, 1894).

Stephen, James, *A History of the Criminal Law of England, Vol II* (Macmillan, London, 1883).

Stoljar, Natalie, 'Counterfactuals in Interpretation: The Case Against Intentionalism' (1998) 20 *Adelaide Law Review* 29.

Stoljar, Natalie, 'Is Positivism Committed to Intentionalism?' in Tom Campbell and Jeffrey Goldsworthy (eds), *Judicial Power, Democracy and Legal Positivism* (Aldershot, Dartmouth, 2000) 169.

Stoljar, Natalie, 'Vagueness, Counterfactual Intentions and Legal Interpretation' *Legal Theory* (forthcoming).

Stoljar, S J, *Groups and Entities: An Inquiry into Corporate Theory* (Australian National University Press, Canberra, 1973).

Stone, Julius, *Legal System and Lawyers' Reasonings* (1968).

Strawson, Peter, *Freedom and Resentment, and Other Essays* (Methuen, London, 1974).

Sunstein, Cass, 'Five Theses on Originalism' (1996) 19 *Havard Journal of Law and Public Policy* 311.

Sunstein, Cass, *Legal Reasoning and Political Conflict* (Oxford University Press, New York, 1996).

Sunstein, Cass, *One Case at a Time: Judicial Minimalism on the Supreme Court* (Harvard University Press, Cambridge University Press, 1999).

Sunstein, Cass, *The Partial Constitution* (Harvard University Press, Cambridge, Mass, 1993).

Sykes, Gresham and David Matza, 'Techniques of Neutralization: A Theory of Delinquency' (1957) 22 *American Sociological Review* 664.

Ten, C L, *Crime, Guilt and Punishment* (Oxford University Press, Oxford, 1987).

Thornton, Margaret, 'Historicising Citizenship: Remembering Broken Promises' (1996) 20 *Melbourne University Law Review* 1072.

Thornton, Margaret, *Dissonance and Distrust: Women in the Legal Profession* (Oxford University Press, Melbourne, 1996).

Thornton, Margaret, 'The Cartography of Public and Private' in Margaret Thornton (ed), *Public and Private: Feminist Legal Debates* (1995) 2.

Thornton, Margaret, 'The Judicial Gendering of Citizenship: A Look at Property Interests During Marriage' (1997) 24 *Journal of Law and Society* 486.

Treitel, G H, *The Law of Contract* (Sweet & Maxwell, London, 9th ed, 1995).

Trindade, Francis and Peter Cane, *The Law of Torts in Australia* (3rd ed, Oxford University Press, Melbourne, 1999).

Tuomela, R, *The Importance of Us* (Stanford University Press, Stanford, 1995).

Tushnet, Mark, 'Symposium on the Trends in Legal Citations and Scholarship: Interdisciplinary Legal Scholarship: The Case of History-in-Law' (1996) 71 *Chicago-Kent Law Review* 909.

Tutu, Desmond, *No Future Without Forgiveness* (Rider, London, 1999).

UK, Criminal Law Revision Committee, *Offences Against the Person* (HMSO, London, 1980).

UK, Law Commission, *Codification of the Criminal Law* (HMSO, London, 1985).

Unger, Roberto Mangabeira, *The Critical Legal Studies Movement* (Harvard University Press, Cambridge, Mass, 1983).

Uniacke, Suzanne, *Permissible Killing: The Self-Defence Justification in Homocide* (Cambridge University Press, Cambridge, 1994).

Vallacher, R R and D M Wegner, 'What do People Think They're Doing? Action Identification and Human Behaviour' (1987) 94 *Psychological Review* 3.

Wachtel, Ted and Paul McCold, 'Restorative Justice in Everyday Life' in Heather Strang and John Braithwaite (eds), *Restorative Justice and Civil Society* (Cambridge University Press, Melbourne, forthcoming).

Wagatsuma, H and A Rossett, 'The Implications of Apology: Law and Culture in Japan and the United States' (1986) 20 *Law and Society Review* 486.

Waldron, Jeremy, *Law and Disagreement* (Oxford University Press, Oxford, 1999).

Waldron, Jeremy, 'Legislators' Intentions and Unintentional Legislation' in Andrei Marmor (ed), *Law and Interpretation* (Oxford University Press, Oxford, 1995) ch 9.

Waller, Louis and Charles Williams, *Brett, Waller and Williams Criminal Law: Text and Cases* (7th ed, Butterworths, Sydney, 1993).

Waluchow, W J, *Inclusive Legal Positivism* (Oxford University Press, Oxford, 1994).

Waring, Marilyn, *Counting for Nothing: What Men Value and What Women are Worth* (Allen & Unwin, Wellington, 1988).

Weinrub, Ernest, *The Idea of Private Law* (Harvard University Press, Cambrdige, Mass, 1995).

Weir, Tony, *A Casebook on Tort* (8th ed, Sweet & Maxwell, London, 1996).

Weir, Tony, *Economic Torts* (Clarendon Press, Oxford, 1997).

Wightman, John, 'Intimate Relationships, Relational Contract Theory and the Reach of Contract' (2000) 8 *Feminist Legal Studies* 93.

Wilhelmsson, Thomas, 'Questions for a Critical Contract Law—and a Contradictory Answer: Contract as Social Cooperation' in Thomas Wilhelmsson (ed), *Perspectives of Critical Contract Law* (Dartmouth, Aldershot, 1993).

Williams, Bernard, *Ethics and the Limits of Philosophy* (Harvard University Press, Cambridge, Mass, 1985).

Williams, Glanville, *Criminal Law* (2nd ed, Stevens & Sons, London, 1961).

Williams, Glanville, 'Oblique Intention' (1987) 46 *Criminal Law Journal* 417.

Williams, Glanville, *Textbook of Criminal Law* (2nd ed, Stevens, London, 1983).

Williams, Glanville, *The Mental Element in Crime* (Hebrew University, Jerusalem, 1965).

Williams, John and John Bradsen, 'The Perils of Inclusion: The Constitution and the Race Power' (1997) 19 *Adelaide Law Review* 95.

Windschuttle, Keith, 'The Myths of Frontier Massacres in Australian History' Pt I (2000) 370 *Quadrant* 8; Pt II (2000) 371 *Quadrant* 17.

Winterton, George, 'Extra-Constitutional Notions in Australian Constitutional Law' (1986) 16 *Federal Law Review* 223.

Wittgenstein, Ludwig, *On Certainty* (Denis Paul and G E M Anscombe (trans)) (Blackwell, Oxford, 1969).

Wittgenstein, Ludwig, *Philosophical Investigations* (G E M Anscombe (trans)) (3rd ed, Blackwell, Oxford, 1968).

Wittgenstein, Ludwig, *Tractatus Logico-Philosophicus* (D F Pears and B F McGuiness (trans)) (Routledge and Kegan Paul, London, 1961).

Yeatman, Anna, 'Contract, Status and Personhood' in Glyn Davis, Barbara Sullivan and Anna Yeatman (eds), *The New Contractualism?* (Macmillan Education Australia, South Melbourne, 1997) 39.

Index